N

With best wishes
Pam
September 2025

NOSHTALGIA

The Bloom's Story, 1921–2010

PAM FOX

People and Places
London

First published in 2025 by People and Places

124 City Road,
London
EC1V 2NX.

British Library Cataloguing in Publication Data:
An entry can be found on request

ISBN 978-1-0683516-0-0 (Paper)

Contents

PART THREE
Aspects of the Bloom's Enterprise

PART FOUR
Conclusions

APPENDICES

Acknowledgements

As with my previous books, I did not write this book on my own. I had the support and help of many people, all of whom I would like to thank for their contribution.

I would like to start my expressions of thanks by saying that the book would not have been written were it not for Stuart Levinson and the Facebook page he administers, Memories of Hessell, Langdale Mans, Cannon Street Rd and Cable St (the 'Hesslers'). It was Stuart's detailed posts on Blooms that sparked my interest in the history of the firm, and which led me to think that there was a fascinating story waiting to be told. Once I started work on the book, Stuart was very supportive of my research, repeatedly encouraging group members to post information and memories. Thank you, Stuart.

In writing this book I have worked with several members of the Bloom family, who have all been very helpful, but especially Martin Malin, grandson of Morris and Rebecca Bloom who founded the firm. His input has been pivotal, providing a window into the Bloom family, without which the book would have lacked a vital ingredient.

In addition, being a writer himself, Martin understood and was supportive of my research and writing. His encouragement and positive feedback were very motivating. I enjoyed each of my many conversations with Martin and valued his insightful comments on my drafts. I would also like to thank Michelle Spencer (Martin's sister), Jonathan Tapper (a Bloom's great-grandchild) and Marc Green (a great-nephew) for their respective contributions.

In addition to the generous assistance of the Hesslers, I also received a great deal of information and many lovely memories from members of a number of other Facebook pages, including: I Grew up at Golders Green Station in the 60s and 70s (thank you Penny Freeman); Jewish Britain (thank you Laurence Epstein); Memories of Petticoat Lane and Surrounding Areas (thank you Jaquie Kutcher Golstein); East End of London and East London,

History and Memories (thank you Maureen Locke); The Jewish East End of London (thank you Adele Schlazer Lester); You Don't Have to be Jewish (thank you Barry Shamplin); East London Days Gone by (thank you Lesley Love); Bethnal Green and East London (thank you Joe Ellis); and the Jewish Historical Society of England (thank you Richard Cohen). Throughout the research process, Mark Nagle promoted the research I was carrying out using social media and encouraged contributions. I am indebted to you Mark.

The compilation of this book has been heavily reliant on those kind people who agreed to be interviewed about their knowledge and memories of Blooms, some of them more than once. Altogether, I carried out over a hundred interviews, each one of them added value to the book. I would like to thank everyone I interviewed (including those people who preferred to remain anonymous – you know who you are!), but there are a few people whose contribution was outstanding: Norman Bookbinder; David Rein (without the conversations with Norman and David the sections dealing with Bloom's manufacturing and wholesale activities would have been very 'thin'); Alan Dein (I had superb conversations with Alan about 'the meaning' of Blooms); Philip Baigel (such a gifted storyteller!); Professor Geoffrey Alderman (who, as with previous books, enlightened me on communal history); Professor Panikos Panayi (who was especially helpful in relation to food history); Professor Tony Kushner (who guided me on the historiography of the Jewish East End and commented on my conclusions); and Connie Stanton whose memories went back a long way. May her memory be for a blessing.

I would also like to acknowledge the help provided by family members in generating the 'pen portraits' of those particularly memorable people who are mentioned in detail in the book: Esther Piper and Julia Gowers (may her memory be for a blessing), Paula Allen, Marsha Bloom, Jeremy Dein and Vivienne Thompson. Thank you to the many people who sent me stories via Facebook Messenger and WhatsApp, particularly Sheila Finesilver, Anna Grantham-Gold, Martine Kaufman and Paul Stewart. In addition, I would like to thank the *Jewish News* for publishing my call for memories and anecdotes, which resulted in several people contacting me. Thank you Alex Gabinski for facilitating this. My friend Fiona Hulbert was conscientious in finding people with delightful stories to tell me.

Several people kindly contacted me with snippets of information they thought I would find interesting, or which had eluded me. I would like to thank John Morrison for providing me with information on the identity of the man who secured financial backing for Morris Bloom (see image 31 on page 39); Daniel Gleek, who told me about the tenants of 58 Brick Lane prior to Blooms establishing their business there (see image 32 on page 60); Barbara Poluck for identifying the man in the photo of the bagel sellers (her father-in-law, known as 'Elmo' who worked in the taxi trade) (see image 38 on page 72).

In addition to Martin Malin, some very kind people agreed to read a draft of my book. I invited them to be brutal! Thank you to Hannah Jacobs, Alan Dein, Professor Geoffrey Alderman and (yet again) my husband Michael Hart for being 'critical friends'; the book was vastly improved because of your comments and feedback.

As with my previous books, David Jacobs kindly gave me access to his impressive library and archives, signposted me to numerous sources of information and offered oodles of encouragement. In this context, I would also like to mention my friend Amy Shevitz, who in addition to reading Chapter Eleven and providing extraordinarily erudite comments, also (very patiently) used her connections to obtain relevant articles and other material for me.

To a much greater extent than any of my books, the story of Blooms is told through images of various kinds: photos, announcements, advertisements, editorials and articles in the *Jewish Chronicle* (thank you to the editor for giving me the permission to do this) and other newspapers, informal photos provided by former customers and those taken by professional photographers, such as Trevor Paul. I must also thank Michelle Spencer and Martin Malin for providing the delightful family photos and Jonathan Fishburn for his search for relevant images and for coming up with some gems. I would also like to thank Sharon Allin for agreeing so readily to my including images of her father's (John Allin) paintings of Bloom's café and factory (see

Plates Section, Plates 1 and 5) and to Philip Baigel for allowing me to reproduce his wonderful picture of the Golders Green restaurant (see Plates Section, Plate 7). Towards the end of my research, I was contacted by Ruth Plaut who has a veritable treasure trove of Bloom's photographs, particularly of the waiters and counter staff. Ruth, I can't thank you enough for allowing me to reproduce your photos and I am sorry that there was not enough space to include more of them!

The talented Elissa Aldous-Hughes, with whom I have worked on several projects, was meticulous in producing the Bloom family trees included in Chapters One and Two. The whole book was designed by Hannah Read. I was very impressed by her skills and by her outstanding determination to get it right. I recognise that it was a very complicated project she took on, but she went the 'extra mile' and was a delight to work with.

Once again, this book has been greatly enhanced by the artistic talent of Beverley-Jane Stewart. Having read my book in draft and as the result of several conversations with me and her own research, Beverley-Jane created the truly wonderful image that became the front cover of this book, capping those that she painted for my Golders Green and Bournemouth books. The painting captures the essence of the history of Blooms. In addition to the painting for the front cover, Beverley-Jane has also contributed a series of beautifully executed line drawings, which have been incorporated into the body of the text. Beverley-Jane, I feel privileged to have such a talented friend, and one with whom it is a great pleasure to work. I can't thank you enough.

Producing this book has been a challenge because of the vast amount of information I have had to synthesise to produce a narrative and because of the literally thousands of items of information that I had to check for their accuracy. Throughout the process, my husband Michael Hart has, as always, supported and encouraged me. I have promised him that I will take a break before embarking on another book. I am not sure that he believes me!

Pam Fox

Glossary of Hebrew and Yiddish Terms

Ashkenazi (plural *Ashkenazim*): Literally 'German' but used to refer to Jews stemming from the Rhine area and settling in a territory extending from Alsace to Smolensk and from the Baltic to the Black Sea. Jews from Germanic lands are designated Western Ashkenazim. Those from the Slavic territories are described as Eastern Ashkenazim.

Bar Mitzvah: Literally 'son of the commandment'. Refers to the ceremony marking the time at which boys become responsible for their actions in Jewish law, usually aged thirteen.

Beth Din: Literally 'house of judgement' but used to refer to a body that adjudicates on Jewish law. In orthodox Judaism, a *Beth Din* consists of three observant Jewish men, at least one of whom is knowledgeable in Jewish Law, *halachah* (*q.v.*).

Challah (plural *challot*): Plaited bread loaf, used to welcome *Shabbat* (*q.v.*) and festivals.

Chametz: Leavened products, which are forbidden during *Pesach* (*q.v.*)

Chanukkah: Literally 'dedication'. The eight-day, midwinter Festival of Lights commemorating the rededication of the Temple at the time of the Maccabees.

Charedi (plural *charedim*): A relatively recent umbrella term for describing Jews who are very observant in their Judaism. Its literal meaning is 'the fearful' or 'trembling in the face of God'.

Cheder: Literally 'room' but used to refer to a part-time religion school for younger children, usually attached to a synagogue.

Daven: Pray.

Dayan (plural *dayanim*): Religious judge(s).

Glatt kosher: The technical definition of *glatt* kosher is meat from animals with defect-free lungs, but it is often applied to products that have been processed under the stricter standard of *kashrut* (*q.v.*) set by the Kedassia licensing body.

Heimische: Literally 'homely', but sometimes used to mean observant.

Kaddish: Prayer for the dead said during the period of mourning.

Kashrus Commission: Supervising authority attached to the United Synagogue now called Kosher London Beth Din (KLBD).

Kashrut (Ashkenazi *kashrus*): Jewish dietary laws.

Kiddush (plural *kiddushim*): The act of declaring a day as holy, often accompanied with wine and food.

Kippah (plural *kippot*): Skullcap. Sometimes *cappel* or *yarmulke*.

Kosher: English version of Ashkenazi Hebrew word *kasher* meaning 'fit' but used to mean food adhering to Jewish dietary laws.

Pesach: Passover, the festival celebrating the freedom gained for Jews with the Exodus from Egypt.

Porging: Kosher law forbids Jews from eating this nerve, because in Genesis, the first book of the Old Testament, Jacob wrestles with an angel and the angel touches Jacob's hip socket, putting the joint out of place and rendering Jacob limp – thus, 'to this day the people of Israel do not eat the sinew of the thigh that is on the hip socket' (Genesis 32:22-32).

Rosh Hashanah: Jewish New Year.

Schlep (Yiddish): Carry or to make a difficult journey.

Schmooze (Yiddish): Flatter to make a social connection.

Seder (plural *sedarim*): Literally 'order'. The name of the service for the first night of *Pesach* (*q.v.*) using symbolic foods. Orthodox Jews outside Israel observe two nights.

Sephardi (plural *Sephardim*): Literally 'Spanish' but used to describe Jews who originate from the countries around the Mediterranean and from Islamic countries, their culture and their pronunciation of Hebrew. Sephardi Jews who subsequently settled in Italy, Holland, England and the Americas are designated Western Sephardim. Those who settled in the Balkans and Mediterranean areas are known as Eastern Sephardim. The term has now been extended to include Jews from the Middle East, North Africa and Asia, who are also referred to as *Mizrahi* (Eastern) Jews.

Shabbat (Ashkenazi *Shabbos*): Jewish Sabbath.

Shechita: Jewish laws relating to the slaughter of animals.

Shiva: Prayers for the dead following a funeral.

Shochet: Butcher certified by the Jewish religious authorities.

Shomer (plural *shomrim*): Religious supervisor(s).

Shtetl (Yiddish, plural *shtetlekh*): A small Jewish town or village in Eastern Europe.

Simcha (plural *s'machot*): Celebration e.g., a *Bar Mitzvah* (*q.v.*).

Treif (Yiddish): Literally 'forbidden' but meaning not in accord with Jewish dietary laws.

Yeshivah (plural *yeshivot*): A place of study for young Jewish men, seminary.

Yom Kippur: Day of Atonement, occurring ten days after *Rosh Hashanah* (*q.v.*) on which observant Jews fast.

Tzedakah: Refers to the religious obligation to do what is right and just, which Judaism emphasises as an important part of living a spiritual life.

Foreword by Steven Berkoff

I first came across Blooms in Aldgate when I was a teenager living just off Commercial Road in London's post-war East End. I seldom chose to visit the establishment since there were many other small Jewish delis where I could fulfil my desire for that special and unique flavour of Jewish nosh. But Blooms did seem to fulfil a fantasy for many Jews, here and abroad, to satisfy that innate craving. So, one day I did venture in, and famous as the waiters are for their outlandish *chutzpah*, I did enjoy my lunch.

I passed Blooms many times and decided one day to grab some takeaway lunch, I went to the counter and ordered my chicken soup, chopped liver and *heimische* (homely) pickled cucumbers and keenly waited. I was actually going to eat it at the counter, but to my shock my soup was served in a cardboard container even though I was eating there. I left, sadly never to return.

Blooms did satisfy, most certainly, that deep, inner longing to connect with mama's table, and that compulsive desire to share the same noisy air as our beloved brethren. Best of all … it was safe!

Whenever I visit a foreign city, one of the first things that I do is to check out the best Jewish delis and I must say America does them better. My favourite being the sensational Cantors in Los Angeles. And, believe it or not, it's a 24-hour deli, with the menu as long as the Old Testament. One could almost live in there.

Our milder, meeker Blooms does hold a place in Jewish hearts, especially for those who had never tasted the ecstatic flavours from Goldenberg in the Rue des Rosiers, Paris or Cantors in LA or Katz's amazing deli in Lower East Side, New York, where they shot that scene from *When Harry Met Sally* – a must to be visited before you die. As long as you don't die by eating their oversize salt beef sandwiches!

I did stray into the Blooms branch in Golders Green. What a difference. Wonderful chicken soup, potato *latkes*, pickles and chopped liver and most of all so friendly! I guess the East End still carried too much the *tsoorus* (distress) of the past. Great shame they have both gone. But there is always Reuben's of Baker Street. Thank God, it's terrific. Read this book. It will surprise you!

Author's Preface

Writing This Book

This book came as a bit of a surprise. With my previous books there was a link from one to another, but I did not see this book coming! In the summer of 2022, I was browsing social media groups focusing on Jewish social history, my specialism, when I noticed that there were recurring and interesting posts relating to the history of Blooms and the memories of people who ate at the firm's restaurants in Aldgate and Golders Green.

After some preliminary research, it appeared that although very little had been written about Blooms, its history would be a worthy subject for a full-length book. From the moment I started suggesting this as a possibility in conversations with professional contacts and on social media, the response was a resounding 'Yes!'

Once I set out on detailed research for the book, I discovered that the amount of material available was enormous, in fact there was so much that it was going to be a challenge to examine it all and distil it into a book. However, the enthusiasm I encountered as I went about my research spurred me on, as did the interesting story of Blooms that gradually emerged, the potency of which far exceeded my expectations. It has been a wonderful book to write.

Structure of the Book and its Coverage

The book is organised into three main sections. Part one of the book (Chapters One and Two) deals with the family history of the Bloom family – its roots in Eastern Europe and how the family fared after their migration to London. Chapter One contains the results of detailed genealogical research, which may be of particular relevance to those with an interest in genealogy, but which is worth reading since it provides a valuable insight into how Morris Bloom led his life in his adopted country and how his outlook, shaped in Lithuania, permeated the Bloom family business. Chapter Two provides the background to what was happening in family life as the Bloom's restaurants became internationally renowned and the firm's manufacturing and wholesale activities secured national coverage.

Part two of the book (Chapters Three to Six) consists of a series of chapters charting the history of Blooms, both its restaurants and its manufacturing and wholesale arm, over the ninety years of its existence. Chapter Three describes the operation of Blooms from its inception in 1920 until the immediate post-war years, drawing attention to its rapid success and the various ways in which it developed over that period. Within fifteen years of the firm being established, a small neighbourhood snack bar had become a restaurant, attracting customers from outside the East End, and Morris's meat products, which were initially produced in the backyard of premises in Brick Lane, were being manufactured in a 'modern electric factory' supplying outlets across London and in the Home Counties.

Chapter Four provides information on the opening of Bloom's restaurant in Whitechapel High Street and the early years of its operation when it quickly became 'The Most Famous Kosher Restaurant in Great Britain', and the opening of a 'sister' restaurant in Golders Green in 1965, highlighting their different characteristics and the contrasting environments in which the two restaurants traded.

Chapter Five offers an insight into the workings of Bloom's factory in its first location in Wentworth Street and after it moved to Tunmarsh Lane in Plaistow, showing how its activities steadily expanded, especially its cannery, and how its business shifted from largely supplying traditional kosher butchers and delicatessens to stocking supermarket shelves up and down the country. The 1970s and 1980s were boom time at the factory.

The final chapter in part two, Chapter Six, outlines the gradual demise of Blooms and mentions the factors that led to its decline. It describes the lead-up to the closure of the restaurant in Aldgate in 1996, the selling of the company's main assets, including its manufacturing and wholesale arm, and the continued operation of the Golders Green restaurant for a further sixteen years, until it too closed in 2010.

Part three of the book (Chapters Seven to Ten) deals with various aspects of the Bloom's enterprise. Chapter Eight looks at the many people employed by Blooms over the years, providing 'pen portraits' of some of the most interesting and memorable characters. The legendary Bloom's waiters (deservedly) have a chapter of their own, Chapter Eight.

Chapter Nine details the evolving customer base for both the restaurants and Bloom's meat products, citing the social, economic and technological reasons for the changes. The chapter discusses the egalitarian nature of the restaurants, particularly the Aldgate branch, where Jews from many backgrounds and walks of life rubbed shoulders with the rich and famous.

Chapter Ten examines the food served at Bloom's two restaurants and how and why its menus changed, especially in the post-war years, and changes in the range of goods produced at the factory. The chapter also describes the rise and decline in the popularity of Eastern European Jewish food and the shift towards a more cosmopolitan diet within the Jewish community.

The final chapter in the book reflects on the historical significance and legacy of Blooms, showing how its role and contribution to Anglo-Jewish history changed over the ninety-year lifespan of the company. Particular attention is drawn to Bloom's role in enabling several generations of descendants of Jewish immigrants to remain in touch with their roots and providing a 'Jewish space' that served different purposes at different points in Bloom's history, and the way in which it supported assimilation.

A section of Chapter Eleven shows how the nature of Blooms was influenced by its British environment by comparing and contrasting its development to that of the famous New York delicatessens. Another section examines the reasons for the success and demise of Blooms, looking especially at the pivotal part played by the Bloom family, as well as social and economic factors. It is suggested that while the family might have overlooked some important business opportunities and traded for too long on its celebrity status, perhaps failing to recognise changing market conditions, in fact Blooms was, in part, the victim of its own success. By contributing to the creation of an assimilated, self-confident and thriving Jewish community, Blooms was no longer necessary.

The penultimate section of Chapter Eleven analyses the legacy that has been left by Blooms, including the way in which it put kosher food on the map and introduced non-Jews to Jewish food, the sense of pride that surrounds its achievement of celebrity status – it is a big Jewish success story – and its role in shaping a distinctive Anglo-Jewish identity and supporting and catalysing assimilation. This section also highlights how Blooms imparted skills and experience that has helped to keep its legacy alive, and how Bloom's legacy lives on through its meat products, which continue to sell in large quantities.

The final section of Chapter Eleven looks at the future of *heimische* food, concluding that although there appears to be a comeback in the types of food served and produced by Blooms, there is unlikely to be a role for Blooms as it existed in its heyday. Times and tastes have changed.

A Note on Sources

This book draws on information gathered from a range of sources, including correspondence, mentions in biographies, autobiographies and memoirs (such as Harry Blacker's *Just Like it Was*[1]), obituaries, contemporary accounts (such as A. B. Levy's evocative *East End Story*[2]), articles and stories in national and local newspapers and periodicals, Bloom's marketing materials and menus, genealogical resources and databases (notably those made available by Ancestry.co.uk, JewishGen and Findmypast, the YIVO *Encyclopaedia of Jews in Eastern Europe*, the National Archives at Kew, the *London Gazette*, the General Register Office, the United Synagogue's database of marriage authorisations) and records kept by family members.

To provide contextual material for the Bloom's story, I consulted a number of specialist websites and secondary sources, especially those relating to the history of the East End, such as Rachel Lichtenstein's helpful book on the history of Brick Lane,[3] Raphael Samuel's *East End Underworld*,[4] the Memory Map of the East End compiled by Rachel Lichtenstein *et al.*[5] and Aumie and Michael Shapiro's *The Jewish East End*.[6]

I was able to circumvent some research by drawing on information I had gathered for my previous books on the history of the Rinkoff bakery,[7] the Jewish Hotels of Bournemouth[8] and the Jewish community of Golders Green.[9] However, I did carry out new, specialist research for the chapter on Bloom's food and to draw the comparison between Blooms and the New York delicatessens set out in Chapter Eleven. Invaluable in providing the information I needed were David Sax's *Save the Deli*,[10] Panikos Panayi's article 'The Anglicisation of East European Jewish Food in Britain',[11] Hasia Diner's *Hungering for America*,[12] Ted Merwin's *Pastrami on Rye: An Overstuffed History of the Jewish Deli*,[13] Claudia Roden's *The Book of Jewish Food*,[14] Massimo Montanari's *Food Is Culture*,[15] John Cooper's *Eat and be Satisfied*[16] and Ruth Glazer's 'The Jewish Delicatessen'.[17]

However, the three main sources I used in writing this book were oral history interviews, the archives of the *Jewish Chronicle* and social media, especially Facebook and Facebook Messenger. Over the last decade, I have been developing a special interest in using memories and anecdotes to inform the telling of Jewish history and I quickly discovered that the Bloom's story lent itself to an oral history approach since there are still many people around who either experienced Blooms first hand, or people who were closely acquainted with those that did. During a nine-month period I conducted more than one hundred interviews and had shorter conversations with a wide range of people, which produced not only wonderful memories and anecdotes to bring my text alive, but also factual information about Blooms. Most of these interviews I organised myself, but several interviewees also kindly referred me to other people who were willing to assist me. A letter placed in the Jewish press appealing for stories and anecdotes relating to Blooms was very productive.

The material produced by my interviews and conversations was quite outstanding in terms of both its quality and quantity. However, as I have discovered previously, despite careful questioning and sensitive probing, people tend to talk about the things they know about and what interests them rather than with a view to furnishing a coherent historical account. I have sought to fill obvious gaps and imbalances in information in a variety of ways, such as by carrying out further rounds of interviews with people able to provide missing information, or recontacting interviewees to request additional material, judicious editing and drawing on information from other sources.

The other potential drawback of oral history material is that people's memories are not infallible. People remember things in different ways and facts get distorted or embellished with the passage of time. I have therefore endeavoured to ensure that the content of this book is as accurate as possible by checking and rechecking information and by using triangulation processes. This is where my second main source of information came into its own. At the start of my research, I entered the word 'Blooms' into the search engine for the digital archives of the *Jewish Chronicle*, which resulted in over 10,000 hits. When I added other words to my search term, such as the names of key players in the Bloom's story, the number of hits increased significantly. I experimented with different ways of narrowing my search, such as looking at just a sample of the references, but I soon realised that being selective meant that I was missing important information. Over a period of three months, I therefore looked at all the references and the investment of my time produced dividends. The pages of the *Jewish Chronicle* are filled with a wealth of advertisements charting the evolution of Blooms and the environment in which it operated. This information is supplemented by numerous editorials, articles and letters that provide a treasure trove of details. The digital archives of the *Jewish Chronicle* are a wonderful resource for social historians.

When carrying out research for my Bournemouth book, for the first time I drew upon information contained in Facebook posts.

The material available proved to be so useful, especially in injecting new perspectives on my subject matter, that I became committed to using social media in future research. In fact, the history of Blooms relies to a far greater extent on content of relevant Facebook posts than my previous book, and to much greater effect. This book would not have been the same without the material available in a number of Facebook pages, but especially Memories of Hessel, Langdale Mans, Cannon Street Rd and Cable St; I Grew up at Golders Green Station in the 60s and 70s; Jewish Britain; Memories of Petticoat Lane and Surrounding Areas; East End of London and East London, History and Memories; The Jewish East End of London; You Don't Have to be Jewish; and East London Days Gone by; Bethnal Green and East London; and the Jewish Historical Society of Great Britain.

However, I discovered that, despite their undoubted contribution, Facebook posts, and to a lesser extent the many follow-up comments I received via Facebook Messenger, social media posts do have certain drawbacks. Like oral history interviews, Facebook posts are very subjective, but they also have a propensity for reinforcing myths (the repeated comments about Bloom's waiters being self-employed is a case in point), and for being nostalgic and occasionally over-simplistic in their interpretation of events. I understand and am sympathetic to the nostalgia that surrounds Blooms, it was an iconic Jewish institution. However, I had to see past the emotion and overcome the other complications to distil from the posts a more factual historical picture and to balance Facebook comments with information obtained from other sources. My book is therefore a, hopefully, judicious, blend of historical research and people's cherished memories.

The Literary Context for This Book

Although, as I quickly discovered, there is copious material relating to Blooms, it largely consists of brief mentions in disparate places, which have never been synthetised, supplemented where necessary, to produce a coherent and dedicated, full-length publication. I made it my pleasurable task to address this notable gap in Anglo-Jewish history. It remains a mystery to me why such a legendary institution has until now been neglected.

In addition to filling an obvious gap, I had another, wider aim in producing this book. From previous research, I was aware that despite its importance in Anglo-Jewish history, detailed and penetrating studies on the Jewish East End are still in their infancy, and however small it might be, I wanted to contribute to addressing this situation.

Until the 1960s, the experience of the Jewish immigrants who had settled in the East End of London since the 1880s was largely overlooked. Few of the first generation of immigrants were able to write their own history as they were struggling to survive in a new environment. A. R. Rollin, a radical labour leader involved in the Jewish clothing trade unions, who gathered material relating to Jewish socialism in the East End, was a rare exception.[18] It was therefore left to social investigators, such as Charles Booth and spokespeople from the established Jewish community to tell a 'top down' story of the immigrant experience in the Jewish East End. Most of the communal commentators lacked the inclination to focus on social, working-class history since, at best, the Eastern European Jews were 'an embarrassment'.[19] Almost exclusively, the commentators confined themselves to showing how Jews had always been a productive, patriotic and well-integrated element of British society, fully deserving of the emancipation they had achieved over the course of the nineteenth century. If the Eastern European immigrants were mentioned at all, it was only in the context of describing how well the communal authorities had coped with the tide of 'foreign' Jews by settling them as quickly as possible or sending them on their way, either back to Russia or to America and other western countries.

Most of the second generation of Jewish immigrants still lacked the skills and education to record their own history and those Jews who had 'escaped' from the East End were generally focused on assimilating and becoming part of the establishment rather than telling their own story. For many of these upwardly mobile Jews, it suited their self-image to buy into the dominant narrative of rapid anglicisation. However, in the early decades of the twentieth century, there emerged a group of talented, working-class Jews, who had been born and brought up in the Jewish East End. Known retrospectively as the 'Whitechapel Boys', this loosely-knit group, who met at the Whitechapel Art Gallery, included the artists David Bomberg, Clara Birnberg (the only woman in the group) and Mark Gertler; the poets Isaac Rosenberg and Joseph Leftwich; and the radical novelists Simon Blumenfeld, Barnett Sheridan (the pen name of Lazar Shrensky) and Willy Goldman.[20] They used their respective skills to portray (often with a tinge of anger) the poverty and brutality as well as the bravery and warmth of East End life during their formative years. Their avant-garde depictions challenged Anglo Jewry's defensive aims to downplay differences between Jews and gentiles and therefore found themselves condemned within and outside the Jewish community.

There was a hiatus in the literature relating to the Jewish East End during the Second World War, but in the immediate post-war years a new generation of novelists, notably Arnold Wesker, Wolf Mankowitz and Bernard Kops, began to write novels based on their East End backgrounds. However, as Tony Kushner has pointed out, they had no counterparts in the world of history and ironically it was left to an American scholar to reveal the richness and importance of the East End Jewish experience in Britain and to challenge prevailing tropes about the Eastern European immigrants.[21] Lloyd Gartner's *The Jewish Immigrant in England, 1870–1914*, which was published in 1960, assessed the reasons for the immigration of European Jews, challenging the common portrayal that they were mainly the victims of persecution and arguing that many were economic migrants seeking a better life. Gartner also contested the long-held assumption that the newly arrived Jews generally settled rapidly and swiftly prospered and experienced upward mobility.

Initially, Gartner's pioneering work fell on stony ground, but it gradually inspired a series of publications that sought to present a new picture of immigration history, critically re-examining widely promulgated myths about Eastern European immigrants. Included amongst these studies, which Tony Kushner refers to as 'revisionist',[22] were some ground-breaking books about the Jewish East End written by the descendants of the immigrants. Particularly seminal was William ('Bill') Fishman's *East End Jewish Radicals, 1875 – 1914*, published in 1975, which focused on the nature of immigrant labour. Fishman (mentioned in several places in this book), who had grown up in the East End, drew upon Yiddish newspapers to demonstrate the existence of Jewish radicals as a significant element of the East End Jewish community prior to the First World War.

Fishman's publication was revolutionary, both in its content and its approach, and led to several leading scholars (both Jewish and non-Jewish) presenting a wide variety of insights into life in the Jewish East End, notably *Economic History of the Jews in England*, published in 1982, in which Harold Pollin set out to show that immigrant Jews rarely prospered, and that those who did were the exception. It was largely their children and their grandchildren who made it into the ranks of the middle classes, and they mainly did not do so until after the Second World War.

Also notable was Jerry White's *Rothschild Buildings: Life in an East End Tenement Block, 1887–1920*, in which he sought to capture the memories of those who could recollect life in the East End during the period covered by the book. Using oral history interviews and written testaments, White aimed to reconstruct life in the tenement and succeeded in uncovering vital information, mainly from second-generation Jews, on the way of life of their parents. This was one of the first studies in which Jews were encouraged to engage with their own history. It is matter of regret that such studies were not carried out until many of the records relating to the Jewish East End had been lost.

The work of the first wave of historians focusing on the social history of the East End was taken forward by a new generation of professional historians spearheaded by David Cesarani and Tony Kushner, who sought to address what they saw as the imbalances and misrepresentations in the existing Anglo-Jewish historiography, notably in the volume edited by David Cesarani, *The Making of Modern Anglo-Jewry*, published in 1992. These historians often gave their attention to the East End of London, such as in *Remembering Cable Street, Fascism and Anti-Fascism in British Society* (published in 2000), edited by Tony Kushner and Nadia Valman.

However, alongside the work of these academics, there grew up another strand of Jewish social history largely drawing on memories to shed light on previously unexplored aspects of life in Whitechapel and Spitalfields. This new wave of interest was part of what is sometimes referred to as the 'memory boom' of the 1970s and 80s, which was not always taken seriously by some traditional, academic historians. With Jewish life in the East End fast disappearing, it was seen by some (notably David Jacobs, Monty Davidson, Harriet Karsh and Alan Dein) as being imperative to gather first-hand accounts of life in the area. Under the guidance of Bill Fishman, the Jewish East End Project (JEEP) was founded to explore marginalised histories of the area, resulting in publications such as Lara Marks's study of the experience of Jewish prostitutes.[23]

Until the latter part of the twentieth century, few memoirs had been authored by Jewish women. However, with the rise of gender studies and heightened interest in oral history, during the 1980s the voices of women were increasingly being recorded. One particularly notable project was carried out by the Jewish Women in London Group. Some of their work was brought together in *Generations of Memories: Voices of Jewish Women*.[24] It showed that previous accounts of life in the Jewish East End had tended to downplay the role of Jewish women outside the home and in supporting their husbands' businesses. Interestingly, one of the themes in the Bloom's story is the significant contribution made by female family members to the success of the firm (see Chapter Eleven).

Perhaps due to the lack of an institutional structure to support, nurture and maintain these initiatives, several oral history initiatives either failed to be analysed or to be used to produce coherent narratives. Others, however well intentioned, fell into the trap of presenting a romanticised view of the Jewish East End (for example, often evident in the publications of the Springboard Trust, such as *Memories: the Jewish East End*), which risked creating a 'historical theme park'.[25] However, other oral history interviews resulted in publications that skilfully avoided being distorted by nostalgia, such as the book on the work of Boris, the celebrated East End photographer,[26] which acknowledged the harshness of life in the East End. Although it faced many difficulties, the Museum of the East End of London, which emerged from JEEP, helped to stimulate this progress as well as preserving many vital artefacts relating to the Jewish East End.

Since the 1980s, there has been a variety of studies focusing on the East End, including Rachel Lichtenstein's book on the history of Brick Lane and my own history of the Rinkoff bakery, which have aimed to contribute to the understanding of life in the Jewish East End. These studies have included new and innovative ways of exploring the Jewish East End – through literature, music, such as Alan Dein's work on rediscovering East End Yiddish jazz scene,[27] and other media, including Rickie Burman and David Mazower's work on the Yiddish theatre in London.[28]

Particularly interesting is the work of an interdisciplinary research team headed by Professor Nadia Valman of Queen Mary College, which has been exploring the Yiddish culture of Jewish immigrants that flourished in the East End in the early twentieth century and subsequently became a formative influence on Jewish culture after the Second World War. The project team has been drawing on a body of rarely used sources (which are often incomplete) in Yiddish and English-language popular culture – literature, periodicals, theatre, songs and oral history recordings.[29] This new generation of research is much more concerned with the inner life of the Jewish community rather than the relationship between the immigrants and non-Jews and between the immigrants and the established Jewish community.[30] There can now be detected an air of confidence in writings about the Jewish community with all its foibles and idiosyncrasies.[31]

Despite this accumulation of studies, much work still needs to be carried out. My hope is that this book, an example of the micro-history and 'history from below' methodology developed by Richard Cobb,[32] and adopted by Bill Fishman, will contribute in some small way to the literature on the Jewish East End and the process of Jewish assimilation that has steadily been building up over the last fifty years or so. The research, and the material on which it is based, may be seen as akin to the more recent studies of which Nadia Valman has been a leading proponent. Hopefully, it will stimulate further studies.

My Approach

This book is no hagiography or a vanity publication. Although I have worked closely with some Bloom family members in its productions, and the book has benefitted enormously from their involvement, I have attempted to take an even-handed approach, celebrating the achievements of Blooms, but not shying away from mentioning things that went wrong. In my view, if I had avoided mentioning minor scandals and negative developments that are common knowledge, it would have both undermined the credibility of the narrative and excluded some important and interesting historical information. As with previous books, on sensitive and potentially contentious matters, the approach I have taken is to include, usually without comment, information that is already in the public domain on the basis that it adds to rather than detracts from the story and gives it authenticity.

Use of Hebrew and Explanations of Jewish Customs and Practices

Hebrew words used in this book are transliterated from the Sephardi pronunciation, unless the Ashkenazi pronunciation was used by the person being quoted (for example, if she/he said *Shabbas* rather than *Shabbat*) or is so common that almost everybody uses it for the word in question, such as *kosher* rather than the Sephardi *kasher*. Likewise, Ashkenazi names of congregations are retained. There are several reasons for the use of Sephardi pronunciation as the basis for transliteration. Here are three of them:

> Jewish schools, excepting some of the most orthodox ones, teach the Israeli pronunciation, which is Sephardi. It is standard in classes on spoken Hebrew, as well as in secular scholarship and at British and American universities.

> Furthermore, not only Sephardi and progressive synagogues (Liberal and Reform) but also Masorti ones and even some constituents of the United Synagogue, at least in part, use the Sephardi pronunciation, especially for the reading of the Torah.
>
> Possibly a greater justification for transliterating Hebrew according to the Sephardi pronunciation is that it is almost always the same irrespective of the speaker. This is not the case for the Ashkenazi pronunciation of Hebrew, which varies depending on the tradition of a community and the origin of the speaker.

Throughout the book, there are references to Jewish customs and practices that will be familiar to most Jewish readers. However, to assist non-Jewish readers, who may be less conversant with Jewish laws and ways of life, I have provided explanations. Where it is possible to give brief explanations, I have included information within the text. However, where the explanations are long and would therefore be intrusive, I have referred readers to the glossary included at the beginning of this book, which provides information on both Hebrew and Yiddish words used in the text. Where a word appears only once in the book, I have explained it in the text rather than included it in the glossary.

Read and Enjoy!

Like my previous books, writing the history of Blooms has given me intense pleasure. Not only have I once again had the privilege of speaking with many interesting, helpful and informative people, many of whom share my enthusiasm for Jewish social history, but I have also learned a lot from my various interviews and conversations. Since I am a social historian by background and inclination, I found it especially rewarding to write about what I think of as the Bloom's 'cast of characters', the fascinating people who ran, worked in, and ate Bloom's produce. I also enjoyed gathering information on the food served and produced by Blooms, which called for a significant amount of primary and secondary research and analysis. I hope that you will find these and other aspects of this book equally captivating. The story of Blooms, like its food (which, incidentally, I never sampled!), is one to savour either in one sitting or in bite-size portions, a concept that I am not sure was understood by Blooms!

Notes

1. Harry Blacker, *Just Like it Was: Memoirs of the Mittel East* (London: Vallentine Mitchell, 1970).
2. A. B. Levy, *East End Story* (London: Vallentine Mitchell and Co. Ltd., 1951).
3. Rachel Lichtenstein, *On Brick Lane* (London: Penguin, 2007).
4. Raphael Samuel, *East End Underworld: Chapters in the Life of Arthur Harding* (London: Routledge and Keegan Paul, 1981).
5. Rachel Lichtenstein, Peter Guillery, Duncan Hay, and Laura Vaughan (2020). 'A Memory Map of the Jewish East End', Bartlett Faculty of the Built Environment, UCL. Https://jewisheastendmemorymap.org/.
6. Aumie and Michael Shapiro (eds), *The Jewish East End* (London: The Springboard Education Trust, 1996).
7. Pam Fox, *History in the Baking, The Rinkoff Story* (London: Rinkoff Bakery, 2019).
8. Pam Fox, *Jews by the Seaside, The Jewish Hotels and Guest Houses of Bournemouth* (London: Vallentine Mitchell, 2022).
9. Pam Fox, *The Jewish Community of Golders Green, A Social History* (Stroud: The History Press, 2016).
10. David Sax, *Save the Deli, In Search of the Best Pastrami and Rye* and *the Heart of the Jewish Delicatessen* (Toronto: McClelland and Stewart Ltd, 2010).
11. Panikos Panayi, 'The Anglicisation of East European Jewish Food in Britain', in the *Journal Immigrants and Minorities*, 30.2-3.
12. Hasia R. Diner, *Hungering for America: Italian, Irish and Jewish Foodways in the Age of Migration* (London: Harvard University Press, 2001).
13. Ted Merwin, P*astrami on Rye: An Overstuffed History of the Jewish Deli* (New York and London: New York University Press, 2018).
14. Claudia Roden, *The Book of Jewish Food, An Odyssey from Samarkand and Vilna to the Present Day* (London: Penguin Books, 1999).
15. Massimo Montanari, *Food Is Culture* (New York, Chichester, West Sussex: Columbia University Press, 2006).
16. John Cooper, *Eat and be Satisfied: A Social History of Jewish Food* (Northvale, NJ: Jason Aronsen Inc, 1993).
17. Ruth Glazer, 'The Jewish Delicatessen: The Evolution of the Institution', *Commentary*, Vol. I, (March 1946).

18. Tony Kushner, 'The End of the "Anglo-Jewish Progress Show": Representations of the Jewish East End, 1887–1987', in Tony Kushner (ed.), *The Jewish Heritage in British History: Englishness and Jewishness* (London: Frank Cass, 1992), p.82.
19. *Ibid.*, p.79.
20. *Ibid.*, p.82. For further information about the Whitechapel Boys, see https://en.wikipedia.org/wiki/Whitechapel_Boys.
21. *Ibid.*, p.79.
22. Conversation with Tony Kushner, 18.5.2023.
23. Lara Marks, 'Jewish Women and Jewish Prostitution in the East End of London', *Jewish Quarterly*, 34(2): 6–10.
24. Jewish Women in London Group, *Generations of Memories: Voices of Jewish Women* (London: Women's Press, 1989).
25. See Kushner, 'The End of the "Anglo-Jewish Progress Show": Representations of the Jewish East End, 1887–1987', p.78. The work of oral historians continued to be rejected and regarded as unreliable by many academic historians.
26. Juliet Duff, *Boris: The Studio Photographer, 1900–1985* (London: The Jewish Museum of London, 1986).
27. See https://spitalfieldslife.com/2018/10/09/east-end-yiddisher-jazz/.
28. David Mazower and Rickie Burman, *Yiddish Theatre in London* (London: The Jewish Museum of London, 1996).
29. See https://www.qmul.ac.uk/makingthejewisheastend/. The project team members are Nadia Valman, Queen Mary, University of London (Principal Investigator); David Feldman, Director, Birkbeck Institute for the Study of Antisemitism (Co-Investigator); Vivi Lachs, Research Fellow and historian of the Jewish East End; Katy Pettit, historian of the East End.
30. Conversation with Tony Kushner, 18.5.2023.
31. *Ibid.*
32. See Cesare Cuttica, 'Anti-Methodology Par Excellence: Richard Cobb (1917–1996) and History Writing', *European Review of History*, 21(1). Cobb wrote a preface to Bill Fishman's book, *East End 1888*.

PART ONE
Bloom Family History

Chapter One

The Bloom Family's Lithuanian Roots

In 1920, Morris Bloom opened a business at 58 Brick Lane, which lay at the heart of the Jewish quarter of the East End of London. The business became internationally famous and endured for ninety years, passing from one generation to the next. In many respects the history of the Bloom family is a typical immigrant success story, achieved through determination and sheer hard work. However, there are several particularly interesting aspects of the family's story, including uncertainties relating to the surname of Bloom.

According to an entry in the 1939 England and Wales Register, Morris was born on 11 March 1891.[1] His 1932 British naturalisation certificate[2] states that his parents were Abraham and Sarah (the anglicised version of their names, Abram and Sore, sometimes Shore). There are no traceable Eastern European records relating to anyone with the name of Morris Bloom, but we are able to learn more about Morris's origins from the records that do exist for his younger brother, Bencelis (born Bentsel and later known as 'Benjamin' or 'Benny'), whose birth was registered in the Lithuanian town of Birzai on 6 November 1893.[3] The birth record says that his parents were Abram and Shore. Their surname is given as Klein (sometimes Kleinate, Kleyn or Kleinas) rather than Bloom.

Child's Name Date of Birth (D-M-Y) Hebrew Calendar	Father, Paternal Grandfather Mother, Maternal Grandfather	Birthplace (Town Uyezd Gubernia)	Type of Record Place Recorded Year Recorded Record#	Film Link Item # Image # Archive/Fond/ Inventory/File
KLEIN, Bentsel 6 - 11 - 1893 9 Kislev	Abram Gilel, Peisekh Shore , Shmuel	Birzai Panevezys Kaunas	Birth Birzai 1893 M68	2270865 4 1068-1097 LVIA/1226/1/1314

1. Birth Record for Bentsel (sometimes Bencelis or Benjamin) Klein (sometimes Kleinas or Kleyn). JewishGen, Lithuanian Births.

In Bencelis's British 1939 naturalisation papers, and a corresponding notice that appeared in the *London Gazette*, it is stated that Bencelis was by then 'known as Benjamin Bloom', suggesting that Bloom was an assumed surname.[4] Other records show that Benjamin Bloom is the name that this man commonly used for professional purposes when trading as a master butcher with a business in Sidney Street in Stepney.[5] He appears to have retained his original name of Klein in his domestic life. Some extant family members are aware that Morris's brother, Benjamin Bloom, was sometimes known by the name of Klein.[6]

Kleinas, Benceles or Bencelis (known as Benjamin Bloom); Lithuania; Master Butcher; 91, Sidney Street, E.1. 1 September, 1939.
Kleinas, Bencelis. *See* Kleinas, Benceles.
Kleinas, Chaza-Sore (known as Sylvia Bloom). Child of Benceles or Bencelis Kleinas.
Kleinas, Hena. (known as Esther Bloom). Child of Benceles or Bencelis Kleinas.
Kleinas, Motelis (known as Montague Bloom). Child of Benceles or Bencelis Kleinas.

2. Naturalisation notice for Bencelis Kleinas, *London Gazette*, 13 October 1939.

In the 1921 Census, Morris gave his birthplace as Ponevezh, the Russian name for what is now known as Panevėžys. It was the nearest main town to Birzai (Birzh in Yiddish), where Bencelis's birth was registered and also provided the name for the district in which Birzai was located.[7] It was quite common for immigrants to cite in records the name of the area in which they were born rather than the specific town.[8] An approximation of Panevėžys is also given as the birthplace for Morris in his 1934 naturalisation certificate.[9]

Bencelis's birth record tells us more about the Klein family. His father was Abram Gilel (elsewhere 'Hillel') Klein, and that

Abram's father was Peisekh. The name of Sore's father is given as Shmuel, but his surname is not recorded.[10] Other Lithuanian records tell us that Abram and Sore were born respectively in about 1848 and 1866.[11] Their notable age difference suggests that Sore might have been Abram's second wife. It also appears that Peisekh more commonly used the name Girsh (sometimes Girsha). His wife was Beylia Iokhelson.[12]

The 1898 All-Lithuania Revision List (a type of census) provides the additional information that, since 1879, Abram had lived not in Birzai itself, but in Juostaviečiai, a small village with fewer than 200 inhabitants, located a few miles to the north west of Birzai.[13] A 1874 Revision List shows in that year Abram was living in Linkuva about twenty-five miles due west of Birzai.[14] This information is significant.

Date (D-M-Y) Town Uyezd Gubernia	Type of Record Archive/Fond/Inventory/File Microfilm link Film image(s)	Name	Father	Relationship to head of household Sex
- January - 1898 Pabirze Volost Panevezys Kaunas	Families Living Out of Towns; 4th Stan KRA/I-26/1/2 102395788 89-125	**KLEYN**, Abrm	Girsha	Head of Household

3. List of Families Living out of Towns, showing the Kleyn (sometimes Klein or Kleinas) family living in the village of Juostaviečiai. JewishGen.

Another Lithuanian record describes Abraham as a 'poor' and a 'small seller',[15] but a later UK record tells us that Abram was a tailor and died sometime before 1920.[16] Further research indicates that Bloom (or a variation of it) might have been the surname of Morris's mother Sore prior to her marriage to Abram. The All-Lithuania Revision List for 1883 mentions a man named Shmuel (the forename given in Bencelis's birth record) Bliumberg (or Blumberg), the son of Leyb, who lived in Linkuva (the town from which Abram originated). Shmuel died in Linkuva in 1875.[17]

Date (D-M-Y) Town Uyezd Gubernia	Type of Record Archive/Fond/Inventory/File Microfilm link Film image(s)	Name	Father	Relationship to head of household Sex	Age this revision Age last revision
25 - May - 1858 Linkuva Panevezys Kaunas	Revision list KRA/I-214/1/1 102371880	**ZYB**, Girsh	Faytel	Head of Household M	 47
		SHTERLING, Shimel	Leyb	 M	 19
		BLIUMBERG, Shmuel	Leyb	 M	36 30
		BLIUMBERG, Rochel		 F	36

4. All-Lithuania Revision List, showing Shmuel Bliumberg living in Linkuva. JewishGen.

There are two plausible explanations for the different surnames of Morris and Bencelis. The first, and perhaps most compelling, is that Morris was born with the surname of Klein but assumed the name of Bloom to avoid being conscripted into the Russian Army. Although name changes for this purpose did not occur as frequently as some sources have suggested, it was not uncommon for young Jewish men of conscription age either to assume a new surname or to be adopted by another family to escape conscription.[18] If a family with the name of Bloom had sons who had already been conscripted, then younger sons would have been exempt. A Lithuanian draftee list for 1911 includes a son of Abram Gilel Klein called Girsh (probably named after his paternal grandfather). Like Morris Bloom, Girsh was born in 1891.[19] It is therefore not implausible to suggest that Morris might have started life as Girsh Klein rather than as Morris Bloom.

Although the despised 'Cantonist' system that had operated during the nineteenth century had been abolished,[20] Jews conscripted to the Russian Army at the beginning of the twentieth century still faced discrimination and antisemitism. They were recruited in numbers disproportionate to their representation in the population as a whole; they were more frequently posted far away from their homes, and to places where their families were forbidden to join them; they were sometimes denied access to facilities enabling them to observe their Jewish faith; and, like other minority conscripts, they were punished more harshly for deviations from military discipline and more likely to die on the frontline.[21] A twenty-five year sentence in the Russian Army was therefore something to be avoided.

A second, equally plausible, explanation for the surname differences is that Morris was the son of one of Sore's close relatives (perhaps one of her male siblings) who had died, or who for some other reason was not able to raise his son. If this was the case, Sore and Abram might have adopted him (and possibly other siblings) to be brought up with their own children. Adoption of the children of deceased or struggling relatives was quite common amongst Jewish families in Eastern Europe.

Whether the name differences can be explained by either of the suggestions outlined above, or by something completely different, what is clear is that there were connections between the Bloom and Klein families and that those connections centred on the Lithuanian town of Linkuva.

Birzai and the Move to Linkuva

Regardless of how Morris came to be parented by Sore and Abram Klein, his early years would have been spent on the outskirts of Birzai in north-east Lithuania. Birzai was located just fifteen miles to the east of the Latvian border. The village of Juostaviečiai, where the family resided, was even closer to the border. During the nineteenth century, many Jews left Birzai and the surrounding villages for the town of Bauska in the Courland (German name Kurland) area of Latvia. Since Bauska lay outside the boundaries of the Pale of Settlement (that part of the Russian Empire to which Jews were largely confined), Jews settling there were freed of the social and economic restrictions that limited the opportunities of Jews living in the Pale. However, the Klein family apparently chose to remain living within Lithuania.

5. Map showing the location of Birzai, Juostaviečiai and Bauska. JewishGen.

Jews living in the village of Juostaviečiai would have been strongly connected religiously and economically to the town of Birzai, where Jews started to settle at the beginning of the seventeenth century when the town was part of the Polish-Lithuanian Kingdom. In 1795, Birzai was included in that potion of Lithuania that fell under Tsarist rule. It grew and became the main town of the Ponevezh district of the Kovno province of Lithuania. The Jewish population numbered 1,040 in 1760, 1,685 in 1847 and 2,510 in 1897, when Jews formed fifty-seven per cent of the total population.

The Jews of Birzai made their living mainly from commerce, trading in flax and timber. A smaller number worked as craftsmen, farmers and peddlers or in the weaving and spinning factories owned by Jews. There were several synagogues, a Talmud Torah, a few *chederim* (basic religion schools for young children) and a variety of communal bodies.[22] The Jewish community of Birzai with which the Klein family was associated was therefore viable and well-organised.

6. Postcard of the Jewish area of Birzai. JewishGen.

In the years prior to the First World War, the economic opportunities available to Jews living in Birzai expanded, and Jews generally had good relations with their non-Jewish neighbours. Even when *pogroms* were rampant in nearby towns and cities (including Linkuva), the Jews of Birzai had a relatively peaceful life.

7. The synagogue in Linkuva. JewishGen.

Despite the comparatively conducive lifestyle of Birzai, All-Lithuania Revision Lists show that by 1908, the Klein family had moved to Linkuva.[23] The reasons for this move are unclear since the situation of Jews in Linkuva at that time was less favourable than in Birzai, and the smaller community had barely recovered from the fire of 1883 when more than150 families lost their homes and other property.[24]

According to family sources, Morris Bloom was one of nine siblings and the Lithuanian Family List of 1908 showing the Klein family's move to Linkuva also provides information on the identity of some of his siblings. In addition to Girsh (arguably Morris) and Benjamin (listed as Bentsel, his birth name), who have already been mentioned, the record also lists three sisters: Chana Beylia born in about 1885 and probably named after her maternal grandmother; Rocha, born in about 1886; and Genende, born in about 1893.

	KLEYN, Abram Gilel	Girsh	Head of Household	M 21 60			
	KLEYN, Girsh	Abram Gilel	Son	M 17			
	KLEYN, Bentsel	Abram Gilel	Son	M 18 in 1913			
Linkuva Panevezys Kaunas	**KLEYN**, Sora		Wife	F 42	1908	541 543	Family list KRA/I-214/1/9
	KLEYN, Chana Beylia	Abram Gilel	Daughter	F 23			
	KLEYN, Rocha	Abram Gilel	Daughter	F 22			
	KLEYN, Genende	Abram Gilel	Daughter	F 15			

8. 1908 Family List for Linkuva, showing members of the Kleyn (sometimes Klein or Kleinas) family. JewishGen.

We know from other records and family sources that Morris had another sister named Mashka, who was born on 6 January 1903.[25] The ten-year gap between Mashka's birth and that of her sister Genende suggests that other children might have been born to Abram and Sore in the intervening period. However, their identities are unknown. Since Chana and Mashka later emigrated to London, it is possible to trace what happened to them (to be mentioned later), but the fate of Genende and Roche is unknown since they are not mentioned in post-war records for Eastern Europe. It is possible that they either emigrated to another country, such as South Africa or the United States, which were favourite destinations for Lithuanian Jews during this period, or that they are listed under their respective married names.

The Klein Family's Expulsion from Lithuania

The wellbeing of Jews living in the north-east of Lithuania deteriorated rapidly after the outbreak of the First World War. During the spring of 1915, Jews were summarily expelled by the Russian military authorities from towns and villages bordering Latvia amidst accusations that they would act as spies for or collaborate with the advancing German Army. By this time, Germany had already captured parts of neighbouring Courland.[26] The expelled Jews, who were given twenty-four hours (and sometimes even less) to leave, either emigrated to other countries if they had the means and contacts to do so, or were forced to move eastwards, sometimes to the far reaches of the Russian Empire beyond the Pale of Settlement.

By the time of the 1915 expulsion, most of the offspring of Abram and Sore had reached adulthood. Some had already left Lithuania and others would probably have married. It would therefore have been a depleted family unit that was forced to leave Linkuva. As Abram Klein applied for a passport at the beginning of 1915,[27] we know that he was still alive at the time of the expulsion, but it appears that Sore had died sometime between 1908 when she appeared on an All-Lithuania Revision List and 1915 when Abram and other family members applied for passports but not Sore.[28]

From papers relating to Mashka, possibly the youngest of the Klein siblings, we learn something about the family's exile. In 1925, Mashka applied for a temporary passport to leave the USSR for a year to travel to England.[29] On the documentation, her place of habitation is given as Penza, a town in the Volga region in the south-east of the USSR, 350 miles south-south-east of Moscow. It was one of the main places to which Jews were deported in 1915, often travelling in crowded sealed freight trains. Many deported Jews died in transit or arrived in Penza hungry and sick.[30] The existing Jewish community in Penza was unable to support the vast influx of deportees and many of the new arrivals died in epidemics that broke out in the barrack-like accommodation where they were housed. Aged twelve on her arrival in Penza,

Mashka obviously survived, but other family members might have perished there.

Since the homes and property of Jews was ransacked and looted on their departure, few Jews returned to Lithuania when the war ended. Those that did so were not welcomed with open arms by the newly independent Lithuanian government. However, fortunately for historians, the government kept detailed records of its citizens and their movements. It appears that Abram died during the early years of the family's exile,[31] but Morris's brother Bencelis did return to Lithuania, where he married Gita Rocha Kaplinas (sometimes Kaplanaite or Kaplan) on 18 March 1922. The wedding took place in Lygumai, about 20 miles south-west of Linkuva. The marriage record states that Gita's parents were Motilis (Lithuanian for Mordechai) and Sore Kaplanaite (Kaplan).[32] Bencelis's comparatively late marriage at the age of twenty-nine might have been a result of his family's expulsion from Lithuania.

				Abraam Hilelis	Marriage		Linkuva	Lithuanian State Archive
Groom	**KLEIMAS / [KLEIN]**, Bencelis	29	Birzai	Sore	18 - 3 - 1922	DUDMAN		
Bride	**KAPLANAITE / [KAPLAN]**, Gite Rocha	23	Lygumai	Motelis	18 Adar		1922	
				Sore	Lygumai / Siauliai / Kaunas		1	LVIA/1817/1/175

9. Marriage record for Bencelis Klein and Gita Roche Kaplan. JewishGen.

We know that Bencelis returned to Lithuania as early as 1919 since in that year he applied to the Lithuanian government for an internal passport, entitling him to travel within the Russian Empire, which he mislaid.[33] Bencelis made a new application for an internal passport in June 1925.[34] By this time, Bencelis and Gita Roche (later known as Rachel Bloom) had two children: Motel (possibly named after his maternal grandfather), who was born in 14 January 1923, and Khaya Sore (possibly named after one of her grandmothers), who was born on 20 April 1925.[35] Their third child, Hena, was born in 1927.[36] Motel became known as Montague ('Monty'), Khaya Sore became known as Sylvia and Hena became known as Esther, all with the assumed surname of Bloom.[37]

The family lived in Lygumai, where Gite Roche had been born in 1899 and where Bencelis worked as a merchant. There is no record to show when Bencelis left Lithuania, but documentation shows that Gita Roche applied for an external passport for herself and her children in 1932.[38] Bencelis had probably by then established himself in London (with the help of his older brother Morris) and had arranged for his family to join him there. Shortly after the family reunion, Bencelis (now Benjamin) and Roche (now Rachel) had a fourth child named Sydney Joseph, who was born in Stepney in 1933.

Morris Bloom's roots in Lithuania and his early life there were to have a profound impact on his outlook and his way of living in Britain, the country where he forged a new life. This is the subject of the next chapter.

Notes

1. 1939 England and Wales Register, Ancestry.co.uk. It is possible that Morris's actual birth date was slightly earlier than this due to differences between the Julian calendars used in Eastern Europe at the time and the Gregorian calendar then used by western countries.
2. Naturalisation certificate for Morris Bloom, The National Archives, Kew, reference HO 334/136/504.
3. Birth Records, JewishGen.
4. Naturalisation certificate for Bencelis Klein known as Benjamin Bloom at the National Archives Kew, reference HO334/228/1215.
5. See for example, street directories in which he is listed as Benjamin Bloom, master butcher, with premises at 91 Sidney Street.
6. Interview with Marc Green, 21.8.2022.
7. 1921 Census Return, Findmypast.
8. In the above census return, Morris's wife Rebecca (see Chapter Two) gives her birthplace as Lodz rather than the town of Zdunska Wola, where she was born.
9. Naturalisation certificate for Morris Bloom, *op cit.*
10. Birth record for their son Bentsel Klein, JewishGen.
11. All-Lithuania Revision List for 1908, JewishGen.
12. All-Lithuania Revision List, 1874, JewishGen.
13. All-Lithuania Revision List for 1898, JewishGen.
14. All-Lithuania Revision List for 1883, JewishGen.

15. List of Tax Payers and Voters, JewishGen.
16. See wedding certificate for Morris Bloom, reproduced in Chapter Two, in which his father's occupation is given as a tailor and he is described as 'deceased'.
17. All-Lithuania Revision List 1883, JewishGen. On a 1863 map of Linkuva, Shmuel is listed as the tenant of a plot of land in the centre of the town. See http://www.linkuva.com/18cmap2.htm.
18. See https://www.museumoffamilyhistory.com/mfh-jitra.htm.
19. 1911 List of Draftees, JewishGen.
20. Under this system, Jewish children were conscripted to military institutions in czarist Russia with the intention that the conditions in which they were placed would force them to convert to Christianity.
21. Information based on article from YIVO *Encyclopaedia of Jews in Eastern Europe*, 'Military Service in Russia', https://yivoencyclopedia.org/article.aspx/military_service_in_russia.
22. Information taken from JewishGen. See https://kehilalinks.jewishgen.org/Birzai/Birzh_1.html.
23. Family List for Linkuva, 1908, JewishGen.
24. 'Linkuva', *Encyclopaedia of Jewish Communities in Lithuania.* See: https://www.jewishgen.org/yizkor/pinkas_lita/lit_00360.html.
25. 1939 England and Wales Register, Ancestry.co.uk.
26. See:https://www.litvaksig.org/information-and-tools/online-journal/expulsion-of-the-jews-from-lithuania-in-the-spring-of-1915-the.
27. List of Applications for Passports, JewishGen. The record shows that Abram applied for what was referred to as 'white passport' in January 1915. At this time, Russian internal passports consisted of a single sheet of white paper with no cover, hence its name.
28. Sore is not included on the above list of applications for passports.
29. Copies of documentation kindly provided by Marc Green, grandson of Mashka, later Minnie, Green.
30. See https://www.jewishgen.org/yizkor/lita/lit0089.html#9r.
31. There is no Lithuanian death record for Abram.
32. Lithuanian Marriages and Divorces, JewishGen.
33. List of Applications for Internal Passports, JewishGen.
34. *Ibid.*
35. *Ibid.*
36. List of Applications for External Passports, 1932, JewishGen.
37. See Benjamin Bloom's 1939 naturalisation papers. Extant family members believe that the family had a direct relationship with the Sieff family of Marks and Spencer fame.
38. List of Applications for External Passports, 1932, JewishGen.

The Bloom's Lithuanian Origins

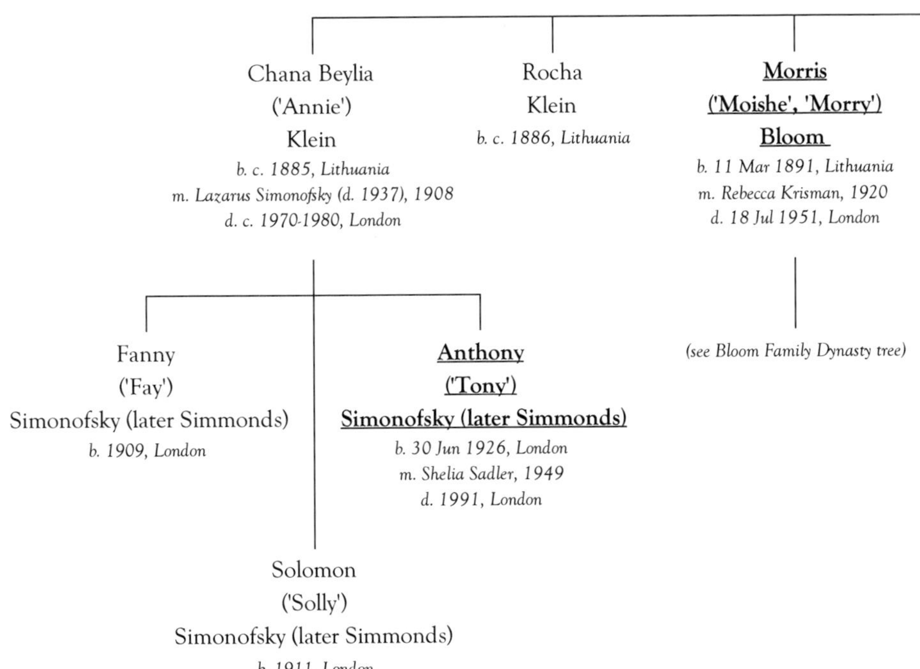

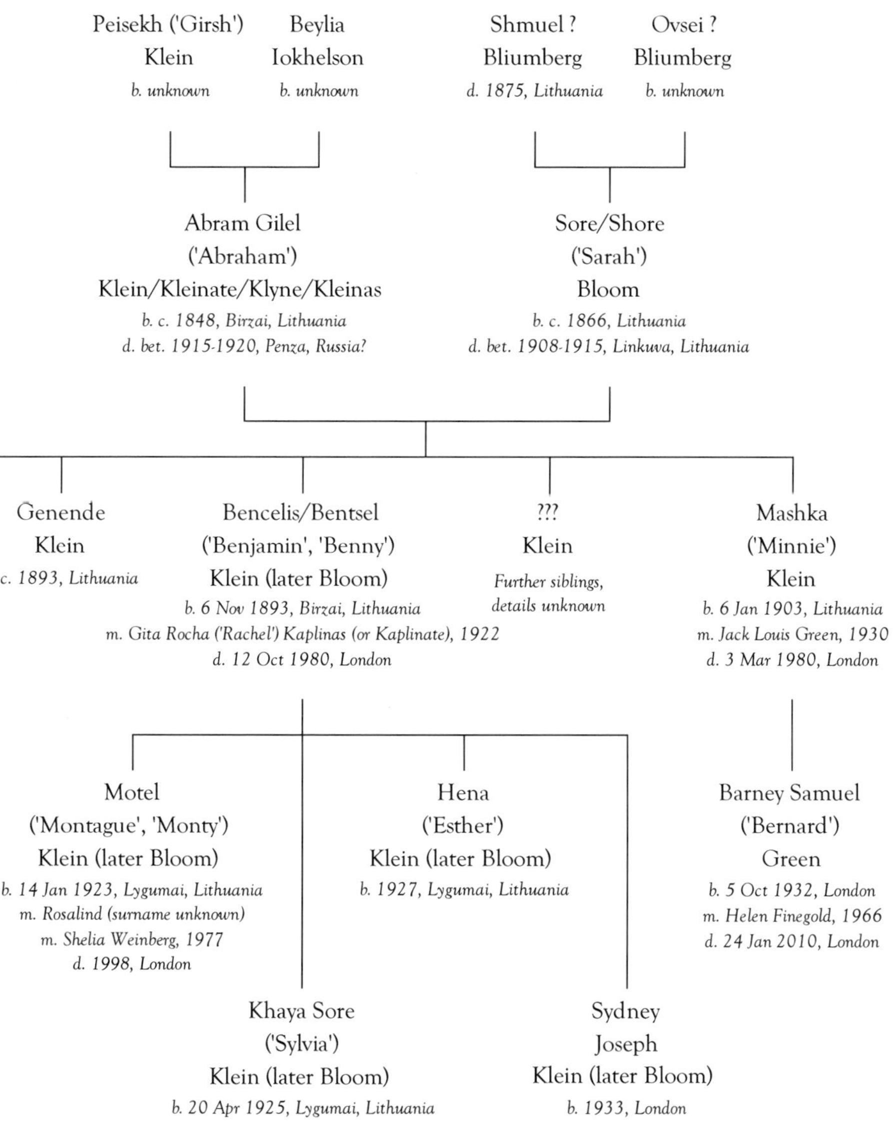

Text ***underlined*** *denotes those actively involved in the family business*

Chapter Two

The Bloom Dynasty

Morris's Migration to London

Morris Bloom arrived in London sometime between 1910 and 1912,[1] about the time that he would have been approaching conscription age for the Russian Army, which was then twenty-one. It is possible that Morris sailed to England from the Latvian port of Libau (now Liepāja), which in the years leading up to the First World War was the most common port of embarkation for Jews leaving the Russian Empire and which would have been accessible for Morris given the proximity of Linkuva to Latvia. However, there are no records to confirm that this is how Morris travelled to England and various family members believe that Morris travelled from Lithuania across mainland Europe, walking for great distances and stopping to work to earn money at various points to pay for his journey.

Like most immigrants from Eastern Europe, Morris is said to have arrived in London speaking only Yiddish and with 'nothing in his pocket',[2] but he was probably assisted in establishing a new life by either extended family members or other migrants emanating from the same part of Lithuania who were already settled in London, known as the *Landsman* system. Morris would have been provided with advice and contacts and a ready-made social circle. However, Morris had not arrived at the most auspicious of times. Although the controversy surrounding the passing of the Aliens Act of 1905 had abated, antipathy towards immigrants from the indigenous Jewish community had been reignited by the Sidney Street Siege of 1911, and the highly assimilated Jewish elite remained appalled by the 'teeming mass' of their co-religionists with their 'alien' religious outlook and separatist tendencies.

Marriage

Most young immigrants married within a short time of their arrival in Britain. The delay before Morris married suggests that during the difficult years of the First World War, he struggled to establish himself sufficiently to consider marrying. In 1920, Morris married Rebecca Krisman (sometimes Kriesman or Kraijsman), probably as the result of a *shidduch* (marriage match). The wedding took place at New Road Synagogue in Whitechapel[3] on 25 February 1920.[4] New Road Synagogue, the members of which were mainly from Poland, was the *shul* to which the Krisman family belonged. On the wedding certificate, Morris was described as a 'sausage maker' and his bride was a 'tailoress'. The couple gave their address at the time of the wedding as 44 Fashion Street, the home of Rebecca's parents. Morris was aged twenty-eight, but he gave his age as twenty-six. He named his father as Abraham Bloom rather than Klein. It is interesting to note that Morris was unable to sign his name ('the mark of Morris Bloom' is recorded) and that the marriage secretary signed the certificate on Rebecca's behalf.

1920. Marriage solemnized at New Road Synagogue in the District of Whitechapel in the County of London

No.	When Married.	Name and Surname.	Age.	Condition.	Rank or Profession.	Residence at the time of Marriage.	Father's Name and Surname.	Rank or Profession of Father.
76	Twenty fifth February 1920	Morris Bloom	26	Bachelor	Sausage Maker	44 Fashion Street	Abraham Bloom (deceased)	Tailor
		Becky Krisman	21	Spinster	Tailoress	44 Fashion Street	Myer Krisman	Tailor

Married in the New Road Synagogue according to the Usages of the Jews by Certificate

This Marriage was solemnized between us, The mark of Morris Bloom, B Krisman; in the Presence of us, L Starkovitz, M Joel; I. Shapiro Minister, Samuel Heller Secretary for Marriages

10. Wedding certificate for Morris Bloom and Rebecca ('Becky') Krisman, 25 February 1920.

Rebecca Krisman, known as 'Becky', was born on 24 May 1898. She was the daughter of Marks (originally Myer) and Toba (known as 'Miriam' or 'Marian') Krisman. According to the 1911 Census,

Rebecca was her parents' only child, even though they stated that they had been married for seventeen years (since about 1894) at the time of the census. Marks (sometimes 'Mark') Krisman was employed as a tailor and the family lived in one room at 45 Pelham Street (now Woodseer Street) in Spitalfields.[5]

The Krisman family originated from Zdunska Wola (Yiddish Zdunske Voyle), the district capital of the province of Lodz in Poland. Lodz itself was the nearest major city to Zdunska Wola. The first synagogue was erected in Zdunska Wola in 1788, but it was not until the 1830s that the Jewish community of the town grew to form a large proportion of the town's population and to extend their presence beyond the confines of two streets. The catalyst for the expansion was the establishment of a Jewish-financed woollen industry. The subsequent rapid industrialisation of the town attracted Jews from surrounding towns as well as many families from Lithuania. It is therefore possible that, like Morris Bloom, the Krisman family originated from Lithuania. While many Jews in Zdunske Wola prospered, others struggled, and it might have been the desire to establish a better life that stimulated the Krisman family to migrate to London. The family has been described as 'very poor'.[6] Marks died young on 18 February 1925 and was buried in Edmonton Federation Jewish cemetery.[7]

Morris and Rebecca's first marital home was 58 Brick Lane in Spitalfields, where soon after their marriage Morris had established a sausage-making business. They lived in two rooms above the business premises (see next chapter for more details of the early business venture). It was here that their first child, Solomon Judah, who was known as 'Sidney', was born on 1 January 1921. At the time of the 1921 Census, when Sidney was just three-months old, the Bloom family shared their home with a young man named Arthur Boothroyd from Portsmouth, who worked as their servant, possibly in both the home and the business.[8] Morris and Rebecca had two other children: Sylvia, who was born on 14 June 1924,[9] and Muriel, who was born during August 1927 and died at the age of three months on 13 November.[10]

11. Rebecca Bloom with Sidney and Sylvia, *c.* 1925. Courtesy of Martin Malin.

Morris's Siblings in London

As Morris's business burgeoned, he was able to assist his brother and two of his sisters who had decided to forge a new life in London. Since All-Lithuania Revision Lists often included family members who were no longer living in the country, it is almost certain that the Klein daughter listed in the 1908 All-Lithuania Revision List as Chana Beylia Klein is Morris's sister who migrated to London several years in advance of Morris. We know this since, on 14 June 1908, Annie (as she now called herself) married Lazarus Simonofsky at the East London (United) Synagogue.[11] Lazarus (sometimes 'Lezer') was a fruit seller from Chernikov (part of modern-day Ukraine),[12] who later adopted the surname of Simmonds. Interestingly, Annie was married under the surname of Bloomberg rather than Klein.

When the 1911 Census was taken, the Simonofsky couple were living at 104 Lucas Street in Stepney.[13] In the census return, Annie gave her year of birth as 1892, but the Lithuanian record mentioned in Chapter One, suggests that she was somewhat older having been born in about 1885. It was not unusual for migrants to change their birth dates, especially if it helped their marriage prospects. Annie and Lazarus had two children soon after their marriage – Fanny (later 'Fay'), born in 1909 and Solomon (later 'Solly'), born in 1911 – but there was a gap in the extension of their family during the First World War when Lazarus served in the British Armed Forces.[14]

After the First World War, Lazarus appears to have struggled to re-establish a livelihood. In 1920, he was arrested for stealing and sentenced to six months imprisonment in Wandsworth Prison.[15] In the sentencing order, it was recommended that Lazarus should be deported, but he clearly managed to stay in the country since he and Annie went on to have more children, including a son named Anthony, born in Marylebone on 30 June 1926, who became known as 'Tony Simmonds'.[16] He worked in the Bloom's business as a restaurant manager for many years.[17] Lazarus Simonofsky died in St Pancras in 1937. Tony Simmonds married Sheila Sadler in Ealing in 1949 and died in the London suburb of Northolt in 1991.[18]

Morris's younger sister Mashka (see above) came to London in 1925, travelling over a thousand miles across Russia to the Latvian port of Libau (modern day Liepāja) to sail to the UK.[19]

Союз Советских Социалистических Республик

ЗАГРАНИЧНЫЙ ПАСПОРТ.

Предъявитель сего, гражданка [illegible]
и Союза Советских Социалистических Республик
Клейн
Машка Абрамовна
отправляется за пределы С.С.С.Р. в Англию гор. London, [illegible]
в удостоверение чего и для свободного проезда дан сей паспорт с приложением печати.
Настоящий паспорт действителен для проживания вне пределов С.С.С.Р. в течение одного года со дня переезда границы.

Выдан 14 ноября 1925 г.
в городе Пенза

СВЕДЕНИЯ О ПРЕДЪЯВИТЕЛЕ:
Время и место рождения 1903, 6/V
Семейное положение девица
ПРИМЕТЫ:
Рост средний Глаза черные
Нос [illegible] Волосы черные
Особые приметы —

UNION
DES RÉPUBLIQUES SOVIÉTISTES SOCIALISTES

PASSEPORT POUR L'ÉTRANGER.

Le porteur du présent, citoyen [illegible] et de l'Union des Républiques Soviétistes [illegible]
Klein
Maschka a
se rend au delà de la frontière de l'U. R. S. S. en Angleterre ville Londres, [illegible] Bulgarie, [illegible]
en foi de quoi et pour le libre passage le présent passeport est délivré avec apposition du sceau.
Le présent passeport est valable pour le séjour hors des frontières de l'U. R. S. S. pour la durée de une année à partir du jour quand la frontière est franchie.
Délivré 14 novembre 1925
ville Penza

SIGNALEMENT DU PORTEUR:
Lieu et date de naissance 1903 6/V Lithuanie
État de famille demoiselle
SIGNES:
Taille moyenne Yeux noir
Nez [illegible] Cheveux noir
Signes particuliers —

№ 105251

12. Travel document for Mashka (later 'Minnie') Klein, sister of Morris Bloom, dated 1925. Courtesy of Marc Green, her grandson.

Like her sister Annie, Mashka anglicised by her first name, becoming known as 'Minnie', but unlike Annie she used the surname of Klein prior to her marriage. On 17 June 1930, Minnie married Jack Louis Green, the son of Judah Solomon Grounine (later Green) and Betsy Geverts (sometimes Giverts). Jack was born in Mile End Old Town on 4 January 1906.[20] He became a ladies' hairdresser, but in 1930 he was working as a 'cartage contractor'. The couple were married at New Road Synagogue (where Morris and Rebecca had married ten years earlier) and Morris was one of the witnesses. According to the wedding certificate, prior to her marriage, Mashka had been living with the Bloom family at 2 Brick Lane.[21]

Minnie and Jack had a son whom they named Barney (later 'Bernard') Samuel (perhaps named after Minnie's maternal grandfather), who was born in Stepney on 5 October 1932. In 1939,[22] Minnie and Jack were living at 86 Gibraltar Walk in Bethnal Green, but the family later moved to Walton Gardens in Wembley where Minnie died on 3 March 1980,[23] and where Jack died in 1988.[24] Bernard married Helen Finegold in 1966, and they had two children: Marc Blair born in 1967 and Simon Anthony born in 1969. Bernard died in Wembley on 24 January 2010.[25] Neither Minnie nor her offspring were involved in the Bloom family business.

Later in life, Benjamin Bloom (sometimes Klein) moved from Stepney to Golders Green, but in his final years he lived with his son Monty in Aylestone Avenue, Brondesbury. He died on 12 October 1980 and was buried in Rainham Cemetery in north-east London next to his wife Rachel, who had died four months earlier.[26] Benjamin and Rachel were buried under the name of Bloom.[27]

13. Headstone at Rainham Jewish Cemetery for Benjamin and Rachel Bloom (sometimes Klein).

Morris and Rebecca's Descendants

By the 1930s, the Bloom family was becoming increasingly affluent and were rapidly assimilating into mainstream society; salt beef and sausage making had obviously proved to be a route to comparative wealth. This upward mobility was indicated by their move from membership of New Road Synagogue to the Great Synagogue in Duke's Place, the oldest Ashkenazi (see Glossary of Hebrew and Yiddish Terms) synagogue in the UK and flagship for the established United Synagogue.[28] The move might have been aided by Lazarus Woolf, a prominent member of the Great Synagogue,[29] who had helped Morris set up in business.[30] According to family members, Morris and Rebecca were intent on their children speaking with 'perfect diction' and having a sound secular education.[31] After attending the Jews' Free School in Bell Lane, Sidney was educated at the Raine's Foundation School in Arbour Square, Bethnal Green.[32] Sylvia attended a comparable girls' grammar school.[33] When the children were young, family holidays were taken at the Kent resort of Cliftonville, then popular with Jewish families living in the East End of London who could afford to take a break from their work.

14. Sidney and Sylvia Bloom at Cliftonville, *c.* 1928. Courtesy of Michelle Spencer.

In January 1934, Morris and Rebecca celebrated Sidney's *Bar Mitzvah* (coming of age) and marked the occasion by making a donation to the Home for Aged Jews.[34] Morris was now in a position to make significant donations to charity, both monetary and in kind, such as his regular gifts of sausages to the Jewish Hospital and poultry dinners for the Home for Aged Jews.[35] Since he had grown up in poverty, throwing away food was anathema to Morris and he therefore ensured that any food left over in his business was given to people who lacked the means to feed themselves. His often-repeated dictum was: 'If the people are hungry, then we must feed them.' For Morris, it was a cornerstone of Jewish life that everyone had something to eat.[36]

Although his father was keen for his son to enter one of the professions, Sidney insisted on joining the family business and left school at the age of sixteen to do so.[37] In the 1939 England and Wales Register, he is described as a 'Beef Salesman'. Sidney's work with the firm was interrupted by the Second World War, during which he worked for three years in a munitions factory run by a firm named Miller.[38] Being employed in a meat factory as the 1939 England and Wales Register said he did, Sidney would have been regarded as working in a 'reserved occupation'. However, he might have come under social pressure to become involved in an activity that contributed more obviously to the war effort.

On the eve of the Second World War, Morris and Rebecca took into their home at 2 Brick Lane a young refugee girl from Germany, who had arrived in the country via Kindertransport. She lived with them until she was reunited with her sister who had been sent to stay with a family in Sussex. Many years later, now married and living in America, Sylvia Schneider wrote about the family's kindness: 'Whenever Mr Bloom passed me in the hall, he would empty his pockets of change and give it to me.' The Blooms continued to write to her and send her food parcels until she emigrated to New York.[39]

In January 1941, Sidney became engaged to Evelyn Radzan.[40] Born in Limehouse in 1923, Evelyn was the youngest daughter of Adolph Radzan (originally Radzanovich), a jeweller and watchmaker, and his wife Annie (née Griver), who lived in Raleigh Lodge in

Raleigh Gardens in Brixton.[41] Both of Evelyn's parents were born in Poland.[42] When Sidney and Evelyn met, Evelyn was working as a shorthand typist with the Ministry of Food.[43] She was to become a pivotal business partner in the Bloom family firm.

Sidney and Evelyn's wedding was held under the auspices of the Great Synagogue at the Porchester Hall in Bayswater, since the synagogue's premises in Duke's Place had been badly damaged by an incendiary bomb on the night of 10–11 May 1941 during the same raid that destroyed 2 Brick Lane. It was the last major raid in the Blitz and resulted in the Bloom family losing their home, a major part of their business and their synagogue.[44]

15. Remains of the Great Synagogue, Duke's Place after the bombing of 10–11 May 1941, the same night that 2 Brick Lane was destroyed. Wikimedia Commons.

Sidney and Evelyn were married on 21 June 1942 when Evelyn was 18 years old.[45] During the early years of their marriage, the couple lived with Evelyn's parents in Brixton. They had two children: Marilyn Felicity, born on 19 December 1943 at the Middlesex Hospital, Marylebone,[46] and Michael David, born on 5 September 1947 at the City of London Maternity Hospital.[47] Both children were to play a future role in the family business.

16. Morris Bloom with his first grandchild, Marilyn, *c*. 1946. Courtesy of Michelle Spencer.

17. Celebration of the *Bar Mitzvah* of Michael Bloom, 1961. Left to right: Rebecca Bloom (paternal grandmother), Marilyn Bloom, Michael Bloom, Annie Radzan (maternal grandmother). Courtesy of Michelle Spencer.

After the war commenced, Morris and Rebecca and their children were evacuated to Brighton. They lived in rooms at the Talbot Private Hotel at 5–6 Regency Square in Brighton with Rebecca's widowed mother Miriam Krisman and their daughter Sylvia.[48] Sidney Bloom, listed separately in the 1939 England and Wales Register, was living at the same address. The hotel, which was 'strictly orthodox', was owned by the Gastman family, who in 1939 were offering reduced rates for long-term guests.[49]

The family remained there for only a short time. By the time that Sidney's engagement was announced in 1941, Morris and Rebecca had returned to live at 2 Brick Lane, where Bloom's restaurant was now located.[50] However, when Sidney and Evelyn's marriage took place in 1942, Sidney's parents, his maternal grandmother and his unmarried sister Sylvia, were living in a house named Roydon Lodge on Woburn Hill in Addlestone near Runnymede in Surrey since, as mentioned above, their home in Brick Lane had been destroyed in the Blitz.[51]

18. Recent estate agent's photograph of Roydon Lodge, Addlestone, Surrey.

Roydon Lodge was a very large property (it is now a block of flats), which Morris had purchased rather than rented. According to family sources,[52] working closely with Rabbi Solomon Schonfeld and the Chief Rabbi's Religious Emergency Council, Morris and Rebecca opened their Surrey home to provide temporary accommodation for young refugees who had escaped Nazi Europe without their families. Morris and Rebecca were also involved in finding longer-term homes and jobs for young people who arrived in the country alone via Kindertransport and other means. Some of these refugees went on to work for Blooms.[53]

The Surrey countryside apparently held little appeal for Morris and Rebecca. By the time they celebrated their silver wedding anniversary in February 1945, the family had made their home in a substantial house at 10 Gloucester Gardens in Golders Green, north-west London. Morris and Rebecca had clearly missed living at the heart of a vibrant Jewish community since by this time Golders Green was recognised as a 'Jewish place'.[54]

19. Recent photo of 10 Gloucester Gardens in Golders Green, the house once owned by Morris and Rebecca Bloom. Author's photo.

Having moved to Golders Green, Morris became a member of the strictly orthodox synagogue, Golders Green Beth Hamedrash, known as 'Munk's Shul' after the long-standing rabbi who led the community. It was located close to Morris and Rebecca's new home in Gloucester Gardens where many other members of the *shul* (Yiddish word for synagogue) also lived.[55] Morris is said to have been very prominent in Munk's Shul. He was one of the wardens who sat at the front of the congregation wearing a top hat.[56] Although Sidney and his family became members of Finchley (United) Synagogue ('Kinloss Gardens'), due to its location Sidney also *davened* (prayed) in Munk's Shul with his father and was a member there.[57]

While Morris and Rebecca might initially have felt comfortable living amongst their co-religionists, in 1948 they experienced a major trauma. In the early hours of 24 December, five armed and masked men broke into the Bloom's home. They viciously attacked the family members living there (Morris, Rebecca, Miriam Krisman and Sylvia Bloom), ransacked the house and stole jewellery. It was thought that the thieves were looking for the takings from the business, which were transported home every night to be stored in a safe. Miriam Krisman (referred to as '*Bubbe*', grandmother) was beaten so badly that she lost the sight in one eye. Morris, who was rendered unconscious by his attackers, never fully recovered from the incident.[58] The crime and the subsequent trial were covered extensively in both the Jewish and non-Jewish press.[59] The family never spoke about the burglary, but steel bars were installed on the windows of the house.[60] The pain inflicted on the family by the burglary was exacerbated when a year later a nurse employed by Rebecca, probably to care for her mother, was convicted of stealing household goods.[61]

Twelve months after the burglary, Sylvia Bloom, who was now working full time in the family business, became engaged to Archibald ('Archie') Malin, a car dealer with a business at 55 Warren Street, then the 'Hatton Garden' for car dealerships. Archie, who was ten years older than Sylvia, was born in Stepney on 27 March 1915. He was the son of Abraham (a poultry dealer) and Esther Malinofsky (née Levy), who had married in 1907. Esther had been married previously, but her first husband died in an accident. Some of Archie's older siblings were therefore children from Esther's first marriage.[62] Having left home at the age of fifteen, Archie was very successful and throughout his life he supported his less fortunate siblings and never forgot his humble East End roots. His son recalls: 'He used to tell me stories about how he had been at the Battle of Cable Street, putting marbles under the hooves of the police horses so that they could not charge.'[63]

The wedding of Sylvia and Archie took place at Hendon Synagogue on 6 June 1950,[64] when Sylvia was twenty-five years old, and Archie was thirty-four. The marriage was witnessed by Sylvia's bother Sidney Bloom and Archie's father Abraham Malin. It was such a large wedding that the reception was held at Wembley Town Hall. With the help of Morris, the couple set up their first home in Hendon Lane, Finchley. They subsequently moved to Hazelmere Gardens, close to Finchley Synagogue, of which (like Sidney and Evelyn) they became very active members. Sylvia Malin donated a vestibule for the synagogue and Sidney gave a stained-glass window.[65]

20. Wedding of Sylvia Bloom and Archie Malin at Hendon Synagogue, June 1950. Courtesy of Michelle Spencer.

The marriage was timely. On 18 July 1951, Morris Bloom died shortly after his 60th birthday. The notice placed by the family in the *Jewish Chronicle* read:

> **BLOOM:** On Wednesday July 18, 1951, Morris Bloom, aged 60 our dearly beloved husband and father. Deeply mourned by his sorrowing wife. Rebecca (Becky), son Sidney, daughter, Sylvia (Mrs. A. Malin), brother, sisters, son-in-law, daughter-in-law, mother-in-law, grandchildren (Marilyn and Michael), relatives, all members of staff, and a large circle of friends. His memory will never be forgotten. May his dear soul rest in everlasting peace.[66]

In his will, Morris left a shareholding of fifty-one per cent of the family business to his son Sidney. The remaining forty-nine per cent of the shares were to be divided between his daughter and his grandchildren, including those yet to be born, who had equal voting rights in relation to the business; they were 'preference shareholders'. However, with his majority shareholding, Sidney made most of the business decisions until his retirement in 1986. Morris died an affluent man, which is remarkable considering his humble beginnings and that apparently, he never became fully conversant with reading and writing in English.[67]

Sadly, Morris did not live to celebrate the birth of the two Malin grandchildren, Michelle Yvonne, born on 11 February 1952 and Martin David, born on 20 May 1955.[68] To commemorate Morris's life, several endowments were made by the Bloom family. In May 1953, Sidney Bloom dedicated a room in his father's name at Menorah Primary School in The Drive, Golders Green,[69] and in 1957 a consecration service was held in the newly erected Morris Bloom Hall, paid for by Rebecca Bloom and Sidney Bloom, at the Hasmonean Grammar School for Boys, which was to be attended by one of his grandsons and two great-grandsons.[70] Later, an Ark [71] covering (*parochet*) depicting the Tribes of Israel was donated to Munk's Shul in Morris's name by two of his grandchildren, Marilyn and Michael.

Rebecca outlived her husband by eighteen years, continuing to work for many of them on the counter at the Aldgate restaurant. Michelle Spencer (née Malin) spent a great deal of time with her grandmother while her mother was working and remembers Rebecca as an outgoing woman who loved socialising and following fashion trends.

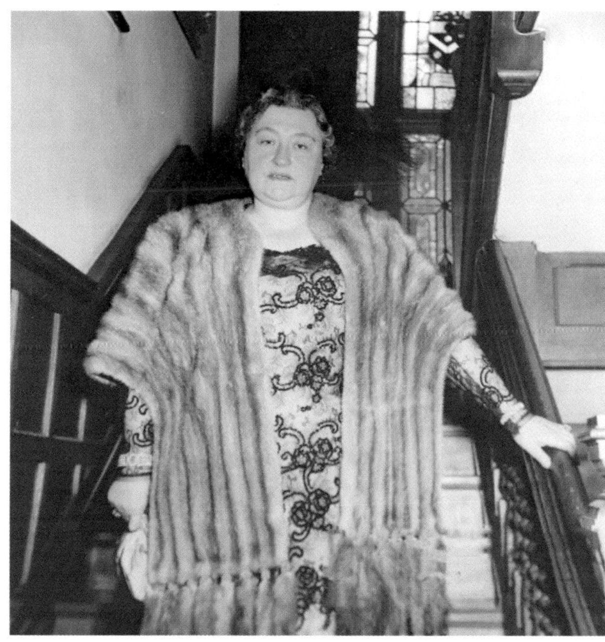

21. Rebecca Bloom at 10 Gloucester Gardens, Golders Green, *c.* 1960. Courtesy of Michelle Spencer.

Rebecca died on 31 March 1969.

> **BLOOM.** Rebecca, dearly beloved mother of Sidney and Sylvia (Malin) passed peacefully away on Monday, March 31 (Nisan 12). A gracious and compassionate lady who was loved and respected by all who had the privilege to know her. Deeply mourned by her heartbroken son, Sidney, daughter, Sylvia, daughter-in-law, Evelyn, son-in-law, Archie, grandchildren, Marilyn, Michael, David, Michelle and Martin, and great-grandchildren, Alan and Jonathan. A true Jewish mother, grand-mother and great-grandmother, whose memory and way of life will always be cherished. Words cannot describe our broken hearts.[72]

Martin Malin, who had celebrated his *Bar Mitzvah* shortly before his grandmother's death, recalls that on the night she was dying, his parents were 'speaking to each other in Yiddish, which was always a bad sign – it meant that there was something that they did not want us children to understand'. So many people wanted to attend the *shiva* (seven-day period of mourning following a funeral (see Glossary of Hebrew and Yiddish Terms), which was held at the family home in Gloucester Gardens, long queues formed outside the house, stretching back to Golders Green Road.[73]

Morris and Rebecca were buried together in at Willesden Jewish Cemetery, where Morris had the foresight to invest in several plots prior to the cemetery becoming full. Buried alongside them was Miriam Krisman, Rebecca's mother, who had died shortly after Morris on 28 October 1952.[74] After her death, Rebecca and Sidney Bloom had endowed a room in Miriam's name at the Hasmonean Grammar School for Girls in Parson Street, Hendon.[75]

22. Miriam Krisman, 1950. Courtesy of Michelle Spencer.

23. Headstone for Morris and Rebecca Bloom at Willesden Jewish Cemetery. Courtesy of Hannah Jacobs.

During their lives, both Morris and Rebecca had together been very involved with the charitable activities of the Wolfson family (Sir Isaac and Edith), and Rebecca was particularly close to Lady Wolfson.[76] Until his death, Morris also contributed to a wide range of other charities, including the Sportsman's Aid Society, a body that raised money for various Jewish charities.[77]

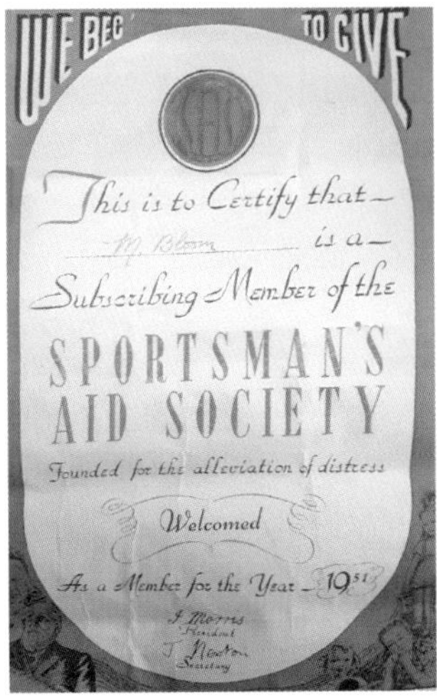

24. Certificate of charitable giving, 1952. Courtesy of Martin Malin.

Following Morris's death, Rebecca continued her charitable activities in what was described as 'a quiet and unobtrusive manner'.[78] She was noted for the money she donated in support of Israel. Her grandson, Martin Malin, speaks with pride about the photo of Rebecca shaking hands with the Israeli statesman, Levi Eshkol, at a Youth Aliyah function in the 1960s.[79] Rebecca received a certificate for her outstanding contribution to a Youth Aliyah children's home in Israel. She was a vice-president of the charity.

25. Rebecca Bloom shaking hands with the Prime Minister of Israel, Levi Eshkol, *c.* 1965. Courtesy of Martin Malin.

Among the British causes dear to Rebecca's heart were the Home for Aged Jews and Highbury Home for Babies. Many years after her death, it came to light that she had donated sufficient money to the Highbury Home for Babies to provide a 'chicken dinner for *Shabbat*, as a very special treat' for thirty years. This support was only discontinued when the home closed in 1982, by which time Rebecca's generosity had been enjoyed by 1,400 children and the staff of the home.[80]

With financial support from Morris, in 1949 Sidney and Evelyn Bloom, had moved from south London to 'Bexleigh', at 2 Fitzalan Road in Finchley. Annie Radzan lived with them there until her death in 1970. Marilyn and Michael remained living in this house until their respective marriages. In September 1962, Marilyn became engaged to David Tapper,[81] the son of Morris ('Morry'), a refugee from Austria, and Maisie (Morry's second wife, née Block) Tapper. The Tapper family co-owned a well-known fashion company named Carnegie of London, located in Osborn Street, the continuation of Brick Lane, around the corner from the Bloom's restaurant in Whitechapel High Street, which is where the couple met.[82] Given that Marilyn and David both came from successful and well-known families, their marriage was seen as 'quite a match'.

Marilyn and David Tapper had two sons: Alan, who was born on 5 January 1964, and Jonathan who was born on 10 June 1967.[83] The Tapper family lived in Chessington Avenue in Finchley, close to Sidney and Evelyn and to the Malin family. Alan, who sadly died suddenly at the age of forty-five, initially worked in the Bloom's restaurant, but he later went into his father's fashion business. In 1999, Jonathan became the managing director of the firm, which by then had been reduced to ownership of the Bloom's restaurant in Golders Green that had opened in 1965.[84]

Jonathan Tapper was the last member of the Bloom dynasty to be involved in the running of the family enterprise. He entered the family business full time at the age of sixteen and learned the skills involved in every aspect of the trade, first at the factory in Tunmarsh Lane and then at the Aldgate restaurant. By the mid-1990s, he was working as a general manager at the restaurant and was also a member of the company's management team. He was very close to his grandfather, Sidney Bloom. Jonathan was the fourth generation of the Bloom family to work in the business founded by his great-grandfather Morris Bloom.[85]

In 1975, Michael Bloom married Caroline Berman at Finchley (United) Synagogue and they had two sons: Daniel Lee, born on 12 April 1976, and Adam Paul, born on 18 April 1980. The family lived in Edge Hill Avenue in Finchley. Michael was involved with the family business from the time that he left school and eventually became its managing director, taking over from his father in 1986.[86] He became a member of the board of management at Finchley Synagogue and like his father, he was charitably inclined. He was a member of the Celebrity Guilds' Committee, which organised events to raise money to buy equipment for people with disabilities.[87]

Michael also became one of the country's leading numismatists, making headlines when he paid £2,200 for a £1 coin. It was the first £1 coin to be struck by Prince Charles (as he was at the time) at the Royal Mint. The proceeds of Michael's purchase were donated to the National Fund for Research into Crippling Diseases, and to celebrate his acquisition, Bloom's famous salt beef sandwiches were sold for £1 at the Aldgate restaurant one Saturday night.[88]

The Bloom family were very close and spent a great deal of time together and celebrated lifecycle events in style, often at the Savoy Hotel or the King David Suite (now known as the Grand Ballroom) in Marble Arch.[89] As they became more affluent, the extended family holidayed several times a year in Bournemouth, staying at the upmarket Cumberland Hotel. Morris and Rebecca Bloom were family friends of Isaac and Bluma Feld who owned the hotel and were therefore given preferential treatment. Geoffrey Feld, the son of Isaac and Bluma, recalls: 'They came to the hotel each year for *Pesach* [Passover] and the other major festivals; they were like part of our family. We put the red carpet out for them!'[90] It is said that Morris and Rebecca Bloom strongly encouraged Isaac and Bluma to buy the hotel.[91]

The Bloom family continued to gather in Bournemouth after the death of Morris. Sheila Finesilver, who stayed at the hotel when she was a teenager, recalls:

> The table next to us in the dining room was occupied by the Bloom family. Sid and Evelyn were there with Michael and Marilyn, with various aunts and uncles. I enjoyed listening in to what they were saying to each other. Michael was only a little boy then, a real *lobus* young mischievous person. And as for the ladies' outfits! Oh, my word, it was a wonderful fashion show for eight days. We saw their outfits arrive in a huge pantechnicon from London. In the vehicle were rails and rails of clothes.[92]

The Six-Day War in 1967 led to an upsurge in support for Israel and, like many other Jewish people who had previously stayed in hotels in Bournemouth,[93] Sidney and Evelyn began taking their main holidays in Israel. They bought a holiday home opposite the Accadia Hotel on the seafront in Herzliya and were often joined there by other family members and friends.

Although Sidney and Evelyn worked very long hours in the business, and like the whole family were *Shomer Shabbat* (obeyed Jewish laws relating to the Sabbath) partly as a way of ensuring that Blooms retained its kosher licence. Nevertheless, they still found time to socialise. They had a very wide circle of friends with whom they regularly spent their leisure time.

Amongst their closest friends were Sam and Gertie Greenspan, with whom they holidayed in Bournemouth and later also in Nice and Juan-les-Pins in the south of France, and in Italy. The Greenspan family lived in Finchley and were members of the same synagogue (Finchley Synagogue), where Sam was a warden for many years. The Greenspan family became manufacturers of meat products themselves and were therefore competitors, but they and the Blooms remained good friends.[94]

26. The Bloom family at Juan-les-Pins, *c.* 1956. Left to right: Rebecca Bloom, Sylvia and Archie Malin and their children, Martin and Michelle. Courtesy of Michelle Spencer.

Sidney liked horseracing and often attended races with Evelyn and their friends. At one point he owned race horses, including one named Nicolaus Silver, which had won the Grand National in 1961 and a flat racer named Galen.[95] Stories are told of an off-course bookmaking business being run from the back of the Aldgate restaurant in the days before it was legal: 'My father placed a bet on a horse in the Derby and the Blooms gave him odds of 60-1. The horse won and Sidney was keen to find out where he got his tips!'[96]

Sidney also liked visiting nightclubs and casinos in the West End and playing cards with his long-standing friends and close colleagues.[97] He was an ardent supporter of Tottenham Hotspur Football Club ('Spurs'). In the 1960s, a large photograph of the 1961 'double winning team' hung on the wall behind the takeaway counter in the Bloom's Aldgate restaurant.[98]

27. The Bloom family and their friends. Left to right: Archie Malin, Sidney Bloom, Gertie Greenspan, Sam Greenspan, Sylvia Malin (née Bloom), Rebecca Bloom, Evelyn Bloom (née Radzan), *c.* 1955. Courtesy of Martin Malin.

When Annie Radzen died on 29 December 1970, there was an outpouring of loss for a woman who had been noted for her kindness and charitable involvements. Her husband, Adolph, had died 15 years earlier in 1956. Annie was legendary amongst the staff and customers of Bloom's restaurant, where she had spent a great deal of her time. Archie Malin played practical jokes on her, which she took in good part:

> When we once stayed at the Cumberland in Bournemouth, he put *matzot* [plural of *matzah*, unleavened flatbread] underneath her mattress, which crackled when she laid down, making her think that she had broken a bone![99]

She was fondly referred to as 'Annie Rad'.[100]

Evelyn Bloom died aged sixty-seven on 4 December 1990. She was by then regarded as the matriarch of the renowned Bloom family. At her funeral, Rabbi Cyril Shine commented that her death had 'saddened the entire north-west London Jewish community'. Several hundred people attended her funeral, including many who had benefitted from her advice and support.[101] After her death, Sylvia Malin, became 'a sort of surrogate mother to Marilyn' and they spoke by telephone several times a day.[102]

Sidney outlived both his wife and his sister, Sylvia Malin, who was known as 'Auntie' by everyone who knew her. Sylvia died on 28 July 2000, having devoted approaching sixty years of her life to working for the family firm. She was noted for her sense of humour and her devotion to her children, Michelle and Martin, and her grandchildren.[103] Sylvia's husband, Archie, died on 12 June 2007 and was buried alongside his wife in Willesden Jewish Cemetery in a Bloom family reserved plot.

28. Headstone for Sylvia Malin (née Bloom) at Willesden Jewish Cemetery.

29. Headstone for Archie Malin at Willesden Jewish Cemetery.

Both Michelle and Martin Malin spent time working in the family business. When she left school, Michelle went to secretarial college and then worked behind the counter at both the Aldgate and the Golders Green restaurants before going on to other jobs. After Martin Malin left university in the mid-1970s and was still in the process of establishing his career as a writer, he worked in the family firm. He started by working in the factory,[104] by then located in Plaistow, and then moved across to the Aldgate restaurant to learn about the different aspects of running a kosher restaurant. He says: 'I was a Jack of All Trades!'[105]

Sidney Bloom died, aged eighty-two, on 1 June 2003 at the Wellington Hospital in St John's Wood. Throughout the illness that preceded his death, he had been 'nursed and cared for like a king' by his daughter Marilyn.[106] After his death, tributes poured in for the 'King of the Kosher Restaurants'. His passing was noted in both the

Jewish and non-Jewish press, including *The Times*, *The Guardian* and *The Daily Telegraph*.[107] Obituaries also appeared in foreign newspapers and he received a mention (the only Jewish restaurateur to do so) in the *Oxford Dictionary of National Biography*.[108] He was frequently described as a 'shy, modest man' and noted for his charitable giving to schools and *yeshivot* (plural of *yeshivah*, Jewish seminary).[109] He was utterly dedicated to the business he had made a success, continuing to visit the Golders Green restaurant (and more particularly its kitchens) until shortly before his death. Sidney was buried alongside his wife Evelyn at Willesden Jewish Cemetery.

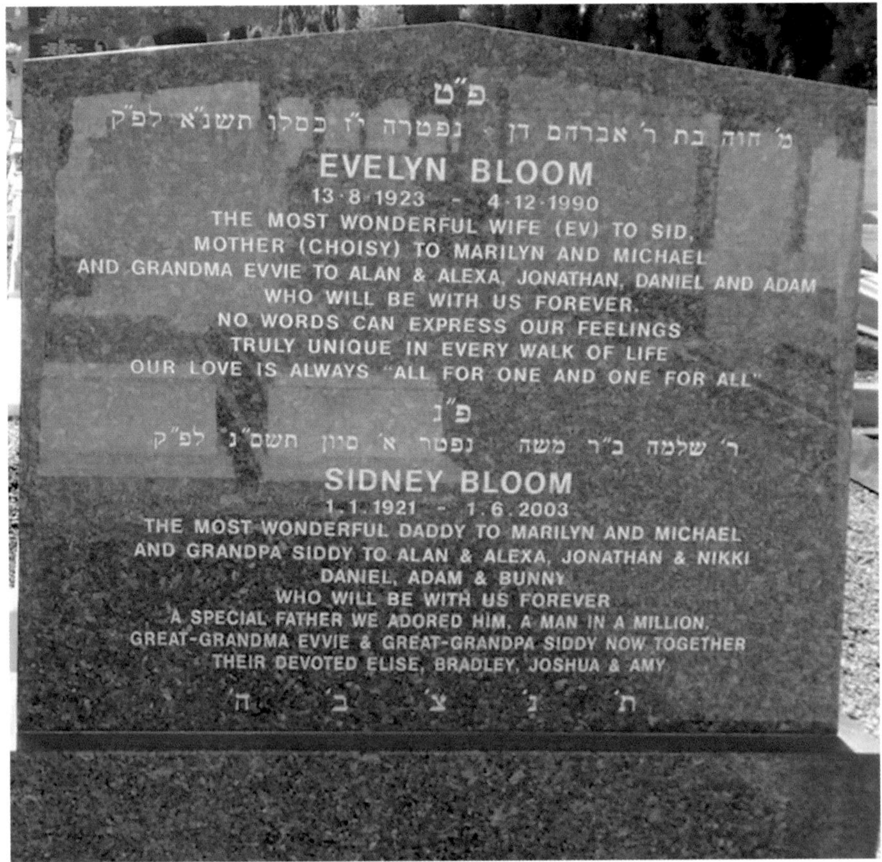

30. Headstone for Sidney and Evelyn Bloom at Willesden Jewish Cemetery. Author's photo.

Notes

1. Different sources cite different years for Morris's arrival.
2. *JC*, 13.7.1962.
3. Established at 115 New Road in 1892, this synagogue was a member of the Federation of Synagogues. It was one of the Federation's 'model', purpose-built synagogues. In Jewish tradition, a couple was married in the synagogue to which the bride's family belonged.
4. See wedding certificate dated 25.2.1921. The witnesses at the wedding were M. Joel and L. Starkovitz. The ceremony was performed by the minister, J. Shapiro.
5. 1911 Census, Ancestry.co.uk.
6. Post by Mavis Miller Shapiro in Facebook page Memories of Hessell, Langdale Mans, Canon Street Rd and Cable St, 27.12,2016.
7. JewishGen Online Worldwide Burial Registry (JOWBR).
8. 1921 Census, Findmypast.
9. Ancestry.co.uk. Given the gap between the births of Morris and Sylvia, it is possible that the couple lost a child.
10. JewishGen Online Worldwide Burial registry (JOWBW). Muriel was buried at Edmonton Federation Cemetery, burial plot P-46.
11. United Synagogue Marriage Authorisation Records. This is remarkable since many immigrants of this period eschewed the anglicised and what they regarded as lax United Synagogue congregations.
12. 1921 Census, Findmypast.
13. 1911 Census, Ancestry.com.
14. Short Service Attestation, Ancestry.co.uk. In 1915, the family were living Lemon Street in Whitechapel.
15. UK Calendar of Prisoners, 186801929, Ancestry.co.uk.
16. There was also a son named Sidney Simmonds, date of birth and death unknown.
17. See Chapter Seven.
18. Death and marriage records, Ancestry.co.uk. The date of Annie's death is not known.
19. Copies of travel documentation kindly provided by Marc Green, grandson of Mashka, later 'Minnie' Green.
20. 1911 Census, Ancestry.co.uk and England and Wales Registration of Marriages, Ancestry.co.uk.
21. Copy of marriage certificate kindly provided by Marc Green, grandson of Mashka, later 'Minnie' Green.
22. 1939 England and Wales Register, Ancestry.co.uk.
23. Copy of death certificate kindly provided by Marc Green, grandson of Mashka, later 'Minnie' Green.

24. England and Wales Registration of Deaths, Ancestry.co.uk.
25. *Ibid.*
26. Index of Wills and Administrations,1858–1995, Ancestry.co.uk.
27. It is interesting to note that Rachel and Benjamin's two sons and his daughter Esther are mentioned on the headstone, but not his daughter Sylvia. She might already have died or there was a family estrangement. She was still alive in 1939 at the time of Benjamin's naturalisation.
28. This move is confirmed by the fact that when Sidney Bloom married in 1942 (see later in this chapter), he and his new wife placed a notice in the *Jewish Chronicle* to thank the Duke's Place community for its wedding present (*JC*, 26.6.1942). Also, Morris, his wife and their immediate family and descendants were buried in United Synagogue plots at the Willesden Jewish Cemetery.
29. Email from Lazarus Woolf's grandson, John Morrison, 26.11.2022.
30. See Chapter Three.
31. Interview with Martin Malin, 22.9.2022.
32. The school had been founded in 1716 by Henry Raine, a wealthy alcohol merchant, who was committed to ensuring that the poorer children living in the East End of London had access to a decent education. The intake included a large proportion of Jewish children. Although the school aimed to prepare its pupils for the professions, Sidney left school prior to his matriculation.
33. Extant family members are not certain which school Sylvia attended, but it might have been the nearby Central Foundation Girls' School in Spital Square, close to the family home.
34. *JC*, 2.2.1934.
35. See for example, *JC*, 29.6.1923 and 2.2.1934.
36. Interview with Martin Malin, 22.10.2022.
37. David Feldman, 'Bloom, Solomon Sidney', in *Oxford Dictionary of National Biography*, Oxford University Press, March 2009.
38. Obituary for Sidney Bloom, *The Daily Telegraph*, 7.7.2003.
39. Letter from Sylvia Schneider to Michelle Spencer, 17.10.2001. The letter contains the information that the whole of Sylvia's family left behind in Germany died in Auschwitz. Letter in the family archives kept by Michelle Spencer.
40. *JC*, 17.1.1941.
41. They had married in Bethnal Green in January 1911.
42. Adolph was born in Poland on 12 December 1886. Annie Griver was also born in Poland on 18 October 1887.
43. See David Feldman, 'Bloom, Solomon Sidney'.
44. A temporary structure was erected on the site of the Great Synagogue in Duke's Place, which was used until 1958.

45. *JC*, 19.6.1942. See also notice of silver wedding celebration for Sidney and Evelyn, *JC*, 16.6.1967.
46. *JC*, 31.12.1943.
47. *JC*, 12.9.1947.
48. 1939 England and Wales Register, Ancestry.co.uk. When they were evacuated to Brighton, the residential accommodation of 2 Brick Lane was let out to several workers – a chef, possibly working at the Bloom's restaurant, and two domestic servants.
49. *JC*, 14.4.1939.
50. See Chapter Three.
51. Obituary for Sidney Bloom by Tom Jaine, *The Guardian*, 24.6.2003. Although they had moved to the Surrey countryside to be safe, ironically, they found that they were living close to the Vickers factory where armaments were being manufactured and which was a target for German bombing.
52. See https://en.wikipedia.org/wiki/Solomon_Schonfeld.
53. Interview with Martin Malin, 22.9.2022. See Chapter Seven for further details.
54. For information on the move of Jews to Golders Green see Pam Fox, *The Jewish Community of Golders Green, A Social History* (Stroud: The History Press, 2016).
55. For information on Golders Green Beth Hamedrash see *ibid.*
56. Interview with Martin Malin, 20.9.2022.
57. After his father died (see below), Sidney went to Munk's Shul to say *Kaddish* (prayer for the dead) during the period of mourning.
58. Interview with Martin Malin, 22.9.2022.
59. For example, the *Gloucester Citizen*, 17.1.1949 and the *Hampstead News* 24.2.1949.
60. Interview with Martin Malin, 22.9.2022.
61. *Hampstead News*, 5.1.1950.
62. Interview with Martin Malin, 20.9.2022. Abraham died in London on 3 August 1956. Esther died in London on 30.1.1959.
63. Interview with Martin Malin, 22.9.2022.
64. It is thought that Finchley Synagogue was not at that time large enough to accommodate the number of people invited to the wedding. Interview with Martin Malin, 1.12.2022.
65. Interview with Martin Malin, 3.11.2022.
66. *JC*, 27.7.1951.
67. Interview with Martin Malin, 3.11.2022.
68. Sylvia Malin was pregnant with Michelle when Morris died. Michelle married Anthony ('Tony') Spencer in St Marylebone in 1972 and they lived in Shirehall Close in Hendon. Both Michelle and Martin were born in Marylebone.

69. *JC*, 29.5.1953.
70. *JC*, 4.10.1957.
71. A cupboard in which the scrolls of the Pentateuch (the five books that form the Torah) are placed.
72. *JC*, 11.4.1969. There is an error in the *JC* entry. If the David referred to is David Tapper, then he was not a grandchild of Rebecca. Perhaps there is a stray comma after Michael's name since Michael's middle name is David.
73. Interview with Martin Malin, 23.9.2022.
74. *JC*, 7.11.1952.
75. *JC*, 4.10.1957.
76. Interview with Martin Malin, 22.9.2022. For further information on the Wolfson family see https://en.wikipedia.org/wiki/Wolfson_family.
77. See for example, *JC*, 3.11.1950.
78. *JC*, 11.4.1969.
79. Interview with Martin Malin, 22.9.2022. Youth Aliyah Child Rescue is an Israeli charity that offers a ladder of opportunity to Israel's most vulnerable children, including immigrants and their children. See https://youthaliyah.org.uk/about.
80. Letter to Sylvia Malin from the home, 24.11.1982, in the family archives kept by Michelle Spencer.
81. *JC*, 21.9.1962.
82. Carnegie of London closed in 1984, but the company's designs are now regarded as vintage clothing. Where the Carnegie factory premises ended was where Blooms was situated before it was bombed in May 1941.
83. Born at the time of the Six-Day War, he was given the middle name of Dayan in honour of Moshe Dayan, Minister of Defence during the war.
84. See Chapter Six.
85. Interview with Jonathan Tapper, 2.10.2022.
86. See Chapter Six.
87. *JC*, 5.9.1986.
88. *Aberdeen Press and Journal*, 10.1.1983.
89. Interview with David Rein, 2.5.2023.
90. Interview with Geoffrey Feld, 9.9.2022. It is said that, at one point, Isaac Feld asked Morris Bloom to go into business with him, but Morris refused. Interview with Martin Malin, 7.4.2023.
91. Interview with Michelle Spencer. 29.4.2023.
92. Sheila Finesilver, post on Jewish Britain Facebook page, 15.5.2016.
93. See Pam Fox, *Jews by the Seaside: The Hotels and Guest Houses of Bournemouth* (London: Vallentine Mitchell, 2021).
94. Interview with Martin Malin, 7.4.2023.
95. Obituary for Sidney Bloom, *The Daily Telegraph*, 7.7.2003 and interview with Esther Piper, née Gowers.
96. Anonymous interviewee, 10.1.2023.

97. See Chapter Seven.
98. Lilian Dullberg, response to author's Facebook post on Jewish Britain page, 21.8.2022.
99. Interview with Martin Malin, 22.9.2022.
100. *JC*, 8.1.1971.
101. *JC*, 20.12.1990.
102. Interview with Martin Malin, 1.12.2022.
103. *JC*, 4.8.2000.
104. See Chapter Five.
105. Interview with Martin Malin, 3.11.2022.
106. Death notice in *JC*, 6.6.2003.
107. See *The Times*, 19.6.2003, *The Guardian*, 24.6.2003 and *The Daily Telegraph*, 7.7.2003.
108. See David Feldman, 'Bloom, Solomon Sidney'.
109. See various obituaries for Sidney Bloom.

The Bloom Family Dynasty

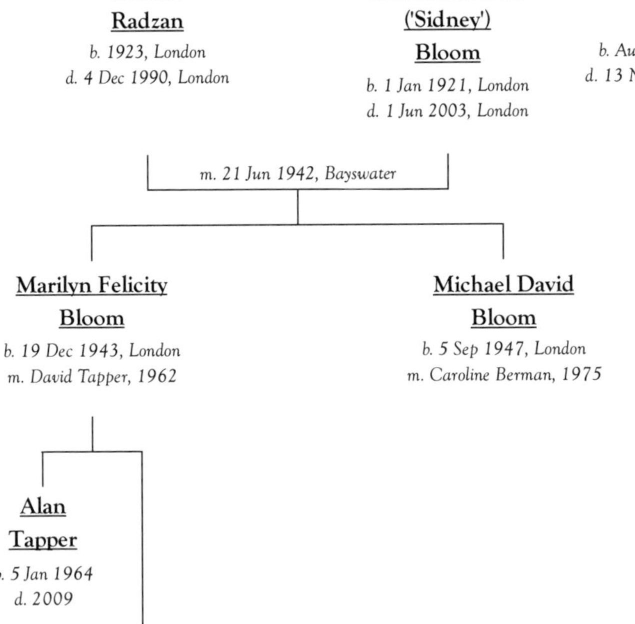

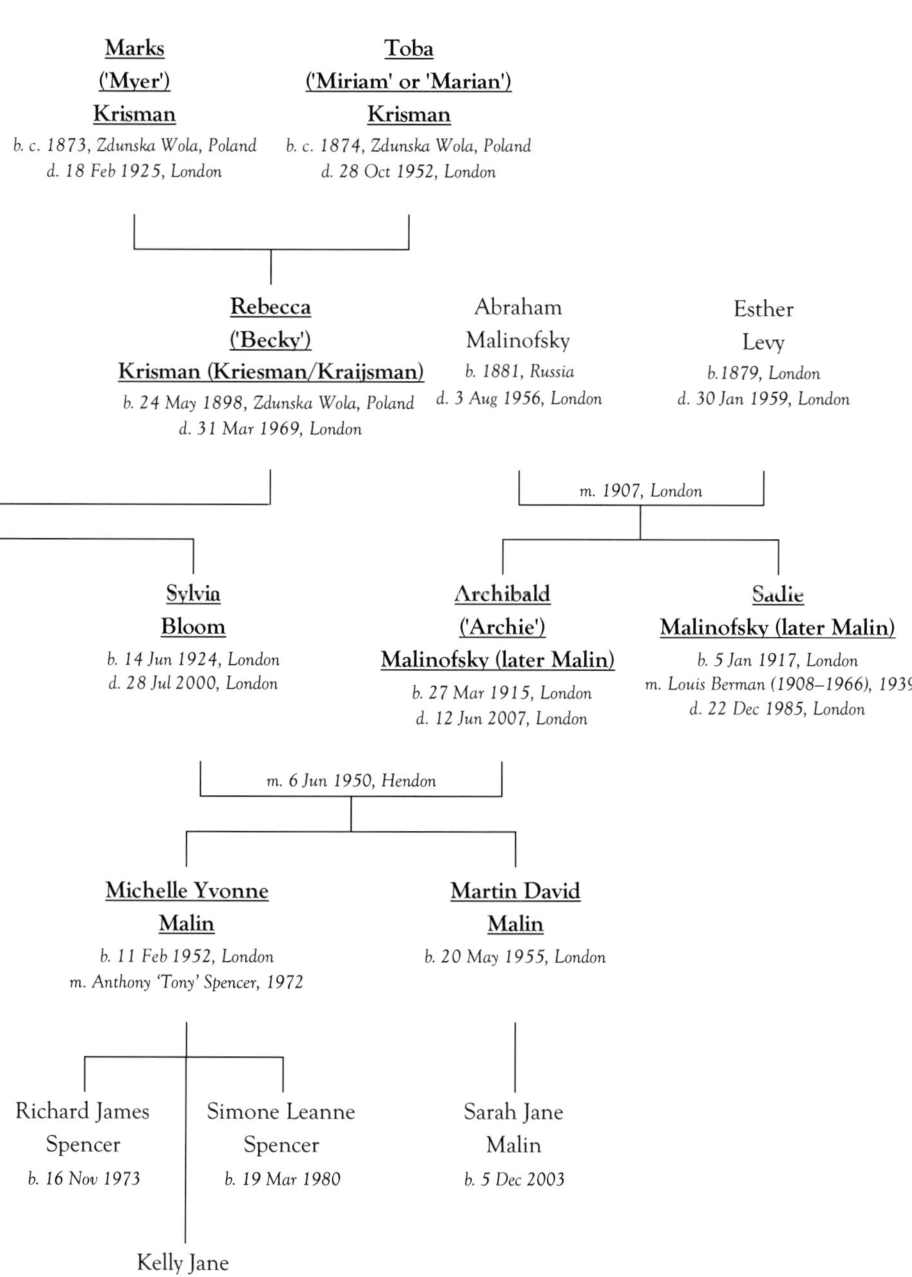

Text **underlined** *denotes those actively involved in the family business*

PART TWO
The Rise and Decline of Blooms

Chapter Three

Blooms: The Early Years

Morris's Early Employment in London

By the time that Morris Bloom arrived in London, the passing of the Aliens Act in 1905 had significantly reduced the tide of Jews from Eastern Europe entering Britain. However, finding work and accommodation was still very difficult in the years leading up to the First World War. We know that Morris had acquired skills in pickling meat prior to arriving in England,[1] and he was therefore able to obtain employment with a firm of butchers soon after he settled in the East End.

It is not known for certain by which firm Morris was employed, but it is possible that he worked for the long-standing and thriving firm of E. Barnett & Co. at 79–83 Middlesex Street since, at that time, it was one of the few kosher meat establishments in the East End involved in producing and selling salt beef and German sausages. The firm had been established in the middle of the nineteenth century when Barnett and Co. (along with other kosher butchers) was in Aldgate, where the Jewish community, largely made up of Jews from Central and Southern Europe, had mainly resided prior to the wave of immigration of Jews from Eastern Europe. It is possible that Samuel Barnett, who founded the firm, learned about sausage making from Jewish butchers who originated from Central Europe and about producing salt beef from Irish people living in the near vicinity. He passed on his skills to his son Emanuel ('Manny'), who was running the firm when Morris arrived in London. By this time, eating salt beef while standing at Barnett's shop counter had 'become a vogue'.[2]

The story of Morris's early years in the East End of London, transmitted down through several generations of the Bloom family, is that he worked long hours and was able to save money by sleeping on a pile of sacks in the same premises as he worked, a common practice amongst recent immigrants. Morris is said to have earned three shillings a week, one shilling of which he sent to his family in Eastern Europe, another of which he donated to his synagogue.[3] The third shilling he retained for meeting his own modest needs.[4]

Morris continued to toil hard during the war years. As an unnaturalised 'alien' he was not liable for conscription to the British Armed Forces, but even if he had been, butchery was a 'reserved trade'. Although the date is uncertain, at some point prior to 1920, Morris tired of selling other people's products and set up his own small business, experimenting with making his personal brand of sausages and using his own recipe for salt beef, which he sold around the Spitalfields neighbourhood. Like most of his co-religionists, Morris was intent on becoming his own master and aspired to be known as a 'connoisseur of table delicacies'.[5]

Bloom's First Premises in Brick Lane

Morris was helped to become self employed by a man named Lazarus ('Larry') Woolf (original surname Lipshutz), who was born in Wentworth Street in about 1890. He was a successful businessman and helped to found what became the famous Houndsditch Warehouse. His descendants were told that Lazarus supported Morris in procuring a loan to supplement his meagre savings by acting as a guarantor. The loan probably came from either a Jewish friendly society, of which there were many at this time, or from the Board of Guardians of British Jews, which in the early decades of the twentieth century made thousands of loans averaging £7 to people seeking to set themselves up as independent traders.[6] Lazarus's assistance is said to have been much appreciated by Morris, who ensured that Lazarus ate in Bloom's restaurant free of charge for the remainder of his life. He did so regularly, and he was known by the waiters and other staff as 'Cockeye', possibly on account of the slight cast in one of his eyes.[7]

31. Lazarus ('Larry') Woolf, c. 1920, who helped Morris Bloom set up his business. Courtesy of John Morrison, his grandson.

Shortly before his marriage in 1920, Morris acquired premises at 58 Brick Lane to provide accommodation for his soon-to-be wife and to open a shop. The premises were purchased from Sophie (previously Sasha) Isow (later Somers),[8] who between 1916 and 1920 ran a patisserie named 'Sophie's' at 58 Brick Lane where, helped by her sisters Tilly and Zena and her brother Jack, she sold salt beef bagels, chicken soup, *borscht* and *latkes* (for all food items, see Glossary of Eastern European Jewish Food at Appendix One) as well as the strudels she made herself that gained her a reputation as 'the queen of strudels'. Morris had been her meat supplier, perhaps trundling a barrow-load of his goods around the East End.[9] Morris renamed the premises 'Bloom's', which he ran in partnership with his wife Rebecca and with the practical support of Rebecca's parents, Mark and Miriam Krisman. Miriam was the cook[10] and Mark helped Morris with selling the meat products. Mark is listed in the 1921

Census as being Morris's assistant in the 'provisions store'.[11] The new enterprise quickly became well-known in the Spitalfields area.

32. Sophie Somers (seated right of photo), née Isowitsky (later shortened to Isow) and her sisters, *c*. 1918. Courtesy of Daniel Gleek.

At the time that Morris was establishing his business, Brick Lane was the centre of a vibrant Jewish community. The area as it was in Bloom's early years is evocatively described by the writer Emanuel Litvinoff, who was born there in 1915, in his book *Journey Through a Small Planet.*[12] Capturing the complexity of Jewish life in the East End, he describes the area as: 'A village remote in spirit from the adjacent cosmopolitanism of the great city'. Its way of life was 'that of the smallest Jewish towns scattered across the land of eastern Europe', more like Odessa and Krakow than London, where the inhabitants 'shared the same sabbaths and festivals ... sang traditional songs in the same minor key, laughed at the same Jewish jokes'. Copies of the Jewish newspaper, *Die Zeit* ('The Time'), were passed around from family to family, to be read avidly in search of scraps of news of the 'Old Country'.

Almost all of the shops in Brick Lane were run by Jews and most of the shop signs were in Yiddish. As a result, the street was known as 'Little Jerusalem'. The shop owners sold a variety of goods: they were drapers, wine sellers and leather manufacturers, and they offered a variety of services, such as the hairdressing and boot repairs. However, the most abundant traders were the purveyors of Jewish food. The numerous small grocery stores were supplemented by the food stalls of Brick Lane market.

For many centuries there had been a market in Brick Lane, but when thousands of Jews started to coalesce in Whitechapel and Spitalfields from the 1880s onwards, the nature of the market changed dramatically. Its customers became almost exclusively Jews living in the neighbouring streets and alleyways, and the main market day became Sundays rather than Saturdays. The vendors spoke in rapid Yiddish and, according to Rachel Lichtenstein who researched the history of Brick Lane, in the early twentieth century Brick Lane 'resembled a scene from an Eastern European ghetto'. One of Rachel Lichtenstein's interviewees, Sally Flood, who was born in Brick Lane, recalled that it was a Jewish meeting place as well as place to shop. When Sally went there with her mother, it took hours to walk through the street because they kept stopping to gossip with neighbours and friends. The street was redolent with the odour of ripe fruit and vegetables and the aroma of Eastern European food: *challot*, *schmaltz* herrings and salt beef (see Glossary at Eastern European Jewish Food at Appendix One). The sounds of the live animals were apparently a great attraction.[13]

Morris and Rebecca Bloom's new enterprise fitted well into this environment. The exterior of the restaurant was probably quite basic, blending into the street amongst the other buildings. To start with, there probably would not have been any prominent signs of the business's ownership since Morris and Rebecca did not yet have any economic success to display. There might however have been Jewish symbols, such as Yiddish lettering on the windows.

The ground floor of 58 Brick Lane was initially used for the sale of cured beef and other meat products, including Morris's distinctive brand of Vienna sausages, which became his signature product.

Until then, the Jewish community had eaten sausages made of beef, but Morris decided to make his with veal. Since they were therefore much paler than sausages sold elsewhere, the community was initially suspicious of the new brand. However, from the outset, Morris was a canny salesman and when he started giving away free samples of his veal sausages, people quickly became convinced of both the quality and taste of his product.[14]

Soon after Morris acquired 58 Brick Lane, he and Rebecca opened a small café, described as 'a tiny little place',[15] fronting Brick Lane, from where takeaway snacks were sold and customers were able to sit down to eat simple meals. Advertisements from those very early days show that the café was open from dawn until after midnight. Morris is said to have snatched just a few hours sleep before making his way to buy meat and other supplies at the kosher market that then flourished in Aldgate. He took his purchases in a wheelbarrow back to Brick Lane, where he made his sausages and salt beef in the yard of his premises before the café opened.[16] Initially, the work involved in running the business would have been unrelenting, and it is likely that Morris and Rebecca and Rebecca's parents snatched food in between serving and preparing food for their customers or, given the marginal social differences at this time, sat down briefly to eat with them.

Within a few years of opening, the café was attracting customers from across Spitalfields and Whitechapel, and Bloom's salt beef sandwiches were becoming 'a household word'.[17] Reflecting on his Whitechapel childhood in the early 1920s, Harry Blacker referred to 'Bloom's Salt Beef Emporium'.[18] However, at this time, the café was still an adjunct to the main business of manufacturing meat products and throughout the 1920s, Morris continued to describe himself as a 'sausage maker'.

Early Success

As Morris's 'table delicacies' became more popular, he decided to acquire additional premises. As early as 1923, notices relating to the business show that Blooms owned 2 Brick Lane as well as number 58. Since the café did not move from 58 Brick Lane for a few more years, it seems that the new accommodation was initially used mainly for manufacturing and storage purposes as well as an additional outlet for Morris's meat products.[19]

People brought up in the area recall being taken to buy produce at wholesale prices. The premises at 2 Brick Lane were in a small alleyway just off the main thoroughfare before it turned left into Old Montague Street. Street directories for the mid-1920s confirm Bloom's double presence in Brick Lane and tell us who the firm's neighbours were at that time. On one side of number 58 was Gordon Marks and Son, woollen manufacturers and on the other side was Mrs Annie Margolis, a grocer. At 2 Brick Lane, Bloom's neighbours were Gold and Sons, trimming merchants.[20]

MAP P 7, P 8.
EAST SIDE.
2 & 58 Bloom Morris, sausage mfr
4 Gold N. & Sons, trimming mers
6 Reuben Mrs. Fanny, milliner
8 Freeman Simon, dyer & cleaner
10 Gordon Louis, tobacconist
12 Shlaen & Sons, tailors
...... *here is Finch street* ......
18 Kitsberg Jsph. fancy goods dlr
20 Figgett H. & Co. costumiers
22 Circus & Benjamin, who. drapers
24 Levin R. & Sons, butchers
26 & 122 Bernstein Charles & Son, bakers
28 Harris Mrs. Rachael, leather sllr
30 Goldberg Benjamin, ladies' tailor
30 Heller Julius, dentist
30 Flastig Jos, who. milliner
32 Levenstein Israel, confectioner
34 Adler A. & Co. booksellers
36 Dekovnick Mrs. Rachael, drug stores
38 Gales Mark, woollen merchant
38 Krause Myer, dentist
.... *here is Osborn place* ....
40 *Bell*, Goodman King
42 Roberts Madame Dora, milliner
44 Myers David, tailor
46 Mautner Simon, provision mer
48 Isaacs Joseph, fruiterer
50 Gershcowit Simon, upholsterers' warehouseman
52 Goldstein & Son, builders' mers
54 Baranofsky Solomon, mantle ma
56 Margolis Mrs. Annie, grocer
58 & 2 Bloom Morris, sausage mfr
60 & 62 Gordon Marks & Son, woollen merchants
64 Lipschitz Neiman, chndlr.'s shp

33. Brick Lane, Post Office Directory of London, 1927.

Such was the growing demand for Morris's kosher provisions that during 1930 he acquired larger premises at 111 Wentworth Street, which ran parallel to Brick Lane. These premises, which became the base for what was now a thriving wholesale business as well as a retail outlet, had formerly housed the City of Norwich public house.[21] Described as a 'Model Electric Sausage Factory', the expanded business opened in time for *Pesach* in 1931. Until then, Morris had not advertised his products, but he now took out a full-page advertisement in the *Jewish Chronicle* to announce the opening of the new factory. He explained:

> Hitherto, M. Bloom's Produce has not been advertised, but owing to consistent high quality and general excellence, it has found favour through recommendation alone and obtained a large and increasing sale. It is desired now, through the medium of this journal, to make this superiority known to the whole Jewish Community.[22]

Morris thanked his friends and customers for their support and congratulations on the new venture, which placed him on another rung up the economic ladder. Aided by technological developments, he was now an established manufacturer and wholesaler, not just a 'master'. The factory was set up to produce greater quantities of Bloom's 'celebrated' goods and a wider range of goods, including, 'special' garlic and plain *worsht*, breakfast sausage, both veal and beef, pickled tongues, pickled beef, smoked beef, liver sausage, postrema (pastrami), salami and pressed beef (see Glossary of Eastern European Jewish Food at Appendix One). Several of these new products, available directly from the factory or from the takeaway counter at the café, had hitherto been unavailable in Britain. It is notable that while many Jewish businesses experienced a downturn in custom during the Great Depression, Blooms expanded. The Bloom's wholesale and manufacturing side of the business was now a significant undertaking and Morris was employing twenty-five staff,[23] which included a team of nine van drivers who delivered Bloom's products, with 'prompt attention' , throughout London and 'The Provinces'.[24]

34. Full-page advertisement in the *Jewish Chronicle*, 6 March 1931.

At the beginning of the 1930s Wentworth Street was almost entirely Jewish and noted for being the location of businesses involved in every aspect of the *schmatte* (clothing) trade: gown and corset makers, hosiers, boot and shoe shops, milliners, tailors and trimming merchants.[25] During the week, there was another Jewish street market in Wentworth Street. On Sundays, this market became part of the bustling 'Petticoat Lane' market centred on Middlesex Street and contiguous streets.

Following the opening of the new factory, regular advertisements were placed in the *Jewish Chronicle*, extolling the quality of Bloom's products and Morris developed a strapline for his wholesale business: 'Buy Bloom's and Buy the Best!!', which was to remain the firm's slogan for most of its existence. He stressed that his products were manufactured 'under the most ideal hygienic conditions', and customers were invited to inspect the production processes.

By the 1930s, the London Beth Din (see Glossary of Hebrew and Yiddish Terms) was licensing the purveyors of produce described as kosher, and Blooms was amongst the first firms to be supervised by the Kashrus Commission (see Glossary of Hebrew and Yiddish Terms) that had been set up in 1920 as a division of the United Synagogue following a series of scandals relating to *kashrut* (Jewish dietary rules) at public and communal events. Initially, the Kashrus Commission was 'light touch' in its supervision, but by the early 1930s, the Commission was becoming more stringent in its requirements as it came under the influence of the ultra-orthodox Rabbi (later Dayan) Yechezekel Abramsky, a recent refugee from Stalinist oppression in Belarus.[26] As a result, in addition to the trained porgers (see Glossary of Hebrew and Yiddish Terms) employed by Blooms, who prepared the meat in line with the requirements of *kashrut*,[27] compliance with Jewish dietary laws was overseen by a *shomer* (religious supervisor) employed by the Jewish licensing authorities rather than by the firm. The first known *shomer* who oversaw *kashrut* at the factory was Rabbi Chait from Brighton. Rabbi Chait (originally Chaitovitz) continued to work at the factory during and immediately after the Second World War.[28]

The limited number of establishments licensed by the London Beth Din in the 1930s included Feld's restaurant and salt beef shop at 128 Whitechapel Road.[29] As previously mentioned, Morris and Rebecca were connected to the Feld family who ran the business. Alexander (originally Zisken) Feld and his wife Annie came from the same *shtetl*, Zdunska Wola, as Rebecca's family, and the two families were related.[30] Geoffrey Feld, the grandson of Alexander Feld, tells the story that it was his grandfather, a trained butcher, had taught Morris Bloom to slice salt beef.[31] The two kosher establishments were not in direct competition with each other because they operated in different parts of the Jewish East End and Felds, which became famous in the 1930s, had closed before Blooms reached its heyday two decades later.[32]

Commission for Kashrus

Appointed by the CHIEF RABBI and BETH DIN.

President: The Very Rev. Dr. J. H. HERTZ, Chief Rabbi.
Vice-President: Dayan Dr. A. FELDMAN, B.A., Ph.D.

Chairman:	*Treasurer:*	*Secretary:*
REUBEN LINCOLN.	E. DEYONG.	I. DAINOW.

Only the following firms are under the strict supervision of the above Commission for whom the Beth Din hold themselves responsible for their Kashrus:

SALT BEEF SHOPS.

M. Bloom, 2, Brick Lane, E.1
Z. Feld, 128, Whitechapel Rd., E.1
M. Marks, 56, Whitechapel Road, E.1
J. Rabbinowitch, 102, Commercial Road, E.1
L. B. Rashberg, 251, Commercial Road, E.1
M. Strongwater, 2, Black Lion Yard, E.1
P. Strongwater, 66, Middlesex Street, E.1
I. Tobin, 4, Court Street, E.1
Mrs. Wooff, 197, Mile End Road, E.1

RESTAURANTS.

S. Z. Abrahamson, Ltd., 49, Whitechapel Road, E.1
Abrahamson's, 4, Denman Street, Piccadilly, W.
Cohn's, 154, Houndsditch, E.1
B. Feld, 128, Whitechapel Road, E.1
First Avenue House, 27, First Avenue, Hove.
J. Goide, Ltd., 87, High Street, Whitechapel, E.1
Herman, 9, Leman Street, E.1
Hotel Central, Aldgate, E.1
Ostwind & Co., 77, Wentworth Street, E.
S. Stern's Hotel, 9, Mansell St., E.
Waltuch's, 28, Garlick Hill, E.C.4

CATERERS.

S. Applebaum, 172, Sandringham Road, E.8
A. Barnett, 7, Leyden Street, E.1
A. Bernstein, 26, Brick Lane, E.1
Mrs. A. Blumstein, 1, Devonshire Road, E.9
J. Goide, Ltd., 87, High Street, Whitechapel, E.1
B. Kleinman, 2, Glaskin Road, E.9
D. Lichtman, 142, Queen's Road, E.8
Monnickendams, Ltd., 44, Victoria Street, S.W.
H. Myers, 39, High Holborn, W.C.
V. Schaverein, 298, Romford Road, E.7
A. Spielsinger, 11, Mile End Road, E.1

Functions supervised by the above Commission can be arranged [illegible] of the West End Hotels if application is made in advance to the Secretary, Mr. I. Dainow, 141, Cannon Street Road, E.1.

35. Notice in the *Jewish Chronicle*, 3 March 1933.

Bloom's closest kosher competitors in the firm's early years were Barratts in Middlesex Street (already mentioned) Strongwaters in both Middlesex Street and Black Lion Yard, Mossy Marks at 56 Whitechapel Road, S. Z. Abrahamson at 49 Whitechapel Road, J. Rabbinowitch at 102 Commercial Road, L. B. Rashberg at 251 Commercial Road, Ostwind and Co. at 77 Wentworth Street, Herman at 9 Leman Street and J. Goide at 87 Whitechapel High Street. However, at this time, the Jewish population of the area was still sizeable and there was plenty of custom for all of these businesses.

The Expansion of Bloom's Activities During the 1930s

When Blooms first relocated its manufacturing activities to 111 Wentworth Street, the firm occupied only the ground floor and basement of the premises. Street directories for the early 1930s show that the upper floors were occupied by small Jewish businesses: Morris Pizzer a dressmaker and Zappa and Collins, mantle makers. However, as the business expanded, Blooms gradually took over the whole building and the rooms on the first floor were used as the firm's headquarters.

During 1935, Bloom's increased the range of meat products manufactured in Wentworth Street to include what were called 'picnic snacks' and cooked meats preserved in glass containers. The firm was also offering luxury lines of food, such as roast duck, roast chicken and minced meat, which could be obtained either directly from the factory in Wentworth Street or from an increasing number of shops supplied by Blooms. In addition, canned goods of Bloom's products started to appear in the mid-1930s. Many of the goods available were now branded with the Bloom's 'logo'.[33]

By 1933, Morris had disposed of 58 Brick Lane, which became part of a redevelopment site,[34] and the café was moved to occupy the whole of the ground floor of the premises at 2 Brick Lane. The café was now surrounded by some colourful Jewish enterprises. Just past the relocated café was a small courtyard called Frostic Walk, where there were a few houses and a shop run by two women, selling pickled herrings and cucumbers from barrels, who were apparently always arguing loudly and publicly. Around the corner in Old Montague Street was the Warsaw Hotel, known as 'Snevlar's Restaurant', where all the Jewish gangsters gathered. Before the Second World War, many of the shops, particularly the dress shops, had what was known as a *schlepper* poised to 'yank people into the shops'.[35]

Opposite Blooms at 2 Brick Lane was a café run by a man named Curley Carr (full name Morris Kersch Carr), who then lived at 106 Cable Street. Curley Carr was also a boxing promoter, and the walls of the café were adorned with pictures of famous boxers. The café had a reputation for being the meeting place of some of London's 'biggest villains'.[36] Many men involved in racing and betting frequented this café as well as the illegal gambling clubs that Curley ran.[37] The café was known for serving all of its food with chips and is said to have been the inspiration for Arnold Wesker's 1962 play, *Chips with Everything.*[38]

On the nearby corner of Chicksand Street there was a cinema, the Brick Lane Cinema, where silent films and later the first Technicolour films were shown to an entirely Jewish audience. During the week, there was a market along Old Montague Street. In 1981, the East End historian Raphael Samuel described the 1930s street scene:

> … the smell was raw fish and poultry both live and dead. The shops were small, and the street was so narrow that when a cart came through there was often a row and the language was very forceful.[39]

A man known as 'Moishe the Gonoff', the most famous Jewish pickpocket of the time, lived in Old Montague Street and when he appeared round the corner into Brick Lane, passing Blooms, the shopkeepers and stallholders would warn each other: 'Watch out, here comes Moishe the Gonoff'.[40] Nevertheless, the area around Blooms was seen as being not as rough as other parts of the East End: 'The kids were well behaved, it was a close-knit community'.[41]

During the 1930s, the corner of Brick Lane and Old Montague Street became known as 'Bloom's Corner'. It was the regular rendezvous for Sunday morning open-air political gatherings, which both attracted customers to Bloom's café and provided entertainment for them. William Myers, who was a delivery boy in the area, recalls going to listen to the speakers outside Blooms and then, if he had money to spare, going inside the café to treat himself to a large saveloy sandwich.[42] William ('Bill') Fishman, who became a well-known chronicler of the history of the Jewish East End,[43] recalls watching as 'communists, socialists and the Labour Party put up a platform and spoke passionately to those who gathered there'. Although he was a small child and did not understand all that was said, the speeches aroused his interest and influenced his political orientation for the remainder of his life.[44]

The gatherings at Bloom's Corner, often consisting of opposing groups of communists, socialists and Zionists, both Jews and non-Jews, were sometimes advertised and reported in the *Jewish Chronicle.* One *Jewish Chronicle* correspondent commented: 'The Fascists, I was told, never dare to speak in such a Jewish and anti-Fascist district.'[45] This publicity was welcomed by Morris Bloom as free marketing.[46]

SUNDAY, OCTOBER 17

[illegible] JEWISH MUSEUM, Woburn House, W.C.1. Open from 10.30 to 1.

HARCOURT SOCIAL CLUB, Ramble. Leader: Maurice Bowman. Meet Liverpool Street Station, Platform 1, 9.30 a.m.

JEWISH BOARD OF DEPUTIES, Board Meeting, Woburn House, 10.15.

[illegible] Y., Mass Propaganda, East End of London, Open Air Platforms at Bloom's Corner, Stepney Green, Fulbourne Street, Eric Street, Philpot Street, 3 p.m., onwards. Mass Meeting, Whitechapel Art Gallery, 7.30 p.m.

HAMMERSMITH J.L.B., Dance, Hammersmith Syn. Hall, Brook Green, 7.30 (2/-)

JEWS' FREE SCHOOL OLD BOYS' CLUB, Opening Dance, Adolph Tuck Hall, Woburn House, Upper Woburn Place, W.C.1, Fox trot Competition, 7 30 to 12 (Admission 3/-).

S.E.L. Y.I.S., supporting Borough Ladies' Guild, Grand Charity Dance, Barnett Ringold Communal Hall, Borough Synagogue, Wansey Street, Elephant and Castle, S.E.17, Dancing 7.30 to 12, Prizes, Comps., Novelties (Admission 2/-)

WELLINGTON SOCIAL AID SOCIETY, Opening Dance, Salon Bal, Harringay, 7.30

36. Notice in the *Jewish Chronicle,* 15 August 1937.

Famous speakers were attracted to speak at Bloom's Corner, some of whom spoke in Yiddish. Sally Flood (mentioned above) recalled hearing the American heavy-weight Jewish boxer Max Baer, who visited the East End before the Second World War,[47] speak outside Blooms about the persecution of the Jews of Russia.[48] During the politically turbulent 1930s, the meetings sometimes developed into mass meetings that became quite hostile, making it difficult for diners to leave the restaurant and the police had to intervene. Sheila Finesilver reminisces: 'I remember the huge crowds listening to the speakers outside Blooms. *Oy vey*! How did I ever get out of there alive!'[49]

The meetings were disturbed by a small but organised group of young Communists. At the meeting at Bloom's Corner, Hanbury Street, where there was a crowd of over 300; the organised interruption became so violent that about 5 o'clock the police were forced to intervene. The crowd however, was not deluded by this interference, and the stewards were informed by many members of the audience that the tactics of the Communists were deeply resented. Similar tactics were adopted at the large meeting held in the White chapel Art Gallery, at 8.30, on the same evening, where Professor Brodetsky and Mr. M. Rosetté spoke.

37. Report in the *Jewish Chronicle*, 20 August 1938.

However, after heckling each other at Bloom's Corner, the opposing groups often joined forces to fight Mosley's 'Blackshirts'. The scenes outside Bloom's restaurant were captured in a painting by the artist John Allin (see Plates Section, Plate 1).

During the week, garment trade workers would congregate outside Blooms, looking for work.[50] The street in front of Blooms was also enlivened by the bagel sellers, who sat on the pavement outside the restaurant during its busiest times, plying their wares to customers. The bagels, which were stored in hessian sacks, were sold for sixpence a dozen. Since the bagel sellers were paid only for what they sold, they often worked late into the night and in all weathers.[51]

The bagel sellers, Esther and Annie Bloomfield, became legendary East End characters. They were mother and daughter but were in fierce competition with one another. The East End historian, Aumie Shapiro, once commented: 'Their relationship was one of pure hatred'.[52] Esther and Annie are immortalised in the autobiography of Harry Blacker:

> Seated on upturned orange-boxes, enveloped in voluminous overcoats that came up to their ears and knitted caps that came down over them ... The bulging sacks of bagels pressed up against their slipper-shod feet, looked like an integral part of their bodies. Here, in all their glory, were the bagel queens of the Lane.[53]

Esther and Annie were famed for the vicious Yiddish curses they would hurl at those who refused to buy their bagels: 'I was told by my mother that their cursing was so strong that even people with thick skins would be quaking in their boots'.[54] Esther died in 1950 when she was in her eighties, having injured her leg in a street accident, but her daughter, who became known as 'Bagel Annie', continued to sell bagels outside Blooms for many years after the death of her mother.[55]

38. Esther Bloomfield with her daughter Annie (top right), the bagel sellers who sat outside Bloom's restaurant. Leaning over Annie is a man named Mike Poluck. The photo, taken by Humphrey Spender, was included in a 1938 special edition of the *Picture Post* magazine, documenting life in Whitechapel. Copy of the article from which the image is extracted provided by Alan Dein.

Established in its new, larger premises at 2 Brick Lane, the café started to attract a wider range of customers,[56] and by the outbreak of the Second World War, it was obviously moving upmarket. The restaurant (no longer a café or snack bar) with its attached takeaway counter had increased its repertoire and was offering 'Luncheon, Dinner and Supper' as well as 'tasty snacks'. By the mid-1930s, Blooms had become so well-known that its regular customers made up a song about the firm's produce, which was sung to the tune of a 1930s song by Bing Crosby, 'Love in Bloom':

> Maybe it's the *chrayn*
> That fills The Lane
> With rare and magic perfumes.
> Oh no, it isn't the *chrayn,*
> It's salt beef from Bloom's.[57]

The takeaway section of the restaurant lay to the left of the door as customers entered the premises. Behind the counter hung a selection of Bloom's meat products. Long tables and chairs for diners were arranged on the right-hand side of the ground floor. The tables were marble topped and uncovered: 'There were no tablecloths in those days and everybody sat down together!'[58] There was a full kitchen at the rear of the premises, but apparently the menu of food produced there was not extensive[59] and it was still relatively inexpensive. It was possible to have a three-course meal for half-a-crown (12.5p).[60]

The entertainment inside the restaurant is said to have been as good as the street cabaret outside. William Myers recalls being enthralled by watching the salt beef being cut before being smothered with mustard.[61] Many of the early waiters are said to have been 'natural comics', who provided a free floor show.[62] Morris and Rebecca's son Sidney Bloom once recalled that his father was a terrific host: 'He liked to see people enjoying themselves, eating and drinking. And he would heap another portion and another portion on the plate.'[63] More than fifty years later, the older customers visiting the 'new Blooms' run by Sidney would still be saying, perhaps predictably, that it was not as good as when Morris was still alive and would be reminiscing about his 'up-front' role and his banter, saying that those who were trying to carry on 'Morrie's' tradition were failing to match his style.[64]

On the eve of the Second World War, Morris started opening his 'High-Class Restaurant' on the 'intermediate days' during *Pesach.* In August 1939, he also announced that the restaurant would be opening after the end of *Shabbat* during the winter months.[65]

Since the early 1930s, Bloom's had been supplying food, prepared in the kitchen at 2 Brick Lane, on a small scale for functions 'upon the shortest notice'.[66] In 1939, the firm increased its catering activities, providing food for both indoor and outdoor events, such as engagement parties, weddings, *Bar Mitzvahs* and other life cycle celebrations. Rather immodestly, Morris declared that this new service constituted 'Good News for the Jewish Public'.[67] This development might have been the result of Sidney Bloom having joined the family firm and providing another pair of hands to expand the business.

Blooms During the Second World War

MR. M. BLOOM AND FAMILY OF

BLOOM'S RESTAURANT

2, BRICK LANE, E.1 ('Phone: BIShopsgate 6311)

Under the supervision of the Beth Din.

desire to thank their innumerable customers and friends for their continued patronage in these difficult and trying times, and, in extending

NEW YEAR GREETINGS

express the hope that the coming year will see the speedy end of Hitlerism and the re-establishment of peace and order among all the nations of the earth.

All our Services functioning as usual: LUNCHEONS, DINNERS, SUPPERS, SNACKS, &c.

Delicatessen Counter. Outdoor and Indoor Catering for All Functions.

M. BLOOM, Wholesale Sausage Manufacturers

Send your orders direct to

111, WENTWORTH STREET, E.1. 'Phone: BIShopsgate 3937

AND BE ASSURED OF SATISFACTION

Ask your local shopkeeper for our two new delicatessen products

CRACOW WORSHT ——— FRANKFURTERS

39. Advertisement in the *Jewish Chronicle*, 27 September 1940.

Bloom's restaurant and its manufacturing activities continued to operate throughout the Second World War, despite the bombs that rained down on the East End. Morris placed advertisements in the *Jewish Chronicle* to confirm this and as a platform to express his horror at the atrocities taking place in mainland Europe.

Owing to the shortage of kosher meat supplies due to the war, in May 1940 Blooms and a number of other meat purveyors, which had come together to form, the Licensed Kosher Salt Beef and Delicatessen Association under the auspices of the Beth Din and the Kashrus Commission, decided to discontinue Saturday evening opening.[68] However, even after 2 Brick Lane was razed to the ground by a fire bomb in May 1941.

However, even after 2 Brick Lane was decimated by a fire bomb in May 1941, Morris was obviously determined to go on feeding his loyal clientele.[69] He relocated the restaurant to the ground floor of the factory at 111 Wentworth Street and announced that it was 'business as usual' as far as the provision of meals was concerned, even though the Bloom family was commuting to the East End from Surrey.[70]

M. BLOOM **RESTAURANT AND DELICATESSEN STORE**

Mr. M. Bloom begs to inform his numerous customers that they will be served in future at his factory at

111, WENTWORTH STREET, E.1

'Phone: BIShopsgate 3937 Under Supervision of the Beth Din

40. Announcement in the *Jewish Chronicle*, 16 May 1941.

Despite the efforts that were made by the kosher food purveyors to co-operate with one another and agree a common line on business issues, this did not prevent the odd outbreak of controversy. In 1942, Morris Bloom placed a notice in the *Jewish Chronicle* to express his anger about allegations that had apparently been made about the way in which he conducted his kosher business. Morris offered a reward for information on the source of the allegations to enable to take legal action.[71] It is not known either what the slander was about nor how this dispute was resolved.

Morris Bloom

Formerly of 2, Brick Lane & 111, Wentworth Street

Now at 111, Wentworth St., London, E.1

'Phone : BIShopsgate 3937

Late premises destroyed by enemy action.

WHOLESALE AND RETAIL SAUSAGE MANUFACTURER AND COOKED MEATS

NOTICE—SLANDER

It has come to my knowledge that serious allegations, which are entirely false and absolutely unfounded, have been and are being circulated with regard to the conduct of my business. I have determined to issue legal process against the originator of these allegations immediately I discover his or her identity. I therefore hereby offer a very substantial reward to any person who provides me with such information as will enable me to punish in a court of law the person originating such false statements or repeating them. For over 20 years I have been supplying the Jewish Community with the best qualities of various Kosher commodities. I have given complete satisfaction to the community in the conduct of my business, which I have always carried on, as I still do, under the strict supervision of the Kashruth Commission of the Beth Din, and I hold their certificate.

M. BLOOM.

41. Notice in the *Jewish Chronicle*, 12 June 1942.

With Sidney Bloom involved in war time munitions work, the restaurant squeezed into 111 Wentworth Street and Morris and Rebecca opening their home in Surrey to refugees, there were few further developments at Bloom's for the remainder of the war other than the appearance of two new meat products: 'Cracow Worsht' and 'Frankfurters'.[72] However, Alan Lever recalls visiting the Wentworth Street premises in the 1940s with his grandfather, Benjamin Lesser, who knew Morris Bloom and had travelled to the East End to pick up supplies of kosher food from Blooms: 'With great pride, Morris Bloom told my grandfather that he had just purchased the freehold of the premises.'[73] Morris was clearly continuing to invest in his business and preparing for better times after the war.

In the immediate post-war years, Bloom's trade was not as brisk as it had been before the war due to unemployment and continued rationing. Sidney Bloom had returned to the business towards the end of the war, and by 1949 the name of the business had been changed to M. Bloom (Kosher) and Son Ltd, reflecting the more prominent role that Sidney was now playing.[74] Despite the fact that Sidney is said by family members to have sometimes disappeared to attend race meetings when he was supposed to be working, he was nevertheless very committed to and had ambitious plans for the development of the family business. However, his plans did not come to fruition until after the death of his father in 1951 when Sidney's vision led to Blooms being transformed from a colourful Whitechapel institution to a nationally and internationally famous Jewish icon.

Notes

1. See various obituaries for Sidney Bloom on his death in 2003. One family member recalls being told that Morris Bloom had been an innkeeper in Lithuania. Interview with Martin Malin, 22.9.2022.
2. *JC*, 2.9.1966. The firm was originally located at 4 Stony Lane in Aldgate. Emanuel Barnett was succeeded in 1917 by his son Harry. The firm closed in 1966.

3. It is not certain which synagogue he belonged to but given his orthodoxy, it could have been Machzike Hadass, known as Spitalfields Great Synagogue, located on the corner of Brick Lane and Fournier Street.
4. Interview with Martin Malin, 22.9.2022.
5. 1960s marketing brochure for Blooms, courtesy of Jonathan Fishburn.
6. 'The Jewish East End', https://www.jack-the-ripper.org/jewish-history.htm.
7. Email from Lazarus Woolf's grandson, John Morrison, 26.11.2022.
8. She was born in Krasnapol in about 1894.
9. The premises were subsequently occupied by S. Schwartz. Sophie was born with the surname Krasnapolski but after her father was killed by Russians, her mother married a man named Isowitsky, which was anglicised to Isow. The Isow family later opened a famous Jewish-owned but non-kosher restaurant in Brewer Street in Soho. Information provided by Daniel 'Gee' Gleek via Facebook Messenger on 5 September 2022.
10. *JC*, 18.6.2010.
11. 1921 Census., Findmypast.
12. Emanuel Litvinoff, *Journey Through a Small Planet* (London: Penguin Modern Classics, 2008).
13. *Ibid.*, p.300.
14. *JC*, 23.2.1996.
15. Interview with Esther Piper and Julia Gowers, 31.8.2022.
16. David Feldman, 'Bloom, Solomon Sidney', in *Oxford Dictionary of National Biography*, Oxford University Press, March 2009.
17. 'History of Blooms' inside cover of restaurant menu, *c.* 1965. Menu from family archives kept by Michelle Spencer.
18. Harry Blacker, *Just Like it Was, Memoirs of the Mittel East* (London: Vallentine Mitchell and Co, 1974). p.16
19. *JC*, 6.3.1923. It is not clear why the advertisement states that 2 Brick Lane was the only Bloom's address since Blooms also traded from 58 Brick Lane at this point.
20. Post Office Directory of London, 1927.
21. Post Office Directory of London, 1925.
22. *JC*, 6.3.1931.
23. *East London Observer*, 25.4.1936, p.1.
24. See Chapter Seven for more details.
25. Michael Brodz, 'Memories of Chicken Soup and Barley', https://magazine.esra.org.il.
26. Conversation with Professor Geoffrey Alderman, 20.8.2020.
27. See Chapter Five.
28. Anonymous interviewee, 20.12.2022.
29. See *JC*, 3.3.1933.
30. Interview with Michelle Spencer, 29.4.2023.
31. Interview with Geoffrey Feld, 9.9.2022.

32. For more information on Feld's restaurant see Pam Fox, *Jews by the Seaside, The Jewish Hotels and Guest Houses of Bournemouth* (London: Vallentine Mitchell, 2022), p.335.
33. See for example, *JC*, 29.6.1923 and 2.2.1934.
34. See *JC*, 26.5.1933. In 1933, numbers 50–58 Brick Lane were being offered for sale by the estate agents Crosby and Co Ltd for redevelopment as a large shop with flats above.
35. Rachel Lichtenstein, *On Brick Lane* (London: Penguin, 2007), p.238.
36. Interview with Stephen Sinclair, grandson of Curley Carr, 26.3.2023.
37. *Ibid.*
38. *Ibid.*
39. Raphael Samuel, *East End Underworld: Chapters in the Life of Arthur Harding* (London: Routledge and Keegan Paul, 1981).
40. *Ibid.*
41. Memories of Pip and Sara Goldstein quoted in Lichtenstein, *On Brick Lane*, p.242.
42. 'Original Blooms', Memory Map of the Jewish East End, recording of interview with William Myers conducted by Rachel Lichtenstein.
43. See mentions of Bill Fishman in Author's Preface.
44. 'Original Blooms', Memory Map of the Jewish East End, recording of interview with William Myers conducted by Rachel Lichtenstein.
45. *JC*, 5.11.1937.
46. Interview with Martin Malin, 22.9.2022.
47. See further mention in Chapter Nine.
48. See Lichtenstein, *On Brick Lane*, p.143.
49. Sheila Finesilver, post on Facebook page Jewish Britain Facebook, 11.1.2016.
50. See Lichtenstein, *On Brick Lane*, p.238.
51. A. B. Levy, *East End Story* (London: Vallentine Mitchell and Co. Ltd., 1951), pp.20–21.
52. *JC*, 29.4.1989.
53. See Blacker, *Just Like it Was*, p.16.
54. Interview with Martin Malin, 22.9.2022.
55. See Levy, *East End Story*, p.21. The mother and daughter are said to have lived in a tenement block on the large, post-war Ocean Estate in Stepney and to have been Holocaust survivors. People recall that during the 1930s Esther was heard to shout 'drei bagels a phenig', which suggests that she originated from Germany or Austria. See Chapter Four for further mention.
56. See Chapter Nine.
57. 'Original Blooms', Memory Map of the Jewish East End, recording of interview with Polly Weiss conducted by Rachel Lichtenstein. *Chrayn* (or sometimes *chrain*) is a spicy paste made of grated horseradish and beetroot. See Glossary of Eastern European Jewish Food at Appendix One.
58. Interview with Connie Stanton, 7.10.2022.
59. *Ibid.* See Chapter Ten for further information.

60. See Lichtenstein, *On Brick Lane*, p.238.
61. 'Original Blooms', Memory Map of the Jewish East End, recording of interview with William Myers conducted by Rachel Lichtenstein.
62. *The Stage*, 28.3.1996. See Chapter Eight for further information on the waiters.
63. *JC*, 16.7.1965.
64. Drew Smith (ed.), *The Good Food Guide 1987* (London: The Consumers' Association and Hodder and Stoughton, 1987), p.33.
65. *JC*, 30.8.1939.
66. See for example, *JC*, 25.3.1931.
67. *JC*, 11.3.1939, 1.3.1940 and 29.3.1940.
68. *JC*, 31.5.1940.
69. The story is sometimes told that Bloom's Corner was specifically named as a Luftwaffe target, since many Jewish intellectuals and dissidents met there. Interview with Martin Malin 22.9.2022.
70. *JC*, 16.5.1941.
71. *JC*, 12.6.1942.
72. *JC*, 27.9.1940.
73. Email from Alan Lever, 9.1.2023. With property prices deflated by the war, this was probably an opportunistic purchase.
74. See *JC*, 30.9.1949.

Chapter Four
Bloom's Restaurants in Their Heyday

The New Aldgate Restaurant and its Environment

During the 1930s Morris Bloom began to invest in property in the East End. His portfolio included premises at 90 Whitechapel High Street, a few doors away from Aldgate East underground station and Whitechapel Art Gallery, opposite the landmark of Gardiner's Corner.[1] The property had remained vacant in the years immediately following the end of the Second World War due to war damage, but in 1951 Sidney Bloom oversaw the repair of the fabric of the building and equipped the interior to become a restaurant to replace the one that had been operating at 111 Wentworth Street. The move to Whitechapel High Street marked a new era in the history of Blooms. The family-run restaurant had left the side streets of Spitalfields and was now housed in a substantial building in a main thoroughfare.

42. Map showing position of Bloom's restaurant at 2 Brick Lane and at 90 Whitechapel High Street, indicated by stars either side of the name Whitechapel. Rachel Lichtenstein, Peter Guillery, Duncan Hay, and Laura Vaughan (2020). A Memory Map of the Jewish East End.

Prior to the acquisition of 90 Whitechapel High Street, the premises had been occupied by typical Jewish clothing firms on the ground floor, with a doctor's practice and a dental surgery on the upper floors.[2] To the right of the building was a cobbled alleyway which widened out into Gunthorpe Street where Canon Barnett School primary school was located.[3] Gunthorpe Street, which was formerly known as George Yard, was the site of the murder of one of Jack the Ripper's victims, Martha Tabram, in 1888. Gunthorpe Street was used as a shortcut between the restaurant and the factory in Wentworth Street.

On the other side of the alleyway was Albert's Menswear,[4] which gained a reputation for the high-quality, hand-made, men's clothes that it sold: 'It was the place that all the Mods bought their Gabicci and Pringle jumpers.'[5] As a sideline, the owner, Albert Collins, sold Jack the Ripper T-shirts. Albert Collins spoke five languages and was employed as a police interpreter during the Second World War.[6] He was a regular lunchtime diner at Bloom's restaurant.[7] The shop closed in 1996.

43. Albert's Menswear shop next door to Blooms at 88 Whitechapel High Street. Vici MacDonald, https://shopfrontelegy.wordpress.com

The rooms above Albert's had briefly housed the editorial office and printing machines of the *Jewish Daily Post*, the first (and only) daily Jewish newspaper written in English in the country. The building is noted for the sign of a *Magen Dovid* (Star of David) supported by two lions of Judah rampant and wielding sabres above the door of the ground-floor shop, which was designed as the badge for the newspaper by the famous Polish artist Arthur Szyk.[8] The newspaper went bankrupt a few months after it was founded in 1935. By the 1950s, the upstairs rooms were occupied by the solicitors T.V. Edwards and Co, which mainly represented local Jewish people 'from the little old ladies down the Lane to the infamous *goniffs* [thieves].'[9]

To the left of Blooms was Gelkoff's confectionery and tobacconist shop run from 1956 by Max and Eva Gelkoff. Later they also ran a kiosk in the foyer of Whitechapel underground station. Their son, Barry, joined the business in 1966. The shop sold high-quality chocolates, some of which were flown into the country at customers' requests. Gelkoffs was particularly noted for its *Pesach* chocolates. It also stocked a large range of cigarettes and Havana cigars. The Bloom's waiters bought their cigarettes there and sometimes also goods ordered by Bloom's diners. However, diners often purchased confectionery and cigarettes themselves on their way in or out of the restaurant.[10] Squeezed in between Gelkoffs and Blooms was 'half shop' named J. Zilkha and Sons Ltd, a luggage and fancy goods store.

44. Max Gelkoff outside the shop he ran with his wife Eva and their son Barry, *c.* 1988. Courtesy of Barry Gelkoff.

Sidney Bloom was followed out from the backstreets and alleys of Spitalfields by a number of businesses that had also lost their premises as a result of enemy bombing, including Curley Carr's café[11] with its entourage of shady characters, which relocated to the south side of Whitechapel High Street, opposite the new Bloom's restaurant. Sidney was also soon to discover that he had been followed by the bagel seller Annie Bloomfield.[12] Sidney recognised that she was 'part of the furniture' and good for business and refused to move her on, as some people suggested.[13] When potential customers passed her on their way into Blooms, Annie called out: 'Bagels for the rich and bagels for the poor. When I've sold out there won't be anymore.'[14] Geoffrey Alderman recalls: 'I remember her bagels. You could break your teeth on them because they'd been sitting around all day.'[15] Monica Finlay recalls that Annie wore 'an old mac with string tied around the waist and a woolly hat. She looked to me, even as a child, as if she'd had a very hard life.'[16]

Annie's presence outside the restaurant became such an integral part of Blooms that after she stopped selling bagels on the restaurant doorstep, she was immortalised in a large photograph of her mother Esther and herself, which hung just inside the front door of the restaurant. Alan Dein comments: 'The photograph reinforced the image Blooms wanted to convey to its customers that the establishment was rooted in the East End and was preserving the world of the immigrants who had once settled there. That picture played a very important role.'[17] Annie died penniless (but still cursing) in 1988 at Charles Clore House (now the Spring Lane Jewish Care home) in Muswell Hill. Several people who remembered her from her days outside Blooms, clubbed together to buy a headstone since she had no living relatives.[18]

There was great competition for occupying the step outside Blooms and in the early 1960s Annie was replaced by Israel ('Issy') Cohen, who had previously run a chain of grocery stores called Cohen's Cash Stores. On his retirement, Issy was looking for something to occupy his time. He usually took up his post outside Blooms at 2pm on a Sunday after the market in Wentworth Street had closed.[19]

45. Issy Cohen selling bagels outside Blooms. Courtesy of the *Jewish Chronicle,* 11 February 2011.

At the time of the opening of the new restaurant, the East End was still ravaged by the war. Due to a shortage of building supplies and the bureaucracy involved in obtaining building permissions, the clearance work had barely commenced, and the East End was blighted by tracts of wasteland and empty spaces. The German bombing had demolished whole streets and injured thousands of people, hastening the exodus of Jews from the area. Even Jews who hitherto had been reluctant to leave the community they knew and the traditions it represented, now resigned themselves to departing for the suburbs. In 1951, the Jewish community of the East End was barely a quarter of the size it had been prior to the First World War. Those who remained were mainly older people who could not face the prospect of leaving, even though many of the communal organisations had been destroyed during the war. Several Jewish businesses continued to operate in the area, but most of their owners commuted to them from the suburbs.

Inside the New Restaurant

The layout of the new restaurant was similar to that at 2 Brick Lane, with the counter and takeaway area to the left of the door, but the 'lozenge-shaped' dining area was much larger than the previous restaurant, providing seating for 145 people. The décor of the restaurant remained largely unchanged for the forty-five years of its existence. There were ranks of tables, squeezed closely together, which were covered with white tablecloths. The tables on the left-hand side were slightly higher than those on the right. At the back of the restaurant there were three large tables that provided seating for parties of diners of up to twenty people, which were used for family parties who were celebrating birthdays, anniversaries, weddings and other events. The Bloom family often gathered around these tables. Some of the seating was arranged in booths with brownish-orange banquette seating, set at right angles to both outer sides of the restaurant, which were ideal for smaller family groups.

In the late 1950s, the right-hand wall of the restaurant was adorned with a black and white photomural of Petticoat Lane Market, shot from the air.[20] It featured some well-known local characters. Hilary Prais recalls that her grandfather, Lew Rosen, the owner of a clothing firm in Whitechapel named Rosen's Menswear, was featured on the mural: 'I always wanted to sit on a table next to the photo of him when we ate at Blooms.'[21]

46. Part of the photomural in Bloom's restaurant, with Lew Rosen (centre of image). Courtesy of Hilary Prais.

Similarly, Hannah Jacobs says: 'The street scene photomural had a lot of meaning when I used to go to Blooms as a child since my parents owned a stall in Petticoat Lane.'[22] Jeremy Cohen recalls: 'When I went in one Sunday evening many years ago with my dad, I asked him about the photomural, "What's that market, Dad?" and he answered in jest, "It's the Common Market son".'

The right-hand wall of the restaurant was covered entirely with mirrors, which reflected the lively street scene depicted in the mural, heightening the East End atmosphere of the dining space. The mirrors also allowed customers to watch each other, which was especially welcome when the diners included well-known people.[23] Devoted to his family, Sidney Bloom hung a large photo of his father in a place of honour in the restaurant, later to be joined by a photo of his mother after her death in 1969. The paintwork was once described by the architectural historian Marcus Binney as 'pure GWR Great Western Railway – chocolate and cream'.[24]

The upper floors of the building were used as offices by and workspace for several different firms, including at one time a shipping company, a clothing firm and a leather business run by Maurice Arnold. At one point, the infamous Kray twins had an office on the floors above the restaurant.[25] Later on, the top floor was left empty for many years and became dilapidated.

The Early Years of the Aldgate Restaurant

Although its surroundings were unpropitious, the restaurant was an immediate success. As a result of the Holocaust and the violence surrounding the establishment of the Independent State of Israel, the mood of the Jewish community in the immediate post-war years was very sombre, but by the early 1950s a corner had been turned. While Jews could never forget what had happened, many were ready to move on and have some fun. Sidney Bloom was quick to sense the change of mood and set out to provide a winning formula of inexpensive, comforting, *heimische* (homey, unpretentious) food.[26]

On the restaurant's opening night there was a celebratory party, at which a band, the Magnetic Dance Band, played.[27] The band was led by Harry Gold, who became a celebrated jazz band leader and the violin player, who was on his way to fame, was Joe (originally Joshua) Loss. Joe Loss had grown up in Grey Eagle Street close to Brick Lane and he knew the Bloom family well.[28] The band members were paid half-a-crown (12.5p) and received a free salt beef supper. They were accompanied by the 1930s child star known as Baby Rita Carr (and sometimes 'Little Rivka'), who had 'a rich mellow voice'.[29] Her family lived close to the new restaurant and were also close friends of the Bloom family. Rita Carr's father was Curley Carr, whose café has been previously mentioned. The restaurant was apparently full to overflowing.[30]

BLOOM'S
RESTAURANT & SNACK BAR
Ready once again to serve the Public!
OPENING DEC. 2nd
UNDER SUPERVISION OF LONDON BETH DIN
Bloom's (late of Brick Lane, E.1), universally famed for salt beef, welcomes you to visit the new Restaurant and Snack Bar, where you can enjoy a variety of sandwiches or a full-course meal cooked at its best.
OPEN UNTIL MIDNIGHT
M. BLOOM (KOSHER) & SON, LTD.
90, High St., Whitechapel, London, E.1. 'Phone : BIShopsgate 6835.
(ONE MINUTE FROM ALDGATE EAST)

47. Announcement of the opening of the new Bloom's restaurant in Whitechapel High Street, *Jewish Chronicle*, 28 November 1952.

48. 'Baby' Rita Carr, who sang at the opening night of Bloom's Aldgate Restaurant. Photo taken outside her father's, 'Curley' Carr, café in 1951. Rita is with her daughter Amanda and her father is in the background on the right. Courtesy of the Carr/Sinclair family.

Sidney Bloom had perhaps underestimated how successful his new venture would be. With rationing still in force, by the end of December 1952 he had to advise his customers that he was unable to obtain enough meat supplies to feed all of those who wanted to dine at the restaurant and therefore had to reduce the advertised opening hours.

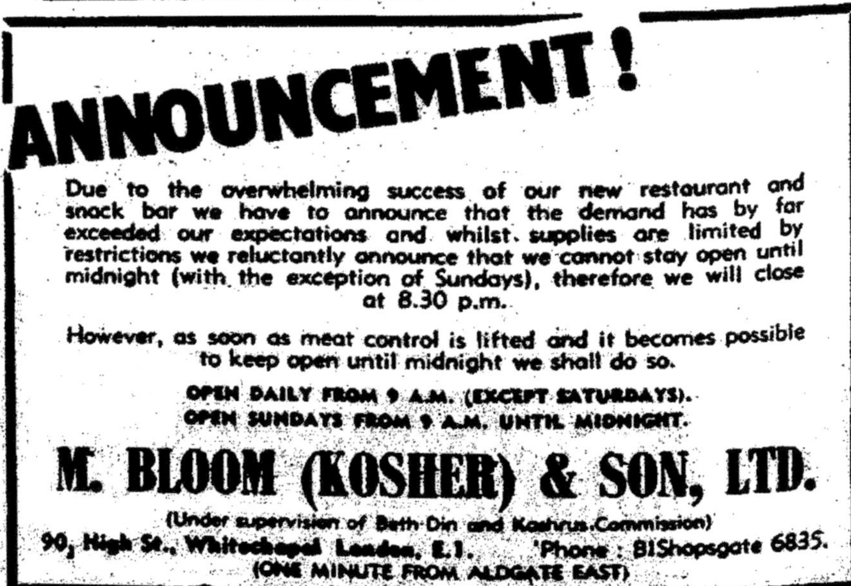

ANNOUNCEMENT!

Due to the overwhelming success of our new restaurant and snack bar we have to announce that the demand has by far exceeded our expectations and whilst supplies are limited by restrictions we reluctantly announce that we cannot stay open until midnight (with the exception of Sundays), therefore we will close at 8.30 p.m.

However, as soon as meat control is lifted and it becomes possible to keep open until midnight we shall do so.

OPEN DAILY FROM 9 A.M. (EXCEPT SATURDAYS).
OPEN SUNDAYS FROM 9 A.M. UNTIL MIDNIGHT.

M. BLOOM (KOSHER) & SON, LTD.

(Under supervision of Beth Din and Kashrus Commission)
90, High St., Whitechapel London, E.1. 'Phone: BIShopsgate 6835.
(ONE MINUTE FROM ALDGATE EAST)

49. Notice in the *Jewish Chronicle*, 12 December 1952.

Evelyn ('Ev', or to her children, 'Choicy') and Sidney Bloom proved to be an excellent team in the running of the Aldgate restaurant. With Evelyn's charm and outgoing personality, she was well suited for her 'front-of-house' role, meeting, greeting, reassuring and *schmoozing* (in this context, welcoming enthusiastically) the customers as the need arose. Stuart Singer comments: 'She was the face of Blooms, and was pivotal to its success; she was the powerhouse behind the business.'[31] People loved it when they were escorted to their table by the famous Mrs Bloom. Evelyn was once quoted as saying: 'Coming here to Blooms should be like coming into my home, because being a *Yiddishe momme*, I want our customers to enjoy themselves.'[32]

Evelyn is remembered for her glamour, stylish clothes, immaculate grooming and year-round suntan. It is often said that she looked like a film star. One admirer comments: 'When I was sixteen, I fancied her like mad and loved all her gold rings.'[33] Simon Alexander, a former customer, comments that, 'wearing all her finery, Evelyn looked somewhat out of place when the East End was at its most run down.'[34] Some customers regarded Evelyn Bloom as something of a celebrity and felt flattered when she spoke to them. Others have remarked on her open and friendly manner. Philip Luxembourg recalls: 'Mrs Bloom often worked behind the delicatessen counter at lunchtimes. It was her warm welcome that initiated me into Blooms and kept me coming back.'[35] When Evelyn was once asked about the secret of her success, she memorably replied: 'Rappaport is chemistry.'[36]

Sidney (known as 'Sid' or 'Siddy' by those who knew him well) was more reserved and emollient than his wife. He is remembered for his kindness and very dry sense of humour. Vivienne Thompson tells this story:

> My brother was Sid Bloom's right-hand man. One day, my brother called Sid to the phone and said that Lloyds Bank wanted to speak to him. Scratching his head and looking quizzically at my brother, Sid said: "Micky what can they want from me, we bank with Barclays? Perhaps they want a loan."[37]

Like Evelyn, Sidney was always immaculately dressed, wearing a well-tailored suit and tie. It is said that he 'ran a tight ship' and that he was particularly rigorous in his oversight of the restaurant's kitchen.[38] He was sometimes described as being 'rotund' and was therefore a good advertisement for his business.[39] To Sidney, every customer mattered, and he loved making friends with them.[40] He particularly liked it when young people came into the restaurant. Michael Georgiou recalls that when he once went to the restaurant after school to wait for his father, Bambos Georgiou,[41] who worked on the delicatessen counter, Sidney Bloom asked him who he was and took him to a nearby toyshop and bought him a chemistry set.[42]

Like his father before him, Sidney was skilled at marketing. As well as the regular notices in the *Jewish Chronicle*, the restaurant was now being advertised in the *Jewish Chronicle Travel Guide*, which increased the restaurant's burgeoning customer base.[43]

Although Sidney Bloom was sometimes described as being 'parsimonious' in his business affairs, he was also generous and very charitable, epitomising the Jewish concept of *tzedakah*.[44] Mildred Charlotte recalls how he willingly supplied her with free tins of chicken and barley soup when she produced Arnold Wesker's play of the same name at the Half Moon Theatre, which added authenticity to the scenes.[45] Stories abound of the large quantities of food that, with Sidney's authority, were given to those in need regardless of their religion.[46] Pamela Kaye recalls that food was regularly donated to homeless people living in the nearby Salvation Army hostel: 'They were given salt beef and smoked salmon sandwiches, and I found the idea of homeless people dining on expensive food quite pleasing'.[47] Martin Malin tells this story:

> When I was about eleven or twelve, my mum would take me on the train to Aldgate to have lunch at the restaurant. We were often there on a Friday just before the restaurant closed for *Shabbos*. Somehow, I once found myself in the delivery area at the back of the restaurant, where I noticed a queue of about forty or fifty people, waiting by the kitchen door. I asked my mother: "What are all those people doing here?" She told me that they were poor Jewish people from around the East End, of which there were quite a few at that time. "We give them something to eat," she said. I asked her why and she explained that it was something that Grandfather Morris had done, and the tradition had been passed down to my Uncle Sidney.[48]

Late at night, after the last paying customers had left, homeless people were often treated to a free bowl of soup and a plate of chips.[49] Like his father before him, Sidney also employed a number of people in the business whom he knew were in need of an income.[50] Another indication of Sidney's generosity was that a number of valued staff members lived in houses provided by the company and several employees had the use of company vehicles.[51]

Sidney Bloom, who was always much more involved in the running of the restaurant than in the management of the factory, was very 'hands on' and was often to be seen serving behind the takeaway counter, slicing seemingly endless portions of salt beef with 'virtuoso relish'.[52]

In June 1953, just six months after the restaurant had opened, its trading hours were extended to mark the coronation of Queen Elizabeth.[53] However, at this stage, announcements were placed in the *Jewish Chronicle* to say that the 'High-Class Restaurant' was closed for extended periods during the main Jewish festivals such as *Sukkot and Pesach* (see Glossary of Hebrew and Yiddish Terms).[54] Sundays were very quickly established as the busiest days for both the restaurant and the takeaway counter, with people flocking to the East End for various purposes,[55] and combining their trips with a meal at Blooms. There are many recollections of the restaurant on Sundays being noisy, crowded, warm and steamy and filled with the smell of cigarette and cigar smoke:

> The waiters were always yelling to each other across the restaurant – "Pass me the sugar!", or something similar – and shouting orders to the kitchen staff. Customers who knew each other would exchange loud greetings. And there was a general hustle and bustle of enthusiastic and animated conversations, with everyone speaking at once.[56]

The writer John Sandilands once commented that the noise in Bloom's restaurant was so extreme that 'you could stand up and sing an operatic aria without attracting much attention.'[57]

By 1955, the restaurant was remaining open until midnight on Sunday evenings to cater for its numerous customers.[58] With Bloom's strict adherence to *kashrut*, it had few competitors at the time. Strongwater's in Middlesex Street and Black Lion Yard had a loyal following, but these two salt beef restaurants were smaller and did not provide such an extensive menu as Blooms. Feld's restaurant had closed and several other former competitors had departed for the suburbs, mainly to Golders Green. The exception was Barnetts, for which it has been suggested that Morris Bloom might have worked on his arrival in London.[59] Barnetts was providing lunch for thousands of City workers in its restaurant in Middlesex Street and was also supplying meat, poultry, sausages, pies and patties to Jewish households across the country.[60] However, this did not seem to have detracted from Bloom's success. The firm was already on its way to becoming a household name and in 1966 Barnetts closed, which gave Blooms the impetus to expand its manufacturing and wholesale activities to be discussed in Chapter Five.

Illustration 1: People teeming out of Aldgate East station into Blooms. Copyright Beverley-Jane Stewart.

A Family Débacle

During the mid-1950s, advertisements for Bloom's restaurant stressed that 'the only' addresses for Morris Bloom (Kosher) and Son Ltd were 90 Whitechapel High Street and 111 Wentworth Street. This was to avoid confusion with Sidney's cousin Monty Bloom's butchery business in Sidney Street, which he had taken over from his father Benjamin Bloom. It was also to avoid confusion with the much smaller restaurant named Blooms operating at 61 Berwick Street in the West End, which was run by a man with the name of Bloom. Although some customers assumed that the Soho restaurant was part of the same enterprise as Blooms in Whitechapel High Street, the two restaurants were not connected in any way and Bala Baruch Bloom, who owned the Berwick Street restaurant, was no relation to Sidney Bloom.[61]

M. BLOOM (Kosher) & SON
LIMITED
(Under the supervision of the London Beth Din)

OUR ONLY ADDRESSES :
HIGH-CLASS RESTAURANT
90, Whitechapel High Street, E.1
BIS. 6835

WHOLESALE DEPT. & HEAD OFFICE
111, Wentworth Street, E.1
BIS. 3937

50. Advertisement in the *Jewish Chronicle Travel Guide*, 1957.

However, of greater concern to Sidney was the setting up of a salt beef bar and delicatessen by Monty Bloom, who had moved from the East End to live in Gloucester Place near Baker Street. In 1954, Monty announced to his 'numerous friends, customers and the general public', whom he said had been aware of him as a 'well-known East London butcher and poulterer', that he was starting a new venture at 237 Baker Street, opposite Baker Street station.

MONTY BLOOM

21, MELCOMBE STREET, N.W.I

(opposite Baker Street Station) WELbeck 5161

takes great pleasure in announcing the

OPENING DATE – NOVEMBER 20

of the

ONLY KOSHER BUTCHER IN THE BAKER STREET AREA

(Licensed by Board for Shechita and under the supervision of the London Beth Din)

DAILY DELIVERIES IN ALL DISTRICTS

All our prices will be in line with those recommended by the Special Committee set up by the Board of Deputies.

SALT BEEF BAR & DELICATESSEN

at our other branch :

237, BAKER STREET, N.W.I

(HUNter 0584)

51. Advertisement in the *Jewish Chronicle*, 16 November 1956.

Initially, Monty traded under the name of Klein, his original surname as discussed in earlier chapters, and the kosher delicatessen was supplied by Monty's own butchery business.[62] This development would probably not have been seen as any threat by Sidney Bloom.

However, within two years, Monty's business was operating under the name of M. Bloom (Kosher) Ltd, a name similar to that of the Aldgate restaurant, which could not be ignored. Believing that his cousin was trading on the success of his restaurant in Whitechapel High Street, Sidney took out an injunction against Monty to force him to change the name of his business.[63]

The problem did not go away. In 1964, Monty Bloom entered a partnership with a man named Sturgess and opened a substantial kosher restaurant at 114 Baker Street, formerly the premises occupied by the well-known Harry Gold's restaurant. Although advertisements for the new enterprise gave the name of the business (described as 'gleaming and spotless' with over a hundred items on the menu[64]) as Bloom and Sturgess, the name of Monty Bloom was still prominent in its advertising and when people rang to make a booking, the phone was apparently answered: 'Hello, Blooms.'[65] This could explain why, at the beginning of the 1970s, Bloom's advertisements were once again stressing the addresses at which the firm operated.[66]

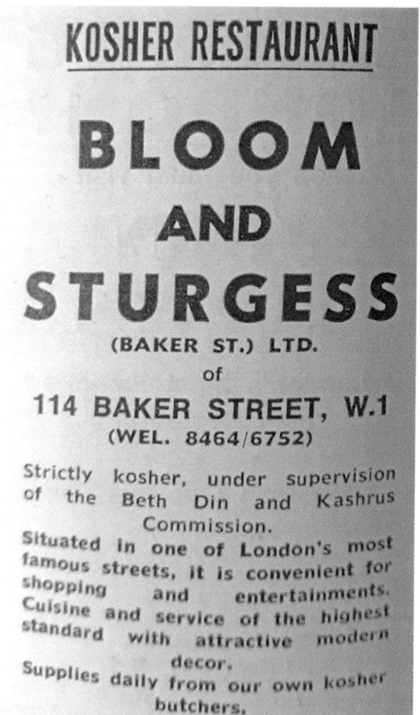

52. Advertisement in the *Jewish Chronicle Travel Guide*, 1967.

The Bloom and Sturgess restaurant closed in about 1972 and became the famous Reuben's kosher restaurant at 112 Baker Street.[67] By 1983 Monty Bloom had moved his butchery business to Sidmouth Parade in Brondesbury, NW2. He relinquished his licence as a kosher butcher in 1985.

The Continuing Success of the Aldgate Restaurant

Notwithstanding this family dispute, by 1960, the success of the Aldgate restaurant looked assured and Sidney was obviously feeling sufficiently confident about its future to declare that Bloom's restaurant was 'The Most Famous Kosher Restaurant in Great Britain'.[68] This was a real achievement in less than a decade. The bold claim was added to the signage on the exterior of the premises. The restaurant was often so busy that it ran out of salt beef, a 'Jewish catastrophe'.

At the beginning of 1961, the restaurant extended its weekday opening hours to 10pm (except for Fridays when it closed after lunch) to accommodate the ever-increasing trade.[69] From 11am on Sundays, queues formed outside Blooms, snaking into Gunthorpe Street. Amanda Myers, whose family (the Sinclair family[70]) still lived in the East End at this time, says: 'I remember the clamouring hordes on a Sunday morning, lining up to get their salt beef sandwiches. It was a place wonderfully full of life. I was a little child, but I can still sense the atmosphere created by the throng.'[71] Even though the restaurant was always busy on Sundays, Sidney Bloom made sure that there was a table free for former soldiers who had participated in the AJEX (Association of Jewish Ex-Servicemen and Women) Jewish Service of Remembrance at the Cenotaph on the Sunday following Remembrance Sunday.[72]

Many people recall that as the queues formed, Evelyn Bloom, or another family member, would emerge from the restaurant with a tray laden with slices of *worsht* or *latkes* to keep would-be diners happy and their hunger at bay until tables became free. Some people recall that they ate so many of the free snacks that they no longer had an appetite by the time they sat down at a table. As young children, Martin Malin (son of Sylvia and Archie Malin) and Jonathan Tapper (son of Marilyn and David Tapper) were both brought into service on a Sunday to hand round food to the people in the queue. Jonathan Tapper recalls: 'Since I was very shy as a kid, I really disliked that job!'[73]

Although the interior décor of the restaurant remained quite basic and traditional, in 1964 it was redecorated and a redesigned shopfront was installed. The new blue tables and chairs were a striking contrast to the white tablecloths. An eye-catching picture of beefeaters marching (it was said towards Blooms) was added.[74] For the convenience of its customers, in 1965 the increasingly famous restaurant started to open on the 'intermediate days' of *Pesach*.[75] Although this involved a great deal of work to ensure that the restaurant was *chomotz*-free (see Glossary of Hebrew and Yiddish Terms), this was warmly welcomed by Bloom's customers, who gladly queued for hours for a table.

By this time, Bloom's restaurant was firmly established as a well-known local landmark. Several nearby businesses, such as the Hanbury Press Ltd, now advertised where their location in relation to Bloom's restaurant. The restaurant's growing fame, seen as resulting from its inviting atmosphere, was being praised by writers, such as Jo Joseph, writing in the *Jewish Chronicle* in 1966.

> Blooms is the warm and inviting wink in the pouchy eye of Aldgate; the Shalom peace on the puckered face of Stepney. It's more than a physical landmark with a blazing neon sign beckoning choosy eaters, Jews and Gentiles, to linger a while at its tempting kosher tables; there is an air about it. A prime original, all-time, *heimische* atmosphere; a glow, a special visible electricity generated by magical Yiddisher processes over decades.[76]

The Customer Car Park

In 1965, Blooms opened a customer car park adjacent to its Aldgate restaurant. Initially, the car park was little more than a levelled bomb site, with the craters still visible, but it was highly valued by Bloom's customers as car ownership had become more prevalent. It was used by people who had come a long way to dine at Blooms, and also by those who just wanted to make a quick stop to pick up supplies: 'My father felt quite safe leaving us in the back of the car in the car park while he went into Blooms to buy food for our Sunday night supper.'[77] A helpful diagram to show how the car park could be accessed was placed in the *Jewish Chronicle.*

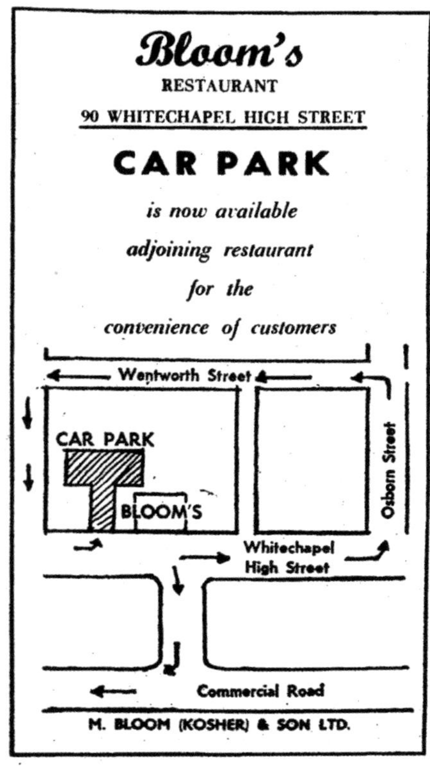

53. Diagram in *Jewish Chronicle*, 12 November 1965, showing access to Bloom's car park.

The car park was usually supervised by a Maltese man named Jimmy (originally Demetrious) Camilleri (a common Maltese name) and by Albert Marmara (also Maltese), who worked in the Bloom's factory and helped in the car park in his lunchtimes and on Sundays. Apparently, Albert was sometimes entrusted with parking the cars belonging to the Kray twins (see earlier mention) for which he was well tipped: 'He had to make sure that they could make a quick exit!'[78] On occasion, 'Michael the Irishman' (Michael O'Power) helped oversee the car park.[79]

The car park provided parking for about fifty vehicles, but at busy times there were long queues of cars waiting to go in. Cars were crammed in and there are memories of people paying the car parking attendants to ensure that their vehicles were kept safe. Philip Baigel recalls:

> When arriving at the Whitechapel restaurant, we parked in the car park, which you accessed by driving through an alleyway between two properties a few shops away. It led to a large open space behind and amongst the surrounding shops which seemed bigger than the laws of nature should allow. This Tardis-like car park was overseen by an entrepreneurial man with a much-weathered, alien-like face, who extracted large amounts of money from people, with more hunger than sense, in return for *protecting* your car from all possible Galactical mishaps. We always made a prompt exit from this spooky space with our children holding tightly to our hands and sped towards the restaurant.[80]

When the restaurant was open after *Shabbat* on Saturday evenings, the car park often contained some very smart cars.[81] Diners sometimes left the restaurant to find that they been boxed in, and several cars had to be moved to let them out or, even worse, that their cars were badly dented. Beverley-Jane Stewart recalls that she developed almost a phobia about being stuck in the car park and encouraged her parents to finish their meals quickly and to leave a hefty tip to facilitate a fast exit before the car park became overcrowded.[82]

The car park to the left of the restaurant was mainly reserved for customers. There was another, much smaller, car park at the back of the restaurant that was used by the vehicles delivering joints of meat and meat products from the factory and for staff car parking.[83]

Illustration 2: The mayhem in Bloom's car park. Copyright Beverley-Jane Stewart.

Kashrut and Cleanliness

The fact that Blooms operated under the supervision of the London Beth Din and Kashrus Commission was a major reason for its success. For most of its existence the full-time *shomer* at the Aldgate restaurant was Rabbi Moishe (Mordechai) Raben. Although he was appointed and employed by the Beth Din, he was seen as being part and parcel of the restaurant and was fondly regarded by both the staff and its customers. He was a very devout man (he was a member of the orthodox Adath Yisroel Congregation in Hendon), but he was not averse to smoking and drinking alcohol (especially whisky) and he knew (and used) many swear words.[84] He was said to have had a good sense of humour and has been described as 'a portly figure with a copious beard and a pronounced waddle'.[85] He was once quoted as saying: 'It is a nice, friendly atmosphere here in Blooms, otherwise I would have been away a long time before. And the food is better than anywhere else – the quality!', thereby giving the Bloom's menu a culinary as well as a religious blessing.[86] Rabbi Raben is remembered as being generous towards the local school children who came to the back door of the restaurant looking for free food.[87] He was saddened by the fact that he never had children himself.[88]

When he first started supervising *kashrut* at Blooms, Rabbi Raben had mainly worked at the Wentworth Street factory, porging the meat (see Glossary of Hebrew and Yiddish Terms) on behalf of the London Beth Din. He continued to do some porging after he became the *shomer* at the Aldgate restaurant, working in a small butchery at the back of the restaurant and, when it was busy, also at the factory after it had moved to Plaistow. In the middle of the restaurant, there was a screen, and behind the screen was the entrance to the kitchen, which is where Rabbi Raben sat for large parts of the day. Helen Blairman recalls: 'He scrutinised the food as it left the kitchen, very, very carefully.'[89] At busy times, the restaurant employed a second *shomer* named Rabbi Yisroel Fine, who usually worked at the factory.[90] Once a week, Rabbi A. Silver, the assistant rabbincal supervisor at the Kashrus Commission visited Blooms to inspect the premises.

Since Sidney Bloom was punctilious about *kashrut*, Blooms generally had a harmonious relationship with the Beth Din. However, the licensing authorities did on occasion raise issues about *kashrut.* In January 1961, Stanley Goldberg, the Bloom's company secretary,[91] wrote to Marcus Carr, Secretary of the London Beth Din, confirming that in future all Bloom's tinned soups with a meat content would 'bear a clear indication on the label to this effect'.[92] Similarly, in1978, Stanley Goldberg wrote to Dayan Swift, enclosing copies of receipts for bread purchased by the company saying: 'We hope that you will agree that if this amount is spent on our bread, it is most unlikely that supplementary purchases would be made from unauthorised sources.'[93] However, these were minor skirmishes compared to the difficulties that arose in Bloom's relationship with the London Beth Din in the 1980s and 1990s.[94]

Although Blooms adhered to *kashrut*, its reputation for standards of hygiene was not so impeccable. Hilary Perry recalls: 'I took an American cousin there once and there was a fly in the dish that we had ordered. When we called the waiter, all he said was: "Well it would have been koshered with the chicken." True story!'[95] The implication of this is that the fact that the laws of *kashrut* prohibited the consumption of meat from unhealthy and diseased animals transcended the environment in which it was cooked and served.

Up until the latter part of the twentieth century, concern with cleanliness in catering establishments, both Jewish and non-Jewish, was not the high priority that it has now become, and many food outlets and eateries had a reputation for being less than assiduous when it came to food hygiene. Blooms was therefore not alone in the criticisms it received about cleanliness. A large proportion of the abundant jokes and anecdotes that are told about Blooms relate to standards of hygiene, both in the kitchen and in the dining areas. However, although many former regular customers refer to these matters, most (but not all) say that their concerns did not stop them from eating at the restaurant and that their love of Bloom's food, overrode their qualms about cleanliness. Leslie Green comments: 'The heart doesn't grieve over what the eye can't see. I am sure that many of us enjoyed Blooms regardless of the *schmutz* [dirt]!'[96]

54. Cartoon by Harry Blacker, *The Stage*, 28 March 1996.

Opening of the Golders Green Restaurant

During 1964, Blooms took out several full-page advertisements in the *Jewish Chronicle*.[97] Business was clearly booming, which is remarkable given that the departure of Jews from the East End was continuing apace, and the streets of the former Jewish quarter were becoming ever-more dilapidated as they waited for the bulldozers to move in to demolish the slum housing that Hitler's bombs had missed. Roads such as Old Montague Street became epitomised by decaying staircases, shattered windows and rubbish piled high. When the wrecking machines did eventually move in, roads and alleys that had been at the heart of the former Jewish enclave disappeared in a matter of days, and their inhabitants scattered across the East End as depicted in Richard Vas's moving documentary, *The Vanishing Street*.[98]

When the process was complete, only a few vestiges of the Jewish East End remained, such as Katz's string and paper bag shop in Brick Lane, which were surrounded by small businesses run by the more recent immigrants, mainly single men from East Pakistan (later renamed Bangladesh).

It was Bloom's acknowledgement of the pace of change that led to the most significant development in the family firm during the 1960s: the opening of a second Bloom's restaurant in Golders Green, now the home of London's largest Jewish population. One journalist commented that the opening of the Golders Green restaurant was the Bloom family's 'belated recognition of the continuing flight to the suburbs as Whitechapel acceded to a new wave of immigrants, this time from Asia'.[99]

Despite the size of the Jewish community of Golders Green, until the arrival of Blooms in July 1965, there was no substantial kosher restaurant in the area. There were only traditional delicatessens, such as Cohen's (Smoked Salmon) Ltd and its rival Flax, and cafés selling salt beef sandwiches and *gefilte* fish (see Glossary of Eastern European Jewish Food at Appendix One), including Godfreys run by Ben and Kitty Godfrey, Biedek's in Golders Green Road and the Kettle of Fish opposite the Hippodrome Theatre, which was run as a partnership between Mr Stoller, who owned fish shops, and a Mr Leslie. Later, Ben and Kitty Godfrey's son, Leslie and his wife Anita, opened a popular salt beef bar in Temple Fortune. More significantly, before Blooms opened, there had been only one small kosher establishment in Golders Green that served sit-down meals: Silver's snack bar in Golders Green Road, which was run by the former German refugee, Herbert Bruck.[100]

Bloom's Golders Green restaurant was located at 130 Golders Green Road, previously occupied by the delicatessen run by the Godfreys. The sign above the door read: 'Taste the Quality.' The premises, which unlike 90 Whitechapel High Street were rented rather than owned by Blooms,[101] were much smaller than the Aldgate property. The space available for dining provided seating for only eighty customers.

The Golders Green restaurant was decorated with nostalgic photographs of the Jewish East End, including a reproduction of the same photomural of Petticoat Lane market that hung in the Aldgate restaurant; it was on the left-hand wall, adjacent to the banquette seating: 'When we took our children, they always preferred to sit next to the mural to look at the interesting characters from "the olden days".'[102] However, with its matted, glass-topped tables and the artificial greenery at the rear, the new restaurant had a more modern feel than the Aldgate establishment. Philip Baigel recalls that the washrooms were located down a flight of stairs, at the end of a very long corridor and customers sometimes joked that the two restaurants shared toilet facilities.[103]

55. Bloom's restaurant in Golders Green, showing the photomural. Courtesy of the *Jewish Chronicle*, 18 June 2010.

When the restaurant in Golders Green opened on 14 July 1965, queues stretched back along Golders Green Road as far as the former ABC cinema. From the outset, business was brisk, especially on Sundays when people came to Golders Green to shop from across London and even further afield.[104] Since there were fewer tables, the queues outside were even longer than at the parent restaurant.

OPENING

WEDNESDAY, 14th JULY, 1965

BLOOM'S RESTAURANT

AT

130 GOLDERS GREEN RD.

THE ONLY BRANCH OF

90 WHITECHAPEL HIGH STREET, LONDON, E.1
BIShopsgate 6001

Under the Supervision of the London Beth Din

Head Office: 111 Wentworth Street, London, E.1
BIShopsgate 3937

56. Announcement in the *Jewish Chronicle*, 9 July 1965.

Just a year after the restaurant opened, an editorial writer in the *Jewish Chronicle* commented: 'Blooms, with its eternal queue in Golders Green, has demonstrated that the kosher butcher and restaurateur can prosper beyond Whitechapel.'[105] Another writer quipped: 'The housewives in the north-west belt are rumoured to have breathed a sigh of relief and said, "now we can stop cooking".'

Illustration 3: Bloom's restaurant in Golders Green. Copyright Beverley-Jane Stewart.

In theory, customers were able to book a table at Blooms in Golders Green, but even if they did so, it did not make any difference; they still had to wait until a table became free.[106] Because of the queues, which sometimes obstructed the pavement outside the restaurant, the urgency for diners to finish their meals and leave was even greater than in Aldgate. David Ziants recalls that the hot water machine for making lemon tea and coffee was always broken in Golders Green on a Sunday because the staff wanted the customers to leave as soon as possible.[107]

The Golders Green branch, like at Aldgate, was also 'frantically busy' at lunchtimes. People coming to buy takeaway food sometimes created mayhem by 'triple parking' outside the premises since the new restaurant did not have the benefit of a car park. Helen Blairman, who worked on the delicatessen counter, recalls: 'It was quiet when you first arrived in the morning. You were mainly preparing the salads rather than serving the customers. But late morning things went mad and there was no respite until about 2pm.'[108]

Although the Bloom family tried hard to replicate the 'magical' atmosphere of the Aldgate restaurant and transferred some of its more experienced waiters and restaurant managers to the new enterprise to address this,[109] many of its customers agreed that it was 'not the same; it just didn't have the same atmosphere',[110] and 'it was always much quieter, not that you are ever going to get silence in a Jewish restaurant!'[111] Many people also recall that the food was never as good, perhaps because the more experienced Bloom's chefs remained in the East End. Mike Levy, who lived with his wife in Golders Green when they were in their early twenties recalls:

> We were delighted when Blooms opened around the corner, and we went there regularly. However, it never seemed to have the charm or ambience that the Whitechapel restaurant had. The waiters were not as outrageous at the Golders Green location and somehow the food always seemed to taste better at Whitechapel.[112]

As a result, despite its success, especially in its early years, Bloom's second restaurant never reached the celebratory status of the Aldgate restaurant.

The Golders Green restaurant was largely overseen by Sylvia Malin, one of the Bloom's company directors, although she also sometimes worked at the Aldgate restaurant. Unusually for the time, Sylvia had a full-time role while bringing up a family. Her son Martin Malin recalls that after he started attending Hasmonean

Boys' Grammar School in Holders Hill Road in Hendon, there was just time for him to take a bus to Golders Green, have lunch with his mother at the restaurant and make it back to school for the afternoon lessons. He often returned to school with *latkes* (see Glossary of Eastern European Jewish Food at Appendix One) to sell to his fellow students bored with school dinners, which made him very popular.[113]

Martin's mother, known by many as 'Auntie Sylvia', was popular with both the staff and the customers: 'The staff just adored her and she was good with the children who came into the restaurant, inventing games to keep them amused and to make eating in Blooms appealing for them. She was very self-effacing, and her contribution was sometimes overlooked.'[114] Sylvia was very supportive of the staff, including the Greek Cypriot waiter known as Nick,[115] whom she encouraged to go to the library and learn English so that he could attend college and 'better himself.'[116] When Martin Malin celebrated his *Bar Mitzvah*, as a mark of their affection for his mother, many of the Bloom's staff attended both the synagogue service and the subsequent event held at the King David Suite in central London: 'I remember the rabbi remarking that there had never seen such a large gathering of Greek Cypriots in the synagogue!'[117]

Unlike the Aldgate restaurant, there was no long-standing *shomer* at Golders Green, but a series of short-term *shomrim* (plural of *shomer*) appointed by the London Beth Din, including a man named Alf Charing and another named Henry, 'a statuesque man with a booming voice', who davened at Munk's Shul in Golders Green.'[118]

A significant innovation that followed the opening of the Golders Green restaurant was the holding of *sedarim* (plural of *seder*, the name of the service for the first night of *Pesach* using symbolic foods). The first *seder* was held in 1967. It had been anticipated that demand would be high and potential attendees were advised to book.[119] However, the response exceeded expectations and some people queued for several hours to participate. The experiment was repeated the following year, but it was then decided that holding a *seder* for such large numbers of people was beyond the restaurant's capacity.

At this stage, Sidney Bloom was spending time between the two restaurants and sometimes after the restaurant in Golders Green closed, he stayed on to socialise with friends. Stuart Singer recalls that when he was young, he was taken by his father Ivan, who was a taxi driver, to the restaurant to play cards with Sidney and Michael Bloom and Sidney Ziff,[120] the firm's meat and poultry supplier: 'The game we played was called Klaberjass a trick-taking, ace-ten game that was popular in the Jewish community. My father was obsessed with playing cards, even playing on his own on occasion, so he really enjoyed these sessions at Golders Green.'[121]

Marketing

During the 1970s, the advertisements placed by Blooms in the *Jewish Chronicle* became standardised and ceased to provide helpful insights into developments in the restaurants. They were mainly limited to giving routine information on opening times, contact details and arrangements during the Jewish festivals. The firm had probably decided to economise by dispensing with the large and frequent advertisements it had previously placed in the *Jewish Chronicle* since the business was now being publicised in other ways, including in reviews appearing in Jewish and non-Jewish publications, such as the Consumers' Association's *The Good Food Guide*.

For many years Blooms was the only kosher restaurant that had an entry in this publication. In one review, the inspector counselled against eating steak at Blooms, saying 'there is no way that in which steaks at Blooms will be any good', but thoroughly recommended the *bortsch*, salt beef and *latkes*, and *tzimmes* (see Glossary of Eastern European Jewish food) and noted that the shoulder of veal and sweet and sour cabbage and the brusque, noisy service were equally popular.[122]

The two Bloom's restaurants were also reviewed in the widely-read 1960s magazine *London Life*.

OPEN EVERY DAY

BLOOM'S, 90 Whitechapel High Street, E1 (**BIS 6001**). Golders Green Road, NW11 (**SPE 1338**). The East End restaurant is bigger and better known. Drive there (car park for patrons) or if you go by train get out at Aldgate East, exiting to High Street North Side. Only the Whitechapel place accepts reservations, which are advisable on Sundays. It's as well to take a really late lunch at the Golders' Green Bloom's, say between 4 and 5 pm, since earlier admission is often pretty difficult without long queueing. Both are open Monday to Thursday from 11 am right through to 10 pm, Friday 11-3, and Sunday from 11 am right through to 11.30 pm, serving all the time. No licence: bring your own – or they can usually send out – beer, etc. Most things are good: for example *gefilte* fish (better boiled, 3s 6d); chopped liver or chopped herring (2s 6d). Among soups try beetroot *borsht* (2s 6d), mixed chicken (4s) or *heimeshe* barley (2s 6d). Hot salt beef (7s 6d) is good, stuffed breast of veal (8s 6d) delicious, stuffed breast of lamb rather fatty (7s 6d). Roast leg of chicken (7s 6d) with stuffed neck (5s) is good and fattening indeed. Always sample some pickled cucumber, sweet and sour (1s 3d). Try to leave room for the *lockshen* pudding (2s 6d), which they serve with a little fruit juice, and is wonderfully light. Wash it all down with lemon tea (1s 6d), which Blooms' do beautifully – Jewish dietary laws forbid milk after meat. Bill for two – around 35s. No credit cards

57. Review of Bloom's restaurants in 1960s, *London Life*, kindly provided by Tom Gillmor at Mary Evans Picture Library.

This change of approach to marketing clearly had no detrimental impact since the reputation of the firm was continuing to grow. *Rosh Hashanah* greetings from Blooms were now addressed to their 'customers throughout the world'.[123]

Intriguingly, in 1976 a report appeared in the Jewish press suggesting that the Bloom family had been exploring the option of selling the 'world-famous restaurant' but had 'drawn a veil of silence' over the matter. The potential sale of the restaurant had been discussed in the 'City' pages of the *Daily Mail*, rumouring that the family would be willing to sell the business, provided that an acceptable offer (estimated as being upwards of £750,000) was made.[124] The report also suggested that possible buyers included J. Lyons, Matthews Holdings and Sydney Ziff and Co.[125] Since the possible sale was not mentioned again, the Bloom family might have been seeking an assessment of the market value of its assets in the light of the firm's increasing fame.

THE TAXI GAME

PLAY THE TAXI GAME AND WIN DINNER FOR TWO

You have to get from the Clock Tower at Golders Green to Bloom's Restaurant in Whitechapel for Sunday lunch. The object is to get there as quickly and directly as possible allowing for speed limits, one-way systems, street markets and other possible obstructions along the way.

To enter the competition, list the roads and streets you would take in route order, indicating left- or right-hand turns (for example, Park Road, left into Marylebone Road) and estimate the time the journey will take. A combination of route and time will be taken into consideration by the judges.

The competition will be judged by experienced taxi-drivers and the lucky winner will recei[illegible] a voucher for dinner for two at Bloom's.

CONDITIONS

Employees of the Jewish Chronicle or their families are not eligible.
No entries are valid without the coupon below.
The Editor's decision is final.
No correspondence can be entered into.

Name

Address

The Taxi Game,
The Jewish Chronicle, 25 Furnival Street, London, EC4A 1JT

58. Notice in the *Jewish Chronicle*, 25 February 1977.

After this mysterious episode, Blooms continued to identify innovative ways of marketing the business, such as by offering a prize of a meal at Blooms for a high-profile *Jewish Chronicle* competition named the 'Taxi Game', which involved entrants identifying the quickest driving route from the clock tower in Golders Green to Bloom's restaurant in Aldgate.

The competition was judged by experienced taxi drivers. The first year, the event was won by Brian Lewis, who recalls:

> Some years ago, we won a competition in the *Jewish Chronicle* to find the quickest way to drive from Blooms in Golders Green to the Blooms in Whitechapel. The prize was as much as you could eat at Blooms Whitechapel. My wife ate so much she was ill in the street afterwards![126]

By the 1970s, Blooms was producing a range of memorabilia, which not only generated income, but also served to raise the profile of the firm and allowed Blooms to shape its image as a 'world-famous' icon. Many former Bloom's customers still own samples of the merchandise, such as the square glass bowl to be used as an ashtray or a pickle plate and even *kippot* bearing the Bloom's logo. See Plates Section, Plates 2, 3, 4.[127]

The prominence of Blooms was also being assisted by its mention in several plays, including productions of Arnold Wesker's *Chicken Soup with Barley*, and from being featured in TV programmes, such as the documentary on Lord Goodman, which was screened by the BBC in June 1970. This showed the broadcaster Monty Modlyn going into Bloom's restaurant in Aldgate and ordering a meal, leading to an explanation of *kashrut*.[128]

Bloom's Restaurants in the Late 1970s and Early 1980s

1977 was the year of the Queen's silver jubilee, which Blooms decided to mark in style, placing prominent notices in the front windows of its two restaurants, congratulating the Queen on the milestone.

59. Michael Jacobs and his niece, Sonia Shugar, outside Blooms in 1977. Photo taken by William Shugar and reproduced courtesy of Hilary Scott.

By coincidence, 1977 was also the twenty-fifth anniversary of the opening of Blooms in Whitechapel High Street and in December that year several special events were organised in the restaurants to celebrate this landmark. The *Jewish Chronicle* commented: 'It will be a *simcha* celebration hugely enjoyed by a vast international clientele, non-Jews as well as Jews.'[129]

Despite the celebrity status of Blooms, the two restaurants retained their somewhat dated, 'no frills' décor. The emphasis continued to be placed on customers eating well and quickly. Alan Dein recalls: 'Blooms was basic; there was nothing pretentious about the restaurants. Nowadays, every restaurant must have a *schtick* [gimmick], like having a Michelin star chef. Blooms was the equivalent of the British standard dish of meat and potatoes.'[130] Sidney Bloom was once quoted as saying: 'There are no orchestras here, no soft lights. I believe in bright lights. Let the people see what they're eating.'[131] By 1980, there had been a few innovations, such as the installation of air conditioning, but the atmosphere remained much the same, as pointed out in a review appearing in *The Good Food Guide*:

> Bloom's is a hangover from the era of heavy overcoats that hung down to your shoelaces. The Eastern-European food would be familiar to anyone from the Circus or a mole on the run. George Smiley would not seem out of place queuing for a glass of cold beetroot bortsch or perhaps the light inside is a little too strong for him to feel comfortable.[132]

While both restaurants continued to prosper, things were changing rapidly in the manufacturing and wholesale arm of the business, to be explored in the next chapter.

Notes

1. Gardiners was a well-known men's clothing store and army outfitters. With its imposing clock tower, it stood on the junction of the five major roads in the Jewish East End, one of which was Whitechapel High Street. It burned to the ground in 1972 and it is said that the blaze was so fierce that the front windows of Bloom's restaurant began to melt. Gardiners is remembered as the rallying point for Jews in the Battle of Cable Street.
2. The building was erected in 1910 by E. Laurance & Sons of Eagle Wharf Road to the designs of E. N. Clifton & Son for Edmund H. Hodgkinson, a retired marine insurance broker and inventor. See https://surveyoflondon.org/map/feature/322/detail/.
3. Many of the guides leading Jack the Ripper walking tours lunched at Blooms.
4. Albert's Menswear moved into the premises in 1942 and refurbished the building following a fire in the 1950s.
5. Rita Adams, post on Facebook page East London in Days Gone By, 15.8.2020.
6. Interview with Barry Gelkoff, 29.3.2023.
7. Interview with Esther Piper (née Gowers), 8.1.2023.
8. Originally, there were Star of David badges on each floor, but only one was retained when the building was refurbished. There is another badge inside the upper rooms. See https://www.londonremembers.com.
9. Anne Martin, post on Facebook page Memories of Hessel, Langdale Mans, Cannon Street Rd and Cable St, 3.4.2020.
10. Interview with Barry Gelkoff, 29.3.2023.
11. See Chapter Three.
12. *Ibid.*

13. Interview with Martin Malin, 22.9.2022.
14. Peter Bloom, post on Facebook page Memories of Hessel, Langdale Mans, Cannon Street Rd and Cable St, 17.8.2022.
15. Interview with Professor Geoffrey Alderman, 31.10.2022.
16. Monica Finlay, post on Facebook page The Jewish East End of London, 8.4.2021.
17. Interview with Alan Dein, 3.1.2023.
18. *JC*, 29.4.1989. The collection was organised by Ann Kaye, a member of the committee for Charles Clore House. Jan Colman, post on Facebook page Memories of Hessel, Langdale Mans, Cannon Street Rd and Cable St, 30.3.2023.
19. Howard Cohen, post on *ibid.*, 26.12.2021. Israel Cohen had shops across north London and in Peckham.
20. The image came from the photo archive kept at the Guildhall Picture Gallery, https://www.londonpicturearchive.org.uk/.
21. Hilary Prais, response to post by author of Facebook page Jewish Britain, 21.8.2022. It is not known what happened to the photomural.
22. Conversation with Hannah Jacobs, 5.5.2023.
23. See Chapter Nine.
24. Marcus Binney, *Evening Standard*, 19.5.1992.
25. Interview with David Rein, 2.5.2023.
26. See Chapter Ten.
27. *The Stage*, 13.3.1997.
28. Aumie and Michael Shapiro (eds), *The Jewish East End* (London: The Springboard Education Trust, 1996), p.41.
29. Rita Carr (later Sinclair), who was born in Whitechapel in 1926, went on to become a popular singer performing with Lew Stone's orchestra. She played for the troops with the big wartime bands during the Second World War. She was one of the first women to enter the Bergen Belsen death camp after its liberation. She died in 2016.
30. Amanda Myers (daughter of Rita Carr), post on Facebook page The Jewish East End of London, 8.9.2021.
31. Conversation with Stuart Singer, 21.4.2023.
32. *JC*, 2.9.1988.
33. Terrence Keating, post on Facebook page The East End of London and East London, History and Memories, 25.6.2020.
34. Simon Alexander, post on Facebook page The Jewish East End of London, 13.11.2020.
35. Interview with Philip Luxembourg, 10.10.2022.
36. Quoted in *JC*, 18.3.2005.
37. Vivienne Thompson, post on Facebook page The Jewish East End of London, 19.11.2018.
38. David Feldman, 'Bloom, Solomon Sidney', in *Oxford Dictionary of National Biography*, Oxford University Press, March 2009.

39. *JC*, 13.7.1967.
40. 1960s Bloom's marketing brochure, courtesy of Jonathan Fishburn.
41. See Chapter Seven.
42. Interview with Michael Georgiou, 3.4.2023.
43. See Chapter Nine.
44. This concept embraces not only charity, but also a commitment to social justice.
45. Mildred Charlotte, post on Facebook page The Jewish East End of London, 23.8.2020.
46. Mildred Charlotte, post on *ibid.*, 29.10.16.
47. Pamela Kaye, post on Facebook page The Jewish East End of London, 20.10.2013.
48. Interview with Martin Malin, 22.9.2022. The people queuing at Blooms continued to be given food parcels, known as *rachmones* (compassion), well into the 1980s. See *JC*, 6.12.1985.
49. *JC*, 14.6.2022.
50. Interview with Martin Malin, 22.9.2022. See Chapter Seven for further information.
51. Interview with Jonathan Tapper, 2.10.2022.
52. *The Stage*, 27.11.2003.
53. *JC*, 29.5.1953.
54. *JC*, 8.10.1954.
55. See Chapter Nine.
56. Anonymous interviewee, 22.8.2022.
57. See https://web.archive.org/web/20061018044059/http://www.eastlondonhistory.com/blooms.htm.
58. *JC*, 5.12.1955.
59. See Chapter Three.
60. *JC*, 2.9.1966.
61. Bala Baruch Bloom emigrated to London from Hungary and was operating as a 'provisions dealer' for many years before Morris Bloom set up in business. See city directories and census returns, Ancestry.co.uk.
62. *JC*, 25.6.1954. By 1956, Monty Bloom's butchery business had also moved from the East End to Melcombe Street (opposite Baker Street Station) to make it the only kosher butcher in the Baker Street area (see *JC*, 16.11.1956).
63. Interview with Martin Malin, 22.9.2022.
64. *JC*, 12.6.1964.
65. Interview with Martin Malin, 22.9.2022.
66. See, for example, *JC*, 12.11.1971.
67. Reubens commenced trading in about 1973 and moved from 114 to 112 in 1995 following a fire. Owing to a bereavement in 2019, the firm stopped trading for a few months until it was taken over by the Israeli Landau chain.
68. *JC*, 19.2.1960.
69. *JC*, 20.1.1961.

70. Amanda Myers is the daughter of Rita Sinclair who sang at the opening night of Bloom's restaurant.
71. Amanda Myers, post on the Facebook page The Jewish East End of London, 26.1.2023.
72. Interview with Martin Malin, 28.4.2023.
73. Interview with Jonathan Tapper, 2.10.2022 and Interview with Martin Malin, 22.9.2022. See Chapter Nine for more information on customers queuing for Bloom's restaurant.
74. *JC*, 10.7.1964.
75. *JC*, 2.4.1965.
76. *JC*, 15.7.1966.
77. Anonymous interviewee, 22.8.2022.
78. Interview with David Rein, 4.5.2023.
79. Derek Morris, post on Facebook page East London in Days Gone by, 30.6.2020. and interview with Martin Malin, 3.11.2022. See Chapter Seven for further information.
80. Message from Philip Baigel, 24.3.2023.
81. Glenys Johnson, post on Facebook page East End of London and East London, 6.1.2020.
82. Conversation with Beverley-Jane Stewart, 14.4.2023.
83. Interview with Martin Malin, 1.12.2022.
84. Interview with Martin Malin, 3.11.2022.
85. *JC*, 2.9.1988.
86. *Ibid.*
87. Robin Das, post on Facebook page The Jewish East End of London, 13.11.2020.
88. Interview with Martin Malin, 22.9.2022.
89. Interview with Helen Blairman, 1.9.2022.
90. For information on Rabbi Fine, see https://www.jewishgen.org/jcr-uk/Profiles/minister_profiles_orthodox_F.htm#Fine_M.
91. See Chapter Seven.
92. Copy of letter dated 20.1.1962, in the possession of David Newman.
93. Copy of letter dated 31.10.1978, in the possession of David Newman.
94. See Chapter Six.
95. Hilary Perry, post on Facebook page Jewish Britain,15.5.2016.
96. Leslie Green, post on *ibid.*, 16.4.2016.
97. See *JC*, 10.7.1964.
98. The film documented the demolition of the Hessel Street market area, which had once been a bustling Jewish commercial centre, almost as celebrated as Petticoat Lane.
99. Tom Jaine writing in *The Times*, 24.6.2003.
100. For more information on the early eateries in Golders Green, see Pam Fox, *The Jewish Community of Golders Green, A Social History* (Stroud: The History Press, 2016), pp.126–127.

101. The premises were leased (never purchased) from Stewart Cohen, the owner of the well-known butchery and restaurant, La Boucherie, trading at Cat Hill in East Barnet. Stewart Cohen later opened a branch in Stanmore.
102. Interview with Philip Baigel, 7.12.2022. Bloom family members believe that the mural was torn down during the restaurant's makeover in 2006.
103. Email from Philip Baigel, 14.11.2022.
104. See Chapter Nine.
105. *JC*, 26.8.1966.
106. Dorothy Kilner, post on Facebook page Memories of Hessel, Langdale Mans, Cannon Street Rd and Cable St, 7.8.2022.
107. David Ziants, post on Facebook page The Jewish East End of London, 29.10.2016.
108. Interview with Helen Blairman, 1.9.2022.
109. See Chapters Seven and Eight.
110. Interview with Marilyn Lovell, 28.3.2023.
111. Interview with Connie Stanton, 7.10.2022.
112. Mike Levy, response to post on author's Facebook page, 19.8.2022.
113. Interview with Martin Malin, 20.9.2022.
114. Interview with Martin Malin, 22.9.2022.
115. See Chapter Eight.
116. Interview with Martin Malin, 3.11.2022.
117. Conversation with Martin Malin, 7.5.2023.
118. Interview with Martin Malin, 3.11.2022.
119. *JC*, 24.3.1967.
120. See Chapter Five.
121. Interview with Stuart Singer 2.5.2023. Stuart is the son of Benita Singer (née Bloom), who worked for many years on the counters at the two Bloom's restaurants. See Chapter Seven. Klaberjass, pronounced Clobyash meaning Jack of Clubs (also known as 'Bela'), emanates from the Netherlands. See https://en.wikipedia.org/wiki/Klaberjass.
122. Christopher Driver (ed.), *The Good Food Guide 1976* (London: The Consumers' Association and Hodder and Stoughton, 1976), p.392.
123. See Chapter Nine.
124. *JC*, 18.6.1976.
125. See Chapter Five.
126. Brian Lewis, on Jewish Britain Facebook page in response to post by author, 21.8.2022.
127. Bloom's marketing brochures and advertisements were designed and written by a Jo Joseph. (See 1960s marketing brochure, courtesy of Jonathan Fishburn), but it is possible that the merchandise was designed by a freelance designer with the surname of Stewart. Message from Paul Stewart, 25.3.2023.
128. *JC*, 3.7.1970.
129. *JC*, 15.7.1977.

130. Interview with Alan Dein, 3.1.2023.
131. *JC,* 16.7.1965.
132. Drew Smith (ed.), *The Good Food Guide 1980* (London: The Consumers' Association and Hodder and Stoughton, 1980), p.55.

Chapter Five

The Wholesale and Non-Restaurant Aspects of Blooms

The Wentworth Street Factory in the 1950s and 1960s

After the end of the Second World War, the premises in Wentworth Street continued to provide the base for Bloom's manufacturing and wholesale activities. It was also the headquarters for the firm, although its registered office was at 114 Baker Street.[1] Wentworth Street was by now referred to as the 'East End food court', since it was the location for fifteen kosher butchers, many delicatessens and bakeries, including well-known firms such as Mossy Marks' delicatessen, Mendel the salmon cutter, Ostwinds, Bonn's and Goide's bakeries as well as Blooms (see Plates Section, Plate 5). As a child, Martine Kaufman bought goods for her mother at Bloom's factory:

> The factory was very long but not very wide. You easily could miss it as you walked past. There were no big signs. Young people lingering outside the factory at the right time (and if the factory people liked you), received free Viennas. Over the decades, like the surrounding area, the front of the factory deteriorated and became a bit shabby.[2]

Inside, the premises were divided into several different areas. The butchery was in the basement. The meat arrived from the abattoir in Canning Town in the Ziffs's (the Blooms main supplier of meat and poultry) delivery lorry, which was parked in the street immediately outside the front of the factory. David Rein, who started working in the factory in1953 when he was twenty-four, recalls:

> The quarters of beef were offloaded from the lorry straight onto the pavement where people walked. Not very hygienic! The delivery men hefted the meat onto their shoulders and

> shoved them through an open window and pushed them down a hole to the basement, where they arrived onto a big table where six butchers of many different nationalities worked. This is where the porging was done. When I first went to work in the factory, meat was still rationed and the meat wholesalers were paid "a little bit extra" to ensure that Blooms received a ready supply.[3]

The butchers separated the meat that was to be used in the restaurant from the meat that was to be used for manufacturing purposes (see further explanation later in this chapter). The cuts to be used for making meat products was put into large pickling barrels, which were loaded onto a lift that was operated by ropes on the ground floor. David Rein says:

> Because the barrels were so big and heavy, it took two of us to haul them up. They weighed too much for one person to get them off the lift and roll them into the factory, which was at the back of the premises. It was very, very heavy work, even for a fit young man, as I was then.[4]

Once the meat arrived in the factory, it underwent several stages of manufacture, which were overseen by Sigmund Sichel, a former German refugee.[5]

> The meat was put into the grinder and when it was ground, it was placed in what we called "the chopper", a big circular machine fitted with electric knives, which whizzed round like a high-speed car. The chopped meat was tipped into troughs with the mixer and then the filling machine, which dispensed the mixed meat onto a big table with people standing each side of it making the products.[6]

At the very back of the factory there was a smokery, consisting of two brick compartments built into the wall in which the Viennas were smoked. Norman Bookbinder[7] provides a detailed description of the smoking process:

> You would have to walk the Viennas hanging from sticks over to the smokehouse, sit on the edge of the smokehouse wall and slide the Viennas across the rails that stretched the width of the compartments. You closed the steel doors, and they hung inside for fifteen to twenty minutes to be dried and smoked. The floor of the smoking compartments was covered with sawdust, delivered in great quantities each day. The sawdust smouldered away, giving the Viennas their smoky taste. The Viennas were then slid out again and transferred to a large bath of hot water to be cooked. It was an archaic process![8]

After they had been cooked and cooled, the Viennas were stored in the refrigerators that lined one wall of the factory until they were dispatched. The process for producing the salami was similarly unmechanised: 'You had to tie and hang the salami by hand. Morris Bloom wasn't very keen on automation. Today, you just press a button and a machine does everything!'[9]

Illustration 4: Inside Bloom's factory in Wentworth Street. Copyright Beverley-Jane Stewart.

During the 1950s, Bloom's owned only a small number of delivery vans and a large proportion of the meat products were mainly sold to kosher butchers from the factory rather than being delivered. The front of the ground floor, which was about forty-feet long, was used for the packaging of the goods and assembling them for collection. When meat was still rationed, the butchers queued for a long time to get their *worsht* and Viennas.[10] The wholesale operation was managed at this time by David Levy, described as 'a very religious man from Stamford Hill'.[11] There was a small office on the ground floor where the butchers paid for their goods and placed future orders.

60. 'Showcard' for Bloom's outlets, *Jewish Chronicle*, 30 December 1960.

While the Aldgate restaurant was rapidly moving the family business into the spotlight, the wholesale activities continued to generate the most profit. With more space available following the restaurant's move to Whitechapel High Street, the manufacturing activities were able to expand, and Blooms introduced new marketing techniques, such as the 'showcard' to be displayed by the butchers, delicatessens and other outlets stocking Bloom's meat products.[12] Potential customers were advised to look for the showcard to avoid being sold imitations of Bloom's goods. New lines were introduced including liver sausages and 'frying *worsht*'. The advertisements for the goods provided helpful guidance on how to prepare Bloom's products.[13]

Upstairs were the administrative offices where Stanley Goldberg, the company secretary, and clerical staff worked. In 1961, he was joined there by his son Melvin, who later became the manager at the Aldgate restaurant.[14] In the 1950s, the restaurant and takeaway counter were closed during *Pesach*, but the Wentworth Street factory produced vast quantities of 'Passover goods' in the lead-up to the festival.

During the 1960s, Bloom's manufacturing and wholesale business based in Wentworth Street continued to expand and the factory became a very busy place. By this time, Blooms had invested in more vans and hired additional drivers, enabling most of its goods to be delivered. Early in the morning, the van drivers congregated in the front section of the ground floor. They weighed the various products and packed them into crates. The drivers would then help each other to stack the crates ready for loading into the vans. Blooms now had use of an area of land belonging to the Etz Chaim Yeshiva in Thrawl Street backing onto Wentworth Street, which is where the vans parked. The land stood between Bloom's factory and the premises of Ellis and Goldstein, the famous textile factory.[15]

Once the vans were loaded, the drivers departed on their respective rounds. Some went north to Ilford; others made their way to south London; and some served Golders Green and the adjacent suburbs of north-west London. The delivery operation was managed by a man named Morrie Moss.[16]

The Bloom's vans,[17] of which the firm appears to have been very proud, featured prominently in its 1960s promotional materials. They contained old-fashioned scales with weights and on their arrival at their customers, the drivers would weigh the goods before issuing the butchers or shopkeepers with a handwritten invoice. This was in the days before the coming of the major supermarket chains, but larger shops, such as Sainsbury's, were just starting to spread across London, creating an increased demand for Bloom's meat products.[18]

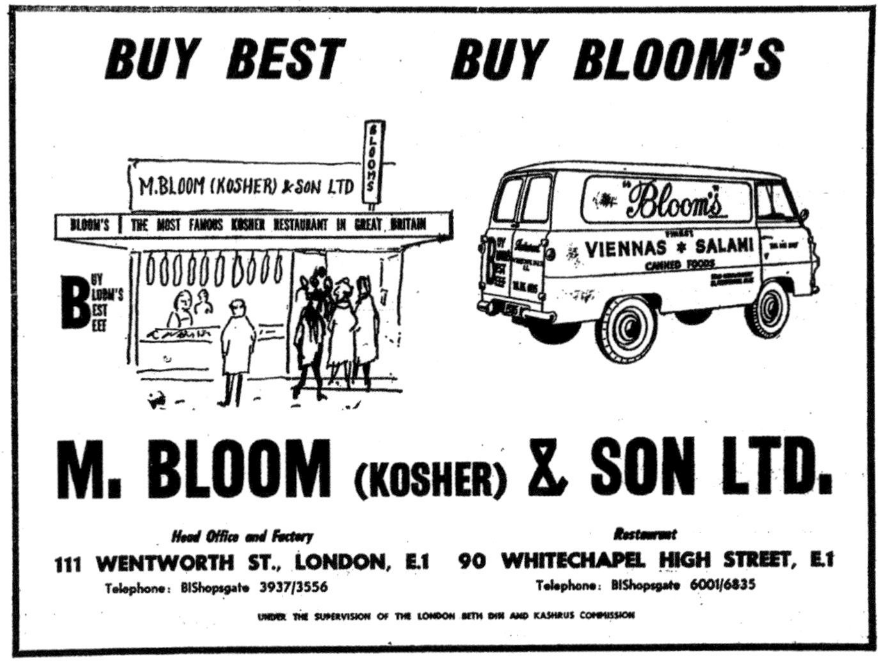

61. Advertisement in the *Jewish Chronicle*, 1 January 1964.

One of the largest stockists of Bloom's products during the 1960s was the long-established firm S. Greenspan, a kosher butcher and poulterer (and, as previously mentioned, owned by a close friend of Sidney and Evelyn Bloom), which advertised that it sold only Bloom's goods.[19] This was a vote of confidence for Blooms, but the firm was still clearly experiencing problems with imitation of its products. An advertisement placed in the *Jewish Chronicle* in the summer of 1966 stated: 'Notice to our provincial customers; to prevent imitation, our Viennas are now available in 8-ounce packets', which prevented the sausages being sold loose and being passed off as the product of another manufacturer.[20]

In 1964, the 'Buy Bloom's Best Beef' slogan became a registered trademark,[21] which appears to have raised Bloom's confidence in being able to protect its brand since the warnings were discontinued.

62. Advertisement in the *Jewish Chronicle*, 29 October 1965.

The Cannery

In response to public demand, the canned and packaged goods that had been introduced on a small scale in 1935, became a much larger element of Bloom's merchandise with the opening of a dedicated canning section in June 1960.[22] The first manager of the expanded canning operation was a man named Mr Berlinger, who had previously worked at the famous kosher Skrek's canning firm in Cardiff.[23] All the canned goods were stamped with the Bloom's name, and they were often marketed separately from Bloom's other products.

63. Advertisement in the *Jewish Chronicle*, 15 January 1965.

The canned goods enabled people all over the country to enjoy many of the same dishes as regular diners at Bloom's restaurant: chicken soup, beetroot *borscht*, cabbage *borscht*, barley soup, dumplings, pickles and *lokshen* (see Glossary of Eastern European Jewish Food at Appendix One).

DELICIOUS KOSHER SOUPS

TAKE *barley soup, or thick pea soup or nice clear chicken soup, beetroot borsht, cabbage borsht; they are typically Jewish (though there is no reason why non-Jewish people should not eat and enjoy them). Kneidlach soup, kreplach soup, these items you just can't buy in the normal way, and people have not got the time to make the soups quite suddenly as they fancy it.*

Already there are over a dozen varieties of soups and canned foods.

ALL of these tasty soups and the wonderful cooked meats are also eaten in hospitals, institutions, holiday camps, and orphanages, because of their quality.

64. Extract from 1960s Bloom's marketing brochure. Courtesy of Jonathan Fishburn.

When Blooms embarked on canning its popular products on a large scale, the cannery was based in two self-contained rooms in a building at the rear of the restaurant in Gunthorpe Street, known as St George's Residence. The cannery was accessed either via the alleyway to the right of the restaurant leading off Whitechapel High Street or through the restaurant kitchen. Some rooms in St George's Residence were used for domestic accommodation.[24]

At this time, most aspects of the canning process were carried out by hand. Norman Bookbinder, who became the cannery manager in the latter part of the 1960s, recalls:

> A measuring jug was filled with soup or whatever was going to be canned, and the contents of the jug were poured into the cans. Holly, who was Bloom's best sealer, would place the cans onto the revolving platform of the canning machine, bring down a handle that lifted a can up towards the can lid and seal it in place.[25]

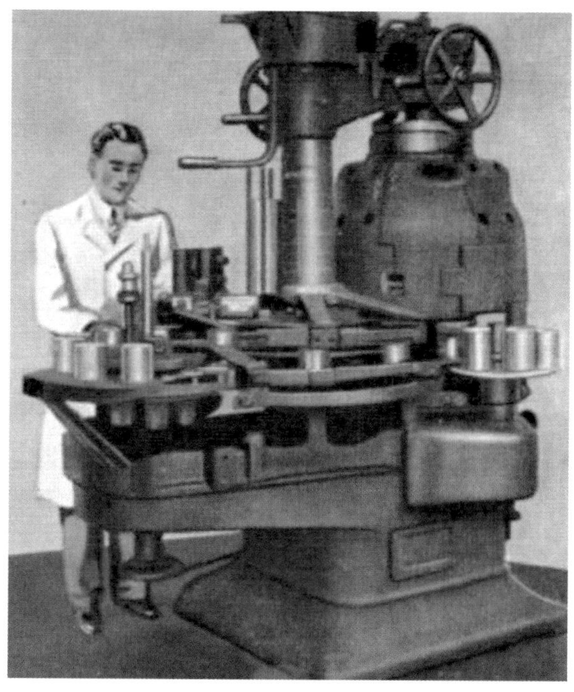

65. Canning machine similar to the one used by Blooms in the 1960s.

The food to be canned was prepared in the same premises as the canning took place. There were six cooking stands onto each of which 600-gallon vessels were lifted for cooking the soup and other products. The meatballs were rolled and shaped by hand before they were cooked by a team of four women who worked in the rooms above the cannery.[26]

Subsequently, the canning process, and some but not all of the preparation of the canned food, was moved to Bloom's new factory in Plaistow (see below).

Outside Catering

After the end of the Second World War, Sidney Bloom decided to discontinue catering for 'outside events' to concentrate on developing other aspects of the business. However, by 1965, Blooms was again offering to provide kosher food for Jewish events.[27] The catering operation, based at the Aldgate restaurant, became one of the mainstays of the family business.

Bloom's 'kitchen-to-home delivery service' is described in a 1960s marketing brochure. The brochure points out that a large proportion of Bloom's products required either no or minimal cooking, which made them ideal for events such as *kiddushim* (plural of *kiddush*, see Glossary of Hebrew and Yiddish Terms) and life-cycle celebrations. The suggestion is that a wedding, *Bar Mitzvah*, *bris* (circumcision), or a *shiva* would not have been complete without Bloom's popular brands.

One of the regular catering deliveries made by Blooms was to Jewish students studying in various parts of London and also in the Home Counties. Dori A. Schmetterling recalls: 'Blooms used to deliver to our J.Soc by black taxi. The food arrived in large metal containers.'[28]

01-247 6001 or 01-455 3033
for BLOOM'S
KITCHEN-TO-HOME DELIVERY SERVICE

LET us suppose a lady has to hurriedly give a small dinner party. She may suddenly have to provide a meal for six people, nebbesh; well she can't be bothered, or she hasn't the time, or she may be at business.

So she rings 01-247 6001; she says she wants a roaster, some tongue, sliced salt beef or salami, coleslaw, latkas, potato salad, maybe some viennas, cocktail viennas, or anything like that (or the Delicacies that only BLOOM'S can supply).

She can then without any preparation at all provide a very good meal—within two hours—and everybody loves her for it. How many times has a lady struggled with a barmitzvah lunch, anniversary supper, engagement or birthday party, or a kiddush. All she has to do is ring 01-247 6001.

So you dial 01-247 6001 and if it's not a very small order, you can get it within a couple of hours on any day of the week except Saturday.

The vans are going out all the time helping the housewife cope with friends and relatives who are visiting and have to be suitably entertained.

REMEMBER 01-247 6001

WHEN you dial 01-247 6001, you would not believe it, but you soon become aware that BLOOM'S actually have something like a milk round in London and the Provinces. Vans deliver food early and promptly each day which guarantees that the food is beautifully fresh and wholesome.

Here's a tip. If you sometimes find it difficult to get to the restaurant, why not ring 01-247 6001 or 01-455 3033 and have the same food sent round to you.

66. Extract from 1960s Bloom's marketing brochure. Courtesy of Jonathan Fishburn.

The Move to Tunmarsh Lane

After the excitement surrounding the opening of the Golders Green restaurant, during the latter part of the 1960s Blooms largely focused on consolidating its successful business. Sidney and Evelyn's children, Marilyn and Michael, were now involved in the family firm, despite their parents' attempts to persuade them to pursue other careers. Marilyn Tapper (née Bloom) recalled: 'I worked there from the age of ten – unofficially. I started properly when I was seventeen and I learned everything from the ground up – how to cut salt beef, how to cook *latkes*.'[29] Their father also insisted that Marilyn and Michael washed dishes and swept the floor, and spent time in both the factory and the restaurant.[30] By the 1970s, they were ready to contribute to the management of the firm and became directors of the company, but while Marilyn married young and withdrew from day-to-day involvement in the business, Michael went on to become its managing director.

By the late 1960s, the premises in Wentworth Street that Blooms had occupied for approaching thirty years had become 'too small, too old and too decrepit'.[31] The decision was therefore taken to relocate the manufacturing and wholesale activities to a much larger factory, the West Factory at Tunmarsh Lane in Plaistow, north-east London.[32] Sidney Bloom was aware that the meat manufacturing industry was changing rapidly, and he was keen for the younger generation, especially his son, Michael Bloom, and Norman Bookbinder (the staff member previously mentioned), to take the business forward into a new era, using modern production methods.[33] Blooms now referred to themselves as 'Meat Product Manufacturers and Restauranteurs'.[34] The firm had once again gone up in the world.

The transfer of the manufacturing and wholesale undertakings to Plaistow took place without any public fanfare. Blooms had acquired the new premises, which had previously been a sweet factory, for about £65,000 in 1968.[35] However, the move did not take place until December 1970 due to the time needed to equip the new premises.

The two-storey building had a floor area of 18,000 square feet, which provided space for the company offices on the upper floor and for the manufacturing and wholesale business on the ground floor.

Soon after the move, Martin Malin, Morris's grandson and Sidney's nephew, worked in the new factory, learning about butchering and food processing. He recalls:

> On the ground floor there was a smokery and a canning department, where the tinned soups and goulashes and so on were canned, and a packaging department where all of the Viennas and salamis were vacuum packed to be sent out to the delis and supermarkets. There was also a butchery section, where the meat from the slaughterhouse was processed and koshered. But there was still space left over for further development.[36]

The move to the new factory allowed Blooms to expand its wholesale business, both in London and beyond. Martin Malin, who sometimes drove the delivery vans, also recalls:

> The more profitable side of the business was selling kosher goods to Jewish butchers in places like Leeds, Manchester and Glasgow. We even supplied outlets in Scotland. Wherever there was a Jewish community, there would be a demand for Bloom's products. Beyond London and the Home Counties, Bloom's products were mainly sent by freight transport since the Bloom's vans of those days were not made for long journeys and they often broke down! I delivered goods to traditional kosher butchers in the East End, who would often give me a very hard time on the price and quality of the meat products, and to top-of-the-range shops like Harrods and Selfridges that had kosher sections in their food halls. While the kosher butchers mainly bought the less expensive goods, the upmarket stores purchased a wider range of products.[37]

Most of the meat and poultry used by Blooms was still being supplied by Sidney Ziff and Co. from its large slaughterhouse in Canning Town. Sidney Ziff and Sidney Bloom, who were close friends, often had lunch together in the Aldgate restaurant.[38] Norman Bookbinder tells this story about the 'two Sidneys':

> One day, there was a shortage of cattle to be slaughtered and we didn't have enough meat to keep our team of butchers going for the next day. Michael Bloom phoned Sidney Ziff and said: "Sidney, Sidney, you've got to help me. We don't have enough cattle for tomorrow. Can you phone round your contacts? Maybe ring a few farms to ask if they have any cattle to spare." Sidney Ziff said: "Okay, I'll see what I can do. Don't worry, I won't let you down." The next day the truck arrived at Tunmarsh Lane containing sixty or seventy sides of beef. We were amazed that Sidney Ziff had managed to lay his hands on that amount of meat so quickly. And what's more, it was top-quality meat. The butchers immediately started boning and processing it. At about half past ten, Sidney Bloom came into the factory to see what was happening. Just a few minutes later, Sidney Ziff walked in and said: "Well, how did I do?" Sidney Bloom replied: "I can't believe you did this in such a short time. What a simply amazing feat!" The other Sidney said: "Yes. I got it from Mars." We looked at him in surprise and asked: "What do you mean you got it from Mars?" I turned to Hassan, the head butcher, and said to him: "This meat is out of this world!" After a pause Sidney Ziff smiled and explained: "Not Mars the planet, but Mars the people who make the chocolate bars!" It turned out that Mars had some cattle farms and Sidney Ziff was very friendly with the people who ran them. To this day, I still laugh when I think of Sidney Ziff standing there saying that he had got his meat from Mars.[39]

On a daily basis, the Ziff meat delivery truck backed into the factory so that the meat was not unloaded in the street and to facilitate the unpacking of the meat carcasses. The large pieces of meat would be taken immediately off the truck and hung on a rail system, which transported the meat into the butchery section where seven highly skilled 'speed boners' (butchers) worked. Once the meat had been boned and porged, it was placed in large stainless-steel vats of cold water where it would soak for half an hour as part of the koshering process.[40] The lower parts of the animal (the hindquarters below the tenth rib) were set aside for sale to the non-kosher market. The forequarters were prepared for use in Bloom's meat products, or for use in the various dishes served in the two restaurants, such as the 'prime bola' from the shoulder of the animal, which was used for roasting, 'top rib' used in *cholent*, oxtail used in soups and the rib-eye steaks. The aim was to deliver the meat to the restaurant as quickly as possible since kosher cuts of meat, which are not as tender as non-kosher cuts, needed to be eaten within two or three days.[41] See Plates Section, Plate 6.

One of the manufacturing processes that was radically updated after the move to Tunmarsh Lane was the smoking of the Viennas.

> The new smoking process was much more efficient. The brick-built smokers were replaced by a steel cabinet. The Viennas were still hung on sticks, but instead of being taken by hand to be smoked, they were loaded onto trolleys. When the trolleys were full, they were wheeled into the smoking cabinet and the doors were closed behind them. After the Viennas were dried and smoked, they were placed in large, gas-fired water baths in which they were cooked at pasteurisation temperature, about seventy-two degrees centigrade.[42]

There was a team of six women who packed the cooked Viennas and sliced the salt beef ready for sliding into packs for sale in shops and a widening range of other outlets.[43] There were also two in-house engineers, who kept all the machinery and equipment working smoothly, and two men, who prepared the orders for the van drivers. For many years, the goods were checked out of the factory and onto the delivery vans by a man named Aubrey Goldstein.[44]

Installed in its new location, the cannery was able to expand and to produce an increased range of canned goods, including products such as chicken *blintzes* (see Glossary of Eastern European Jewish Food at Appendix One).[45] The cannery was located in a dedicated section of the factory, but some of the food to be canned continued to be cooked at St George's Residence in Gunthorpe Street, which was one of the reasons why there was a company van making frequent trips between Aldgate and Plaistow.[46]

With the increased scale of production that accompanied Bloom's move to Plaistow, the company now needed to pay for two *shomrim*. One of the long-standing *shomrim* was Rabbi Yisroel Fine and the other was Bengeo (first name unknown), a younger man, who was a Sephardi Jew from Morocco. Bengeo was an expert porger (*menaḳḳer* in Hebrew) and oversaw the porging process after the butchers had boned the meat. In addition, the *shomrim* approved the ingredients used in the meat products, inspected the machinery to check that it was kosher and that it was regularly cleaned to keep it that way and ensured that milk products were not brought into those parts of the factory producing kosher meat products.[47]

Upstairs in the West Factory, there were five offices housing the receptionist, the bookkeepers and the invoice clerks. Stanley Goldberg, the long-standing company secretary and later, Michael Kallenberg, the financial director, and his assistant also had offices on this upper floor.

Boom Time at the Factory

During the late 1970s and early 1980s, business was booming at Tunmarsh Lane, with Blooms delivering to approaching 500 kosher butchers and delicatessens throughout the country. The firm was proud of the fact that it was able to deliver raw or cooked meat anywhere within twenty-four hours. Each week, the boners handled up to twenty-five tons of on-the-bone and boneless beef, three tons of lamb and a ton of poultry.[48] The Bloom's factory was particularly busy in the lead-up to *Pesach*, preparing festival goods. Factory production was halted for thirty-six hours while the sixty staff working in the factory ensured that the premises were thoroughly koshered and nothing was overlooked. Michael Bloom once explained:

> Every piece of equipment in the building is koshered. The ovens are scraped and burned out so that all the *chometz* is eliminated – and all of this is on top of the normal cleaning. Inspectors from the Beth Din come down to ensure that everything is as it should be. We have a secluded Passover storeroom, where we can store *chometz* things until the festival is over.[49]

Some of the Bloom's goods manufactured at the factory contained dough and production of these ceased during *Pesach*. Any food left over from pre-*Pesach* was frozen. However, Bloom's customers did not go hungry; production of goods such as *blintzes* and *kneidlach* (see Glossary of Eastern European Jewish Food at Appendix One) continued. In the ten days before *Pesach*, the factory was open twenty-four hours a day to cope with the extra demand for salt beef, salami, Viennas, *latkes*, canned soups and other Bloom's products.[50] The quantities of meat handled by the butchers during *Pesach* doubled.

In this boom period, the Bloom's catering division was equally busy during *Pesach*. Blooms catered for *sedarim* in synagogues and those organised by other bodies. Between Jewish festivals, the firm provided catering for a wide variety of customers and events, including for the cast of *Yentl* when they were filming at Lee International Studios in 1983. Barbra Streisand,[51] the star of the film (who also dined at the Aldgate restaurant), was interviewed the following year by *The Sunday Times Magazine* about her experience of filming *Yentl*. She commented that it had been hard not to think about eating with mountains of food, cooked by Bloom's French chef Robert,[52] being brought in daily from the restaurant and 'left lying decadently across the film set'.[53] According to one family member, during the filming they discovered that 'Barbra had a quiet hankering for *gefilte* fish'.[54] The whole Bloom family were invited to the première of *Yentl* in London and the catering by Blooms was mentioned in the film credits.[55]

Similarly, Elizabeth Taylor is said to have dined on salt beef sandwiches brought in from Blooms when she was recording her narration for the film *Genocide*a a year earlier.[56] Blooms also provided kosher catering for many major events in London that were not specifically Jewish, such as the men's fashion show held in London in 1983, at which Michael Bloom himself oversaw the catering.[57]

By 1985, Blooms had reached its zenith, but its fame was about to plateau and although it might have not yet been fully recognised, a range of factors were already at play that were to lead to the firm's decline, and eventually its demise.

Notes

1. See Bloom's headed paper. The registered office was the offices of Bloom's long-standing accountants, Stoy Hayward.
2. Message from Martine Kaufman, 23.8.2022.
3. Interview with David Rein, 2.5.2023.
4. *Ibid.*
5. See Chapter Seven.
6. Interview with David Rein, 2.5.2023.
7. See Chapter Seven.
8. Interview with Norman Bookbinder, 5.12.2022.
9. *Ibid.*
10. Interview with David Rein, 2.5.2023.
11. *Ibid.*
12. See, for example *JC*, 18.2.1955.
13. *JC*, 5.12.1955.
14. See Chapter Seven.
15. Interview with David Rein, 2.5.2023.
16. *Ibid.*
17. In addition to the delivery vans, at its zenith, Blooms also ran a fleet of fourteen company cars used to support its various business activities.
18. See Chapter Nine for further discussion.
19. *JC*, 29.10.1965. Greenspans had been established in the East End in 1890. It relocated to Lyttleton Road in Hampstead Garden Suburb.
20. *JC*, 15.7.1966.
21. *JC*, 7.2.1964.
22. *JC*, 31.3.1989.

23. Anonymous interviewee, 20.12.2022. For information on Skrek's see https://wp-research.aber.ac.uk/nsrefugeeswales/history/life-for-refugees-in-wales/food/.
24. Interview with David Rein, 4.5.2023.
25. Interview with Norman Bookbinder, 9.12.2022.
26. See Chapter Seven.
27. *JC*, 22.1.1965.
28. Dori A. Schmetterling, post on Facebook page, Jewish Britain, 14.5.2016. The J.Soc met in the basement of a block of flats close to the Albert Hall.
29. *JC*, 18.6.2010.
30. Obituary for Sidney Bloom in *The Times*, 19.6.2003 and *JC*, 5.9.1996.
31. Interview with Martin Malin, 20.9.2022.
32. The last time that the Wentworth Street location was given as the head office address was November 1970 and the first time that the new address was used was January 1971.
33. Interview with Norman Bookbinder, 5.12.2022.
34. Strapline on Bloom's headed paper.
35. *JC*, 29.9.1967. At the time, it was a 'buyers' market' and this was said to have been 'a good price'.
36. Interview with Martin Malin, 3.11.2022.
37. Interview with Martin Malin, 20.9.2022.
38. Interview with Martin Malin, 3.11.2022.
39. Interview with Norman Bookbinder, 5.12.2022.
40. *Ibid.*
41. *JC*, 4.2.2011.
42. Interview with Norman Bookbinder, 9.12.2022.
43. See Chapter Nine.
44. See Chapter Seven.
45. *JC*, 7.7.1978.
46. Interview with Norman Bookbinder, 9.12.2022.
47. Interview with Professor Geoffrey Alderman, 31.10.2022. See Chapter Ten for the reasons for this.
48. *JC*, 31.3.1989.
49. *Ibid.*
50. *Ibid.*
51. See Chapter Nine.
52. See Chapter Seven.
53. 'Streisand's One-Man Show', *The Sunday Times Magazine*, 4.3.1984.
54. Interview with Martin Malin, 22.9.2022.
55. Interview with Martin Malin, 30.12.2022.
56. *JC*, 14.1.2022.
57. *JC*, 25.2.1983.

Chapter Six

From Boom to Demise

A Change of Management

The year 1985 marked a watershed in the history of Blooms. In that year Sidney Bloom decided to retire as managing director of the family business and to hand over the reins to his son Michael, who had been working as co-managing director for several years. Although Sidney stepped back from day-to-day management of the firm, he continued as a company director and visited the restaurant most days to support Michael and keep a watchful eye on the business.

In addition to Michael Bloom and his parents, the other directors of the company at this time were Sylvia Malin (Sidney's sister) and Michael Kallenberg, the company's financial director, who had been a close friend of Michael since their school days at Christ's College School in Finchley.

After Michael Bloom took over, it was soon recognised that he would be taking a more informal approach to his leading role in the business. Whereas his father had always been addressed as 'Mr Bloom', Michael asked staff to use his first name,[1] and he was quoted as saying: 'I try to think as he does [his father Sidney], but I am not as cautious.'[2]

The '*Kashrut* War'

One of Michael Bloom's first major decisions as managing director was to enter into an agreement for Blooms to have sole use of an abattoir in Cardington, Bedfordshire, which was owned by Canvin International. His aim was to enable the wholesale side of the business to become more self-sufficient and to improve the quality and reduce the price of the meat used by the firm. The move to the abattoir at Cardington was seen as 'a matter of survival' in an increasingly competitive environment. Michael Bloom explained: 'We had been brought to our knees by inflated prices and limited meat supplies ... we were a team without option. If you are going to die, you may as well die fighting.'[3] However, Michael soon found himself caught up in a major disagreement between the London Board of Shechita and the Joint Shechita Authority of the Federation of Synagogues, a battle which became known as the '*Kashrut* War'.

Illustration 5: 'The *Kashrut* Wars'. Copyright Beverley-Jane Stewart.

The Joint Shechita Authority of the Federation of Synagogues was set up in May 1984 as a joint initiative of the Federation of Synagogues and the Luton Shechita Board. It was this body that licensed the abattoir in Bedfordshire that had been taken over by Blooms. The Joint Shechita Authority was a rival body to the London Board of Shechita,[4] which was established in 1804 to oversee the supply of kosher meat and poultry to the Anglo-Jewish community. The London Board had several parent bodies, of which the United Synagogue was the senior partner. This meant that, in practice, its activities were overseen by the *dayanim* (plural of *dayan*, religious judge) of the London Beth Din, an arm of the United Synagogue. The Federation of Synagogues, the main partner in the Joint Shechita of the Federation of Synagogues, had its own Beth Din, set up in 1966, through which it issued its own *kashrut* licences, rather than via the London Beth Din, as had been the case previously. In 1981, the London Board of Shechita decided not to allow products certified by the Federation Beth Din to be sold in butcher shops and other outlets licensed by the London Board of Shechita.

The announcement in 1986 that Blooms, together with a number of major kosher food manufacturing firms,[5] had defected to the Federation of Synagogues, depriving the London Shechita Board of further income, escalated the tensions between the two warring bodies. With its sole use of the abattoir in Bedfordshire, Blooms became the wholesale supplier for the defecting firms, who styled themselves 'the Federation of Kosher Butchers '86'. Blooms reported an immediate upsurge in wholesale business resulting from cheaper prices, with its retail customers apparently queuing for hours to buy the cheaper meat.[6] The move was viewed by many as a brave one, with 'Michael Bloom and his band of jolly butchers' being seen as 'the Yiddisher answer to the Tolpuddle Martyrs, who struck out against injustice'.[7]

JEWISH CHRONICLE AUGUST 22 1986 7

NOTICE TO THE JEWISH PUBLIC

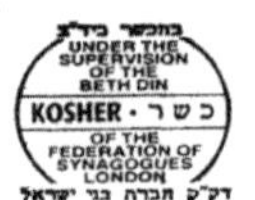

The public is informed that the following Wholesale Butcher and Manufacturer, Retail Butchers and Poulterers, have been granted the Licence of the Joint Shechita Authority of the Federation of Synagogues.

M. BLOOM of
M. BLOOM (KOSHER) & SON LTD
Trading as **BLOOM'S**, Wholesaler,
Tunmarsh Lane, London E13 9NB.

S. COHEN trading as
LA BOUCHERIE
4 Cat Hill, East Barnet,
Herts EN4 8JB.

S. COHEN
93B Upper Clapton Road,
London E5.

NORMAN GOLDBERG (BUTCHERS) LTD
12 Claybury Broadway, Ilford,
Essex.

IVOR SILVERMAN
4 Canons Corner, London Road,
Stanmore, Middlesex.

The following establishments have in addition been granted the Licence of the London Kashrus Board of the Federation of Synagogues.

BLOOM'S RESTAURANT
90 Whitechapel High Street, E1 7RA.

BLOOM'S RESTAURANT
130 Golders Green Road, NW11 8HB.

LA BOUCHERIE
4 Cat Hill, East Barnet, Herts, EN4 8JB.

SILPAK KOSHER FOOD CENTRE
360 Uxbridge Road, Hatch End, Middlesex.

All the above are now under the supervision of the Beth Din of the Federation of Synagogues, which is fully responsible for their kashrus.

STEVE'S of 228 Station Road, Edgware and
5 Canons Corner, London Road, Stanmore,
continues to hold our licences.

NOTICE TO THE JEWISH PUBLIC

BLOOM'S
LA BOUCHERIE
STANLEY COHEN (E.5)
NORMAN GOLDBERG BUTCHER'S LTD
IVOR SILVERMAN
SILPAK

Are pleased to announce their association with the Beth Din of the Federation of Synagogues through the grant of licences by the Joint Shechita Authority and/or the London Kashrus Board.

All other licences have been ***voluntarily relinquished.***

We are happy to assure all our customers of our continued service.

BLOOM'S ***have also been appointed the sole wholesale licensee of the Joint Shechita Authority for the supply of kosher meats to the trade.***

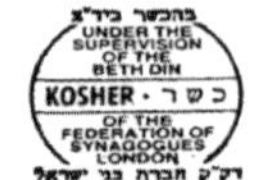

67. Notice in the *Jewish Chronicle*, 22 August 1986.

The London Beth Din instructed Blooms to remove its seals from Bloom's products and the London Board of Shechita ordered poulterers it licensed not to supply Blooms and the other rebels.[8] There was talk of reverting to the secular courts to resolve the dispute, which would have been a major departure from the Jewish tradition of resolving disputes within the community.[9] In the end, a Joint Rabbinic Authority was set up to oversee *kashrut* licences granted to meat manufacturers and purveyors, with increased representation of *dayanim* from the Federation of Synagogues.[10] Professor Geoffrey Alderman explains: 'The Farm Animal Welfare Council was targeting *shechita* and the argument was put to the United Synagogue and to the Federation of Synagogues that the war between them was not doing much for the Jewish community, that there needed to be a united front.'[11] However, the new joint body was stillborn due to continuing disagreement between the communal bodies and it was not until 1992 that a workable settlement was finally reached.

The aim of ending the monopoly of the London Board of Shechita and reducing meat prices, a cause that had been spearheaded by Blooms, had apparently been achieved. However, it had been a trying time for the Bloom family, who placed a notice in the *Jewish Chronicle*, thanking their customers for their 'magnificent support during the past few difficult weeks.'[12] The move to the abattoir in Bedfordshire would have meant taking business away from Sidney and Evelyn's long-standing friends, the Ziffs, which could not have been easy for them. However, they appear to have remained on amicable terms. An article in the *Jewish Chronicle* stated that Blooms had continued to purchase some of its meat supplies from Ziffs.[13]

The Aldgate Restaurant and its Changing Environment

In 1978, the East End docks in the Port of London, which had been declining for many years, finally closed. The London Docklands Development Corporation (LDDC) was set up in 1981 to oversee a comprehensive regeneration of the area, taking advantage of the proximity of the City of London with its burgeoning banks and finance houses. LDDC regeneration projects, especially the building of Canary Wharf, a huge commercial and housing development, had a knock-on impact on the streets that had once housed dispossessed Jews. They now became a desirable place to live, and renovated houses and flats began to sell for unimaginable amounts, mainly to young professionals seeking to live close to their workplaces in the City. Most of the children and grandchildren of the post-1880 Jewish immigrants, even those who had been successful, could no longer afford to buy property in the area.

Many of the tower blocks built with haste after the Second World War were either renovated or demolished to make way for privately owned, low-rise housing, which hastened the gentrification of the former Jewish quarter of the East End. Even the newer Bangladeshi immigrants, who had replaced the Jews, found themselves being squeezed out by the development, despite the significant contribution that they had been making to the local economy. The opening of the Docklands Light Railway (DLR) in 1987 improved rail communications in the area and helped to accelerate the rising fortunes of the East End.

The impact of the redevelopment of the East End sealed the irreversible decline of the Jewish community in the area and there were growing concerns about the way in which Jewish heritage and culture were being obliterated. There was pressure from academics, historians and conservationists to preserve the few Jewish landmarks that remained. Several guides began to lead heritage walks to make people aware of what had been lost and to preserve memories of Jewish life in the East End. By the end of the 1980s, just 2,000 Jews remained in the area, many of whom were aged and housebound. Bloom's restaurant in Whitechapel High Street, together with Connie Shack and Lou Morrison's famous Kosher Luncheon Club in Greatorex Street[14] stood out as the last bastions of the Jewish community that had once dominated Spitalfields and Whitechapel. Blooms was now described by *The Good Food Guide* as 'a faded outpost of Ashkenazi cooking', and the Guide was saying that it seemed that the firms 'famous Ashkenazi cooking had become tired of fame' and the at the waiters had taken to 'prowling unattractively', which was not good for business.[15]

These developments had far-reaching consequences for the custom of Bloom's Aldgate restaurant, which will be discussed in detail in Chapter Nine. By the late 1980s, the restaurant had reduced its opening hours and had ceased opening during *Pesach*, since it was no longer economically viable to do so. To boost trade, the company pursued other business opportunities. As an extension of its still-buoyant takeaway trade, in the early 1990s Blooms was making deliveries of lunch orders to offices and banks in the City. One recipient comments: 'Blooms was my lifeline for kosher food at bank luncheons.'[16]

In addition to changing demographics, the Aldgate restaurant (and the restaurant in Golders Green) was affected by the increasingly stringent requirements of the Beth Din and the Kashrus Commission. As it became more and more expensive for them to meet the standards set by the licensing bodies, reports in the press and elsewhere suggested that the restaurant was economising, such as the less frequent laundering and replacement of the waiters' trademark uniforms and the tablecloths. In 1990, the Kashrus Commission started requiring licensed caterers such as Blooms to provide a certificate of hygiene issued by an inspector, which was an additional expense for the restaurant at the time of a rapidly narrowing customer base.[17]

Bloom's Wholesale and Manufacturing Business

Following the '*Kashrut* War', Michael Bloom appears to have been feeling optimistic about the future of the manufacturing and wholesale side of the business. At the end of 1987, he predicted that the abattoir in Bedfordshire would expand.[18] However, his optimism proved to be unfounded. The ever-increasing competition in the kosher meat trade meant that, by the late 1980s, the activities based at Tunmarsh Lane were beginning to struggle, despite the initial boost that the business had been given by access to cheaper and higher quality meat when Blooms took over the Cardington abattoir.

One sign of the financial strain was evident in the advertisements appearing in the *Jewish Chronicle*, offering competitive prices and discounts for Bloom's goods and services, but especially its catering activities. In 1987, Blooms was advertising a range of three-course party menus of its 'world famous' kosher products at less than £5 per head. The ready-packed, freshly prepared food was delivered free of charge, and Blooms also supplied disposable crockery and cutlery. To tempt customers, Bloom's financial director Michael Kallenberg, reminded readers that 'we are famous for our very generous portions!'[19]

In 1988, Blooms announced that the firm now held two *kashrus* licences, one from the Kashrus Commission of the Beth Din and the other with the Kashrus Board of the Federation of Synagogues in London. This move had been made to retain the custom of those who would eat only at restaurants and buy products licensed by the London Beth Din.[20] Funding *kashrut* licences and *shomrim* from both Beth Dins would have been very expensive and a major drain on company finances, but Blooms stated that it intended to remain loyal to the Federation of Synagogues. By 1990, Blooms was licensed only by the Kashrus Commission of the London Beth Din, which had by then taken over the supervision of the abattoir in Bedfordshire.[21] This must have come as a relief for the company.

In the late 1980s, the factory's weekly turnover included ten tons of manufactured products and four tons of canned soups. In the wholesale side of the business, Blooms was handling thirty tons of beef and five-and-a-half tons of lamb a week.[22] However, an article in the *Jewish Chronicle* in 1988 hinted that the Tunmarsh Lane factory might have been failing to move with the times. It compared some of the largest kosher factories in London, pointing out that several were investing in modern machinery and abandoning traditional processes to reduce costs and increase production. Blooms, however, were proud of having retained some long-standing ways of manufacturing meat products. The Tunmarsh Lane factory housed a now out-of-date smoking house and a mix of modern and new machinery. Michael Bloom was quoted as saying: 'We maintain that some of the old ways of manufacturing are still the best as far as we are concerned.'[23] Despite concerns raised by consumers about additives, Blooms had decided to continue using colouring and preservatives in several of its products. Michael Bloom declared: 'Nobody will try white salami or eat white Viennas. They still want to see them red.'[24]

Confirmation of Bloom's struggle to keep up with competitors came at the end of 1989 when the canning equipment at the factory broke down and production of Bloom's canned goods ceased. Michael Bloom explained that the cost of replacing the canning machine (which lacked a refrigeration system and therefore did not meet EEC requirements) ran into six figures, and the investment in installing new equipment at Tunmarsh Lane was not worthwhile at that time. The firm had been advised that it would need to move to new premises before 1992 if it wished to continue exporting Bloom's products since many other aspects of the factory, not just the canning machine, did not meet EEC regulations. However, Michael Bloom hinted that the firm was considering investing in other projects, including new restaurants, rather than replacing out-of-date equipment.[25]

When the canning equipment failed, Michael Bloom stressed that anyone suffering from *kreplach* (see Glossary of Eastern European Jewish Food at Appendix One) withdrawal could buy freshly made soups to take away at Bloom's restaurants. However, the discontinuation of Bloom's canned goods particularly affected people living in small communities outside London, who had difficulty in accessing fresh kosher products. Within a year, the production of Bloom's soups and other canned goods had recommenced since the firm was apparently 'being driven barmy by customers asking for them'.[26] Blooms had arranged for the canned goods to be produced under licence by a third-party company.[27]

After the closure of the Tunmarsh Lane factory at the end of 1991, Blooms entered into an agreement with Greenspans to manufacture Bloom's meat products at the Greenspan's factory located at the Millmead Industrial Centre in Tottenham.[28] The arrangement was that Greenspans used the factory during the day and Blooms occupied it overnight, using the firm's own staff to make the products and continuing to source meat from the abattoir in Bedfordshire.[29] Apparently, this joint use of the factory in Tottenham proved to be unworkable in the long term. Having failed to locate alternative premises,[30] in 1995 Blooms licensed Gilbert's Kosher Meats Technology to produce two of its products for the expanding Safeway supermarket chain. The remainder were produced under a licence by Greenspans.[31]

The manufacturing and wholesale side of the Bloom's business operated under these licensing arrangements until 1996, despite the various challenges that it (and other kosher meat manufacturers) faced during that time: the boycott of kosher meat products by some supermarket customers because of their objections to the Jewish ritual methods of *shechita* (see previous mention);[32] worries over Bovine Spongiform Encephalopathy (BSE), known as 'Mad Cow Disease'), which led to customers switching to poultry rather than meat;[33] and the escalating costs of meat resulting from increased production expenses.[34] However, Michael Bloom remained optimistic that customers would still eat kosher meat for health reasons[35] and continued to look for new business opportunities. In January 1995, he stepped in to avoid a kosher famine in Leicester following the sudden retirement of a kosher butcher there. He arranged to supply not only of kosher meat, but also some kosher groceries to Jewish families living in Leicester and outlying villages.[36]

The Closure of the Aldgate Restaurant

Given the extensive coverage of the pressures on meat manufacturers, it is therefore somewhat ironic that the eventual demise of Bloom's manufacturing and wholesale activities was to result from problems elsewhere within the company that had not come to the attention of the press.

Well into the 1990s, it appeared that the Aldgate restaurant was withstanding the many pressures that seemed to indicate the end of this culinary landmark.[37] However, it was soon to become evident that the business had been failing for some time as the result of a forty per cent reduction in its turnover.[38] The first warning of an impending crisis occurred in January 1996 when it was reported in the Jewish press that the *shomer* had discovered an 'attempted breach of *kashrut*' on the premises at the restaurant, and that the London

Beth Din had revoked Michael Bloom's *kashrut* licence.[39] It later emerged that the *shomer* had discovered a consignment of meat stored in pickling vats that was cut in a way that was unfamiliar to him, and which did not bear the seals and markings verifying that the meat had come from a licensed source.[40]

This news sent a shockwave through the community and was highly embarrassing for the Bloom family since the restaurant had traded on its kosher credentials for seven decades and had become the symbol of kosher food in Britain. Rabbi Jeremy Conway, director of the Beth Din's *kashrut* division, hastened to reassure diners: 'The public can remain confident in the *kashrut* controls of the London Beth Din and the continuance of this much-loved kosher establishment – the oldest kosher restaurant in Britain.'[41] He stressed that Blooms remained open for business as usual, the *kashrut* licence having been transferred to Sidney Bloom. The London Board of Shechita temporarily halted the production of Bloom's sausages by withdrawing Michael Bloom's manufacturing licence, but the sausages were back in production a week later after the licence was again transferred to Sidney Bloom.[42] The ruling of the Beth Din was that Michael Bloom would cease direct involvement in the day-to-day running of the business.[43]

The emergency measures offered only a brief respite. Without any notice, on 15 February 1996 Blooms at 90 Whitechapel High Street ceased trading. An announcement was placed on the door saying: 'Closed for essential repairs until further notice. Golders Green open as usual.' Unaware of what had happened, on the wet and windy Sunday after the closure, many regular diners arrived to partake of their favourite dishes. They expressed a range of reactions to the shutting of the restaurant – astonishment, shock, anger, disappointment – but all agreed that it had been legendary.[44] A regular street trader, who had arrived to sell his wares, was quoted as saying: 'It's good for me because disappointed customers have ended up having a quick look at what I am selling.' However, even he confessed that he was disappointed at having missed out on the chicken soup that the restaurant usually gave him free of charge.[45] One former, non-Jewish customer on hearing of the news wrote to the *Jewish Chronicle* with the following lament, published two weeks following the closure:

> Sirs:
>
> As a *goyischer* aficionado of Jewish cuisine (how's that for a linguistic mish-mosh?), I was much saddened by the demise of the Whitechapel Blooms. When I came to London from America thirty years ago, it was the only decent restaurant open on Christmas Day, so I went there for my first Christmas dinner in England. It was a long holiday bus ride from South Kensington, but it was worth it. When I told the waiter why I was there, I was treated like visiting royalty. Never in history has hot salt beef been served with such aplomb or eaten with such relish! If there is a *broche* [prayer] for the death of a great restaurant, let it be said.
>
> John Whiting[46]

When the restaurant closed, it was the oldest and last kosher restaurant in the East End, the Kosher Luncheon Club, the only other remaining kosher eaterie, having closed two years previously. The *Jewish Chronicle* pronounced that the closure represented 'the end of an era', and that without Blooms, the East End would be 'like one of its famous salt beef sandwiches without the mustard.'[47]

Over the next few weeks, it was revealed in the press (both Jewish and non-Jewish) that the company, M. Bloom (Kosher) and Son Ltd, had debts of around £200,000 and had called in Ian Franses Associates, a company specialising in insolvency. Ian Franses advised the directors of the company to sell its assets to prevent it going into liquidation. A Company Voluntary Arrangement (CVA),[48] a company rescue tool, was established with Ian Franses designated as the 'supervisor' of the CVA.

The decision to sell its main assets was obviously a very painful decision for the Bloom family, entailing as it did the immediate loss of seventeen jobs, including many drivers and waiters who had worked for the firm for thirty years or more, and who were familiar to generations of Jewish and non-Jewish customers.[49] A member of staff was quoted in the press as saying: 'Business has been declining for years, but it is a sad day for the Bloom family and for the East End of London.'[50] It was reported that Sidney Bloom had broken down in tears at the creditors' meeting held on 11 March 1996 as Ian Franses read out a statement pledging that the family would 'do all they can' to see that creditors were paid in full.[51] At this meeting, creditors were told that if they were to accept the proposals drawn up by Mr Franses, they would receive 54p in the pound, whereas if Blooms were to go into liquidation, they would receive just 14p in the pound. Not surprisingly, the creditors opted for the former course of action.

Over the next few weeks, it emerged that the front part of the building housing the Aldgate restaurant was owned by two members of the Bloom family (Sidney Bloom and his sister Sylvia Malin), while the premises to the rear of the restaurant, the kitchen and St George's Residence (sometimes referred to as 'St George's House') in Gunthorpe Street, were owned by the company.[52]

Several firms expressed an interest in purchasing the company's assets. The bidders included Stewart Cohen, owner of La Boucherie, who offered an immediate payment of £250,000 to buy both the restaurants and the manufacturing and wholesale business. Despite the fact that Ian Franses had predicted that the Aldgate restaurant was likely to be turned into flats, Stewart Cohen indicated that if his bid were successful, he would not only be reopening the Aldgate restaurant, but that there was also 'a very good chance' of him opening other Bloom's eateries.[53] Gilbert's Kosher Foods and Greenspans, who were already manufacturing meat products under the Bloom's label, made individual offers for the Bloom's manufacturing and wholesale activities.

Shortly after the creditors' meeting at which the bids were submitted, Bernard Greenspan stated that he wished to buy the whole of the Bloom's business. When further 'substantial' bids were subsequently submitted, and the three original interested parties increased the amount of their bids, Ian Franses extended the submission deadline and placed a notice in the *Jewish Chronicle* to elicit yet more expressions of interest.[54]

On the instructions of the Supervisor I Franses Esq FCA FIPA FSPI of Messrs Ian Franses Associates

RE: M BLOOM (KOSHER) & SON LIMITED – T/A BLOOMS (IN COMPANY VOLUNTARY ARRANGEMENT)

A unique opportunity to acquire, in respect of the above named company, it's Good will and Clients Lists, Leasehold Interest premises known as 130 Golders Green Road, London NW11, Freehold Property known as St Georges House, Gunthorpe Street, London, E1, and Restaurant and Kitchen Plant and Equipment, as listed below.

Lot 1: Freehold property known as St Georges House, Gunthorpe Street, london, E1

Lot 2: The business of a restaurant carried on by the Vendor under the names or style of "Bloom" ("the Name") together with all the assets (subject to any claim) in relation to that business.

Lot 3: The right to use the Name in relation to the business of the manufacture and distribution of kosher food products.

Lot 4: The use of the Name in relation to the business of a restaurant.

For further information please contact Mr R Cohen at:

James Owen & Co.
Valuers & Auctioneers
James Owen House
136/144 Granville Road
London NW2 2NL
Tel: 0181-458 5545 Fax: 0181-458 0696

68. Notice in the *Jewish Chronicle*, 22 March 1996.

Eventually, the Aldgate restaurant business was sold to Burger King after it had been deemed too small for use by the McDonald's chain. Burger King took out a twenty-five year lease on the restaurant building, but vetoed a suggestion that a plaque should be mounted on the outside marking Bloom's long connection to the premises.[55] The much-loved Petticoat Lane photomural was retained for a while but was eventually removed. The upper floors of the building were converted from offices to flats.[56] St George's Residence was sold separately to a developer and became a block of flats.[57] The customer car park was sold and became a lucrative NCP car park.

Initially, it was agreed that the manufacturing and wholesale arm of Blooms would be sold to Greenspans but the deal foundered as a result of Greenspan's concerns about its profitability due to the continuing drop in the sale of beef products because of the BSE scare.[58] However, it was soon purchased by Gilberts, who had the previous year invested in a state-of-the-art meat processing factory in Bletchley, Milton Keynes that met EEC requirements. It was described in the *Jewish Chronicle* as a 'squeaky-clean factory, housing huge steel cabinets, hoppers and drums, that brings in beef quarters on butchers' hooks and sends them out as wrapped slabs, slices and cylinders to some 60 supermarket outlets as well as delis'.[59]

This factory became the base for the manufacture of Bloom's meat and canned products, overseen by the Managing Director Norman Bookbinder, who had previously worked at the Bloom's factory in Tunmarsh Lane.[60] Norman Bookbinder was more optimistic than Greenspans that the recently introduced regulations regarding beef would restabilise the kosher meat market,[61] and announced immediate plans for expanding the range of Bloom's products.[62]

69. Advertisement in the *Jewish Chronicle*, 4 September 1996.

Although the sale of company assets had at first included the leasehold of 130 Golders Green Road, it was subsequently decided to retain the Golders Green restaurant since it had been running at a profit. After the creditors had all been paid, sufficient funds remained to provide a cashflow to enable the restaurant to continue in business.[63] While other company assets were being sold, the Bloom family were at pains to point out that the Golders Green restaurant was still open and still in family hands. The family must have felt beleaguered when later in the year, the restaurant was engulfed by a fire and had to be closed for three months for refurbishment.

70. Notice in the *Jewish Chronicle*, 26 April 1996.

After Michael Bloom's licence was revoked by the London Beth Din, he made several attempts to clear his name and to recover his *kashrut* licence. Two years after the decision was taken to transfer the licence to his father, he was still unable to take an active part in the management of the remaining part of the business – the Golders

Green restaurant – although he was still a company director. When he once visited the restaurant for lunch, he was reminded by the *kashrut* division of the London Beth Din that he was debarred from the premises.[64] He appealed to the London Beth Din after one of the Bloom's drivers, Peter Mitchell, came forward to say that he was responsible for taking the non-kosher meat to the Aldgate restaurant. However, since at that time Peter Mitchell was not willing to disclose his identity to the Beth Din, his confession was deemed inadmissible.[65]

When the Beth Din refused to change its ruling, in November 1997 Michael Bloom applied to the High Court for a judicial review of the decision. The judge, Gavin Lightman, showed some sympathy for Michael Bloom's case, saying that 'he has grounds for a genuine sense of grievance, that he was unable at the original hearing to present the defence he could have done if Mr Mitchell's evidence had been available to him.' Nevertheless, Judge Lightman failed to rule in Michael Bloom's favour, largely it seemed because he perceived that it was not a matter for the secular courts but for the rabbinical court.[66] The London Beth Din agreed to a further hearing, but this was no more successful for Michael Bloom than previous hearings. The Beth Din maintained that Michael Bloom was responsible for the presence of the non-kosher meat in the Aldgate premises in December1995, even if he did not put it there himself.[67]

Having lost his long battle against the London Beth Din, in 1999 Michael Bloom decided to open an eighty-seater, 'kosher-style' eaterie in Grenville Street, a 'ramshackle' street off Farringdon Road on the edge of Hatton Garden, the centre of London's jewellery trade. Michael Bloom was assisted in the running of the restaurant and takeaway by two Bloom's former staff, whom he referred to as 'The Original Bloom's Eastenders': Peter Nicholas, who had been a very competent general manager, turning his hand to anything,[68] and Milton (originally Militiades) Charalambous, a highly experienced waiter. Between them, they had over sixty years of working with Blooms, but they were now working in a very different environment. They had 'hung up their bow ties' and were 'working in their shirt sleeves'.[69]

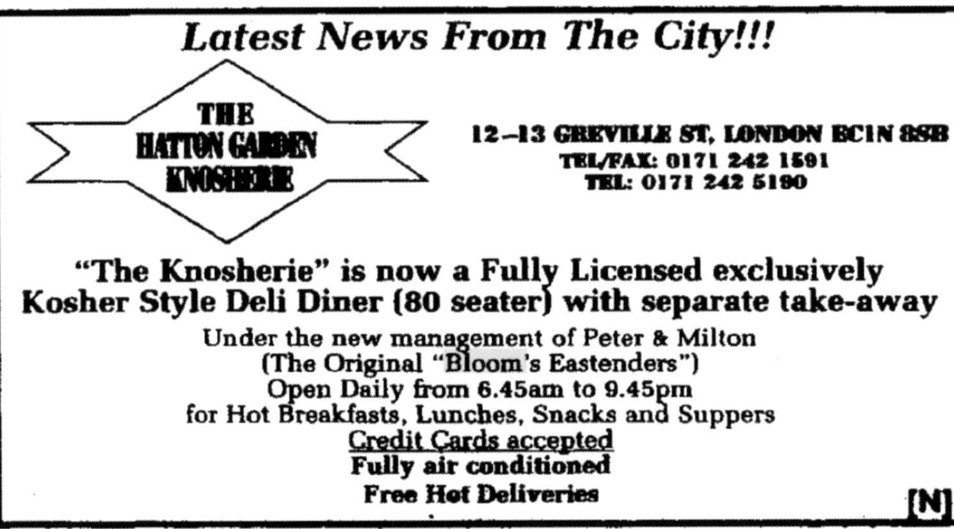

71. Advertisement in the *Jewish Chronicle*, 9 July 1999.

Named the Hatton Garden Knosherie,[70] Michael Bloom bought the restaurant from the long-standing proprietor Esther Berker and added the letter K to its previous name. The eaterie was successful despite its lack of a *kashrut* licence. In 2000, Michael Bloom announced that the restaurant, which he referred to as a 'New York-style deli', was open twenty-four hours a day, seven-days a week (including during the Jewish festivals and holy days), serving two-course meals of 'kosher-style food' for £10 per head, mainly to diamond dealers.[71] Many of Bloom's kosher meat products were available, but bacon and eggs and bhajis were also on the menu.[72] Milton Charalambous commented: 'We don't have to worry about the rabbis,'[73] and Michael Bloom said: 'There's none of the *chazerai* [rubbish] here now.'[74]

Malcolm Ian Goodall who ate at the Knosherie comments: 'I remember the restaurant. It was opposite Brown's Felt Dealers. It renewed my faith in salt beef sandwiches. They were so lovely and thick.'[75] Michael Bloom ran the restaurant until the death of his father in 2003.

72. Advertisement for the Hatton Garden Knosherie in the *Jewish Chronicle*, 21 July 2000.

The Golders Green Restaurant

During the late 1980s, business at the Golders Green restaurant was stable and the restaurant was withstanding the competition created by the proliferation of kosher eateries within the area. Potential diners were warned: 'Be prepared to bump into relatives you never knew you had, and for a volume of animated conversation that could match the Beastie Boys' output decibel for decibel.'[76]

Rather than being challenged by the new restaurants and takeaways and the rising ascendancy of 'Israeli-style' Jewish food,[77] the directors of Blooms felt that the restaurant's position was strengthened by being in a 'kosher epicentre'. In addition, Michael Bloom was not ruling out the possibility of Blooms opening a third branch.[78] However, the staff of the restaurant were less sanguine about increased competition. In 1991, following the opening of a kosher butcher next door to the Golders Green restaurant, Melvin Goldberg, the long-standing restaurant manager,[79] was quoted as saying: 'All butchers now sell a range of delicatessen, and I don't think it is right for the licensing authorities to let one shop open in direct competition to the next-door shop. I think this is a moral issue.'[80]

Whether the company perceived itself to be threatened or not, it is obvious that Blooms felt the need to reach out and attract new customers. In May 1991, the decision was taken to open the Golders Green restaurant after the end of *Shabbat* until 4am, with the aim of providing a meeting place for young people who would otherwise have gathered on the streets of Golders Green. The initiative was prompted by a late Saturday opening earlier in the year to raise money for the Appeal for Israel, a cause dear to the hearts of the Bloom family, mounted by Finchley Synagogue where the Bloom family were members. It was reported that on a January evening, in the region of 1,000 customers 'munched their way through salt beef sandwiches and *latkes* to raise a total £5,250'.[81] All of the staff at the restaurant donated their services free of charge.

The extended opening after *Shabbat*, which brought in large numbers of hungry young people, was seen as an opportunity by Finchley Synagogue to persuade Jewish teenagers to participate in synagogue-based activities.[82] For six Saturday evenings running, Aubrey Ross, a board member of the synagogue, mingled with young people eating at Blooms. Although he was said to have 'stood out like a fox in a chicken coop', he was successful in compiling a list of potential congregants.[83] The initiative continued for several years in Golders Green, but it was never trialled in the Aldgate restaurant with its very different catchment area and clientele.

BLOOM'S

MOTZAEI SHABBAT: 19th SEPTEMBER 1992

AFTER THE SELICHOT SERVICE, FANCY A HOT, LATE-NIGHT, EAT IN OR TAKE-AWAY "NOSH"? THEN COME TO US IN GOLDERS GREEN

OPEN TILL 4 A.M. - EVERY SATURDAY NIGHT

Bring this coupon with you and you will receive a special 10% Discount.

Alternatively, phone us when you get home on

081-455 1338/3033

and we'll try and arrange a special delivery for you.

LOOK FORWARD TO SEEING YOU!

UNDER THE SUPERVISION OF THE COURT OF THE CHIEF RABBI, LONDON BETH DIN [S]

73. Notice in the *Jewish Chronicle*, 18 September 1992.

Under the day-to-day management of Melvin Goldberg[84] and Leon Nicholas, the highly experienced head waiter,[85] trade was brisk. The restaurant had many loyal customers, including Philip Baigel, who lunched there regularly. His experience motivated him to use his artistic talents to paint a three-dimensional picture of the restaurant, capturing its main features and the people who ate and worked there. Later, he had the picture made into a jigsaw.[86] See Plates Section, Plate 7.

In 1997, the Bloom family celebrated 75 years of 'continuous control of Blooms'. The restaurant was to operate for another fourteen years with a few twists and turns in its fortunes.

THE BLOOM FAMILY IS PROUD TO CELEBRATE 75 YEARS CONTINUOUS CONTROL OF

Still the oldest – still the best and still the most famous Kosher Restaurant name in the world

For all enquiries, including bookings, free deliveries, etc.

Tel: 0181 455 1338 / 3033

Under the supervision of the Kashrut Division of the London Beth Din

74. Notice in the *Jewish Chronicle*, 17 January 1997.

One of the challenges that the restaurant faced was another 'Kashrut War' that took place in the summer of 1998. The new battle was precipitated by the decision of Gilberts, the firm that had taken over the production and distribution of Bloom's meat products, to relinquish its licence with the London Beth Din and to join the Manchester Beth Din. Rabbi Jeremy Conway, head of the *kashrut* division of the London Beth Din, ruled that London outlets licensed by the London Beth Din could only sell products bearing the seal of the London Board for Shechita and not those licensed by the Manchester Beth Din. As the Golders Green restaurant was licensed by the London Beth Din, it therefore could not sell or serve Bloom's products.[87] At the time, Norman Bookbinder, managing director of Gilberts was optimistic that the ban would have only a slight impact on his firm's sales since most of Gilbert's business was with outlets that did not require a kosher licence, including Tottenham Hotspur Football Club, which had a large Jewish following.[88] He recently recalled that the skirmish was resolved as a result of the weight of correspondence to the *Jewish Chronicle*, questioning the reasonableness of the Beth Din's stance.[89] Especially pivotal in reversing the ruling was a letter from a woman named Ann Kent from Edgware, seeking clarification about the point on the M1 motorway where Bloom's sausages would no longer be kosher.

If I went to Manchester and purchased Bloom's sausages, they would be kosher — or so I understand. If I travelled with my purchases to London, the sausages would apparently no longer be suitable to be sold by a kosher butcher or restaurateur.

I would like to know at what point on my journey to London would that which was kosher in Manchester lose its acceptability.

Ann Kent,
Francklyn Gardens,
Edgware,
Middlesex.

75. Letter in the *Jewish Chronicle*, 4 September 1998.

The dispute gained such a high profile that it was covered in the non-Jewish press. Having seen the correspondence and the embarrassing media coverage, the Chief Rabbi decided to intervene, and the decision was reversed.[90]

After the closure of the Aldgate restaurant in 1996, Jonathan Tapper, who had been working as its general manager was made redundant by the CVA Supervisor Ian Franses. Jonathan went to work for the poultry wholesaler Lewco Poultry, but in 1999, at the invitation of the CVA Supervisor, he returned to work at Blooms in Golders Green. Shortly afterwards, he purchased the restaurant for the sum of £72,000.[91]

76. Jonathan Tapper. Courtesy of Michelle Spencer.

The Golders Green restaurant underwent a major refurbishment when Jonathan Tapper took over its running. A street scene of Jerusalem replaced the East End photomural. However, there were few further developments until 2007 when Jonathan Tapper sold the restaurant to a businessman named Laurence Bassini (born Bazini),[92] an old school friend of Jonathan's, who had ambitious plans for the expansion of Blooms and was hoping to benefit from the boom in kosher restaurants. Jonathan Tapper remained as the managing director to provide expertise, experience and continuity, and the restaurant continued to trade under the Bloom's name.

The change in ownership might have been prompted by increasingly critical reviews of the restaurant. In July 2007,

Jay Rayner wrote a highly damaging article in *The Observer*, likening Blooms to a car crash. He said: 'The food I was served in Blooms was, for the most part, very bad bad [sic] food indeed'. He recognised that Blooms was a long-standing institution, but commented: 'Mind you, so is Broadmoor and no one goes there for dinner.'[93]

With an input of capital from the new owner, the Golders Green restaurant had a three-week, six-figure makeover with a view to attracting new custom, which for several years had been noticeably waning, and re-establishing the restaurant's position as Britain's best-known kosher eaterie.[94] What was described as a 'brooding mid-twentieth century establishment' was replaced with a 'light and airy' décor.[95] The Jerusalem street scene was replaced by 'new murals in rainbow shades depicting the wandering of Jews through the desert', and the tables were replaced by 'sleek booths and shiny glass panels'.[96] The menu was also expanded to include a greater variety of dishes, aimed at reflecting the multicultural nature of British society.[97] None of these changes had the desired impact. See Plates Section, Plate 8.

Bloom's Restaurant in Edgware

In September 2007, another Bloom's restaurant was opened in Edgware, where the Jewish community had been growing steadily and the area had been emerging as a kosher centre, attracting clientele from the surrounding suburbs of Mill Hill, Stanmore, Bushey and Borehamwood. The décor of the new seventy-seat restaurant, which took over the space occupied by the former Kinneret Sephardi eaterie together with the premises of a building firm that had been located at 131 Hale Lane Edgware, was a replica of the newly refurbished Golders Green restaurant. The food and wine menus were also the same as in Golders Green and plans were made to introduce a set menu alongside the à la carte menu, which blended *heimische* and contemporary dishes.[98] Jonathan Tapper was optimistic that the Bloom name was sufficiently strong to enable the restaurant to compete with the other eateries that opened in Edgware at the same time.[99] See Plates Section, Plate 9.

The location of the new restaurant had the advantage that customers did not have to struggle with parking as customers did in Golders Green, and the owner worked hard to attract custom to the Edgware restaurant. One initiative was the opening of the restaurant for *Shabbat* dinners hosted by the Chabad rabbi Leivi Sudak and his wife Feige. The Friday night dinners commenced with *kiddush* and *challah* (Jewish bread) and were said to have had a 'spiritual ambience'. The meal was followed by traditional *Shabbat* melodies and discussions on the weekly Torah portion. Rabbi Sudak explained that the idea had come about 'in answer to a conundrum'. While guests enjoyed visiting the Sudak's home for Friday night dinner, they were uncomfortable with doing so regularly if they were unable to reciprocate the invitation. Rabbi Sudak thought that if diners could pay for a meal (the £25 cost being paid before *Shabbat*) at a restaurant hosted by the couple, they would come back time and time again.[100]

Rabbi Sudak had planned to increase the number of people attending the dinners, but this was not achieved before the Edgware restaurant closed less than a year after it was opened. Philip Baigel recalls that when he visited Bloom's restaurant in Edgware, there were very few diners despite reports in the *Jewish Chronicle* suggesting that trade was good and that plans were being made for Blooms to take over Reuben's restaurant (previously Blooms and Sturgess) in Baker Street.[101] One of the reasons for the lack of trade was that the food was seen by diners as being overpriced.[102] The introduction of late-night opening at the restaurant in November 2007[103] did not help the situation, and the restaurant closed in August 2008. It was taken over by Stephen Grossman, then Anglo-Jewry's largest poultry dealer.[104] See Plates Section, Plate 10.

The End of Blooms

Despite the makeover that the Golders Green restaurant had in 2007, trade steadily declined over the next three years. Even those who had been regular customers were eating there less often. The takeaway counter remained relatively busy at lunchtimes, but the dining area often had only a few customers, both during the day and in the evening. In addition, the restaurant continued to receive poor reviews, including in *The Good Food Guide*, which had once highly praised the Aldgate restaurant. It said scathingly: 'The dishes are produced under strict rabbinical supervision, but it would have been much the better for the said rabbis to have tasted them.'[105] By 2009, customers were reporting that the restaurant was no longer accepting credit or debit cards, only cash, because of 'cash flow problems', which they saw as a sign that the establishment 'didn't have long to go'; that the takeaway service was not available because staff were 'too busy'; and that the restaurant was 'deservedly empty'.[106] Alan Dein comments:

> There were now lots of other places where people could go to eat Jewish food. Blooms had been superseded, especially by those *heimische* places that had managed to project more of a New York deli image, like "Uncle Ian's" salt beef bar in Temple Fortune. While there were queues outside other places, Blooms was looking very sorry.[107]

With income dwindling, by the spring of 2010 the restaurant was struggling to pay its staff, especially its team of waiters: 'The waiters were great guys and they got on well with the customers. But at the end of the day if you've got seven or eight waiters, you need to fill the place constantly.'[108] The restaurant closed for the final time on 6 June 2010 and went into liquidation. A notice placed on the door advised creditors that a meeting would be held on 25 September and that David Rubin and Partners had been appointed as the liquidators.[109]

When the restaurant closed, tributes to Blooms flowed from around the world, and several of its high-profile customers commented on its demise. The food critic Matthew Norman commented: 'It is such a shame that it's gone. It's a bit like Radio 3, you never listen to it, but you're sort of glad that it's there. There's sadness because it really was out of its time.'[110] The actor Maureen Lipman said: 'Blooms was past its sell-by date', and Jay Rayner, who had a few years earlier written a damning review of the restaurant said: 'It's like an elderly relative that's died and had lost it towards the end of their life.'[111] Several other people commented that it was not just that people now wanted to eat a different type of food, but also the ambience in which the food was served. A few years before the closure, Geoffrey Alderman, a regular columnist in the *Jewish Chronicle*, had warned Blooms that a better kosher dining experience was needed:

> I do not wish to have a table that is so closely jammed against its neighbour that I have to ask the customers on the adjoining table to move if I want to leave. Nor do I wish to be seated so close to other customers that they are forced to eavesdrop on my conversation, and I on theirs.[112]

At the time of the restaurant's closure, Esther Rantzen echoed Geoffrey Alderman's comments:

> It did deteriorate over the years, there's no question. There are three things about running a restaurant: good food, good value and good service, and if Blooms can't do that, then it has to go.'[113]

The food writer Giles Coren suggested: 'There ought to be a *shivah* for Blooms, we should put a plate of salt beef on a low chair.'[114] As time progressed, the nostalgia surrounding Blooms escalated, but people also began to recognise the legacy left by Blooms and its significance in Anglo-Jewish history, which will be discussed in detail in Chapter Eleven.

Notes

1. *JC*, 5.9.1986.
2. *Ibid.*
3. *Ibid.*
4. See Glossary of Hebrew and Yiddish Terms for explanation of *shechita*.
5. The four butchery firms were: La Boucherie in East Barnet; Norman Goldberg of Ilford; S. Cohen of Clapton and Ivor Silverman of Stanmore.

6. *JC*, 29.8.1986.
7. *JC*, 5.9.1986.
8. *JC*, 22.8.1986.
9. Interview with Professor Geoffrey Alderman, 31.10.2022.
10. *JC*, 19.10.1986.
11. Interview with Professor Geoffrey Alderman, 31.10.2022.
12. *JC*, 26.9.1986.
13. *JC*, 29.1.1988.
14. See Chapter Eight for further details.
15. Drew Smith (ed.), *The Good Food Guide 1988* (London: The Consumers' Association and Hodder and Stoughton, 1988), p.34 and *The Good Food Guide 1988,* p.36.
16. Gary Pickholz, post on Facebook page Jewish Britain, 15.5.2022.
17. See *JC*, 25.1.1991.
18. *JC*, 11.12.1987.
19. *JC*, 10.7.1987.
20. *JC*, 8.7.1988.
21. *JC*, 29.1.1990.
22. *JC*, 29.1.1988.
23. *Ibid.*
24. *Ibid.*
25. *JC*, 9.1.1990.
26. *JC*, 24.8.1990.
27. Interview with Norman Bookbinder, 5.12.2022. The name of the third-party firm is not known.
28. Interview with David Rein, 2.5.2023.
29. *JC*, 17.2.1995. La Boucherie was the only other firm still using this abattoir. Blooms continued to purchase some of its supplies from Ziffs.
30. At one stage, Blooms apparently considered investing in a factory near Tring in Hertfordshire. In the end, it was decided this was too far for employees to travel. Interview with David Rein, 2.5.2023.
31. Interview with Norman Bookbinder, 5.12.2022.
32. Protesters objected to the fact that animals were not stunned before they were slaughtered. *JC*, 7.9.1990.
33. *JC*, 18.5.1990.
34. *JC*, 17.2.1995.
35. *JC*, 27.1.1989.
36. *JC*, 20.1.1995.
37. See Chapter Ten for detailed discussion of these changes.
38. *JC*, 23.2.1996.
39. *JC*, 12.1.1996.

40. *JC*, 23.2.1996.
41. *JC*, 12.1.1996.
42. *JC*, 26.1.1996.
43. *JC*, 23.2.1996.
44. *Ibid.*
45. *Ibid.*
46. *JC*, 1.3.1996.
47. *JC*, 23.2.1996. The closure of the restaurant was paralleled by the closure in March 1996 of the Chicken Shop in Jubilee Street that had been run by the Gold family since 1902, another 'last bastion of the East End'. *JC*, 15.3.1996.
48. For further information on CVAs, see https://www.chamberlain-co.co.uk/company-voluntary-arrangement-cva/.
49. 'Debts put the final bite on Blooms', Will Bennett reporting in *The Independent*, 23.2.1996.
50. *Ibid.*
51. *JC*, 15.3.1996.
52. *JC*, 23.2.1996. The family were apparently unaware that they owned St George's House until the liquidator was appointed.
53. *JC*, 23.2.1996.
54. *JC*, 22.3.1996.
55. *JC*, 2.5.1997.
56. See https://surveyoflondon.org/map/feature/322/detail/.
57. *JC*, 17.5.1996.
58. *JC*, 12.7.1996.
59. *JC*, 19.1.1996.
60. *JC*, 12.7.1996. See Chapter Seven for Norman Bookbinder's career details.
61. After the introduction of the regulations in 1992, kosher butchers started using castrated steers aged between eighteen – twenty-four months, and most offal was removed from kosher menus. Liver and heart were still permitted. All meat had to be traceable with relevant information being provided on a blue label on the packaging. *JC*, 4.2. 2011.
62. Interview with Jonathan Tapper, 2.10.2022 and interview with Norman Bookbinder, 5.12.2022. The sale to Gilberts included a deal that the company would pay the Bloom family for use of the Bloom's name and its recipes on a sliding scale over several years.
63. Interview with Norman Bookbinder, 5.12.2022.
64. *JC*, 5.12.1997.
65. *JC*, 30.1.1998.
66. For further details of the court case see *JC*, 21.11.1997.
67. *JC*, 3.7.1998.

68. See Chapter Seven.
69. *JC*, 23.7.1999. Sadly, Milton Charalambous died in 2010, aged 70, of mesothelioma, an asbestos-related cancer. A court ruled that the disease was due to him being exposed to asbestos dust while working in the basement of Bloom's restaurant, when he would stand near an old boiler, sorting the linen. He worked for Blooms for over 30 years. *The Caterer*, 23.12.2012.
70. *JC*, 23.7.1999.
71. *Ibid.* and *JC*, 21.4.2000.
72. *JC*, 23.7.1999.
73. *Ibid.*
74. *Ibid.*
75. Malcolm Ian Goodall, post on Facebook page The Jewish East End of London, 29.10.2016.
76. *JC*, 10.7.1987.
77. See Chapter Ten.
78. *JC*, 30.1.1987.
79. See Chapter Seven.
80. *JC*, 18.5.1991.
81. *JC*, 1.2.1991.
82. See Chapter Nine for further discussion.
83. *JC*, 3.4.1992.
84. See Chapter Seven.
85. See Chapter Eight for further information.
86. Image of jigsaw kindly sent to the author by Philip Baigel, 14.11.2022.
87. *JC*, 23.8.1998.
88. Julian Kossoff, writing in *The Independent*, 12.9.1998.
89. Interview with Norman Bookbinder, 5.12.2022.
90. *Ibid.*
91. *JC*, 14.5.1999.
92. See https://en.wikipedia.org/wiki/Laurence_Bassini.
93. Jay Rayner, writing in *The Observer*, 1.7.2007. Although it was not published until July, the review appears to have been based on a visit earlier in the year because the refurbishment, which Jay Rayner states followed his visit, took place in April 2007.
94. *JC*, 27.4.2007.
95. *Ibid.*
96. See Rayner writing in *The Observer*, 1.7.2007.
97. See Chapter Ten.
98. *JC*, 29.6.2007.
99. *JC*, 9.11.2007.
100. See https://www.lubavitch.com/blooms-kosher-deli-open-on-shabbos-with-chabad /.

101. *JC*, 28.9.2007.
102. For example, email from Ralph Schiller 27.12.2022.
103. *JC*, 9.11.2007.
104. *JC*, 16.9.2008. Stephen Grossman was a friend of Jonathan Tapper.
105. Quoted by Alastair Little, responding to an article on Blooms in *The Times*, 'Waiters were the stars at celebrity kosher joint Blooms', 13.4.2020.
106. See https://www.allinlondon.co.uk/restaurants/kosher/7602-blooms-kosher-restaurant.
107. Interview with Alan Dein, 3.1.2023.
108. Interview with Norman Bookbinder, 9.12.2022.
109. *JC*, 11.6.2010.
110. *JC*, 18 6.2010.
111. *Ibid.*
112. *JC*, 19.10.2007.
113. *JC*, 18.6.2010.
114. *Ibid.*

PART THREE

Aspects of the Bloom's Enterprise

Chapter Seven

Bloom's Staff

Over the years, Blooms employed hundreds of staff, who were involved in a wide variety of activities. While some of the staff were temporary – students, those in between jobs or people in the process of establishing their career and needing an income while they did so – others stayed with the company for many years, sometimes for several decades. Many of the long-standing staff performed different roles during their employment with the firm, often moving between the factory and the restaurants; others remained in the same job. Across the Bloom's enterprise, staff were drawn from a wide range of backgrounds and the multicultural and international nature of the workforce became more pronounced over time. However, despite these variations, there was something that most Bloom's employees shared: their pride in working for the famous company and an awareness of its uniqueness. Bloom's employees included some fascinating and legendary characters, some of whom are mentioned in detail at various points in the narrative. Throughout this chapter, passing references are made to Bloom's waiters, but they will be the main subject of the next chapter.

The Early Years

When Blooms was first established as a business entity in 1920, as opposed to Morris Bloom working informally on his own, the work involved in running the café and the manufacturing activities was carried out by Morris, his wife Rebecca and Rebecca's parents, but within a few years the expansion of the business made it necessary for Morris to employ people to assist him, particularly with the manufacturing processes.

We do not know the identities of Bloom's earliest employees, but studies of other Jewish businesses operating in the East End of London during the 1920s would suggest that they are likely to have been immigrants whose need for employment was such that they were willing to accept lower wages while they were still in the process of establishing themselves. It was also probable that there were instances of sub-contracting since this was commonplace in the Jewish economy at this time. However, unlike the 'sweated industries' (tailoring, cabinet, boot making and cap making), in which Jews were then employed in large numbers, and often on a seasonal basis, the work with Blooms was likely to have been comparatively constant and the working environment more favourable.

Given the *Landsman* system which, as previously explained, involved Jews already settled in the country helping new arrivals from the same area they had originated, it is possible that some of the early workers were either from north-western Lithuania, where Morris was born, or from the environs of Zdunska Wola in Poland from where Rebecca and her parents had their origins.[1] Wherever they came from, and however long they had lived in the UK, most of the early Bloom's employees are likely to have been men living in the near vicinity of the factory and café. The 1921 Census return for Morris and Rebecca suggests that, from time to time, some of their employees might have boarded with the family.[2] Again, this was not unusual. Due to their commitment to charitable giving previously mentioned, the Bloom family might have fed their early workers, particularly recent immigrants struggling to make a living.

Information contained in Bloom's advertisements and obtained from other sources show that by the time that the sausage factory opened in Wentworth Street in 1932, Blooms was employing staff in several roles, including drivers, butchers, sausage makers and administrative staff. One of the sausage makers in the new factory was Jack Feld from Stoke Newington.[3] However, Morris, Rebecca and her mother Miriam (her father having died) remained 'hands on' and between them possessed the skills required in running the various aspects of the expanding business. It is particularly notable that Miriam Krisman continued to work in the café for several years after the firm became successful and started employing staff to help in the kitchen.[4] The family's direct involvement in the business endured as a salient feature of Blooms throughout its existence, one that was often remarked upon by both its employees and customers.[5]

By the 1930s, Bloom's staff were employed on a more formal basis and were now in a stronger bargaining position regarding their terms and conditions of employment. This was because the Aliens Acts of 1905 and 1914 had resulted in a dramatic reduction in the supply of cheap immigrant labour. An article appearing on the front page of the *East London Observer* in 1936 reported on Morris Bloom's alleged overworking of his delivery men. The article mentioned that the drivers had contracted hours, the duration of which were regulated by legislation. The article also suggested that the employees were sufficiently organised to consider using the threat of strike action to demand more reasonable hours of work. A large proportion of Jewish workers were now members of trade unions[6] and the types of staff employed by Blooms were not as badly affected by the Great Depression of the early 1930s as other tradespeople were and therefore able to challenge their employers. Morris pleaded guilty to six summonses and was fined £65 at Old Street Police Court. In his defence, Morris claimed that the drivers had deliberately falsified their time records to 'cause trouble' for him.[7]

Motor Driver's Terrible Hours

WENTWORTH STREET MANUFACTURER FINED.

Fines and costs totalling £65 were inflicted on Morris Bloom, a whole-sale sausage manufacturer, of Wentworth Street, Stepney, at Old Street Police Court on Tuesday, when he had pleaded guilty to six summonses which allege dthat he permitted drivers to drive a motor vehicle contracted to carry goods for continuous periods amounting in the aggregate to more than eleven hours in a period of 24 hours.

Mr. Douglas Potter (defending counsel) said that Mr. Bloom had carried on business for a number of years and he employed 25 men. The difficulty was to know exactly how long a round would take, and instructions had been given to the men from time to time that records must be properly kept. The real explanation lay in the reluctance of drivers to fill up the time records. So much did the men object that they went so far as to threaten strike action. He suggested that forms were deliberately filled up inaccurately in order to get Mr. Bloom into trouble.

Imposing the fines as stated, the Magistrate (Mr. F. O. Langley) remarked that these sort of offences must stop.

77. *East London Observer*, 25 April 1936.

The Goldberg Family

One of Bloom's earliest employees was Charles Goldberg, whose parents Morris (a tailor) and Esther (née Megalsky) Goldberg both originated from Poland but had lived in England since the mid-nineteenth century.[8] Charles Goldberg, born in Stepney in 1881, worked as the company's office manager based at 111 Wentworth Street. He had previously worked as a stockjobber at the London Stock Exchange,[9] but moved to Blooms when he heard they were looking for a bookkeeper and someone to deal with the administration involved in the buying and selling of the meat products. His appointment marked the commencement of the Goldberg family's long association with Blooms, which spanned three generations. After Charles Goldberg retired just before the Second World War, his son, Stanley Goldberg, was employed as the company secretary and later became a director of Blooms.

Stanley Goldberg is said to have been Sidney Bloom's first right-hand man and confidante. He served in the armed forces during the Second World War and his father Charles returned to the company while Stanley was away fighting on the frontline. The Goldberg family were very orthodox Jews, and both Stanley, who is said to have been 'a very quiet and unassuming man',[10] and his father would have found it uncomfortable to work in close proximity to women in case they accidentally touched them, which would have been 'against their religious principles'.[11] As a result, until they left the company, no women were employed at the factory in Wentworth Street.[12]

Stanley Goldberg's son, Melvin, started working for Blooms in 1961 and remained with the company until the Golders Green restaurant closed in 2010. Initially, he worked alongside his father in the office at the factory, but he became the restaurant manager in the early 1970s. He worked first at the Aldgate restaurant and later in Golders Green, where he was usually referred to as 'Mr Melvin'. During the years that the two restaurants were both open, Melvin travelled backwards and forwards between them.

Melvin is remembered for the signature grey trilby hat he always wore (he was often referred to as 'the man with the hat'), and for his religious observance. Despite the supervision arrangements, he did not trust the *kashrut* of Bloom's food. He relied solely on the Kedassia *hechsher* (the seal of the more orthodox supervising body that had been set up just before the Second World War) and took his own meals to eat at work.[13] However, unlike his father and grandfather, he appears to have been more relaxed about working with women.

Refugees and Holocaust Survivors

The early staff employed by Morris Bloom included several family friends and, as mentioned previously, a number of refugees, several of whom Morris had helped to bring to Britain, including Siegfried Blumhof and Siegmund Sichel (sometimes Sichil). Siegfried Blumhof was born in Grebenau in Hessen, Germany in 1906.[14] When he first came to England, he lived in the Bloom's home in Addlestone, but he was interned and sent to Canada in 1940. He returned in June 1941 and soon afterwards married Sitti Fink.[15] They lived in Kentish Town, Camden. Having been a farmer in Germany, Siegfried trained to become a butcher at Blooms. Siegfried's mother-in-law was the housekeeper in Bloom's Surrey home.[16]

RETD. U.K. 30 JUN 1941

MALE ENEMY ALIEN EXEMPTION FROM INTERNMENT—REFUGEE (B)

INTERNED

(1) Surname (*block capitals*) BLUMHOF.

Forenames Siegfried Israel.

Alias Released 15.9.41

(2) Date and place of birth 25-12-06. Grebenau.

(3) Nationality German.

(4) Police Regn. Cert. No. 775671. Home Office reference if known

Special Procedure Card Number if known

(5) Address prior to Internment 55, Woodseer Street, Stepney.

(6) Normal occupation Farmer.

(7) Present Occupation Butcher (Trainee).

(8) Name and address of employer Unemployed.

(9) Decision of Tribunal Exempted from internment. Date 19-10-39.

(10) Whether exempted from Article 6(A) (Yes or No) No.

(11) Whether desires to be repatriated (Yes or No) No.

[7535] 28717/835 25m 9/39 G & S 704 [over

78. Internment record for Siegfried Blumhof. Ancestry.co.uk.

Born in Wiesbaden in Hessen, Germany in 1897, Siegmund Sichel (always referred to by his surname 'Sichel') came to London with his wife Gerda, his widowed mother Zerline and his older brother Hugo, shortly before the commencement of the Second World War.[17] They lived initially in Drake House in Stepney Way.[18] Sichel was interned until June 1941 when he was released and declared exempt from internment having secured employment with Blooms.

MALE ENEMY ALIEN—EXEMPTION FROM INTERNMENT—REFUGEE

(1) Surname (*block capitals*) SICHEL. INTERNED CIRCULAR 21.6.40

Forenames Siegmund.

Alias

(2) Date and place of birth 7/11/97. Wiesbaden.

(3) Nationality German.

(4) Police Regn. Cert. No. 595058. Home Office reference if known S8905

Special Procedure Card Number if known

(5) Address prior to Internment No. 2, Drake House, Stepney Way, London, E. 1...

(6) Normal occupation Sausage maker.

(7) Present Occupation ---ditto---

(8) Name and address of employer Mr Morris BLOOM, No. 111, Wentworth Street, London, E. 1.......

(9) Decision of Tribunal Exempt from internment. Date 2/10/39.

(10) Whether exempted from Article 6(A) (Yes or No) Yes.

(11) Whether desires to be repatriated (Yes or No) No.

[7535] 28717/835 25m 9/39 G & S 704 [OVER

79. Internment record for Siegmund Sichel. Ancestry.co.uk.

Sichel, who had served in the German Army during the First World War,[19] subsequently trained as a sausage maker, which meant that he came to London with experience that was valuable to Blooms. According to Norman Bookbinder, who worked with Sichel in the Wentworth Street factory for several years, Sichel was multiskilled and could 'turn his hand to every job that needed doing'.[20] Sichel is said to have been an exacting manager and 'everyone feared getting on the wrong side of Sichel'. If he saw someone not doing things according to his own high standards, 'he would push them aside and show them how things were done properly.'[21]

As the result of his various skills, Sichel is said to have generated a significant amount of additional income for Blooms: 'Sichel turned everything into money.'[22] Because of this, he became one of the company directors in the 1960s.[23] By then, he had naturalised and moved to Maida Vale in west London. Sichel and Gerda, who worked in a Jewish care home well into her eighties, had apparently decided not to have any children since they were first cousins.[24] Sichel, described as 'a good-hearted, charitable man',[25] died in Westminster in 1980, aged eighty-two.[26]

One of the butchers (known as *fleischmeisters*) managed by Sichel, was Szepsel Taubenhaus, sometimes known as 'Sam'. Born in Warsaw in 1911, during the Second World War Szepsel served in the Third Division of the Carpathian Shooters, one of the few Jews to do so, and was awarded the Krzyż Walecznych (Cross of Valour).[27] He fought in Palestine and subsequently came to England. Sichel had worked as a weaver in Poland, but he trained to become a butcher on his arrival in Britain. While Sichel was a 'big man with an enormous voice', Szepsel was 'slight and quite timid'.[28]

80. Szepsel Taubenhaus (third from left, back row) with his family in Warsaw prior to the Second World War. Image included in a public family tree. Ancestry.co.uk.

The War Years

With many of their regular staff either evacuated or drafted into the armed forces, it would have been difficult for Morris and Rebecca Bloom to maintain anything other than a basic level of service in the restaurant or minimum levels of production at the factory during the war. The contribution of recently recruited refugees, such as Siegmund Sichel and Siegfried Blumhof, would have been very important, as would that of the drivers, who probably had to drive further afield to deliver supplies to the many regular customers who had been evacuated to the Home Counties. Morris would also have sorely missed the contribution of his son Sidney while he was involved in munitions work, and the continuing part played by Rebecca and Miriam Krisman must have been crucial. During these years, Morris Bloom himself was often to be seen cutting the beef in the window of the restaurant now operating in Wentworth Street. The sandwiches he prepared personally have been described as 'the best ever'.[29]

This situation would have become easier after Sidney Bloom's return to the business, but major changes in the Bloom's workforce did not occur until the early 1950s when Sidney took over the business from his father and started to recruit staff to work in his new enterprise, the restaurant in Whitechapel High Street. Finding staff was probably not too onerous as it would have been during the war years, since having returned from war service, some people had found it difficult to re-establish a regular living and were looking for work. By this time, a large proportion of the London Jewish community was living outside the East End, which meant that many of the new employees travelled to work at Blooms from the suburbs of north and north-west London.

The Post-War Restaurant Managers

Morris Bloom's philanthropy extended to members of his family and prior to the Second World War he brought into the firm his nephew Anthony (known as 'Tony') Simmonds (originally Simonofsky), one of the offspring of Morris's sister Annie previously mentioned. Having spent several years learning about the running of the business, Tony became the first restaurant manager when the new enterprise opened in Whitechapel High Street. He is said to have been very competent and to have been liked by both his colleagues and customers. Towards the end of the 1950s, Tony went to live in Canada for a few years, but returned to Blooms to resume managing the Aldgate restaurant.[30] Apparently, at a later date, he lived in Australia for a while before returning once more to work as a manager at the restaurant in Golders Green.

Tony Simmonds was followed as restaurant manager by Reuben (always referred to as 'Dick' or 'Dickie') Gowers. The youngest of eight siblings, Dick was brought up in Booth Street and then at 56 Brick Lane, next door to the Bloom family, and was a childhood friend of Sidney Bloom. His parents, Jacob and Annie, who were both from Vilnius in Lithuania, ran a fruit and vegetable stall in the market in Brick Lane. Dick continued to live at 56 Brick Lane until his marriage to Julia Barnett in 1948.[31] He was the restaurant manager at Bloom's from the early 1960s until the latter part of the decade.

Dick Gowers's daughter, Esther Piper, recalls that he worked particularly long shifts on Sundays, but took a couple of hours off in the late afternoon to go home to be with his family then living in Stanley Cohen House, part of the Golden Lane Estate in the Barbican: 'He always brought with him chocolate Lindt teddy bears and marzipan from Gelkoffs, the sweet shop next to Blooms. After he returned to the restaurant, he sometimes did not get home until midnight.'[32] Michael Martin recalls that Dick Gowers was once congratulated personally by the food critic Egon Ronay for the quality of the black coffee he had been served at Bloom's restaurant. Ronay said: 'Mr Gowers had told him it was the finest Colombian coffee. Egon Ronay said he had guessed that. He was right, it was Nescafe's finest instant coffee!'[33]

Although he was a Bloom's employee, Dick Gowers continued his close friendship with Sidney Bloom, and they often socialised together:

> They went to the clubs and casinos in the West End. One of my dad's brothers was called Sulky [originally Solomon] Gowers, an actor and singer, who starred in many West End productions, such as 'Oh What a Lovely War'. He ran a small drinking club called The Madelaine where he sang. He had a bit of a reputation and was a character and a half. He knew the Krays. Sid and Dad used to go to my uncle's club and to other places where he had connections, like the Astor Club in Berkeley Square. Dad and Sid, and Sid's wife Evelyn and my mother, often went to the races together, usually to Windsor on a Monday afternoon. The Bloom men were big gamblers as well as fanatic Spurs supporters![34]

81. Dick Gowers, early Bloom's restaurant manager Courtesy of Esther Piper, his daughter.

After he left Blooms, Dick Gowers became a London taxi driver. The restaurant managers who took over from him included Melvin Goldberg (mentioned above), Sam Marks (during the late 1960s and 1970s) and an Israeli man named Yoram, who is said to have been brought to Britain in the 1980s by the Bloom family to manage both the Aldgate and Golders Green restaurants.[35] Sam Marks had a brother named Joe, who worked in the Bloom's factory, and his sister Jean Hizer was a well-known singer in the music halls of the East End.[36]

82. Sam Marks (left), restaurant manager. Jean Hizer is front row left. Courtesy of Michael Hizer, Jean's grandson.

The Chefs and Kitchen Staff

In 1932, Blooms announced that they had employed a 'first-class chef' to supplement the help being provided by their 'excellent kitchen staff'.[37] However, the family remained prominent in preparing the food served in the café until the opening of the grander restaurant in Whitechapel High Street, when a team of four professional and experienced chefs was established.

For several years, the team of chefs was led by Bernard (always known as 'Bob') Rose (originally Rosenberg), who had grown up in Hackney. He had been employed by Blooms since about 1935.[38] The soups sold by Blooms were all made from Bob Rose's own recipes.[39] He was valued so highly by the Bloom family that he was given a company car to enable him to travel from his home in Cheshunt in Buckinghamshire to the East End.[40] He was once described by a journalist as follows:

> Bernard (Bob) Rose presents a hollow-cheeked studious visage, with hard work and dedication written on every furrow of his brow. And don't expect, either, from Bernard any of the aura of mystery about the kitchen. For he is a worker and craftsman with no nonsense about him. "There's no secret in traditional Jewish cooking," he told me. "Recipe? Yes, I can give you a recipe, but it's how you apply it. I stick to the old-fashioned method of cooking to please the customer." Bernard comes from the old-fashioned, put a handful of this and a handful of that school.[41]

Norman Bookbinder, who managed the Bloom's cannery (see more below) for a number of years, recalls that Bob Rose occasionally went into the cannery for a break:

> I didn't drink myself, but I kept a bottle of whisky there especially for Bob because I adored him. When I offered him a drink, he would say, "Excellent idea dear boy." However, when I asked if he wanted water with it, he invariably said: "Actually I find that whisky destroys the taste of the water, so I'll just have the whisky straight." He must have made this same joke a thousand times in the many years that we worked together.[42]

When the cannery moved to the Tunmarsh Lane factory, Bob Rose spent time there preparing the food.[43]

Another long-standing member of the post-war team of chefs was a Frenchman named Robert (surname and origins unknown), the second chef who took over the role of head chef when Bob Rose retired. Robert, who has been described as a 'lugubrious character',[44] apparently ran the kitchen with skill and was a highly talented chef. Little is known about him other than that he was Jewish, oversaw the cannery, and eventually moved to become the chef in the Golders Green restaurant.

The pastry chef in the team was a man named Bambos Pais, an Armenian Cypriot. Norman Bookbinder recalls: 'He made a sensational dessert that had sponge cake as a base with fruit on top. If you ate one, you invariably licked you fingers afterwards to prolong the pleasure.'[45] Bambos became famous in 1966 when he was invited to work at Kensington Palace. In addition to his skills as a kosher chef, Bambos had a good grasp of French and continental cookery and catered private parties when he was not working at Blooms, including several parties organised for Princess Margaret and Lord Snowden. The couple, who also dined at the Aldgate restaurant, were so impressed by Bambos that they suggested that he should contact Kensington Palace to talk about working there.

The story was covered by newspapers across the globe. When he was asked to comment for an article that appeared in the *El Paso Herald-Post* in the United States, Bambos, who had by then naturalised as a British citizen, was quoted as saying: 'I cannot talk about it now or the crumble will be ruined. I will give a press conference at my apartment and tell my decision then.'[46] Bambos appears to have been unfazed about the job offer, and when he was interviewed by the *Jewish Post*, he commented: 'If you can satisfy the tastes of Bloom's customers, believe me, you can satisfy the taste of Kensington Palace.'[47] Having given the matter careful consideration, Bambos decided to stay with Blooms since the Bloom family had been good to him and he felt that working at Blooms was 'like being one of the family'.[48]

The fourth member of the chef team was a Polish man named 'Sid', who had come to the country at the end of the Second World War. Although he spoke English, his first language was Yiddish, with which he sprinkled his conversation. He was an expert on making traditional *heimische* food such as *latkes* and *tzimmes* (see Glossary of Eastern European Jewish Food at Appendix One). Norman Bookbinder recalls:

> Everything Sid made was fantastic, but he had a bad temper. I remember Mrs Bloom once went into the kitchen, saying that a woman customer had commented that the *tzimmes* were a little salty. Sid picked up a chopper and brandishing it he shouted: "Salty, I'll give her salty!" He ran towards the kitchen door, making for the restaurant. Thankfully, bloodshed was somehow averted.[49]

The expert team of chefs became pivotal in the success of the Aldgate restaurant during its heyday. The team was also responsible for training waves of unskilled kitchen staff, including many kitchen porters recruited from the Bengali community, which from the 1950s had started to coalesce around Brick Lane and the adjacent streets, and those from other countries, including a man named Osman from Mauritius. It was 'on-the-job' training; they learned by watching the experienced chefs at work. Some of those who trained at Blooms subsequently worked in the two restaurants, while others established successful careers elsewhere.[50]

After the invasion of Hungary by Russia in 1956, a significant number of Hungarian Jews fled to England, many of whom spent the first few weeks in the country at the Jews' Temporary Shelter now located in Mansell Street, which found work for the refugees in nearby enterprises, including at Blooms. Laszlo Roman, who arrived in London as a teenager in 1957, recalls being sent to work as a porter in the Aldgate restaurant where another Hungarian Jew whom he knew was already working. Although the pay was good and Laszlo was provided with food, he found it difficult to communicate with other staff since he spoke no English. Despite Bloom's track record of employing refugees, Laszlo did not feel welcomed or valued by the chefs or the restaurant manager, but he was able to bear the situation since he viewed the job as only being short term while he established himself and was able to complete his education.[51] For some employees, the kitchen at Blooms was apparently an expedient staging post.

The skills of the chefs and the kitchen staff were supplemented by the team of four women cooks, who worked in St George's Residence to the rear of the restaurant. They cooked food such as the *kreplach*, *kneidlach* and *gefilte* fish for the restaurant as well as food to be canned (see Glossary of Eastern European Jewish Food at Appendix One). The woman who ran the cooking operation was called Mrs Saul, who was born in India: 'She was an amazing woman. She spoke Hebrew, but she also spoke Gujarati and Hindi. Her English was perfect. She was a sensational cook and knew how to cook and make everything.'[52]

Two other members of the team were an Israeli woman called Naomi, and a woman named Mrs Dessa, an orthodox Jew and Holocaust survivor, to whom everyone deferred: 'If you met her going upstairs and she was coming down, you would walk back down so that she could complete her descent first because you did not want to pass close to a very orthodox woman.'[53] Mrs Dessa specialised in frying the fish and producing the chopped liver.[54] The identity of the fourth member of the cooking team is unknown.

The Salt Beef Sandwich Makers

While the teams of chefs and cooks worked largely behind the scenes, the staff who prepared the salt beef sandwiches had a high profile. After the opening of the new restaurant in 1952, one of the first salt beef sandwich makers was Hymie (also known as 'Harry') Stockfeder, a Jew from Poland, where he had worked as a box maker.[55] He lived in Willesden, where he died in 1959, aged sixty-five.[56]

83. Harry Stockfeder, salt beef sandwiches maker in the early years of the Aldgate restaurant. Courtesy of Sybil and Ralph Schiller.

During the 1950s, Blooms employed several Holocaust survivors, one of whom was Laser Josef (universally known as 'Joe') Bojm, another of the salt beef sandwich makers. Joe was born in Kaluszyn in Poland in 1910, the youngest of six children. He was recruited into the Polish Army when he was aged nineteen in 1929, and he fought with the Free Army throughout Europe during the Second World War. He was captured by the Russian Army, but he managed to escape and catch up with the Free Army, which was now under British command. He served in Israel, but after the war ended, he decided to make a new life for himself in the UK. His immediate family – parents, siblings, nieces and nephews – all perished in the Holocaust.[57]

84. Laser Josef ('Joe') Bojm, salt beef sandwich maker at Blooms. Courtesy of Paula Allen, his daughter.

Late in life, Joe married Millie (originally Mindel) Feigenbaum in 1951 and they had two daughters, Paula and Sharon. The family lived in Grindall House in Darling Row, behind the Blind Beggar Pub in Whitechapel (the regular haunt of the Kray twins), which was within walking distance of the Aldgate restaurant. This is probably how Joe came to be employed at Blooms. Joe was a very sociable man and therefore loved working in the restaurant. It gave him the opportunity to meet many people and to use his language skills; he spoke Polish, Yiddish, English, Russian as well as a little Italian, Hebrew and Arabic. His daughter, Paula Allen, recollects: 'He was a hard worker. He did not want to take anything from anyone. He wanted to make his own way in the world. He was more than happy to work long hours.'[58] Paula also recalls being taken to see her father at work in Bloom's restaurant:

> I still have a vivid image of Daddy as he stood behind the counter, wearing a white coat that buttoned up the front and holding a long knife for cutting the thick slices of beef. They were almost an inch thick, not wafer thin with no fat on them like today. I can never fully enjoy a salt beef or a tongue sandwich because no one makes them like Daddy did. He was very skilled at it. At home he could take a side of smoked salmon and cut it so thin that you could see through each slice.[59]

Joe Bojm started working for Blooms in 1953 and remained with the firm for many years before taking up a position in a kosher restaurant in the West End.[60] He died in 1996, aged eighty-six.[61]

Although there might have been some rewarding aspects of the job, the sandwich makers would be slicing with elaborate, almost theatrical, choreography the salt beef repetitively for most of their long shifts. The meat had to be cut with the grain to ensure that the slices had a solid appearance.[62] Working in the front window of the premises, they were very visible to passers-by and people waiting at the nearby bus stop. Heather Bieber recalls: 'I used to watch the huge joints being put on a carving board and a skewer being inserted while they carved thick slices very quickly, which were put on proper rye bread and smeared with hot English mustard.'[63]

THE MOST FAMOUS KOSHER RESTAURANT IN BRITAIN

85.Watching the salt beef sandwiches being made. Extract from 1960s Bloom's marketing brochure. Courtesy of Jonathan Fishburn.

Many of the sandwich makers, who wore long white coats and ties to distinguish them from the waiters, became familiar figures to the takeaway customers. Anne Lesser recalls: 'My dad worked at Blooms behind the salt beef counter. He was quite a large man and became known as "Big Ben".'[64]

Other people who worked as sandwich makers at Blooms over the years were Terry Pulver and two Greek Cypriots, one named Hassan, who was the deputy restaurant manager and carried out several jobs as well as slicing the beef, and Jeff (surname unknown), who was often mistaken for Engelbert Humperdinck because of his long sideburns. Martin Malin recalls: 'Jeff taught me a lot of Greek swear words!' In the late 1970s, Martin Malin himself also sliced the beef for two years.[65]

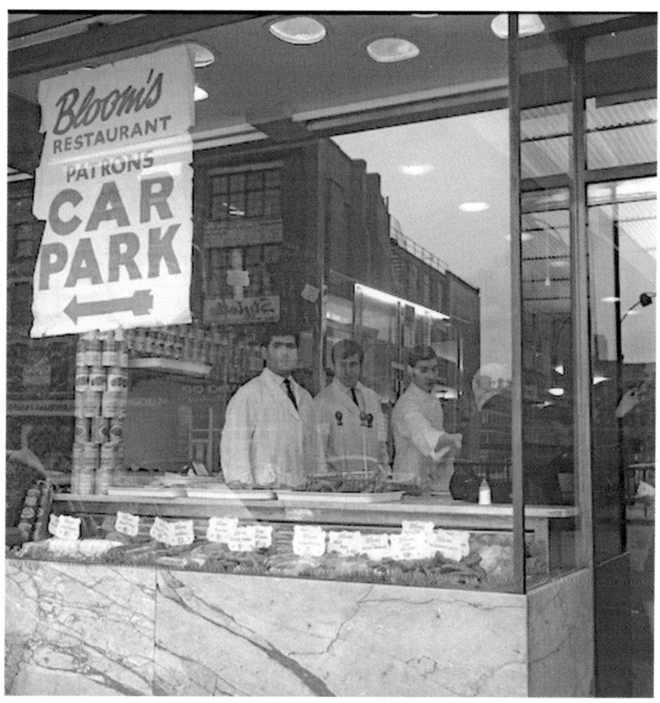

86.The Bloom's counter staff, 1970. Reproduced with the permission of Steven Berkoff.

As a result of their high profile, some of the salt beef carvers developed 'airs and graces' and regarded themselves as 'the kings of the salt beef sandwiches'. Their customers were more than capable of dealing with this:

> My Mother, G-d rest her soul, was an absolute force of nature, with an iron will, prepared to pit it against the hardest of them. She told me that when she was young, Blooms had a rule that you couldn't have a salt beef sandwich at certain times of the day. My good old mum went in at one of those times and asked for a salt beef sandwich. The man at the counter sharply and loudly said, "NO SANDWICHES." My mother being my mother said, "I'll have a plate of salt beef with a

> pickle please. Oh, and two slices of bread." He stared down at my mother and said, "YOU'RE NOT GOING TO MAKE A SANDWICH, ARE YOU?" "Oh, of course not," she said. He brought over the plate with the salt beef and pickle and begrudgingly gave her the two slices of bread. He stood right in front of her and stared at her with a face of thunder. My mother looked him in the eye and took a piece of the bread and started placing the salt beef on the bread, slowly cutting the pickle and putting it on top of the salt beef. Then, without breaking eye contact, she took the other piece of bread and put it on top. At this point he lost his mind and started shouting at the top of his voice: "SHE'S MAKING A SANDWICH, LOOK, A SANDWICH". Undaunted, my mother started eating it. She thinks that he went out to the back of the restaurant and had an embolism.[66]

There were also some long-standing salt beef sandwich makers at the Golders Green restaurant, including a man from Mauritius known as 'BooBoo', who was also a part-time chef and counter hand.[67]

The Drivers

Comparatively little is remembered about the drivers in the post-war years, probably because they spent most of their time on the road delivering Bloom's products. Many of them were long-standing and, as a result, built up good client relations in the areas to which they delivered. The team of drivers included Len (surname unknown), originally from Manchester, who is remembered as 'a smart man who always wore a shirt and tie and had a neatly trimmed moustache'; Eric (surname unknown), who served the Stamford Hill area and parts of the East End; Ian Cohen, who delivered to the Ilford area (he joined Blooms when he was very young and remained with the firm longer than any of the other drivers); Joe (surname unknown), who covered south London; and Lou Tendler, who delivered to outlets in north-west London.

The two drivers who are mentioned most often are Aubrey Goldstein and Benny Winsky. Aubrey Goldstein, who is described as 'an interesting character, who'd volunteered to fight in Israel in 1948',[68] had to give up driving because of a sight impairment, lived in Southgate and was an active member of the Cockfosters and North Southgate United Synagogue, where he taught in the *cheder* (religion school). After he retired from Blooms, he started buying and selling Jewish books.[69] Benny Winsky, often referred to as 'Benny the Worsht', was apparently known by many people in the Jewish community remaining in the East End or those living in Barkingside, Ilford and the other places to which Jews had moved: 'Benny was everybody's friend.'[70] Benny was born in Whitechapel in October 1921 and went to the Jews' Free School with Sidney Bloom. Benny and his wife Hettie lived in Middlesex Street in the East End for many years before moving to Edgware.

Some Memorable People

Over the years, the Bloom's workforce, both in the restaurant and in the factory, included some 'real personalities'. Some of these characters have already been mentioned in passing in previous chapters, such as the Irishman called Michael O'Power (sometimes referred to unflatteringly as 'Mad Michael'). His main job was driving supplies to and from the factory when it moved to Plaistow, but he also did a variety of 'odd jobs' for Sidney Bloom, including working as a kitchen porter and helping with the running of the customer car park at the Aldgate restaurant. He was sometimes handed car keys by the more prominent diners as they arrived. In exchange for a generous tip, he parked their cars and promised to look after them. He is said to have driven several cars into the car park wall.[71]

The well-known employees at the Bloom's factory also included the 'larger-than-life' Hugo Blumenthal, who worked at the front of the factory (first at Wentworth Street and then in Plaistow), helping the delivery people to load their vans. He arrived in England from Poland shortly before the start of the Second World War, possibly via the Kindertransport, and acquired a vocabulary that apparently included most English swear words, which he used liberally and indiscriminately. Norman Bookbinder tells this story:

> During the 1970s, Blooms was seeking to woo the custom of the new supermarkets that were opening all over the country. One day, I had been introducing the buyer for Mac Fisheries, a man named Mr Stass, to our products at the Tunmarsh Lane factory. He was the first supermarket buyer that had been to Blooms. After a tasting session at the factory, I had arranged to take him to the Aldgate restaurant for lunch, and he was very excited to be going to the famous Bloom's restaurant. Everyone had been briefed and I was nicely dressed and was holding a briefcase in my hand. The head waiter, Peter Nicholas, walked forward to greet us, saying, "Norman, your table is ready for you." Hugo, who had been working at the back of the restaurant, started shouting with his strong Polish accent across the packed restaurant: "What table waiting for him. He came from Manchester with his arse hanging from trousers. Now he big man with table waiting for him." Mrs Bloom rushed across the restaurant and, highly embarrassed, quickly ushered Hugo into the kitchen as he was still shouting: "I was not frightened of Gestapo, and I am not frightened of you." Mrs Bloom begged him: "Hugo, just go into the kitchen please. Don't spoil it for Norman." To my great surprise, we were awarded the contract![72]

Hugo Blumenthal, who served in the British Army during the war, married a woman named Inga, a Holocaust survivor, and they set up home in Redbridge. Inga later worked in the Golders Green restaurant, where she became close to Sylvia Malin.[73]

Mentioned several times in Chapter Five was David Rein, who worked in Bloom's factory for over forty years. David Rein (originally Reingwitz) was born in Whitechapel on 26 September 1929. His father was Pinkus, who was a kosher butcher, and his mother was Sarah Dresner (sometimes 'Draisner').[74] His parents came to England from a village near Lodz in Poland in 1920 to join Pinkus's sister, who was already settled in the East End. His father was classified as an 'enemy alien'. David had three older brothers, all born in Whitechapel.[75]

Pinkus's first butcher's shop was at 284 Brick Lane, but shortly before the Second World War, he opened a butcher's shop at 92 Hanbury Street, which was demolished by one of the first bombs that fell on the East End during the Blitz. David attended Robert Montefiore School in Vallance Road and was evacuated with the school to a village near Ely a few weeks before the outbreak of the Second World War: 'I lived on a poultry farm with a family who had never met a Jew before I went there.'[76] David returned to London for his *Bar Mitzvah* in 1942. His family had now moved to Stoke Newington,[77] where David lived until he was called up for National Service in 1947. He served in the Royal Air Force as a radar engineer, stationed at West Malling in Kent.

On his return to London, David went to work in a small firm making televisions, which he did not enjoy, before going to work in the Bloom's Wentworth Street factory. One of David's first tasks at Blooms was to smoke the Viennas. He had planned to become a porger so that he could take over his father's kosher licence, but instead he remained working on the production side of the Bloom's business.

After the Tunmarsh Lane factory closed in 1991, David transferred to work for Blooms when the firm was using the Greenspan's factory in Tottenham, and then for a short while he worked for the Kedassia-licensed Frohwein's firm in its factory on the Staples Corner industrial estate, next to Golders Green, before retiring aged seventy.

David and his family lived in Gants Hill, Ilford. They were very close to the Bloom family, and they attended each other's life-cycle celebrations, including David's marriage to Yvonne Myers at the newly opened Clapton Federation Synagogue in Lea Bridge Road in Hackney in 1955.

87.Wedding of David Rein and Yvonne Myers in 1955, attended by the Bloom family Courtesy of David Rein.

While the Bloom's workforce was undoubtedly male dominated, there were several women employees who worked at the Aldgate and Golders Green restaurants, mainly serving behind the delicatessen counters. As a result, they became well known to the customers. There are particularly fond memories of the 'good-looking twins', Rochelle and Benita Bloom (later Rochelle Berlyn and Benita Singer). They joined the firm when they were fifteen in 1953. Rochelle Berlyn recalls:

> We lived on the Pembury Estate in Hackney, but we knew about Blooms because our older sister Esther was already working there. One day, my father, Harry Bloom, rang Sidney Bloom to ask about vacancies for us. A waiter picked up the phone and my father said he wanted to speak to Mr Bloom. The waiter asked who was calling. My father said, "It's Mr Bloom." The waiter was confused. "But you've just said that you want to speak to Mr Bloom." This went on for some minutes before the waiter realised there were two Mr Blooms. It happened again later on when my uncle, who was called Sidney Bloom, rang the restaurant. The waiter was even more confused![78]

The twins looked very similar and were often mistaken for each other. Norman Bookbinder says: 'I remember often talking to one of them and suddenly realising it was not the one I thought that I was speaking to!'[79] Rochelle worked with Blooms for twenty years and Benita for forty-five years, apart from the time that they took off to have their children. Benita Singer transferred to the Golders Green restaurant when it opened in 1965.[80] She stopped working for Blooms in around 2000.[81] The twins were noted for the speed with which they served food that had been ordered, but also that they always had time to speak to their customers.[82] Benita was entrusted to slice the salt beef for the sandwiches and was particularly skilled in managing the long queues when they formed outside Blooms.[83] At the time that Blooms began experiencing financial problems in the early 1990s, Benita's son, Stuart Singer, a tax specialist, became the firm's accountant and handled the sale of the company's various assets and continued as the Bloom's accountant for several years.[84]

88. Rochelle Berlyn and Benita Singer née Bloom. Courtesy of Stuart Singer, Benita's son.

As a result of the skills, experience and contacts they made working for Blooms, a number of employees went on to become very successful elsewhere, including Norman Bookbinder. Norman was born and brought up in Salford. After leaving school, he went to work with his uncle Bernard, who owned a kosher butcher's shop in Manchester. In 1965, he decided to move to London where he was introduced to Sidney Bloom as a potential employer. He recalls:

> I warmed to him immediately because he was mad about football like me. When I walked into the room and he heard my Manchester accent he said: "Ah, Bobby Charlton, come in. I hear you've come for a job. You can work in the restaurant because you are a charmer and you'll do well there." In fact, when I started work for Blooms, he got me doing some of the worst jobs in the factory![85]

Over the years, Norman became a highly valued employee taking on more responsibility, managing the Bloom's cannery, and then overseeing the selling of the firm's products to the rapidly expanding supermarket chains. On occasion, he was asked to manage the factory in Plaistow. As a result of his success in setting up contracts with supermarkets he was recruited to work for a large, non-kosher meat processing conglomerate, Hazelwood Foods, managing its relationships with supermarkets.[86]

In 1995, Norman Bookbinder (by then running his own company, Roman Foods) set up a meat processing business with David Gilbert,[87] the son of the owner of Gilberts in Stamford Hill, with whom Norman had become acquainted when working for Blooms. Their firm, Gilbert's Kosher Foods, was highly successful having invested in the 'high-tech' factory in Milton Keynes mentioned in Chapter Six.[88] Since the untimely death of David Gilbert in 2005, Norman has been the sole managing director of Gilberts, which has gone from strength to strength and is now an £8 million business.[89]

Another former Bloom's employee who established his own business, was Gerry Commissar, a Polish Jew. After working behind the counter at Blooms for several years, he became a trainee manager, mainly working in the Golders Green restaurant. In 1970, he opened Gerrys, a licensed kosher restaurant and salt beef bar licensed by the Federation of Synagogue's Beth Din and Kashrus Commission. The business, which Gerry ran with his wife Brenda and daughter Samantha until 1979, was located at 11 Lanson House, Whitchurch Lane, Edgware. The restaurant, was recommended by the *Jewish Chronicle* due to the interpersonal and culinary skills of its 'Bloom's-trained owner'.[90]

An Increasingly Diverse Workforce

One of the most remarkable developments in the Bloom's workforce after the Second World War was its increasing diversity. Whereas in the pre-war years Bloom's employees were exclusively Jewish and mainly drawn from the East End Jewish community, by the 1960s, Blooms was employing staff from a variety of religious backgrounds and from many countries. Bloom's Jewish employees became a minority as second and third generation of Jews made their way into the professions and then into a much wider range of occupations.

The increasingly diverse workforce included both Greek and Turkish Cypriots, who migrated to London in the late 1950s and early 1960s for various reasons, including better wages and education, but above all to escape the political situation in Cyprus. Norman Bookbinder comments: 'Although they were unable to get on in their own country, they got on fabulously at Blooms. I was sometimes invited to weddings and other special occasions organised by my Cypriot colleagues, which included both Greeks and Turks.'[91] To start with, there were just one or two Cypriots and then, through their community networks, others found work with Blooms in a similar way to how Jews had secured employment a few generations earlier. The long-standing Turkish-Cypriot waiter Memet Kemal, who worked for Blooms for twenty years, missed his former colleagues after he moved on to other occupations and continued to work at Blooms for four hours on a Sunday 'to see the boys'.[92]

Some of the Cypriots (both Greek and Turkish), who worked for Blooms were able to improve their standard of living and decided to return to their family villages in Cyprus. However, several naturalised (like the pastry chef Bambos Pais mentioned above), put down roots and continued working for Blooms for several decades and went on to open their own businesses, such as Chris Christopoulou, a waiter at the Golders Green restaurant, who opened a salt beef bar, The Sunset, in Finchley Central;[93] the head waiter, Jimmy Nicholas who opened his own kosher-style eaterie in Edgware High Street; and the deputy restaurant manager Hassan, who opened a restaurant in Ballards Lane.

The most successful of the former Bloom's Greek Cypriot staff was Charalambos (always known as 'Bambos') Georgiou. He came to England from Cyprus in 1958 with his wife Katerina, whom he had married in 1955, and their two young children. In Cyprus, Bambos had worked as a carpenter, but he found the English weather too inclement to work outdoors. The family set up a home in East Finchley and Bambos used his contacts in the Greek Cypriot community to obtain work in the catering trade. He worked in Phil Rabin's Nosh Bar and then Carroll's restaurant, both in Great Windmill Street in Soho and both of which served Jewish food. He moved on to work in Bloom's restaurant in Aldgate. He carved the meat for the salt beef sandwiches with great precision, and he often said: 'There are very few carvers, quite a few cutters and a lot of butchers, who don't know how to carve the meat or handle a brisket.'[94] Bambos found the atmosphere at Blooms very conducive. His son Michael recalls:

> He enjoyed the happy-go-lucky atmosphere created by people with the same origins meeting together to eat the same food and speak the same language; it resonated with the culture of the Greek Cypriot community. He understood their immigrant history and outlook.[95]

Bambos struck up a good relationship with both the customers and the Bloom family. He picked up many Jewish customs, *Yiddishe* words (and swearwords) and Hebrew sayings, which he passed on to his offspring: 'On Fridays, when the restaurant closed early, he'd say to Sidney Bloom "It's *Shabbos*, let's go and have a pint!", and they would go to one of the local pubs before going home.'[96] When there were unexplained losses of money on the counter at the Golders Green restaurant, Bambos was transferred there to control the situation. He is fondly remembered by many former customers of the restaurant.

While he was working at Blooms, Bambos was approached by the then owner of Selfridges, Charles Clore, to open a salt beef bar in their Food Hall, which he did in 1966. After successfully establishing the Brass Rail at Selfridges, he became 'the most sought-after deli man in London',[97] working at The Stage delicatessen in Golders Green and Leslie's restaurant in Temple Fortune.

89. Bambos Georgiou (far right) at the opening of the Brass Rail Salt Beef Bar in Selfridges in 1966. Courtesy of the Georgiou family.

When Bambos's wife Katerina died in 1977, leaving him with six teenage children to raise, he decided to invest in his own restaurant. In 1978, Bambos purchased the premises at 11 Lanson House, Whitchurch Lane in Edgware from former Bloom's employee Gerry Commissar (see above) and opened B&K (Bambos and Katerina) Salt Beef Bar, which was very successful. This is where the younger generation of the family learned the salt beef trade and used the skills in carving and pickling passed down from Bambos to develop the business. Bambos died in 2016, aged eighty-five, but decades after B&K was established, his sons, Michael and John (described by a visiting Canadian journalist as 'Deli men through and through'[98]) and his grandsons continue Bambos's legacy, running the two B&K restaurants in Edgware and Hatch End (which opened in 2012) and three eateries in central London (in Wardour Street, Goodge Street and Leather Lane) that have been opened in the last seven years, all operating under the moniker of 'Tongue and Brisket'. See Plates Section, Plate 11.

By the late 1950s, the workforce at the factory was also very diverse and included: a non-Jewish Polish man named Gregory, who was involved in food preparation on the ground floor of the premises; Turkish Cypriot brothers, Hassan and Willie Veli, who were both butchers; a Greek Cypriot named Louis, who worked on the production side; a German-Jewish man named Hans, who was a butcher; and a Maltese man named Albert (originally Alberto) Marmara, who worked both as a butcher and in the production side of the factory. Albert continued to work in the Bloom's factory until a few years before its closure.[99]

As the population of the East End (and the country as a whole) became more multicultural, the Bloom's workforce also included people from Arabic countries, Pakistanis, Bengalis and those from Sri Lanka, the Maldives and Mauritius. The people employed by Blooms were often those who were escaping conflict. Later, the company employed staff who were part of more recent waves of economic migrants, including those from Eastern European countries.

Morris's Legacy

In his will, Morris Bloom included a clause saying that after his death Blooms should continue offering work to those who needed it, or people who might face difficulties in obtaining employment.[100] Sidney Bloom was committed to complying with his father's wishes and, as a result, throughout the remainder of Bloom's existence, the company continued to employ people who for various reasons needed a job. Martin Malin comments:

> If a business analyst had been called in to look at the running of the firm, they would have been totally perplexed by the number of people on the books with no obvious role. Nobody got the sack at Blooms, even if they were not contributing and even when they did something really silly![101]

The supernumerary employees included a man named Hillel, who worked behind the counter at the Aldgate restaurant. He had fought in the Second World War and suffered from shell shock. Martin Malin recalls: 'His hands were too shaky for him to cut the salt beef, but he took the customers' money. As a D-Day survivor he was a prime example of the sort of person that my uncle Sidney wanted to employ. That's what the family did.'[102]

Other employees with a fluid role were Sammy Bush, another former school friend of Sidney Bloom, who pickled all the cucumbers in the restaurant and helped the waiter named Milton[103] with the laundry in the basement, and Solly and Lawrence who worked at the factory.[104]

One of the people that Sidney Bloom took under his wing was a young man named Michael ('Micky') Fuller, the son of continental refugees Rachel and Jan Fulle (later Fuller). Micky had found it difficult to settle in a job, but having been recommended by the waiter Max Strum[105] for a position at Blooms, he was very happy working there. His sister, Vivienne Thompson, recalls:

Sidney needed someone who was good with figures and Micky was a great mathematician. He became Mr Bloom's right-hand man. Sidney knew that Micky wanted desperately to go to Israel to work on a kibbutz and he said to Micky "*Gehgezinterheit* [stay healthy], but you must come back." After three or four months, Micky returned and Mr Bloom put his arms around him and said, "You are like manna from heaven." He treated Micky like a son.[106]

90. Michael Fuller, Sidney Bloom's 'right-hand man' in the 1960s, Courtesy of Vivienne Thompson, his sister.

In addition to Tony Simmonds, another member of the extended family who was brought into the business was Sadie, the youngest sibling of Archie Malin (Sidney's brother-in-law). Sadie had married Louis Berman, who had died young and left without an adequate income. She was employed at the Aldgate restaurant, working on the delicatessen counter for many years. 'She lived in Leytonstone and one of the drivers or one of the waiters would always give her a lift home because they did not like the idea of her travelling alone on the buses.'[107] She is said to have been very popular with the customers, who were saddened by her relatively early death, aged sixty-eight, in 1986.[108]

Employment Practices

As mentioned earlier in this chapter, during Bloom's early years, the firm's arrangements for employing staff were fairly informal. Like other catering and food manufacturing firms at the time, relatively little was committed to paper. However, in 1963, the Contracts of Employment Act came into force, which amongst other stipulations, required employers to issue their employees with contracts, providing information on remuneration, duties, hours of work, holiday provision and other working arrangements. Blooms quickly complied with the legislation, but one example of the contracts that were issued suggests that the terms and conditions of employment were still quite rudimentary. The section in the sample contract relating to 'Sickness and Injury' states rather bluntly: 'You will not be paid for time off.'[109]

Up until the 1970s, Blooms continued to rely on informal methods of recruitment – word-of-mouth recommendations by existing staff, notices posted on the doors of the restaurants – but this gradually gave way to public advertisements for vacancies placed in the press, including in the *Jewish Chronicle*, even though the company was not setting out to recruit only Jewish staff. The wording of the advertisements suggested that, as the business had become larger and more complex, the calibre of staff being sought had become higher, especially for the 'white collar' jobs, and that training was provided if necessary.

YOUNG MAN WANTED
TO TRAIN FOR A CAREER WITH
"BLOOMS"

If you are a bright, willing young man looking for a job with prospects, then why not get in touch with us and hear what we have to offer.

The successful applicant will work in our East London factory and be trained in all aspects of processed food manufacturing. Good initial salary and excellent prospects on completion of training.

Write with brief details to:
Mr. M. Kallenberg, M. BLOOM (KOSHER) AND SON LTD.,
West Factory, Tunmarsh Lane, London, E.13

91. Advertisement in the *Jewish Chronicle*, 19 December 1975.

Bloom's employees were sometimes asked to work beyond their normal roles. When the restaurants were particularly busy, Bloom's staff from other parts of the company were drafted in to help. Norman Bookbinder recalls that when he managed the Bloom's cannery, he was sometimes called to the Aldgate restaurant on a Sunday to work an extra shift, cutting the salt beef for the sandwiches and serving the delicatessen customers, working alongside Evelyn Bloom in her role as the 'meeter and greeter'. He comments: 'I was only too pleased to oblige – anything to get away from the cannery! The atmosphere was wonderful and the cash payment was always welcome.'[110]

Although after 1963 most of the workforce was employed directly by Blooms, the company continued to sub-contract some of its work. For example, several of the delivery drivers involved in the wholesale part of the business were self-employed. Blooms also contracted with a few firms to provide ongoing specialist skills, including plumbers and electricians, whose services appear to have been valued. Nick Callaghan recalls: 'My dad was their plumber and got called out every Sunday morning. Blooms would give him salt beef, *latkes*, chips, barley soup, "new greens" [pickled cucumbers], and orange sorbets, so my mum would leave our Sunday roast until Monday.'[111]

As mentioned above, Sidney and Evelyn Bloom socialised with staff members who were part of the extended family or long-standing friends, but otherwise there were clear boundaries between the Bloom family and the firm's employees. As a result, some employees felt that there was a 'them and us atmosphere' and 'a certain lack of warmth'.[112] Some long-standing employees felt that their contribution was not fully appreciated.[113]

Staffing in Bloom's Latter Years

Until the closure of the Aldgate restaurant in 1996, Bloom's staff were used flexibly between the two restaurants, especially the waiters and the counter staff, and when the Aldgate restaurant closed, several of the staff who had not been made redundant by the liquidator Ian Franses,[114] were transferred to Golders Green. During Bloom's declining years, the company took on fewer and fewer new staff, and one of the main recollections of the final years of the Golders Green restaurant is its ageing workforce. When the Edgware branch was opened in 2007, new staff were employed, who were trained by the long-standing staff at the Golders Green restaurant, but they were made redundant within a year due to the closure of the short-lived restaurant.

When the Golders Green restaurant closed in 2010, the manager Melvin Goldberg had been working for Blooms for fifty years and was still not ready to stop working, even though he was past normal retirement age. He went on to work for another kosher eaterie, one of the two Dizengoff restaurants a few doors away from Blooms.

Notes

1. See Chapter Two.
2. See 1921 Census return, Findmypast.
3. Gary Saffer, post on Facebook page Memories of Hessel, Langdale Mans, Canon Street Rd and Cable St, 31.3.2023. Jack Feld served in the Queen's Royal Regiment during the war. Information on birth certificate for his daughter Julia Feld.

4. This work ethic appears to have been a phenomenon of Miriam Krisman's immigrant generation. For example, '*Bubbe*' Richman continued to cook at the Green Park Hotel in Bournemouth when the hotel was at the height of its success. See Pam Fox, *Jews by the Seaside: The Hotels and Guest Houses of Bournemouth* (London: Vallentine Mitchell, 2022).
5. See Chapter Eleven for further discussion.
6. By this time the small Jewish trade unions that had proliferated earlier in the century were being absorbed into the appropriate British trade unions, which further increased their bargaining power. See Harold Pollins, *Economic History of the Jews in England* (London and Toronto: Fairleigh Dickenson University Press, 1982), p.190.
7. *East London Observer*, 25.4.1936.
8. Information from Ancestry.co.uk.
9. *Ibid.*
10. Interview with Martin Malin, 4.5.2023.
11. Interview with Norman Bookbinder, 30.12.2022.
12. *Ibid.*
13. Daniel Pinner, post on Facebook page Jewish Britain, 21.8.2022.
14. Information from Ancestry.co.uk.
15. *Ibid.*
16. Interview with David Hallgarten, 10.1.2022.
17. We know that the family was still in Germany in 1938 since Hugo's father, Asser, died there in that year.
18. 1939 England and Wales Register, Ancestry.co.uk.
19. German Army records, *ibid.*
20. Interview with Norman Bookbinder, 30.12.2022.
21. Information on Sichel provided by Norman Bookbinder, interviewed 5.12.2022. Szepsel died in Greenwich, aged sixty-three, in 1974.
22. Interview with David Hallgarten, 10.1.2023.
23. See the firm's headed paper during the 1960s.
24. Interview with David Hallgarten, 10.1.2023.
25. *Ibid.*
26. Register of Deaths, Ancestry.co.uk.
27. Information from public family tree, *ibid.*
28. Interview with Norman Bookbinder, 9.12.2022.
29. Interview with Connie Stanton, 7.10.2022.
30. Passenger lists, Ancestry.co.uk.
31. The family were members of the Sandys Road Synagogue.
32. Interview with Esther Piper (née Gowers) and Julia Gowers, 31.8.2022. Dick Gowers married Julia Barnett in Willesden in 1948 and he died in 1988. Sadly, Julia Gowers died as this book was being written. May her memory be a blessing.

33. Michael Martin, post on Facebook page The Jewish East End of London, 30.1.2018.
34. Interview with Esther Piper (née Gowers) and Julia Gowers, 31.8.2022. Sulky Gowers (originally Solomon) apparently operated on the fringes of London's underworld and brokered tickers to the big Tottenham Hotspurs matches. See https://www.independent.co.uk/sport/the-glamour-is-in-the-game-not-necessarily-the-lifestyle-1364044.html.
35. Pamela Kaye, post on Facebook page The Jewish East End of Britain, 20.10.2013.
36. Email from Michael Hizer, 20.1.2023.
37. *JC*, 21.10.1932.
38. *JC*, 16.7.1965. In this article it is stated that Bob Rose had worked for Blooms for 30 years in 1965.
39. Post by Gloria Meyer on Facebook page The Jewish East End of London, 29.10.2016
40. Anonymous interviewee, 20.12.2022.
41. *JC*, 16.7.1965.
42. Interview with Norman Bookbinder, 9.12.2022.
43. Interview with Martin Malin, 9.4.2023.
44. Interview with Martin Malin, 30.12.2022.
45. Interview with Norman Bookbinder, 9.12.2022.
46. *El Paso Herald Post*, 2.2.1966.
47. *Jewish Post*, 18.2.1966.
48. Jewish Telegraph Agency, 10.2.1966.
49. Interview with Norman Bookbinder, 9.12.2022.
50. Interview with Martin Malin, 30.12.2022.
51. Conversation with Laszlo Roman 15.5.2023. Laszlo went on to become a successful chemical engineer.
52. Interview with Norman Bookbinder, 9.12.2022.
53. *Ibid.*
54. Interview with Ruth Plaut, 17.5.2023.
55. 1911 Census, Ancestry.co.uk.
56. Email from Ralph Schiller, 7.12.2022. Harry Stockfeder was the uncle of Ralph's wife Sybil.
57. Documentation provided by Paula Allen, Joe's daughter, 11.12.2022.
58. Interview with Paula Allen, 9.12.2022.
59. *Ibid.*
60. *Ibid.*
61. Public family trees, Ancestry.co.uk
62. If the meat was sliced against the grain, it became stringy and broke up easily.
63. Email from Heather Bieber (née George), 8.12.2022.

64. Anne Lesser, post on Facebook page Memories of Hessel, Langdale Mans, Cannon Street Rd and Cable St, 12.7.2017.
65. Interview with Martin Malin, 22.9.2022.
66. Elliott Morris, response to author's post on Facebook page Jewish Britain, 21.8.2022 by Elliott Morris.
67. Interview with Martin Malin, 30.12.2022.
68. *Ibid.*
69. Conversation with Stuart Singer, 21.4.2023.
70. Interview with Norman Bookbinder, 30.12.2022
71. Interview with Norman Bookbinder, 9.12.2022.
72. Interview with Norman Bookbinder, 5.12.2022.
73. Interview with Martin Malin, 30.12.2022.
74. Sarah died aged forty-seven in 1945 and David's mother remarried.
75. Information for this and following paragraphs provided by David Rein interviewed 4.5.2023.
76. Interview with David Rein, 4.5.2023. David changed his name by deed poll on his return from National Service.
77. David's father later opened a butcher's shop in New Cavendish Street in the West End of London and in 1960 naturalised as a British citizen, *ibid.*
78. Interview with Rochelle Berlyn, 26.8.2022.
79. Interview with Norman Bookbinder, 30.12.2022.
80. Benita Singer, post on Facebook page Memories of Petticoat Lane and the Surrounding Area, 1.9.2016.
81. Benita Singer was made redundant after the Golders Green restaurant was sold to Jonathan Tapper. Interview with Stuart Singer, 2.5.2023.
82. Conversation with Alan Jacobs, 20.4.2023.
83. Interview with Stuart Singer, 2.5.2023.
84. *Ibid.* Stuart took over from Alf Davies, partner with the large Jewish accountancy firm, Stoy Hayward, based in Baker Street, who had been the Bloom's accountants for many years.
85. Interview with Norman Bookbinder, 5.12.2022.
86. Interview with Norman Bookbinder, 30.12.2022.
87. Until David Gilbert went into business with Norman Bookbinder, he had his own meat products business in North Finchley, Gilbert's Kosher Meats Technology, serving the expanding convenience food market, which was separate from but worked closely with his father's traditional family firm. *JC*, 9.7.1982.
88. *JC*, 19.1.1996.
89. Interview with Norman Bookbinder, 5.12.2022.
90. *JC*, 15.7.1977.
91. Interview with Norman Bookbinder, 9.12.2022.
92. *JC*, 2.9.1988.

93. See https://youngandfoodish.com/top-5-salt-beef-sandwiches-in-london/ The business moved to Monkville Parade in Temple Fortune, initially run by his son, also named Chris.
94. David Sax, *Save the Deli, In Search of the Best Pastrami and Rye and the Heart of the Jewish Delicatessen* (Toronto: McClelland and Stewart Ltd, 2010), p.228.
95. Interview with Michael Georgiou, 3.4.2023.
96. *Ibid.*
97. See Sax, *Save the Deli*, p.227.
98. *Ibid.*, p.227.
99. Interview with David Rein, 2.5.2023. From the 1950s onwards, a Maltese community clustered south of Whitechapel Road and around Cable Street. Some of its members made their way to work at Blooms.
100. Copy of the will dated 1951, obtained from the Probate Search Service, https://probatesearch.service.gov.uk/).
101. Interview with Martin Malin, 30.12.2022.
102. Interview with Martin Malin, 22.9.2022.
103. See Chapter Eight.
104. Interview with Martin Malin, 3.11.2022.
105. See Chapter Eight.
106. Interview with Vivienne Thompson, 25.5.2023.
107. Interview with Martin Malin, 9.4.2023.
108. *JC*, 3.1.1986.
109. Copy of 'Particulars of Terms of Employment' for Josef Bojm provided by Paula Allen, 11.12.2022.
110. Interview with Norman Bookbinder, 5.12.2022.
111. Nick Callaghan, post on Facebook page Memories of Hessel, Langdale Mans, Cannon Street Rd and Cable St, 18.7.2021.
112. Interview with Jeremy Dein, 7.9.2022.
113. See further information on Lou Dein in Chapter Eight.
114. See Chapter Six.

Chapter Eight

The Waiters

From Bloom's early years, the waiters were the stars of the show, and very few people sharing their memories of Blooms fail to mention the waiters. They were simultaneously loved and reviled. Above all, they are remembered for their rudeness and off-hand attitude towards customers, whatever their background and station in life. In 1966, the journalist Simon Jenkins wrote: 'From the welcome, "Sit there and wait until I'm ready.", to the final slamming down of the bill, the customer was the enemy.'[1] Bryan Eli comments: 'No *nouvelle cuisine* there [at Blooms], but you could always be sure of some juicy insults.'[2] One writer summed up the 'phenomenally grumpy' waiters as follows:

> Bickering, grumbling, confronting, insulting, and seemingly affronted by the very fact that you had chosen to eat there, it was like being served by a coterie of particularly stroppy cab drivers whom you've asked to take you to South London.[3]

When the Aldgate restaurant closed in 1996, writing in *The Independent*, Will Bennett commented: 'Never again will its famously surly waiters treat customers torn between the Vienna sausages and the fried *gefilte* fish with abrupt scorn.'[4]

Few diners were fazed by the brusqueness of the waiters. Adrienne Nee-chessis Hardwood recollects: 'The main event in Blooms was THE WAITERS. Everybody loved the rudeness of these people. Nobody got offended and expected them to be just the way they were.'[5] The more seasoned Bloom's diners were a good match for the waiters, such as John Goldman: After the Bloom's waiter brought my soup, I asked him to taste it. "Why, didn't you order it?" I repeated, "Taste it." He asked where the spoon was. It was then that I smiled at him!'[6]

Similarly, Helen Freedman recalls that when she once went into the restaurant with her family and wanted her small children to share a Coca-Cola:

> The waiter brought one glass, so I asked for another. "That's not allowed," he said. So, I tipped out the napkin from a glass on the table and poured in some of the Coke. "You can't do that!" roared the waiter. "Too late," I said.[7]

The less battle-hardened tourists and occasional visitors were not so *au fait* with the ways of the waiters and sometimes engaged in seemingly pointless and acrimonious debates about matters, such as about the naming of the food they were served. Jan Shure once wrote in the *Jewish Chronicle* about American tourists arguing long and loudly with a Bloom's waiter about the differences between salt beef and pastrami.[8]

Despite the legendary rudeness of the waiters, people returned to eat at Blooms again and again. In fact, for many people the waiters were the very reason for going to Blooms, or at least were regarded as being an integral part of the Bloom's experience. David Newman says: 'From what I remember, you only went to Blooms in order to be insulted by the waiters',[9] and Geoff Weinberg comments: 'The "unusual" service was part of the charm.'[10] However, not everybody was so tolerant. Looking back in 2010, the food critic, Jay Rayner commented:

> I always found the rudeness of the service absolutely baffling. If I am being really cruel, it was a gift to the antisemites. If people went there and found it funny when they were abused, then they're mugs. What's the point of spending money on it?[11]

In the waiters' defence, some commentators recognised that Jews were not always the easiest of customers. After spending a day with the Bloom's waiters in 1988, Lee Levitt commented: 'Serving Jewish customers tends to be more exacting than I imagine the average waitering job is ... Jewish customers, perhaps more than most, can be demanding and impatient.'[12] Others have explained that most diners were able to discriminate between what were intended to be gratuitously offensive comments or intentionally bad service and what was designed to appeal to a common way of interacting, the raised voices and sarcasm of Yiddish immigrant culture.[13] The behaviour of the waiters, which became the trademark of the Aldgate restaurant, was transferred to Golders Green, although perhaps with less energy and panache, a replica rather than the 'real thing'.

The Bloom's waiters became renowned amongst both the Jewish and non-Jewish communities, and eventually across the world. As a result, many newspaper articles were dedicated to their idiosyncratic ways, often referred to as a 'pantomime' or a 'performance'. The author, columnist, editor and theatre critic Simon Blumenfeld once wrote about his visit to Blooms with Danny Kaye when he (Danny Kaye) was appearing in London:

> Inside was Bloom's repertory company, waiters who must have been at heart actors. They took their jobs seriously, not as a profession but as a vocation. Moishe, the headwaiter, a burly Lithuanian, approached our table. "Yes?" Danny looked around. "Where's the menu?" "No menu," said Moishe stoutly. "I am here. You tell me. I bring." "A menu," said Danny firmly, "I'd like to read the menu." "Dis is a restaurant," Moishe rebuked him, as though speaking to a child. "You come here to eat. So, eat. You want to read, then you go next door to the Whitechapel Library." End of Blooms, Act I.[14]

The Bloom's waiter experience commenced at the front door of the restaurant, where diners were greeted by the waiters tussling with each other in a bid for their custom. The disputes were particularly heated when someone arrived who was known to be 'a good tipper': 'They shouted: "My customer! My customer!"'[15] Philip Baigel recalls:

> When you showed up for your relaxing Sunday family lunch, you were immediately accosted by a bevy of waiters, vying for your attention, and trying quite forcibly to direct you towards

> their tables. It was reminiscent of arriving at some developing world airport, where you were surrounded by dodgy taxi drivers and street hawkers fighting for your attention and custom.[16]

The victorious waiter would apparently '*schlepp* [pull] you by the lapels and drag you into a seat'.[17]

Illustration 6: Bloom's waiters inside the Aldgate restaurant. Copyright Beverley-Jane Stewart.

The waiters were allocated specific tables, according to their status and skills. The head waiters generally had tables numbered one and two just inside the entrance to the restaurant. This gave them the first pick of the customers. For many years, a long-standing waiter named Costa (said to have been a 'big gambler', who often popped out of the restaurant to place a bet on a horse[18]) served the large tables at the back of the restaurant since he had a reputation for being able to carry enormous trays full of food on his upraised hands and was therefore nicknamed 'Bucket Hands'.[19] On occasion, the waiters deigned to work as a team, helping each other if some tables were busier than others. Having witnessed the waiters in action, the *Jewish Chronicle* reporter Lee Levitt, commented: 'Serving four customers at a time, as some waiters do, is no mean feat. Akin to juggling, it requires a steady hand and a confidence born of long experience.'[20]

92. Bloom's waiter, Costa, June 1985. Courtesy of Ruth Plaut.

Customers sometimes managed to slip through the rugby scrum of waiters at the entrance to the dining area, making their own way to a preferred table. Such anarchy was looked upon with askance by the waiters. A *Jewish Chronicle* columnist once told this story:

> A friend of mine was anxious to meet the Yiddish poet Stencl a few weeks ago and we arranged to meet in Blooms. Stencl was on time, but my friend was late, so we sat down at a table to wait and immediately a red-face waiter bore down on us. "You can't sit here you know, it's a table for four." I explained that we were waiting for somebody, and he retreated to glare at us doubtfully from a distance. When a quarter of an hour passed and my friend did not appear, I ordered my meal and Stencl, who is an ailing man and eats like a canary, ordered his *lokshen* pudding and tea. At which the waiter's face turned the colour of Bloom's celebrated *borscht.* "Stop messing me about, you can't sit here." I was about to tell him to go to hell, but Stencl, a modest retiring man, who hates a scene, fled to a small table in the corner and I followed.[21]

The most regular customers were given more choice over seating arrangements; they were allowed to sit at 'their' table and to be served by 'their' waiter,[22] and it is rumoured that a particularly generous tip to a waiter would secure a favoured spot in the restaurant.

At the Golders Green restaurant, a member of the waiting staff would often be seen doing paperwork sitting at one of the dining tables, even though there were fewer tables there than in Aldgate. This increased the pressure on the other tables, especially at peak times. Carole May comments: 'Even if all the other tables were taken, it would never occur to them to vacate the table and offer it up to the waiting customers.'[23]

In most instances, customers were often barely allowed to take their seats before they were approached by a waiter to take their order, but at other times were ignored. In 1986, *The Good Food Guide* relayed an incident reported by one of their inspectors: 'I said: "Have you forgotten us?" The waiter said: "No." and walked off to take the order of someone who had arrived half an hour earlier.'[24]

While taking an order, the waiters rarely stopped to chat or exchange pleasantries unless there was something they wanted to know. Malcolm Westbury recalls: 'Jimmy, the head waiter, was as interested in asking us if we knew the result of the 1.30 at Kempton Park as he was in taking our order!'[25]

By the 1960s, Blooms had produced menus for customers to peruse, but the printed choices were often irrelevant. Stories abound of customers going through the process of consulting the menu, often deciding to order what they usually ate, only to be told by the waiter what they could or could not have. 'Martin Buber' recalls:

> … if they were "long" on something, the waiter would try to persuade the customer to order it. I once ordered X – can't remember what it was – and the waiter went into the whole routine of, "You have X if you want it, but me, no I wouldn't have that, I'd have Y. It's your choice, but I've seen how they cook X and, personally, I wouldn't have it I'd have … a very wise choice sir, you'll just love it!"[26]

Nicole Schlagman shares a similar story:

> Many years ago, I was in Blooms with my husband. When he ordered the mixed grill, the waiter advised the steak, which he said was particularly good. My husband still ordered the mixed grill. When the waiter arrived with the food it was the steak. There can't be many restaurants where the waiter decides what you are going to eat![27]

The waiters' apparent lack of concern for the wishes of their customers is illustrated by Mike Mendoza's recollection: 'I ordered a load of food for my lunch one day, but they forgot a dish. When I mentioned this to the waiter, he said, "You are fat enough. You don't need any more to eat.""[28] Another former diner tells this story about the perversity of the waiters:

> One hot summer evening my husband and two friends decided we really needed a good *heimische* meal at Blooms in Golders Green. That evening, we each ordered the house speciality – salt beef, *latkes* and the works. The waiter, in his own time, plonked a jug of tepid water on the table, at which point we asked for some ice. We waited five minutes and reminded him about the ice. He confirmed it was coming. Another five minutes and another reminder – "Yes, it's coming. We're busy." We were getting hotter and hotter, especially under the collar! After a quarter of an hour or so, a bowl of rice turned up on the table. We said, "Sorry, but we didn't order rice. Where's the ice?" The waiter responded, "Sorry, madam. There is no ice, so I brought you rice." We had no words![29]

Some customers were unwilling to be told what they could or could not eat. Geoffrey Alderman, the former *Jewish Chronicle* columnist and prominent Jewish historian, relates how he stood his ground:

> On one occasion, I went to the Aldgate restaurant with my wife Marion when she was heavily pregnant with our daughter Naomi. Marion did not want a heavy meal, just a plain omelette. The waiter said, "You can't have an omelette. We've got no eggs." So, I said, "What do you mean you've got no eggs?" The waiter told us that the restaurant had run out of eggs. Whether that was true or not, I don't know, but I went across the road to a supermarket, bought half a dozen eggs and I brought them back into Blooms. I told the waiter, "You can show these eggs to the *shomer* and then make my wife an omelette." And they did![30]

The food often arrived at breakneck speed and over the years, speed of service became an end in itself. Philip Baigel, a regular diner at the Golders Green restaurant comments:

> The speed at which the chicken soup and chopped liver arrived at your table gave me the impression that there must be a huge, constantly boiling cauldron of chicken soup and a chopped liver mountain secreted away in that "holy grail" of the kitchen. I never actually saw this mountain with my own eyes, but I was convinced it existed.[31]

Norman Bookbinder explains the reason for the rapid service:

> If a customer sat down and ordered a rib steak, Lou [Dein] told him he could not have one. He'd say something like, "Oh sir, you don't want the steak this week. I had a steak for lunch yesterday and it broke my teeth." This was because serving a steak would have meant him going back into the kitchen and telling the chef to prepare a rib steak. There would then have been a delay while the chef put the steak under the grill and waited for it to cook. As a result, Lou would have only been able to serve one set of customers in an hour when he wanted really to serve two people so he could get two tips. He therefore always encouraged customers to have the salt beef, which was ready on the block and could be served up in two minutes.[32]

On its way to the tables, the food was checked by a 'booker' sitting just outside the kitchen door. A tally sheet listed the names of the waiters working on a shift and recorded against each of their names the food that they had ordered from the kitchen and its price. Family members or the restaurant manager sometimes booked out the food, but one of the regular bookers (first in Aldgate and later in Golders Green) was a man named Bernie Abrahams, another old school friend of Sidney Bloom.[33] The system was that the waiters took the money from the customers and at the end of a shift, they gave the amount recorded on the tally sheet to a family member or the restaurant manager. This is confirmed by Sandra Shelton Adler, whose uncle was a booker: 'My uncle was in charge of the bills. In those days the waiters took the money from the customers, and it all had to be sorted out at the end of the evening.'[34]

It was this booking system, a form of internal auditing, that might have given rise to the often-repeated story that the waiters were self-employed, that they purchased the food they ordered from the kitchen and then recouped the cost from their customers. Research presents a different picture. The families of former Bloom's waiters are adamant that their relatives were paid a salary from which tax was deducted and they made a decent living because of the tips they received. They did indeed collect the money from the customers because for many years there was no cashier in the restaurant. Jeremy Dein, one of Lou Dein's two sons, maintains: 'My father was definitely paid a wage. He collected the cost of the meals ordered by his customers and later paid it to Mr or Mrs Bloom, or to whoever was on duty, keeping his tips because at this time there were no service or cover charges.'[35]

In addition, members of the Bloom family have sometimes been quoted as saying that the story of the waiters being self-employed, albeit a compelling one, is not correct. In 1988, Jonathan Tapper, then general manager of the Aldgate restaurant, asserted that 'the waiters do not work on commission, though they do receive tips from customers', and rejected the rumour that the waiters bought the food then sold it to the customer, saying: 'We buy the meat and we sell it.'[36]

However, there is some evidence to suggest that, earlier in the company's history, the waiters were self-employed, which may be another source of the widely held belief that this was always the case. Marsha Bloom (née Shack) is certain that her father, Connie Shack, who was one of the first Bloom's waiters (see later in this chapter), bought the food and then charged the customer.[37] Her recollection is supported by David Franks: 'My dad worked there pre-war. He told me that to stop the waiters fiddling, they had to pay the kitchen to get the food out and then it was up to the waiter to get his money back from the punters.'[38] It is possible that this practice was discontinued in 1963 with the introduction of the new employment legislation mentioned in Chapter Seven, requiring regular staff to be issued with contracts and paid a wage.

There are stories of the waiters sometimes 'rounding up' the price of a meal in order to earn extra money, but the Bloom family must have been aware of this practice since the food menus included a line at the bottom, encouraging customers to check their bills against the prices given on the menu. It read: 'Patrons are respectfully requested to check their bill against the prices on the menu.'[39]

Once the food arrived at the tables, it was served with little finesse: 'The food was virtually tossed at the table. It was the stuff of legend.'[40] The diners were also encouraged by the waiters to eat their food as quickly as possible. Regular diners knew not to put down their cutlery before they had fished eating to avoid their plates being whisked away. There was no question of a leisurely meal. Barry Shamplin recollects: 'If you weren't eating quickly enough, a waiter would come along and try to take your plate away saying, "Come on, I've got a living to make!"'[41] Ben Azai once commented in the *Jewish Chronicle*: 'Blooms gives me the impression of a circus with every waiter employed as a ringmaster to whip as many people as possible through the hoop in the shortest possible time,'[42] and Marilyn Lovell says: 'It wasn't the sort of place you went to for a special event. You were encouraged to eat as quickly as possible and go.'[43]

After the diners had been encouraged to leave, the table that they had occupied was cleared with great alacrity to make way for the next customers. Philip Baigel recalls:

> If you happen to be sharing a table meant for four people with another couple of diners, and they finished their meal (or the waiter decided they had finished their meal!), within a nano-second, their half of the table had a new (and almost clean) tablecloth and cutlery, and so on, regardless of any interference with the two other people at the table who were still eating their meal.[44]

Laurel Nygate recalls that in 1968, her husband proposed to her in Blooms restaurant: 'He had to do it very quickly before they cleared his plate away!',[45] and Lilian Dulberg comments: 'There was, and still is, a saying when you go to a restaurant and the table is cleared too quickly: "Did that waiter work for Blooms?"'[46] The table clearing process was sometimes quite rudimentary:

> And the other thing they used to do was that they used to come out and not necessarily clean the table They would just take their serving napkin, throw it around a few times, knocking all the bits and pieces from the last people onto the floor. That was how they cleared the table.[47]

It is also rumoured that when clearing a table, the waiters sometimes 'recycled' bread that customers had not eaten, placing the plate of unconsumed bread it on a newly laid table.

Although the waiters were keen to serve as many customers as possible, they did not want the diners to depart so speedily that they neglected to leave a tip. The waiters held firm views on what constituted an appropriate tip and did not hesitate to say so when a tip did not reach their expectations. George Rollinson recalls:

> When I first met my partner, I took her to Bloom's restaurant. Someone left without giving the waiters what they [the waiters] considered to be a proper tip. Talking aloud amongst themselves, they made sure that the rest of the customers got the message.[48]

Sheila Finestone shares a similar story:

> In about 1978, when I had been married for a short time, my husband and I went to Blooms one Sunday for lunch. We had the full traditional works served by an awful waiter. We left a tip – I can't recall exactly how much – and walked out of the restaurant. We were followed by the waiter, who pushed at us the money we had given him, screaming: "You two obviously need this tip more than I do!"[49]

The waiters knew which customers were likely to leave generous tips and they were treated accordingly. The waiters would 'go the extra mile' for those whom they knew to be good tippers. After a bill had been settled and the tip proffered, the waiters would be 'pulling the seats away from underneath the customers', ushering them towards the door and calling the next customers to take a table.[50] They were apparently not interested in receiving feedback from their diners:

> My mum and dad took us to the Aldgate branch occasionally for a special treat. One time, at the end of the meal, my mum told the waiter, "That was the best salt beef sandwich I ever had." He looked at her and shrugged as if to say, "What's that to me?"[51]

Customers arriving early in a shift were served by waiters wearing their smart uniform of black trousers and bow ties and pristine white jackets, emblazoned with the Bloom's logo and to which a badge was pinned giving the waiter's name. Alan Dein comments: 'Their uniforms helped to elevate the dining experience to being a special event, and gave the waiters the appearance of belonging to some kind of fraternity,'[52] and Marilyn Lovell says: 'They were smart looking but always miserable!'[53] Diners who arrived later were greeted by waiters who were somewhat dishevelled and whose jackets and serving napkins bore the evidence of the many meals they had served during the course of a shift.

The waiters worked very long shifts. During the week, they arrived well before lunch to prepare the restaurant, worked through the lunchtime trade until mid-afternoon when they had a few hours rest before returning to the restaurant for the dinner trade. Those waiters living nearby were able to go home for a break, but those who lived further away found other ways of relaxing during their down time. The long-standing waiter Lou Dein (see below) lived in Gants Hill, but he had several friends in the East End, with whom he socialised during his break. His son, Jeremy, comments: 'They probably went for a bet or a drink.'[54] Several of the waiters were chain-smokers and were often to be seen in their less busy moments smoking outside the two restaurants.

93. Waiters outside Bloom's Restaurant, Whitechapel High Street, 1980. Right to left: Milton Charalambous, waiter, 'BooBoo' (surname unknown), counter staff, Konge (surname unknown), waiter, Lou Dein. Reproduction licensed by Paul Trevor.

The waiters sometimes also smoked inside the restaurant. Deborah Ezekiel relates this story:

> Back in the early 1990s, my husband and I went to the Blooms in Golders Green. In those days, smoking was still allowed in restaurants. My husband asked a waiter if it was okay to smoke at our table as no one else was doing so nearby. The waiter couldn't understand why my husband was asking permission. After a confused conversation, he took a cigarette from the box my husband was waving around and sat down at our table and smoked it.[55]

On a Sunday, the busiest day in the restaurants in both Golders Green and Aldgate, there were more waiters working (about a dozen waiters compared to six on weekdays), and they had shorter breaks, running in 'perpetual motion' between the tables and the kitchen. Jon Trevor recalls: 'I loved the waiter called Stan, who was always rushing unless you mentioned West Ham',[56] and Alan Doctors remembers Lou Dein 'rushing through the restaurant with overfilled plates of hot chicken soup, *lokshen* and *kreplach*, spilling soup as he went'.[57]

The restaurant kitchen closed between 8pm and 9pm and, determined to make their way home at a reasonable hour, the waiters hurried the last diners along. Jeremy Dein remembers his father used to say to those who sat down after 7.30pm and asked to see the dessert menu after they had finished their main course: 'Look, can you hurry up, I've got to get home to see my children.'[58] The waiters' shifts were even longer at *Pesach* when the waiters worked from 10am until midnight. Dawdling diners were encouraged to leave by the tired waiters: 'They not only wiped the tables while you were still eating, but they also put the chairs on the tables to get you to go.'[59]

Despite the exercise they had rushing around the restaurant, the waiters were not generally noted for their general level of fitness. The exception was the waiter named Savvas Toufexis, a Greek Cypriot, who had served in the British Army during the Second World War. He had made a point of remaining fit, and for several years he entered a competition that was part of the annual Soho Festival that raised money for charity. The competition entailed waiters running around Soho, carrying trays of plates and glasses laden with food and drink. Savvas won the competition for two years in succession.[60]

94. Savvas Toufexis, the Bloom's waiter who won the 'Round Soho Race' two years running. Courtesy of Martin Malin.

Although they had a reputation for being 'snippy', the waiters also had a softer side. David Long remembers how one of the waiters kindly offered to change the wheel of his father's car when they once went to lunch at Blooms in the late 1960s and arrived with a flat tyre: 'It was a nice gesture since we normally went to the Cosmo!'[61]

Most of the waiters loved children, even if they were rude to the adults. They often presented their young customers with a 'I'm a Bloom's Beefeater' badge at the end of a meal (see Plates Section, Plate 4).[62] Ross Dooley has happy memories of playing chess at the back of the restaurant with one of the older waiters named Max Strum (originally Moses Max Shtrom) while his family enjoyed their meals.[63] Max, who was a German refugee from Halberstadt, appears to have been rather different from the other waiters: 'He was perhaps more cultured and better educated; he did not gamble or bet on the horses.'[64] Marsha Bloom, the daughter of the waiter Connie Shack (see more below), recalls that on a Friday afternoon when the restaurant closed early, she would cycle to Blooms to meet her father: 'My stabilisers were always breaking and when I arrived, several of the waiters came out to fix them.'[65] Frances Shillings also tells a story about the softer side of the Bloom's waiters:

> I always enjoyed the food and the last time I ate there I was pregnant. Amongst the food that I ordered was a slice of stuffed *kishka*, but my fancy was for a whole one. A big smile appeared on the waiter's face when I told him I was pregnant, and he brought me a whole *kishka*. It was delicious, and afterwards he would not take any extra money for it. He told me to keep the money to put in the baby's piggy bank.[66]

The waiters were very kind to the nurses from the nearby hospitals who ate at the Aldgate restaurant. Anna Grantham-Gold recalls:

> When I was nursing at the London Jewish Hospital, I used to go regularly to Bloom's Aldgate restaurant. The waiters always made a fuss of me. When I went back after I was married with

> my husband, they remembered me. My husband commented that it was like having dinner with a celebrity.[67]

The homeless people in the vicinity knew that behind the rudeness of the waiters was a generosity that resulted in free food for the needy of any religion.[68]

However, despite their redeeming qualities and the fact that for many decades they had been a prime attraction (or were merely endured), by the time that the Aldgate restaurant closed in 1996 their charm was wearing thin. The *Jewish Chronicle* reporter, Jan Shure, commented that the 'Fawlty-esque' and 'dour-humoured waiters' were no longer seen as being 'conducive to romance and relaxation' sought by assimilated Jews.[69] Such views appear to have become even stronger by the final years of the restaurant in Golders Green when Geoffrey Alderman commented: 'I do not want to be told in a suburban restaurant in 2007 that my guests and I must gobble up our dinner in 90 minutes because there may be other customers waiting for the table.'[70]

95. The Turkish Cypriot Waiter, Konge, 1981. Courtesy of Ruth Plaut.

96. Peter Nicholas, 1981, Bloom's waiter and general manager, *c.* 1985. Courtesy of Ruth Plaut.

The Best-Remembered Waiters

Connie Shack

A large proportion of the waiters employed by Bloom's remained with the company for many years, some of them for several decades, notwithstanding the hard work, their long hours and the difficult customers they had to handle. Jeremy Dein recalls: 'The team of waiters that I knew during the years that I was growing up and well into my twenties were the same. They were all there for a long, long time.'[71] When he was interviewed by the *Jewish Chronicle* columnist Monty Modlyn in 1981, Connie Shack, by then working elsewhere, was quoted as saying: 'Monty, can you imagine being a waiter at Blooms for sixteen years – what humour, what patience.'[72]

Conan Shack, always known as 'Connie', was born in Whitechapel on 16 August 1922.[73] He attended the Jews' Free School in Bell Lane with Sidney Bloom in the late 1920s and early 1930s, and they had remained lifelong friends. During the Second World War, Connie served in the army and saw active service in Italy and Greece. He became the honorary secretary of the Jewish Services Club in

Athens.[74] Connie worked as a waiter for Blooms as a very young man in the restaurant at 2 Brick Lane, and he was one of the first waiters employed by Sidney Bloom when the new restaurant opened in Whitechapel High Street in 1952.[75] Connie's brother, Ben, worked in Bloom's factory in Wentworth Street.

During the 16 years Connie worked at Blooms in Aldgate, he became many customers' favourite waiter, with some diners being prepared to queue for a long time to be served at his tables, which were on the left of the restaurant. He was described as having 'a smiling, good-humoured and effervescent personality', and was 'known throughout the London Jewish community'.[76] His wartime service in Greece proved to be useful when he was working with the Greek-speaking waiters at Blooms. His daughter, Marsha Bloom, comments: 'They didn't know he could speak Greek, but he was able to tell when they were saying something uncomplimentary about him or the other Jewish waiters. My father always stuck up for the waiter known as "Little Danny", when he was being teased by the Greek Cypriots.'[77]

By the time Connie left Blooms in 1968, he had served customers from all over the world, including Sophie Tucker.[78] He is remembered as the 'waiter with the spoons' since he kept a supply of spoons in his back pocket. People recall that the other waiters could be heard shouting across the restaurant to Connie, asking him to pass them a dessert or serving spoon.[79] Although he worked long hours at Blooms, Connie also had a number of other part-time jobs to earn extra money to support his family.[80] For a short time, he left Blooms to work for the Jewish-owned Isow's restaurant in Soho: 'There was a brief falling out of some kind but he was soon persuaded to return to Blooms.'[81]

While he was still working at Blooms, Connie set up his own catering company, Conmore Caterers, in association with Lou Morrison, who had previously worked in the wine trade. Lou Morrison had been one of Connie's regular customers at Blooms and had always insisted on being served by Connie.[82] When the company became established, Connie left Blooms and, with the help of the Federation of Synagogues, he opened what became known as the Kosher Luncheon Club (mentioned in previous chapters) in the Morris Kasler Hall at the rear of the Great Garden Street Synagogue in Greatorex Street (formerly Great Garden Street).[83] Connie was the 'hands-on manager' and Lou Morrison dealt with the finances.

Connie ran the Kosher Luncheon Club for approaching 25 years with the help of his wife Minnie, who cooked the soups and desserts, and his daughter Marsha, who was one of the waitresses and also the driver when Lou Morrison was not around, since Connie never drove.[84] It is interesting that having worked for many years as part of an exclusively male team of waiters at Blooms, Connie employed only waitresses. The Kosher Luncheon Club became a celebrated institution and was particularly popular with the older Jews who remained in the East End. It was also frequented by local businesspeople and had a reputation as being a place where 'deals were done'.[85] Unlike Blooms, the luncheon club was 'milky' (dairy and fish; no meat) and served mainly fried fish and salads. It was often said that Connie 'fried the best fish in the East End'.[86]

Connie remained a close friend of Sidney and Evelyn Bloom and he and his wife were regularly asked to Bloom family celebrations,[87] along with Joe Mintz, (originally from South Africa), another Bloom's waiter, who was also a close family friend.[88]

97. Connie Shack. Courtesy of Marsha Bloom, his daughter.

In 1961 the Shack family moved from their home on the corner of Brick Lane and Woodseer Street in the East End to Gants Hill, where Connie became involved in various charities and was a prominent member of the 'Beehive Lane' synagogue (officially Cranbrook United Synagogue). He died in King George's Hospital in Ilford on 22 September 1995.[89] Over 400 people attended his funeral.[90]

Lou Dein

No book on the history of Blooms would be complete without saying more about Louis (known as 'Lou') Dein, who has been mentioned several times earlier in this chapter. Lou was born at 30 Langdale Mansions in Samuel Street in the East End of London on 15 August 1919.[91] His father, Abraham Dein, was a tobacco cutter working for the retail tobacconist, Major Drapkin and Co, located at 90 Middlesex Street.[92] Abraham, who was born in Odessa, came to England with his wife Fanny (originally Feige Rosnick) from Kishinev (now named Chișinău) where Fanny was born. Israel, Lou's oldest surviving sibling, was born in Kishinev. Lou was one of seven children, including his twin sister, Ada. The family moved from the East End to West Ham during the 1920s, where Lou grew up.[93]

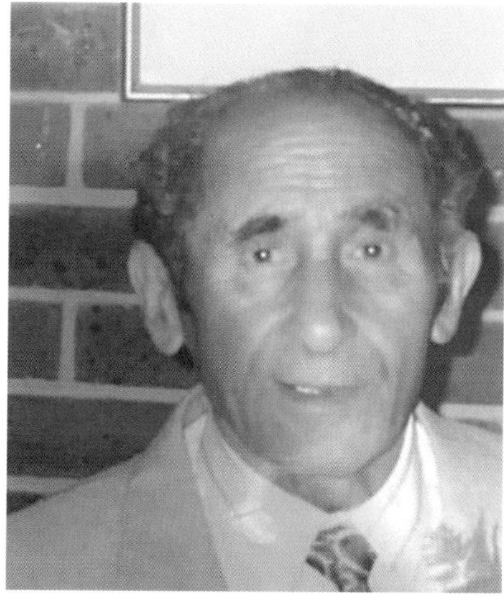

98. Long-standing waiter, Louis ('Lou') Dein. Courtesy of Jeremy Dein, his son.

From his childhood, Lou was an 'ostentatious character', with 'the thickest cockney accent you could ever imagine'.[94] It is not known what he did for a living immediately after he left school, but prior to the Second World War he joined the regular army; he was not conscripted. During the war, he became a sergeant and spent almost three years in a prisoner-of-war camp, having been captured while attempting to save the life of a fellow soldier. When Lou was demobbed, he tried out many jobs. He became a barber and then the manager of a dance hall in East London, which is where he met his wife, Sylvia Adelman. Lou and Sylvia married in Willesden in 1958 and set up home in Gants Hill. They had two sons: Simon, who was born in 1959 and Jeremy, who was born in 1960.

Shortly after his marriage, Lou went to work in Bloom's Aldgate restaurant, and over the years he became the firm's most legendary waiter, known by diners from across the world. Lou is remembered for his particularly shambolic approach to serving food, always having his thumb in the bowl of soup, and dropping food from overloaded plates on his journey from the kitchen to the table. He is also remembered for his unkempt appearance ('He was a bit of a *schloch*, with his ruffled hair and hunched shoulders'[95]); his tendency to be over-familiar and to share with his customers unsavoury details of his ailments, including the corns on his feet; not hesitating to point out when a tip was not acceptable, saying, 'I have a family to raise, next time go and sit on someone else's table'; and not being above telling a sob story to secure a good tip. When he was promoted to head waiter, Lou sometimes plied queuing diners with cocktail Viennas, 'but woe betide them if they dared to take more than one.'[96] Lou worked hard and he wanted people to know it. Vivienne Thompson recalls that, on occasion, 'Lou would dip his hand in the cucumber barrel and wipe the brine on his forehead to show Mr Bloom that he was *shvitzing* [sweating] from his labours.'[97]

Lou was devoted to his family and was very proud of his two sons, often speaking about them to his regular customers. Former Bloom's diners marvel at the fact that Simon became a prominent psychiatrist and Jeremy became a leading criminal barrister. Lou used the contacts he made in the restaurant to further his sons' careers.

Jeremy Dein tells the story of how his father approached the many Jewish barristers who ate their lunch at Blooms to obtain a pupillage for him and was successful in securing an opening with the well-known QC, Eldred Tabachnik, then practising at the 11 Kings Bench Walk chambers: 'I well remember that I had my interview for my pupillage, secured by my father, sitting in the back of Bloom's restaurant.'[98] A regular customer, Anna Grantham-Gold (see previous mention), proved to be a useful contact for Lou's son Simon.

> My favourite waiter was Lou. He was always really kind and looked after me very well. He asked me if one of his sons could come and look round the London Jewish Hospital where I worked as he wanted to become a doctor. I organised that and he did indeed become a doctor, specialising in psychiatry.[99]

Ian Gold shares this memory of Lou:

> Lou served in the war with my uncle, and they remained friends. I was in Blooms once when Leon Brittan came in and was obviously having some business meeting over a meal Lou interrupted and started showing him photos of one of his sons graduating. So funny and so innocent ....[100]

Lou had his own inimitable way of dealing with fussy customers: 'If someone grumbled to my father that the *lokshen* soup was not hot enough, he would say something like "Well, lucky for you, then it won't burn your tongue."'[101] The writer Robert Elms once told this Lou Dein story:

> My favourite story of Bloom's hideous rudeness concerns a man who had ordered mashed potato with his chopped liver or tongue, but instead received boiled potatoes. Upon politely pointing this out to Lou, the famously ferocious waiter, Lou picked up the man's fork from the table and proceeded to crush the spuds while shouting, "You want mashed potatoes, I'll give you mashed potatoes."[102]

Lou apparently had a razor-sharp wit, delivered with a 'Buster Keaton-like, deadpan face'. A former diner, 'Martin Buber', recalls: 'I once took an American to Blooms who wanted *matzoh* ball soup, or as we call them *kneidlach*. "Do you have *matzoh* balls," he asked Lou the waiter. "No, my back is killing me today," came back the quick-as-a-flash reply.'[103] Lou's son comments: 'He was not educated, but he was certainly a sharp cookie.'[104]

Lou's hours were long, and the journey to and from the East End was an arduous one. He never drove and his journey involved taking a bus and train: 'He would ring my mother when he was leaving work and she would collect him at Gants Hill station.'[105] All this meant that Lou had little time or energy for leisure activities. However, he was a fanatical West Ham supporter. Jeremy Dein again recollects: 'The club was embedded in his DNA, as it became for me. We barely missed going to a game together. In fact, the last time I saw him was at a West Ham game.'[106] Lou often told his sons that he almost became a player for the club, having been a member of the West Ham Boys' team. Alan Jacobs, a former taxi driver, who travelled the country with Lou to watch West Ham matches, recalls Lou's kindness: 'On Sunday afternoons we often used to go to the East End to visit my *Bubbe*. Lou always wanted me to call into the restaurant where he had a big bag of food ready waiting for me. I gave him a few quid and there would be enough food to feed us for a week.'[107]

Lou had a fine singing voice, which he used to serenade the queues of people waiting to eat at the restaurant with renditions of the songs of Al Jolson and Tom Jones: 'He was like a 1930s crooner, you could hear him all the way down the street and the customers just loved it.'[108] Norman Bookbinder comments: 'He had a wonderful voice and people used to get out of their Rolls Royce cars, even when it was raining, to hear him sing.'[109] Towards the end of his career, Lou starred on the BBC programme *That's Life*. The presenter, Esther Rantzen, visited the restaurant and Lou was filmed singing 'My Yiddishe Momma', Sophie Tucker's most famous song. He also featured in a book about the TV series, *Eastenders*.[110]

Lou enjoyed working at Blooms, especially the opportunity it gave him to meet Jews of all nationalities and the many well-known personalities who dined at the restaurant.[111] His son recalls: 'He was always bringing home the autographs of the famous people he served.'[112] Although it was not allowed, he also regularly took home bags of food from the restaurant: 'Of course it wasn't good for us and was full of calories, but we loved it.'[113]

Lou worked for Blooms for thirty-four years, latterly as the head waiter, patrolling the four tables at the front of the Aldgate restaurant. He held the keys to the restaurant and went in early to open the premises. On occasion, he was asked to work at the Bloom's Golders Green restaurant, but he did not like it there: 'Golders Green was not the place for him.'[114] Alan Dein comments: 'Uncle Lou was like a character from Central Casting. He was made for the role of the typical surly waiter. He had a face that was evocative of the old Jewish East End. He was a sort of role model for the Greek Cypriot waiters he worked with. He was born an East Ender and that's where he wanted to be.'[115] Lou was often teased mercilessly by the other waiters and other Bloom's staff, but he always took it in good part.[116]

Lou decided to retire when a workplace accident hindered his ability to navigate the gangways. He was also aware that Bloom's heyday was over, which saddened him greatly. During his short retirement, Lou was 'deeply hurt' not to have had any contact from the Bloom family.[117] He died in Ilford on 30 March 1998, aged seventy-eight.

Leon Nicholas

By the final years of the Golders Green restaurant, the 'eclectic' team of waiters (and interestingly, by this time also a waitress), included several who had worked for Blooms for a long time, and they were regarded with affection by their regular customers. Many of the long-standing waiters had acquired nicknames.[118] 'The Walrus' was Leon Nicholas, a Greek Cypriot, named for his distinctive moustache. Jeremy Dein describes Leon Nicholas as a 'tall man with a big moustache. He had a wide smile and a twinkle in his eye.'[119] David Ziants recalls that Leon Nicholas prided himself on having a good memory for the people he served:

> Leon always welcomed our family back and he always seemed to remember the relationship between us. He'd say: "Nice to see you with grandchildren" or something similar. I think one of the last times I was there [in the Golders Green restaurant], my grandparents were either no longer alive or not in a position to be there. Instead, I was with the second husband of a great aunt, who late in life had become involved with his only known family in London – myself and my brother. So, when Leon saw us with a man who was not the "normal grandfather", he was really put off balance.[120]

Leon worked at the Aldgate restaurant for many years before transferring to Golders Green to become the long-standing head waiter there. During the 1980s, many people believed he was called Leo because the 'n' had fallen off his name badge.[121]

Despite Leon's loyalty to the firm, he is said to have had a rather tempestuous relationship with some members of the Bloom family, especially Evelyn Bloom, and the restaurant managers. Stories are told of Leon regularly taking umbrage, ripping off his white coat and storming out of the restaurant, threatening never to return.[122] He worked for Blooms for so long that he absorbed Jewish culture and knew more Yiddish than many of his Jewish customers.[123] He is remembered for his 'slapdash' approach to table service, Sheila Davies recalls:

> When we once took our children and my parents to the Blooms in Golders Green, we were served by Leon the waiter who was very famous there. Harriet, my daughter, couldn't finish her plate, so Leon lifted her plate and scraped the food onto my father's plate without asking him and said: "Don't waste it. You have it." My father was a very "English Gentleman" and you should have seen his face![124]

Leon had a son named Nick, who was also a Bloom's waiter, working alongside his father in Aldgate and then in Golders Green. Apparently, Nick was a very different character from his father –

'much less outgoing and not nearly as flamboyant.'[125] Leon worked at the Golders Green restaurant until he was well into his seventies, leaving just a few years before its closure.

99. Leon Nicholas, *c*. 2000, long-standing head waiter at the Bloom's restaurant in Aldgate and then at the Golders Green restaurant. Image courtesy of Martin Malin.

Waiter Jokes

Over time, as the Bloom's waiters became legendary, they became the source of a large stock of jokes akin to the genre 'Waiter, waiter there's a fly in my soup', or 'Mr Cohen went into a restaurant …' These jokes are still retold to this day. A small selection is set out below:

Customer: 'I asked for my steak to be rare, and it was well done.
Waiter: 'Thank you, sir. We always aim to please.'[126]

Bloom's waiter: 'Would you like dinner?'
Customer: 'What are my choices?'
Waiter: 'Yes, or no.'[127]

Bloom's restaurant often used to get groups of Jewish *bubba*s coming into the restaurant to eat. So, what did the waiter ask them? 'Is ANYTHING okay?'[128]

I once made the mistake of asking a waiter if the orange juice was fresh. 'It was when they put it in the carton, sir.'[129]

Six months after a Bloom's waiter died, his widow went to see a medium since she had promised her husband that she would try to contact him in the great beyond. During the séance, the widow was sure that she saw her husband standing in the corner of the room, dressed in his waiter's outfit. 'Arnold', she cried. 'Come closer and speak to me!' A ghostly voice drifted from the corner, 'I can't, it's not my table.'[130]

The Bloom's waiter served the *gefilte* fish with his finger resting on top of it. When the diner questioned him about this, he replied, 'You want it to fall on the floor again?'[131]

An elderly Israeli man goes into Blooms. He meets the owner at the entrance and is handed on to a waiter who shows him to his table. The waiter is Chinese. In fluent Yiddish, the waiter talks him through the menu and the specials, while chatting about the weather. The man eats and then takes the bill to the owner at the counter. 'That waiter speaks excellent Yiddish,' he said. 'Shush!' says Mr Bloom. 'He thinks it's English!'[32]

Customer: 'Waiter, there are flies in my *kneidlach* soup.'
Waiter: 'Look, sir, there are schmucks [stupid or foolish people] in my restaurant and do you hear me complaining!'[133]

Notes

1. Quoted in https://web.archive.org/web/20061018044059/http://www.eastlondonhistory.com/blooms.htm.
2. Post by Brian Ell on Facebook page The Jewish East End of London, 19.11.2018.
3. Robert Elms, *London Made us, A Memoir of a Shape-Shifting City* (digital edition) (Canongate Books, 2019).
4. Will Bennett, *The Independent*, 23.2.1996.
5. Adrienne Nee-chessis Harwood, response to author's post on Facebook page Jewish Britain, 21.8.2022.
6. John Goldman, response to author's post on *ibid.*, 21.8.2022.
7. Helen Freedman, post on Facebook page Memories of Petticoat Lane and Surrounding Areas, 1.11.2016.
8. *JC*, 23.2.1996.
9. David Newman, post on Facebook page Memories of Hessel, Langdale Mans, Cannon Street Rd and Cable St, 12.7.2017.
10. Geoff Weinberg, post on *ibid.*, 19.3.2021.
11. *JC*, 18.6.2010.
12. *JC*, 2.9.1988.
13. Interview with Alan Dein, 3.1.2023.
14. 'Dooally Danny's Visit to Bloomin' Britain', *The Stage*, 27.11.2003.
15. Interview with Geoffrey Alderman, 31.10.2022.
16. Email from Philip Baigel, 8.11.2022.
17. Interview with Geoffrey Alderman, 31.10.2022.
18. Email from Vivienne Thompson, 21.5.2023.
19. Interview with Martin Malin, 30.12.2022.
20. *JC*, 2.9.1988.
21. *JC*, 9.3.1973.
22. *JC*, 16.7.1965.
23. Carole May, response to author's post on Facebook page Jewish Britain, 21.8.2022.
24. Reported in Drewq Smith (ed.), *The Good Food Guide 1986* (London: The Consumers' Association and Hodder and Stoughton, 1986), p.43.
25. Email from Malcolm Westbury, 14.12.2022.
26. Response to article in *The Times* by 'Martin Buber', 13.4.2020.
27. Nicole Schlagman, post on Facebook page The Jewish East End of London, 29.10.2016.
28. Mike Mendoza, post on Facebook page Jewish Britain, 15.5.2016.
29. Anonymous contributor by email, 20.8.2022.
30. Interview with Geoffrey Alderman, 31.10.2022.
31. Message from Philip Baigel, 14.11.2022.

32. Interview with Norman Bookbinder, 9.12.2022.
33. Interview with Martin Malin, 20.9.2022. The 'bookers' also oversaw the quantities of food that was sold at the delicatessen counter. On busy days, the bookers sat in the kitchen to free up a table.
34. Sandra Shelton Adler, post on Facebook page Memories of Hessel, Langdale Mans, Cannon Street Rd and Cable St, 29.11.2017. One of the other regular bookers in the 1960s was Michael Fuller mentioned in Chapter Seven.
35. Interview with Jeremy Dein, 7.9.2022.
36. *JC*, 2 .9.1988.
37. Interview with Marsha Bloom (née Shack), 13.12.2022. Also mentioned in an interview with Connie Stranton, 7.10.2022, a woman who dined at Blooms in the pre-war years.
38. David Franks, post on Facebook page The Jewish East End of Britain, 30.1.2018.
39. See copy of Bloom's menu kept by the Jewish Museum of London, reference number 2000.45.3.
40. Interview with Alan Dein, 22.8.2022.
41. Barry Shamplin, post on Facebook page You Don't Have to be Jewish, 1.6.2021.
42. *JC*, 9.3.1973.
43. Interview with Marilyn Lovell, 28.3.2023.
44. Message from Philip Baigel, 8.12.2022.
45. Laurel Nygate, post on Facebook page Jewish Britain, 21.8.2022.
46. Lillian Dulberg, post on *ibid.*, 21.8.2022
47. Interview with Philip Baigel, 7.12.2022.
48. George Rollinson, post on Facebook page East End of London and East London, 24.6.2021.
49. Post by Sheila Finesilver on Facebook page Jewish Britain, 15.5.2016.
50. Jeff Wright, post on Facebook page East London Days Gone By, 5.8.2021.
51. Response by Ivor Spitalnik to author's post on Facebook page Jewish Britain, 21.8.2022.
52. Interview with Alan Dein, 22.8.2022.
53. Interview with Marilyn Lovell, 28.3.2023.
54. Interview with Jeremy Dein, 7.9.2022.
55. Deborah Ezekiel, post on Facebook page Jewish Britain, 21.8.2022.
56. Post by Ian Trevor on Facebook page The Jewish East End of London, 25.5.2020.
57. Alan Doctors, post on Facebook page Memories of Hessel, Langdale Mans, Cannon Street Rd and Cable St, 12.7.2017.
58. Interview with Jeremy Dein, 7.9.2022.
59. Adele Liss, post on Facebook page The Jewish East End of London, 29.10.2016.

60. Conversation with Martin Malin, 1.12.2022.
61. David Long, post on Facebook page Jewish Historical Society of England, 8.9.2021.
62. Response to an article in *The Times* by 'EP2017', 13.4.2020.
63. Ross Dooley, post on Facebook page Memories of Petticoat Lane and the Surrounding Area, 14.4.2014.
64. Interview with Martin Malin, 20.9.2022. Max lived with his wife Gertrud ('Trudy') née Levinson, whom he had married in 1941 in Bethnal Green. They later lived in Woodford Green. He was a member of a close circle of émigrés who gathered in Robert's Restaurant in Commercial Road, which was renowned in the 1940s and 1950s as a meeting place for Continental Jews who had arrived in the East End having escaped from Nazism. Max emigrated to Israel where he died in 1998. Interview with Vivienne Thompson, 25.5.2023.
65. Interview with Marsha Bloom (née Shack), 13.12.2022.
66. Frances Shillings, post on Facebook page The Jewish East End of London, 29.10.2016.
67. Message from Anna Grantham-Gold, 21.8.2022.
68. 'Bob O' Job' in response to article in *The Times*, 13.4.2020.
69. *JC*, 23.2.1996.
70. *JC*, 19.10.2007.
71. Interview with Jeremy Dein, 7.9.2022.
72. *JC*, 4.9.1981.
73. Interview with Marsha Bloom (née Shack), 13.12.2022.
74. *JC*, 15.10.1995. Connie served alongside Johnny Simons, Alan Sugar's father, and they remained firm friends.
75. Interview with Marsha Bloom (née Shack), 13.12.2022.
76. *JC*, 15.10.1995.
77. Interview with Marsha Bloom (née Shack), 13.12.2022.
78. See Chapter Nine.
79. Interview with Anthony Gerstler, 6.9.2022.
80. Interview with Marsha Bloom (née Shack), 13.12.2022.
81. *Ibid.*
82. Conversation with Marsha Bloom (née Shack), 27.3.2023.
83. The Kosher Luncheon Club opened on 21 October 1968.
84. Conversation with Marsha Bloom (née Shack), 27.3.2023.
85. Interview with Marsha Bloom (née Shack), 13.12.2022.
86. See Pam Fox, *History in the Baking, The Rinkoff Story* (London: Rinkoff Bakery, 2019).
87. Interview with Marsha Bloom (née Shack), 13.12.2022.
88. Interview with Martin Malin, 30.12.2022.
89. *JC*, 15.10.1995. The Shack family lived close to Lou Dein and his family.
90. Conversation with Marsha Bloom (née Shack), 27.3.2023.

91. Birth record, Ancestry.co.uk.
92. 1921 Census, Findmypast.
93. Death record for Abraham Dein, Ancestry.co.uk.
94. Interview with Jeremy Dein, 7.9.2022.
95. Alan Dein, Lou's great nephew, quoted in Rachel Lichtenstein, *On Brick Lane*, (London: Penguin Books, 2007), p.104.
96. Kevin Greenland, post on Facebook page East London in Days Gone By, 30.6.2020.
97. Email from Vivienne Thompson, 21.5.2023.
98. Interview with Jeremy Dein, 7.9.2022.
99. Anna-Grantham Gold, response to author's post on Facebook page Jewish Britain, 21.8.2022.
100. Ian Gold, post on Facebook page The London East End of London, 29.11.206.
101. Interview with Jeremy Dein, 7.9.2022.
102. See Elms, *London Made Us*.
103. Response to article in *The Times* by 'Martin Buber', 13.4.2020.
104. Interview with Jeremy Dein, 7.9.2022.
105. *Ibid.*
106. *Ibid.*
107. Conversation with Alan Jacobs, 20.4.2023.
108. Interview with Martin Malin, 20.9.2022.
109. Interview with Norman Bookbinder, 9.12.2022.
110. Interview with Jeremy Dein, 7.9.2022.
111. Obituary for Louis Dein, *JC*, 8.5.1998.
112. Interview with Jeremy Dein, 7.9.2022.
113. *Ibid.*
114. *Ibid.*
115. Interview with Alan Dein, 3.1.2023.
116. Interview with Martin Malin, 20.9.2022.
117. Interview with Jeremy Dein, 7.9.2022.
118. Email from Philip Baigel, 14.11.2022.
119. Interview with Jeremy Dein, 7.9.2022.
120. David Ziants, post on Facebook page The Jewish East End of London, 29.11.2016.
121. Ellis Rosen, post on *ibid.*, 19.11.2019.
122. Ricky Tobias, post on Facebook page Memories of Hessel, Langdale Mans, Cannon Street Rd and Cable St, 16.4.2020.
123. Interview with Alan Dein, 3.1.2023.
124. Email from Sheila Davies, 5.5.2023.
125. Interview with Martin Malin, 20.9.2022.
126. Response by '2022RAM' to article on Blooms in *The Times*, 13.4.2020.
127. *Ibid.*

128. *Ibid.*
129. Response by Stanley Cohen in *ibid.*
130. Joe Barnett, post on the Facebook page The Jewish East End of London, 29.10.2016.
131. Response by 'Times Reader' to article on Blooms in *The Times*, 13.4.2020.
132. Message from Brian Ingram, 5.3.2023.
133. Response by 'Frisky' to article on Blooms in *The Times*, 13.4.2020.

Chapter Nine

Bloom's Customers

Charting changes in the clientele of Bloom's restaurant and in the profile of the customer base for the firm's manufactured products provides a clear reflection of what was happening in Anglo-Jewish history. At any point in the ninety years that Blooms endured, examining the make-up of the firm's custom offers a snapshot of what was happening socially, economically and demographically in the Jewish community.

The Early Years

When in 1920 Morris Bloom obtained premises for producing and selling the meat products with which he had been experimenting – his own brand of Vienna sausages and salt beef made to his own recipe – his customers would have been almost exclusively immigrants like himself, originating from various parts of the Russian Empire, and living and working in the crowded streets of Whitechapel and Spitalfields.

The food establishments that existed in the second decade of the twentieth century when Morris Bloom was in the process of establishing his business did not generally have a good reputation. An article appearing in the *Jewish Chronicle* on 3 March 1911 declared that 'ninety per cent of these establishments are unworthy of the name of restaurant or, indeed of kosher'. According to the writer, many were 'unwholesome' and served 'uninviting fare' on 'ill-kept tables'. It is unlikely that struggling immigrants would have been attracted to the 'more respectable kosher restaurants' also referred to in the article since they would have been seen as the preserve of established Jewish elite and beyond their budget. It is also doubtful that, with their poor reputation, already assimilated Jews would have frequented an establishment like Blooms. This is confirmed by an article in *The Caterer* for 15 July 1914, which opined quite bluntly that the 'better class of Restaurants' were for 'English Jews' and the establishments in the East End were only 'frequented by aliens from Eastern Europe'.[1]

However, the Jewish East End was already beginning to change as a result of severe bombing of the area during the First World War. Many Jews lost their homes and were forced to relocate elsewhere. Upward mobility in the Jewish community was also becoming increasingly evident. Jews had mainly come to Britain to achieve a better life, if not for themselves, then for their children. A significant number were now leaving the congested streets of Whitechapel and Spitalfields, moving to the more salubrious areas of Ilford, Clapton and Stamford Hill or, for the more affluent, to the leafy suburbs of north-west London, especially Golders Green. Between 1905 and 1914 the Jewish population of the East End reduced from 125,000 to 100,000.[2]

Due to this dispersal, by the 1920s the Jewish East End community had become almost entirely working class and largely made up of those immigrants still struggling to make a living and to prevent themselves from falling into poverty. The fact that Blooms remained open from dawn until the early hours of the morning reflected the fact that many of its earliest customers were often working almost intolerable hours to earn enough to feed themselves and their families. Blooms sought to provide for this clientele by offering large portions of tasty food at a moderate price; the emphasis was on sustenance rather than cuisine.[3] While some customers might have had the time to sit and enjoy a meal, most of the trade is likely to have been for takeaway food to save time. Blooms (and similar establishments) can therefore be seen as a precursor of the fast-food eateries of today.

The food was only one aspect of why Jews frequented Bloom's café; it also allowed them to remain connected with the world that they had left behind, a world that they were not yet ready to forsake completely. The atmosphere that pervaded establishments such as Blooms in the 1920s was captured evocatively by the writer Emanuel Litvinoff in his book *Journey Through a Small Planet*: '… the cafés resounded with arguments about anarchism and communism, waged over glasses of lemon tea.'[4] Blooms was the type of place where people met their friends and relations and quickly became a nexus of Jewish secular networks – social, economic, psychological and informational. Diners at Morris and Rebecca's café would have sat together on benches at wooden tables reminiscent of the inns that they might have frequented in Eastern Europe, looking for jobs and matchmaking.[5]

At this time, Bloom's customers are likely to have been largely single men, who were seeking to earn as much money as possible so that they could afford to pay for their families to join them or to marry. They would probably have been living in shared rooms or sleeping in the same premises where they worked (as Morris Bloom had done), which made food preparation difficult. Most would also have lacked the skills to provide food for themselves.

Illustration 7: Inside Bloom's original café at 58 Brick Lane. Copyright Beverley-Jane Stewart.

The Jewish tradition in Eastern Europe was to eat at home rather than in public, referred to in Yiddish as *oyessen* meaning eating out.[6] The inns in Eastern Europe were largely places for obtaining liquid refreshment, for socialising and providing accommodation for travellers, rather than commercial eating establishments.[7] However, far from home, the experience of Yiddish-speaking immigrants sitting down to consume food together would have been a bonding experience, helping to mitigate their home sickness. The provision of food by people who had experienced the same scarcities and deprivation as their customers would have enhanced this sense of community.

Although the immigrants might have been looking for a new life, some of the customers would probably have seen eating at Blooms as a temporary measure since it was the accepted role of women to cook for their family, which accounts for the large number of kosher butchers that existed in the East End at this time. However, women might have numbered amongst the takeaway customers if they were also working to sustain family life. This was the reality of immigrant survival, even if it was frowned upon by more traditional and less sympathetic co-religionists.

Given Morris and Rebecca's lifelong philanthropy, some of the first customers might have eaten for free if they were impoverished and hungry, even if they were given only leftover scraps of food. Jewish communal bodies and wealthy philanthropists organised charities for the poor, such as the Jewish Soup Kitchen in Brune Street, but not all initiatives came from the top of the community.

As Bloom's reputation spread, which it quickly did, the café started to attract customers from outside the immediate vicinity, but for the first decade of its operation it remained essentially a neighbourhood establishment. The expansion of the firm's custom beyond the East End was more apparent in its manufacturing activities. In the early years, it is probable that the enterprising Morris Bloom sold bulk amounts of his Viennas and salt beef to barrow sellers, who distributed them around the neighbourhood and beyond. The fact that the products were salted and preserved was key since there was no refrigeration in those days as was the fact that the food was easy to eat by hand, probably wrapped in newspaper. The main customers of the barrow sellers are likely to have been Jews employed in the sweatshops, who ate as they worked at their sewing machines or as they took short breaks, standing on street corners. In the latter part of the 1920s, Blooms started to invest in its own delivery vehicles, allowing Morris to sell his products to a network of kosher butchers and delicatessens opening across London as Jews moved out of the East End. The foundations for what became a significant wholesale business had been laid.

The Pre-War Years

As already mentioned, by the 1930s, the Jewish quarter of the East End became more intensely working class, as those able to do so left in increasing numbers for other parts of London. However, to begin with, many Jews who were now residing elsewhere still had their businesses – shops, workshops, factories, warehouses and professional practices – or jobs in the East End to which they travelled daily. These commuters provided a ready clientele for Blooms, as did those visiting family and friends who had remained in the East End. As a result, trade is likely to have been brisk throughout the day and the restaurant's customers less homogenous than they had been a decade earlier. Blooms was now catering for some diners who were significantly more affluent than its first customers.

Although the Jewish community was dispersing apace, the number of Jews living in the East End was still significant. As Jews relocated, many cafés, restaurants and food shops followed them, which meant that Blooms and similar establishments remaining in the East End experienced an increase in trade. However, there is no evidence of the snaking queues that came to epitomise Bloom's restaurant in the post-war years.[8]

In the late 1920s and early 1930s, something else was happening in the Jewish community that had an impact on Bloom's custom: a generation of Jews who had been born and brought up in Britain, and who had been exposed to anglicising measures, was now coming of age. Although this second generation generally maintained their social and spatial distance from non-Jews, continuing to conduct their work and social activities in a predominantly Jewish environment, their aspirations and outlook were noticeably different from those of their parents.

Judging from the few contemporary accounts that exist, although in the pre-war years Bloom's clientele remained exclusively Jewish, the ambience of the café turned restaurant became less reminiscent of an Eastern European inn, which is likely to have appealed to the younger generation. Bloom's advertisements in the *Jewish Chronicle* during the 1930s appear to have been framed specifically to attract second-generation Jews seeking a congenial gathering place where they could feel at home and escape from the virulent antisemitism of the pre-war years, of which they bore the main brunt. The advertisements placed an emphasis on the restaurant being a place for meeting as well as eating: 'Make Blooms your rendezvous for a delightfully appetising meal at a moderate cost'[9] and 'Meet your friends at Blooms for lunch, order what you like, and you will like what you order'.[10]

The changing ambience is also likely to have found favour with first-generation immigrants still living in the East End. Although they shared Yiddish folkways and a recent Eastern European past, their attachment to the places from which they came and the struggles that had defined them were becoming less potent, and the need for reminders of their origins less pressing. With expectations changing, it would have become less frowned upon for women to buy prepared food from a takeaway, especially a kosher one. However, for still-struggling, post-1880 migrants living in the vicinity of Brick Lane, Blooms restaurant remained a vital lifeline rather than somewhere to celebrate a successful transition from Eastern Europe.

The growing popularity of Blooms during the 1930s did not escape the attention of prominent Jews, both in this country and abroad. One of Morris Bloom's proudest moments in the pre-war years was when the famous American-Jewish professional heavyweight boxer, Max Baer, ate at the restaurant at 2 Brick Lane to celebrate his win against Ben Foord in London in May 1937. This was covered in the press.

MAX BAER.

Cheered By East End Crowds.

Remarkable scenes were witnessed in the East of London last evening when Max Baer, conqueror of Ben Foord, celebrated his victory at Bloom's Restaurant. There were many well-known personalities in the boxing world present.

Long before the guests were due to arrive the roads were congested by hundreds of people anxious to obtain a glimpse, or possibly an autograph, of the ex-world champion.

Baer had a great reception from the crowd, his car being mobbed on arrival. Many times during the dinner given in his honour there were cries from the thousands of people outside of "We want Maxie."

A microphone was fitted up, and eventually the American spoke to the crowd thanking them for the wonderful reception that had been given him.

100. *Yorkshire Observer,* 1 June 1937.

The event was also recorded in an iconic photograph. From their expressions, it is clear that Morris and Rebecca were delighted to have such a celebrity dine with them; it was a public endorsement for their hard endeavours of approaching twenty years. Interestingly, included in the photograph is 'Baby' Rita Carr, who sang at the Aldgate restaurant when it opened in 1952. Morris and his family are looking decidedly prosperous, with Morris clearly in the process of becoming what Claude Montefiore referred to as an 'Englishman of the Jewish Persuasion'.[11]

101. Max Baer at Bloom's restaurant in 1937. Sitting, left to right: Max Baer,' Baby Rita Carr, Morris Bloom, Buddy Baer. Standing left to right: Isadore Green, editor of the Weekly Sporting Review, Rebecca Bloom, Sylvia Bloom, Maxie Solomons, boxing promoter and Sidney Bloom. Photo courtesy of the *Jewish Chronicle*, 23 February 1996.

As described in Chapter Three, the success of the restaurant was enabled by an increase in demand for Bloom's meat products, leading first to the acquisition of additional premises at 2 Brick Lane and subsequently to the opening of a 'state-of-the-art' factory in Wentworth Street in 1932. With its increased production levels and expanding fleet of vehicles, Blooms was well placed to supply the ever-increasing number of butchers and delicatessens opening in other parts of London.

Bloom's Customers During and Immediately After the Second World War

Illustration 8: Blooms open for business during the Blitz. Copyright Beverley-Jane Stewart.

As a result of the evacuation of Jews from the East End and the departure of Jews to fight on the frontline, combined with the privations of war, Blooms experienced a downturn in trade at the beginning of the Second World War. Some evacuees returned to the East End, but the heavy bombing of the East End during the Blitz resulted in the forced relocation of many of those who had frequented Bloom's restaurant and customers who had regularly purchased goods from the Wentworth Street premises. Disruption to transport links caused by the bombing meant that it was difficult for people to travel to the East End from elsewhere, keen as the former loyal customers might have been to partake of Bloom's food. However, Morris and Rebecca encouraged them to make the journey from wherever they were and were clearly determined to stay open to serve their customers whatever the difficulties involved.

Luncheon, Dinner, Supper, or just a tasty snack

North, South, East, or West—wherever you may be, book to Aldgate East Station, which is within three minutes' walk of Bloom's.

102. Extract from Bloom's wartime advertisement, *Jewish Chronicle*, 30 August 1940.

The impact of wartime measures, especially food and petrol rationing, would also have made it difficult for Blooms to maintain supplies to kosher butchers and delicatessens, but somehow the firm managed to obtain enough meat and other goods to do so. In addition, by maintaining its outside catering service throughout the war years, Blooms also ensured that its customers continued to receive food to celebrate family cycle events.[12]

Even after 2 Brick Lane was demolished by enemy bombing in 1941, Morris and Rebecca continued to provide meals for their customers from cramped space in the factory in Wentworth Street. They also explored ways of serving those who had left the East End. An advertisement placed in the *Jewish Chronicle* by the Kashrus

Commission provides the information that Bloom's factory (along with the other larger kosher food firms in the East End at the time, such as Barretts and Strongwaters and Raschburgs) was contributing to the war effort by preparing parcels of kosher food to be sent to evacuees and Jewish troops. This appears to have been a commercial as well as a communal venture since the parcels were offered for sale rather than free of charge.[13]

Customers of the Aldgate Restaurant in the 1950s and 1960s

The 1950s were a good decade for Britain in general and for its Jewish population in particular. There was a new monarch on the throne, the National Health Service had been established and the years of austerity and rationing came to an end. The mood was now much more hopeful than it had been in the years immediately following the end of the war. In general, but not uniformly, the Jewish community was becoming more affluent and many Jews had money to spend on luxuries, such as dining out. Although the rate of assimilation was much more rapid than it had been before the war, Jews were keen to spend time together in 'Jewish' places. At this point, Anglo-Jewry was both at its most numerous and its most homogenous, creating very favourable market conditions for Blooms.

Although the East End Jewish community had been reduced to a rump, the, resilient Jews who stayed in the area provided a niche market for Blooms, but a younger generation, now largely living elsewhere, swelled the ranks of Bloom's post-war customers, lured by the firm's effective marketing strategies. At this stage, a large proportion of those flocked to eat at the new restaurant in Whitechapel High Street, or to buy from its delicatessen counter, were people who still had direct links with the East End. In 1951, the year before the new restaurant opened, the contemporary commentator, A. B. Levy, wrote:

> ... the links between the East End and the greater community are unbroken: Jews and Jewesses keep on pouring into Aldgate and Stepney, by means of underground train, bus, taxi and

> those *kasher* [kosher] conveyances, the 647 and 653 trolleys, to buy or sell, study or teach, go to work or to play, arrange a burial or a marriage, visit a parent, ask a *shaaloh* [question on a religious matter], get a divorce, plan a *simcha*, or order a tombstone.[14]

Blooms provided all these people with somewhere to eat and meet. Already changing prior to the war, the new restaurant was no longer a neighbourhood eaterie.

People with businesses in the vicinity, many of whom were friends or business acquaintances of Sidney Bloom, regularly ate in the restaurant at lunchtime such as Jack Marks the fruit seller in Brick Lane, who supplied Blooms. Ruth Janis Williams recalls: 'My dad, Gerry Williams, also known as "Lord Williams of Lemon Street", used to eat there every day of his working life.'[16] One of the main elements of the lunchtime trade from businesspeople was the market traders, who owned or worked on the stalls in various street markets in the East End, but especially the Brick Lane Market. A review in the Good Food Guide noted that 'the clatter of the market traders' was 'music compared with other places' taped music'.[15] The market traders were also evident amongst the diners at Bloom's restaurant on a Sunday afternoon, the peak day for the street markets. Henry Goodman, who became a well-known actor, recalls:

> I worked on a stall in the East End when I was a kid; I was only about twelve or thirteen. I got up early on cold winter Sunday mornings to work on a watch stall. If we had a good day, we could go round the corner, by Aldgate East station, to get a really great salt beef sandwich. That's how I remember Blooms. It's a taste that lingers in my buds of a good day.[17]

In addition to the Jews with businesses in the East End, numbered amongst Bloom's lunchtime customers during the 1950s and 1960s were people working in offices, finance houses and law firms located in the nearby City of London and the areas adjacent to it. As a result, many deals were struck by diners sitting around the tables at the

Aldgate restaurant. Friday lunchtimes were particularly popular with City workers. Brian Scott Lee recalls:

> In the 1960s, I worked in Bunhill Row, just off City Road. Most Fridays we went to lunch at Blooms. On one occasion, the four of us were discussing where we would go that Saturday night, and someone suggested that we should go the Playboy *schpieller* [club]. An American guy turned to our table and said something like, "Don't be a bunch of *schmucks* [stupid people], you'll lose your money." It turned out that he was Victor Lownes [the head of Playboy Enterprises in the UK at that time]! Apparently, he also dined at Blooms on Fridays.[18]

Many East End and City business people did not dine at the restaurant at lunchtimes, but either bought takeaway food themselves or arranged for junior colleagues to collect food from Bloom's delicatessen counter. Charles Haslett recalls: 'I worked in Mansell Street in 1964 for a tailor's cutter. He used to send me to Blooms most days for a salt beef sandwich and *heimische* cucumber.'[19] Some businesspeople working further away sometimes sent a cab to collect their order,[20] but for others the pick-up arrangement was a grander affair. Pat Cook recalls: 'I always went and got my boss's salt beef sandwich at Blooms. His chauffeur took me in the Rolls.'[21]

Because of this business trade, there were long queues on weekday lunchtimes for the popular takeaway snacks. Helen Blairman recalls: 'The demand was so high that the deli counter in Aldgate was cleaned out every single day. We were unbelievably busy. Trade was constant. We had to make sure we took a break and had something to eat before the lunchtime rush because there would be no time to eat or rest once the rush started.'[22] Those who were short of time had to make sure that they were at Blooms before midday if they wanted to avoid standing in a long queue. Philip Luxembourg recalls:

> I left school at fifteen and one of my first jobs was in Godfried & Paul, a wholesale hosiery firm just opposite Blooms. I used

> to go backwards and forwards between the two. As customers came in, I was asked to go and get them a sandwich. I quite enjoyed doing this – it was a little outing and I liked standing in the queue with everybody else. It didn't matter what day of the week it was, there was always a long queue for the deli counter. It was this experience that initiated me into Blooms.[23]

If they could see that the salt beef was coming to an end, seasoned customers would miss their turn and go to the back of the queue because the meat on the new piece of salt beef that would be brought out was more succulent than the dried-out end of a slab.[24] While most people purchasing from the delicatessen counter bought food to eat elsewhere, a few stayed to make use of the eight bar stools that stood in front of the delicatessen counter: 'You could watch yourself eat your lunch in the big mirrors!'[25]

103. Interior of Aldgate restaurant showing takeaway counter with Joe Bojm and unknown woman, *c.* 1960, Courtesy of Paula Allen, Joe's daughter.

The business trade for the takeaway counter was supplemented by Jews living in the East End. Martine Kaufmann recalls: 'In those days we didn't eat out much, but I can remember queuing to get our takeaways from Bloom's delicatessen counter. I'm sure that they ignored us a bit! My mum liked the takeaways because it meant she did not have to cook.'[26] On Friday lunchtimes, just before the restaurant closed for *Shabbat*, some of the older and frailer Jews would go to Blooms to buy food to enjoy at home on a Friday evening as a weekly treat. Less wealthy pensioners were given the food for free.

Bloom's food was also a major attraction for young Jews living in the East End or nearby. Kelly Sherwood recalls: 'Oh, happy days for sure. We kids used to go in and ask for the skin of the smoked salmon to get the scrapings of the fish. Sometimes we were lucky, but other times we were told to b … off!'[27] Blooms was a particular attraction for the children, both Jewish and non-Jewish, attending the Canon Barnett primary school in Gunthorpe Street. At the end of the school day, they arrived at the rear of Blooms, hoping for free offerings from friendly kitchen staff,[28] which gave some of them a taste for Bloom's food. Barry Silkman recalls that when he was a little older, if he and his friends from the school had the money, they went into the restaurant and dined on *kreplach* soup, salt beef and chips with 'new green' cucumbers: 'We didn't know it then, but they were the best days of our life!'[29] An inspector who had submitted a review to *The Good Food Guide* said that his fondest childhood memories were of sitting with his family 'at the same tables, looking at the same view of Petticoat Lane on the walls, being served by the same waiters eating myself sideways'.[30]

Many of those Jews who had moved to the suburbs, or even further afield, still had relatives and friends living in the East End and either met them in Blooms (or dined at the restaurant having visited them), usually as family groups. Several people born during or just after the Second World War recall being taken there by their parents or grandparents (or more often a combination of both), who had previously lived in the East End. Ian Gold recalls: 'I remember going there on a Sunday for lunch with my grandma and family. It was the only restaurant we ever went to. If you were going out to eat it was always at Blooms!'[31]

For some young people, their early introduction to Blooms led to a loyalty to the restaurant spanning many decades. David

Ziants, who recalls going to Blooms in Aldgate with his parents and grandparents, was still eating with his own family in Blooms in Golders Green when it closed in 2010. The long-standing waiters who served him remembered him as a child.[32] Even some of those younger Jews who had 'married out' or left Judaism (and the number doing so was steadily growing at this time, much to the consternation of Jewish communal bodies) continued to visit Blooms as a reminder of their Jewish origins. After Ernest Leverett married Cicely Petley in All Saints Church in Old Buckingham in February 1954, the wedding reception, which was attended by thirty-five guests, was held at Blooms.[33]

Blooms was a popular venue for family celebrations, such as special birthdays, wedding anniversaries and *Bar Mitzvahs*, which were then less ostentatious and more family orientated than they later became. As previously mentioned, at the back of the restaurant there were large tables that were set aside for large, multigenerational gatherings.

At this point, the regular customers making the compulsive pilgrimage to the East End were very familiar with each other. Jacquie Braham Lynam remembers that her parents, who took her to Blooms on a regular basis, 'seemed to know at least half the other diners.'[34] Blooms offered its customers a prime opportunity for indulging in their propensity for playing 'Jewish Geography'. Alan Dein comments:

> When you went in, you were always likely to meet someone you knew and a conversation would ensue about where they lived, who their friends were, who their son went out with before he married, that kind of thing. If I'd been a bit older when I went there with my parents it might have felt a bit claustrophobic, but at the time it was great fun. The place exuded "Jewishness".[35]

When diners spotted someone whom they knew, they often rushed across the restaurant to greet them, adding to the already chaotic atmosphere of the place and making it difficult for the waiters to navigate the tables.[36]

However, not all families relished the hubbub of Bloom's restaurant, or could afford a sit-down meal. Some people who grew up during the 1960s, have retained fond memories of driving to Blooms with their parents to buy takeaway food and sitting in the family car, or in a nearby park, to devour it. Marilyn Lovell recalls that after a 'nostalgia trip' to the East End with her father and sister, they went to collect *latkes* and salt beef sandwiches from Blooms, which they ate in the car going home: 'We had a Humber Super Snipe, which had tables in the back. We used to put them down and devour the food we had bought from Blooms as we travelled. There wasn't a month went by without us making these trips.'[37]

As mentioned in a previous chapter, in its early years, the décor at Bloom's restaurant was 'basic', and some commentators have suggested that the table manners of some of its diners were not very polished either. Jack White tells this story:

> A man was eating chicken in Blooms, and he picked up the chicken in his hands and started noisily biting large lumps. One of the waiters said: "Please sir don't eat like that, you are upsetting the other customers." The coarse customer replied: "Don't worry, I've got permission to eat like this." "How come?" asked the waiter. "Well," replied the customer. "Last week I was at a wedding at the Savoy. I was eating chicken as I am today and the posh waiter said: "We at the Savoy do not allow such behaviour. In Blooms you can eat like that!"[38]

Adele Winston remembers that in the mid-1960s, the noted Jewish restaurant critic Anthony Blond once described the fun he had watching other diners eating at Blooms and commented that the way they ate informed his perception that Jews eat each meal as though it were their last.[39] Barbara Jacobs has shared a memory of watching Bloom's customers 'folding their sandwich in half and trying to get a pickle in their mouths at the same time'.[40] In a similar vein, Philip Baigel comments: 'A family outing to Bloom's restaurant on a Sunday was imbued with a theme that runs through most Jewish festivities: they tried to kill us; we survived; let's eat!'[41]

While Jews with roots in the East End formed the core of the Aldgate restaurant's initial trade, by the late 1950s it was already on the radar of well-known Jews, especially stars of the stage and the screen, both in Britain and America. Sophie Tucker, who in the pre-war years had dined at Feld's restaurant,[42] became a regular diner at Blooms and a friend of Sidney and Evelyn Bloom. Several of the offspring of the first waiters at the restaurant recall their fathers coming home with a copy of a Bloom's menu signed by Sophie Tucker.[43] The writer and columnist Simon Blumenfeld mentioned that, during the 1950s and 1960s, he had sometimes dined at Blooms with stars, such as Danny Kaye.[44] Reportedly, when Golda Meir, the soon-to-be prime minister of Israel, visited Blooms in 1967, the entire restaurant stood up in her honour.[45]

Amongst those dining in the restaurant at this time were famous people from the past. Simon Schama, who became a renowned historian, tells this story of when he was once eating with his father, Arthur, at Blooms in the early 1960s:

> … mid *kreplach*, Arthur dropped his spoon and nodded his head at a grey-haired gent with a smooshed-in snozz sitting quietly on his own slicing his way through a plate of tongue. "Come on," said Arthur. "Let's pay our respects." "Who is he?" I asked. "Kid Lewis?" "Kid *Lewis*?" Arthur snorted, all incredulous. "That *schlemiel* [fool] signed up with Mosley before he saw the light! That's the other Kid, the good one, Jackie boy, Kid *Berg*." The Kid, born Judah Bergman, who went to America and laid Kid Chocolate and Mushy Callahan low, before he was through himself in 1939. We went over, my father treating Kid Berg like they'd grown up together, and the quiet man with the sideways nose stopped eating his tongue, took a sip of lemon tea, and smiled as he received the noisy accolade.[46]

There were also some important but less prominent diners. In 1965, Sidney Bloom commented that it was not uncommon to see a Russian trade delegation eating at Blooms.[47]

The custom of Blooms during the 1950s and 1960s was at its most diverse on Sundays. In 1962, Tamar Freedman wrote in the *Jewish Chronicle*:

> Today's [Bloom's] customers are as mixed as the menu offered to them. Particularly on Sunday mornings with the attractions of Petticoat Lane just around the corner, the restaurant is crammed with a miscellany of people. An entire cup final winning team has been known to celebrate its victory with *cholent* [see Glossary of Eastern European Jewish Foods at Appendix One] all round on Sunday morning. There is a British field marshal who can occasionally be observed enjoying a plate of chopped liver, followed by *lokshen* soup, and pop fans can observe one of their favourites digging into a salt beef sandwich.[48]

As its reputation as the 'go-to' restaurant spread, long queues often formed outside on Sundays. People arrived earlier and earlier to beat the queues, only to be find that they were already too late. Philip Baigel comments: 'It sometimes seemed that the whole world had got there before us. A whole gamut of guzzlers must have fancied a full lunch at breakfast time!'[49] However, others recall that queuing was part of the 'Bloom's experience' and that diners enjoyed chatting with other people in the queue: 'They all knew each other, so it was a great meeting place. They were willing to wait an hour or even longer to get a table.'[50] Neville Filar recalls that the queuing customers were sometimes entertained by a man named Jonnie Fields 'who did his jumping over the matchbox trick for threepenny pieces', performing on a piece of cardboard.[51] There was also a busker named Dixie, who well into his eighties, 'danced and shuffled on an old sandboard to earn a few coppers.'[52]

Favourite and famous customers, and apparently also pregnant women, were sometimes whisked to the front of the queue, or smuggled in through the back entrance. Anthony Gerstler recalls: 'We were frequent customers, so if we got there and it was very busy, the staff slipped us in through the back where the coats were kept, we didn't have to queue'.[53] However, some prominent customers, including Charlie Chaplin (who was a friend of the Bloom family), insisted on standing in line like everybody else, even when he was invited by the owners to jump the queue.[54]

The Golders Green Restaurant

When it opened in 1965, the clientele of the Golders Green restaurant was notably different from that in Aldgate. During the week, the new restaurant was frequented by younger people living in Golders Green or nearby, many of whom had been born in London, but whose connections to the East End were not as strong as those dining in Aldgate. By this time, the Jewish community of Golders Green was very diverse in its origins rather than people who had arrived there principally from the East End.[55] As a result, the new Bloom's restaurant was also a dining venue for Jews who had settled in Golders Green from a range of provincial cities, from places outside the United Kingdom, including South Africa, India and various Middle Eastern and North African countries, along with a number of former continental refugees and Holocaust survivors. However, Jews living in the suburbs of north and north-east London did not often make the trek to Golders Green, seeing it as the domain of the *nouveaux riches*. They felt more at home in the Aldgate restaurant, which they continued to visit.[56]

Far fewer celebrities frequented the Golders Green restaurant than they did the parent restaurant in Aldgate. A notable exception was the playwright and actor Steven Berkoff, who had grown up in the East End of London. He once commented quite forthrightly:

> I went to the one [Bloom's restaurant] in Golders Green and I thought it was very good. It was pleasant, homely and nourishing and full of those flavours that we like … I used to go to Blooms in Whitechapel. I didn't like it much there, I thought it had a very bad atmosphere. It was sleazy and indifferent – there was no commitment to food.[57]

Other famous people who frequented the Golders Green restaurant in its early days were the actor Ian Hendry, Jack Cohen, founder of the Tesco supermarket chain and his wife Cissy, the actors Jill Gascoine and her husband Alfred Molina, the actor Tony Booth (father-in-law of the future prime minister, Tony Blair) and the football manager Joe Kinnear.[58]

The picture on Sundays was rather different from weekdays, when people came from far and wide. One former Bloom's employee tells the story of two couples from Manchester who, on the first Sunday after the extension of the M6 motorway connecting it to the M1 was opened, drove their cars all the way from Manchester to Golders Green, had lunch at Blooms and then drove home again.[59] During the restaurant's early years of trading, the shopping parades in Golders Green Road were in their heyday and Sunday was the peak shopping day.[60] People came from across London and even further afield to shop there and then queued to eat at Blooms.

Bloom's Wholesale Customers in the 1950s and 1960s

Although they were not as visible as in the restaurants, there were significant changes in the customer base for Bloom's manufacturing and wholesale activities in the post-war years. By this time, only small amounts of Bloom's products were sold to retail customers at the front door of the factory in Wentworth Street, mainly to local people living close to the factory or to friends of the Bloom family.[61] However, there was an exponential growth in the non-restaurant side of the business when Blooms opened its cannery in 1960. The canned goods generated trade throughout the country rather than being largely confined to London and the Home Counties as it had been before the Second World War. The canned goods allowed people who were not able to visit the restaurant, or those who had developed a taste for Bloom's food because of dining there occasionally, to enjoy Bloom's signature dishes.

Also in huge demand was Bloom's wide range of packaged goods, which needed little preparation and were easy to store in the domestic fridges or freezers that were increasingly commonplace. Packaged goods had become available as the result of new technological developments, such as vacuum packing and freeze drying, which had originally been developed as a way of sending food to troops overseas. The American historian Ted Merwin has commented: 'Ironically these technologies were modern analogues of the smoking, salting and drying and spicing that ancient peoples had used to preserve meat fish and vegetables.'[62]

In addition to the dispersal of the Jewish population, the popularity of the canned and packaged goods was also the result of more women entering the labour market and having less time for the domestic roles they had traditionally played: 'It was like Bloom's food was just waiting to be packaged. My mum always had different types of their food in the fridge to provide quick meals.'[63] For many people, the packaged Bloom's goods meant not only having convenient access to the food they liked, but also seemed to be welcomed for their apparent cleanliness which, at the time, was seen as being greater than for fresh produce. These developments mirrored what was happening in the wider food industry.

New distribution networks were established by Blooms to enable its canned and packaged products to be delivered nationwide. Although it was not always viable for the firm to do so, Blooms aimed to ensure that its goods reached those areas where people had difficulty accessing kosher food.

BLOOM EVERYWHERE

INCIDENTALLY, did you know that you can buy BLOOM'S goods anywhere in London and certainly the majority of the larger towns in the United Kingdom. In fact they deliver by road, rail, sea and air.

So almost every part in the United Kingdom there is a spot where you can obtain BLOOM'S foods (90 per cent. of all Kosher Butchers stock them).

If there are families in some isolated parts of the country who require BLOOM'S *foods, a postal service, express post, is used to supply them. This is the service used to supply students at Universities and families in rural areas.*

Canned food, viennas, salamis, even roast chickens are sent to people living away from home and cannot get the food locally (often the family in London will 'phone up or send a postal order asking for the food to be sent on to a relation).

104. Extract from Bloom's 1960s marketing brochure. Courtesy of Jonathan Fishburn.

HOLIDAY FLATLETS AT COAST

HAVE you noticed that it's become popular over the last few years for families to go to Brighton or Westcliff or Bournemouth and to take over a small flat and do their own cooking. Once you get to the coast (say Brighton) you will find that between six to twelve butchers and grocers stock all BLOOM'S foods.

AND BLOOM'S have arranged such a fast service by passenger train that the goods are often there within an hour. They go on the train at London Bridge (for Brighton) or Waterloo (for Bournemouth). The food is then picked up and immediately placed in fridges. It's worth remembering this service when you next take a flat at the coast !

IT seems natural that on holiday, or at home, the Jewish housewife (or the young Jewish bride just starting a home) should plump for BLOOM'S

Their tinned food is something you can't always buy elsewhere.

105. Extract from 1960s Bloom's marketing brochure. Courtesy of Jonathan Fishburn.

During the 1950s, Blooms had started to supply the buoyant Jewish hotels and guest houses in Bournemouth, then the premier holiday destination or Jews. Bloom's signature Viennas served at the Cumberland Hotel after the regular cabaret on a Saturday night became legendary.[64] Later, the New Ambassador kosher hotel in the same resort became known as 'Blooms-on-Sea' because of the amount of Bloom's produce it served and because its menus were remarkably similar to those at Bloom's two London restaurants.

By the mid-1960s, Bloom's canned goods and its packaged products were also becoming popular with families who were now self-catering in increasing numbers at the coastal resorts commonly frequented by Jews. Blooms introduced what it referred to as a 'taxi-service' to transport orders to the resorts 'within a matter of hours' of the orders being received. The goods were transported by van to London Bridge (for Brighton) or to Waterloo (for Bournemouth) and picked up in the resort by the local kosher shopkeepers, who refrigerated the orders to await their collection by the customers.

Bloom's products were also sent to Jewish holiday camps, orphanages and hospitals across the country. Blooms was so committed to delivering its goods to those who wanted them that it even exported its canned and packaged goods overseas, building up a loyal following in Gibraltar, Ghana and Singapore.[65]

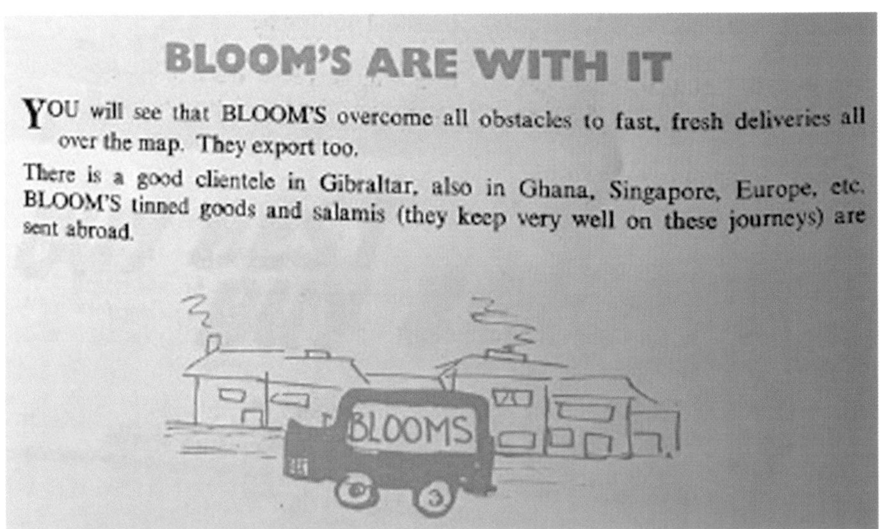

BLOOM'S ARE WITH IT

YOU will see that BLOOM'S overcome all obstacles to fast, fresh deliveries all over the map. They export too.

There is a good clientele in Gibraltar, also in Ghana, Singapore, Europe, etc. BLOOM'S tinned goods and salamis (they keep very well on these journeys) are sent abroad.

106. Extract from 1960s Bloom's marketing brochure. Courtesy of Jonathan Fishburn.

Bloom's marketing materials from the 1960s suggest that the company was keen to develop a new generation of customers amongst young families in a bid to make its success sustainable.

CHILDREN BLOOM ON IT

CHILDEN love nothing better than viennas and chips, or fried salami and eggs, and also when they go to school they ask mummy for salami sandwiches for lunch. Most children turn their noses up at chicken or steak, and even shoulder of lamb; they prefer viennas and chips, nice and hot. Children also love the old traditional frying sausage, or frankfurters, as a quick lunch.

DID *you know that supplies go to Kosher Holiday Camps and children get our good food that way? A large number of schools, private and L.C.C. are supplied with viennas, salami and pressed beef, etc. This has introduced* BLOOM'S *food to the children who really take to it.*

107. Extract from 1960s Bloom's marketing brochure. Courtesy of Jonathan Fishburn.

The Aldgate Customers in the 1970s and 1980s

During the 1970s, the Aldgate restaurant was still at its zenith and was continuing to attract celebrities and tourists and visitors to London from across the world. Geoffrey Alderman comments: 'It was in all the guidebooks. It was the "done thing" to go to Blooms.'[66] The restaurant was particularly popular with American tourists. A story is often told of the American tourist, who on arriving in London, hailed a taxi and gave 'The Beefeaters' as his destination. Without any ado, the taxi driver took him straight to Blooms in Aldgate.[67] Before the 1970s, there were few non-stop, scheduled flights from America to Israel and Americans wishing to travel there flew to London and transferred to an onward flight. When there was time in between their flights, some of the Americans made their way to the East End for a meal at Blooms before taking a taxi back to the airport.[68] Alan Jacobs, a former taxi driver, recalls taking American tourists to Blooms after giving them a 'whistle-stop tour' of the City of London. One of the people he took to Blooms several times when he was visiting London was the comedian, Jackie Mason.[69]

By the late 1960s, the number of Jewish stars, celebrities and prominent people eating at the Aldgate restaurant had increased significantly. The names frequently mentioned include: Dustin Hoffman, Barbra Streisand, the Marx brothers, Ron Moody, Alan Sugar, Elkan Allan, Ronnie Scott, Donald Pleasence and Warren Mitchell. Fiona Griffin recalls: 'My boss, the late agony aunt Marjorie Proops, used to take me there for lunch. Her chauffeur would drive us to Whitechapel from the old *Daily Mirror* building in Holborn Circus.'[70] Some of the 'show biz' diners were born locally, such as the singer Georgia Brown (born Lillian Klot), the song writer Lionel Bart (born Lionel Begleiter), the bandleader Joe Loss, who had played at the opening night of the restaurant in 1952, and the wealthy textile manufacturer and philanthropist Sir Harry Djanogly. In the evenings, before voting in the House of Commons, several Jewish MPs dined regularly at Blooms, including Gerald Kaufman, the Labour MP for two Manchester constituencies, who is said to have been 'very friendly', and Myer Galpern, the first Jewish MP in Glasgow and Deputy Speaker of the House of Commons.

Amongst the celebrities who frequented Blooms, there were many non-Jews, including members of the royal family, such as Princess Diana, one of whose favourite dishes was said to be Bloom's *borscht*, and Princess Margaret.[71] The roll call of celebrities who dined at Blooms at this time included footballers, such as Bobby Moore and, much to the Bloom family's delight, sometimes the whole of the Tottenham Hotspurs ('Spurs') football team, who apparently had a 'terrific weakness' for the *cholent.*[72] The Spurs team were sometimes treated to their meal by Sulky Gowers, the brother of one of the first Bloom's restaurant managers, Dick Gowers.[73] See Plates Section, Plate 12.

Also seen dining in Blooms were Elizabeth Taylor, with both Eddie Fisher and Richard Burton, Tom Cruise, Telly Savalas, John Cleese, Barbara Windsor, Hughie Green, Dickie Henderson, Arthur Askey and Donald Sutherland. When he was in town, Orson Welles often dropped into Blooms for a bowl of chicken soup with *lokshen*.[74] Barry Mingay, who worked in Osborn Street between 1976 and 1986, *lunched* at Blooms on a Friday and recalls:

> One Friday, Arthur Mullard was in Blooms and was being interviewed for a newspaper article. The place was buzzing and when the waiter asked him "What would you like today?" straight-faced, and in a very loud voice, he said, "What I'd like is a nice pork chop, but I might be in the wrong place!" The place erupted into laughter, and it took ages to calm down again.[75]

Stuart Singer recalls that the pop singer Marc Bolan dined at Blooms the night before he died in a road accident in 1977: 'My mother, who worked on the Bloom's counter served him and he gave her his autograph for me. It was shocking when I heard the news the next day.'[76] Stories are also told of the evening that Cliff Richard dined at Blooms. His fans heard about it, and a large crowd gathered outside the restaurant waiting for a glimpse of him. They were so excited that the front window of the restaurant was almost broken in the melée.[77]

The former prime minister, Tony Blair had a fondness for kosher food, and once held a birthday party at Blooms for his father-in-law, the actor Tony Booth.[78] It was subsequently reported in the *Jewish Chronicle* that Tony Blair had enjoyed 'the white thing with carrot on top [*gefilte* fish], salt beef and the potato *latkes*.'[79] Tony Blair was introduced to Blooms by a barrister friend, South African born Eldred Tabachnik, then President of the Board of Deputies of British Jews, who dined regularly at Blooms.[80] Frank Sinatra not only dined at the restaurant, but sometimes also rang the restaurant to have meals delivered to his hotel room at the Savoy. The story goes that, on one occasion, he failed to return to Blooms the silver platter on which his food had been served. Sidney Bloom was apparently not impressed.[81] Charlie Chaplin (previously mentioned) and his wife often dined at Blooms. Sylvia Moe tells this story about their friendliness:

> I remember Blooms so well, it was an annual treat for my father to take my extended family there on Sundays in the summer, and can you ever guess who was in there one year? Charlie Chaplin and his sweet wife Ooana, she saw that I recognised her and smiled back at me. As they left, she stopped by our table to wish me goodbye.[82]

Barry Din recalls seeing the wrestlers Jackie Pallo and Mick McManus going into Blooms together, which he found 'strange since they were always at loggerheads in the ring',[83] and Vivienne Thompson tells this story:

> My brother [Michael Fuller] worked for several years at Blooms and one night when I was there with him, Peter Sellers and Spike Milligan and three beautiful ladies came in for a meal. They sat and sat and made no move to leave. They eventually overstayed their welcome and Mr Bloom said to my brother

> that he should try telling them nicely that it was way past closing time. With his fabulous sense of humour, my brother went over to their table and asked them if they would like to join in with the Blooms theme tune. With that, we all stood up and sang *Goodnight Vienna*. They got it! They left a hefty tip and departed still laughing.[84]

Intriguingly, Jack Chandler comments: 'I sent my commissioned officers there to eat. They loved it!'[85] However, there were also some shadier celebrated characters who frequented Blooms, including the part-Jewish Kray twins (they had one Jewish grandparent), who had been groomed by the Jewish gangster Jack 'Spot' Comer (born Jacob Colmore) and associated with Curley Carr (see earlier mentions) and others operating on the fringes of East End gangs, such as Sulky Gowers the brother of the restaurant manager, Dick Gowers previously mentioned, and many other Jewish 'wheeler-dealers' – cardplayers, illegal bookies and their runners.[86] After the Kray twins were imprisoned, one of their wives visited the delicatessen counter every Thursday to pick up a salt beef sandwich to take to him in prison.[87]

Rochelle Berlyn, who worked on the Aldgate delicatessen counter, recalls underworld characters, who may have been Jack Spot and his minders (probably Morris Goldstein, known as 'Moishe Blueball', and Bernard Shlach, known as 'Sonny the Yank'), coming into the restaurant on several occasions and once witnessing a fracas at the rear of the premises, which she was told to ignore by Sidney Bloom.[89] It appears from these memories that, at this time, disreputable Jews were either discreetly admired or at least regarded as being part of the fabric of the community served by Blooms, which enabled them (the shady characters) to continue to operate within their Jewish milieu.

Despite the restaurant's celebrity diners (both famous and infamous), the restaurant remained surprisingly egalitarian, with multimillionaires rubbing shoulders with the locals, and being subjected to the same idiosyncratic waiter service. A review that appeared in *The Good Food Guide* for 1980 noted: 'There is no main customer in democratic Blooms where the jocular waiters rule and you are treated like (slightly stupid) human being whether you are East End momma in black satin or a rubber neck from Toronto'.[88]

Writing in the *Jewish Chronicle* in 2001, the actor and TV presenter, Larry Viner shared a story about Larry Adler, the American harmonica player, who was apparently known for name-dropping. Adler was once heard to say to a passing waiter: 'I came here forty years ago with Cole Porter.' The waiter looked glumly at him and replied: 'I am serving as fast as I can.' Viner commented that the story exemplified Bloom's approach to its celebrity customers.[90]

Quite often, especially at busy times, diners were asked to share tables with people they did not know and who might have been from a very different walk of life: 'It was all very sociable.'[91] For many of the regular customers, the experience of dining with celebrities and 'movers and shakers' enhanced their sense of having 'arrived' in British society and it was evident that the ability to eat well in Britain had helped to eradicate the divisive class divisions that had existed in Eastern Europe prior to emigration. Sometimes sharing a table at Blooms proved to be good entertainment value. Georgina Phillips tells this story.

> About fifty years ago, my husband and I went to Blooms for lunch one Sunday. As usual, the restaurant was packed, so the waiter asked if we minded sharing a table and showed us to a table where an elderly couple was already seated. When the waiter asked them for their order, the man said he would like to start with chopped liver, his wife said: "He will have chicken soup." The man said nothing but asked the waiter for salt beef and *latkes* to follow. His wife told the waiter her husband would have Viennas and chips. Again, he did not protest, but asked for *lokshen* pudding for dessert. This time, his wife said that he would have fresh fruit. Towards the end of the meal the waiter asked if they wanted anything else, to which the man replied that he would like a glass of lemon tea. His wife said nothing,

> and my husband and I sat there thinking that at last, this man could have something of his own choosing. We were wrong. The waiter served the lemon tea and after a few minutes his wife said, "Solly, take your teabag out, your tea is strong enough." At this point we could not contain our laughter, poor Solly was not even allowed to have his tea at the strength he wanted![92]

Jewish families living outside the East End continued to make regular forays to the area to keep their roots alive, often combining a trip to Blooms with visits to other attractions, such as the street markets (especially Petticoat Lane market, which by now had a reputation for selling stolen goods), the Houndsditch Warehouse, the many jewellery shops in Black Lion Yard and the Whitechapel Art Gallery. For some Jews, the overcrowded and insalubrious area that they had worked so hard to leave had become a sort of shrine. Sheila Finesilver recalls: 'I often got up very early on a Sunday to *schlep* around Petticoat Lane. After several hours in the market, I was famished! I'd fall into Blooms and work my way through the menu like a *chaze*r [a piggish person, a glutton].'[93]

Other people visited the East End more sporadically, but Blooms was still their favoured destination. Nicole Schlagman recalls: 'My dad had a manufacturing warehouse on Middlesex Street. I used to go there sometimes in the school holidays and help put tickets on the skirts. The reward was always a lunch at Blooms.'[94] Jackie Joannides remembers that it was 'heaven' going to eat at Blooms, 'especially on a cold damp market day.'[95] Sometimes, an amount of cunning was involved in plotting a visit to the 'hallowed' restaurant in Aldgate:

> Every Sunday, I would try and plan our family itinerary in such a way as to include a visit to Blooms. My wife was aware of this ruse, but instead of trying to quash my munching machinations she would use them to her advantage. "Let's take the kids to a museum in East London," she would say. "Too much of a *schlepp* [in this context a tedious journey]. Lots of weekend traffic," I would invariably reply. "What about the

> Bethnal Green Museum of Childhood? It's quite near Blooms in Whitechapel," she would slip in innocently. "OK, everyone in the car!" I would announce.[96]

As in previous decades, the restaurant was still seen by many families as a means for connecting young people to their family history. The writer Robert Elms once recalled:

> One Jewish friend, taken to Blooms as a boy in an act of pilgrimage and rite of passage, which seems to have been universal among North London Jews just one generation away from the streets of Whitechapel, was told "Blooms is horrible, you are going to love it."[97]

Similarly, Elizabeth Whycer remembers:

> When I was a teenager in the 1970s, my parents took me there [to Blooms in Aldgate]. We lived in Enfield, but Mum and Dad's early roots were in the East End. My mum in particular remembered absolutely everything about the old East End around Whitechapel. Dad was a Bethnal Green lad, and my great-grandparents Millie and Hyman Silverstone had a grocery store in Hanbury Street. So, for me, Blooms gave me a flavour of the old buzzy community that's now long gone except in living memory.[98]

As a result, the tables continued to be crowded with multi-generational families:

> This was a time when families ate together and talked together. No mobiles, shmobiles here! There was the *Bubbas* and *Zeides* [grandmothers and grandfathers], whose soup was peppered with *lokshen* and whose English was peppered with *mamaloshon* [mother tongue]. They were very much at home with this *heimische* fare. They grew up with this food – it was their bread and butter – their *challah* and *schmaltz*. They were dressed to

> *fress* [eat a large meal]. Also at the table were their *kinderlach* [children] and *eineklach* [grandchildren], who were just as happy to eat their chicken soup with *kneidlach* and *kreplach. Heimische* food was a treat for them and the Sunday outing to Blooms was comparable to a Lourdes pilgrimage or the Haj.[99]

Children and young people were always welcomed by the waiters and were provided with special child-size portions of food.[100] As some of the young people who had dined in Blooms as children came of age, the roles were sometimes reversed. Angela Harell recalls: 'After my mum died, I used to take my father to Blooms almost every week for chicken and salt beef. He just loved it.'[101]

The Aldgate restaurant became the place for families to meet with friends and relatives visiting London, either from elsewhere in the UK or from abroad. This was partly because of its continuing celebrity status, but primarily because it was a place where families could re-bond and share nostalgic stories of the East End. Sandy Slotnik recalls:

> When my family from New York once visited us, they took us to Blooms. Having just come back from New York myself, and having eaten food like I've never eaten before, I was thinking this would be a mistake. But no, they absolutely loved it, the rudeness of the waiters and all.[102]

By this time, visits to Blooms were facilitated by London's improving arterial road system, especially the routes leading to the eastern suburbs. Many Jewish households owned cars and drove to the East End, either specifically to eat at Blooms, or on their way to or from other outings (such as before or after a football match, or on the way back from a holiday), often going out of their way to do so. Paulette Lerman tells us that after working in Oxford Street, every Monday she went to eat at Blooms before driving home to south London.[103] On their way to the Savoy Hotel after their wedding in Rochester, Pauline Halpern and her new husband detoured to the East End to have a meal at Blooms.[104]

As well as the better road networks, increasing car ownership amongst Jews led to a growth in Bloom's takeaway custom. Hazel Capal recalls: 'With less traffic on the road, Dad would drive there on a Sunday night from Stamford Hill to pick up salt beef sandwiches. And they would still be warm on his return!'[105] David Hallgarten remembers: 'Unbelievably, it used to take just twenty-five minutes to get from Hendon to Aldgate to pick up a salt beef sandwich, so it was a regular pit stop.'[106] Some people drove significant distances to Aldgate to eat at Blooms. Georgina Phillips recalls:

> We lived in Brighton and drove to Blooms quite often just for lunch. On one occasion, we walked in and there, sitting at the bar and tucking into a salt beef sandwich, was my mother's cousin and his wife. They told us that they too often drove up from the coast just for a Bloom's salt beef sandwich because it was the best money can buy.[107]

Bloom's takeaway food was popular with patients in the nearby hospitals, some of whom apparently welcomed the food more than flowers and grapes. Peter Beresford recalls: 'When I was nineteen, I was in the London Hospital after a major operation on my ankle. My girlfriend used to visit me there, but she went to Blooms first to bring me salt beef sandwiches.'[108] Some people stopped off at Blooms on their way to hospital. Susan Berman says: 'As I went into labour with my daughter, I was craving for a salt beef sandwich, so my husband drove me to Blooms.'[109] Howard Cohen tells this story:

> In about 1980, an elderly aunt, who lived in Mile End Road, was admitted to the London Hospital and I decided to visit her there. I thought it would be a good opportunity to pop into Blooms for something to eat. Just after I sat down, my two brothers arrived. They obviously had the same idea as me about combining a hospital visit with savouring Bloom's food! We were just ordering when our parents walked in, again without any liaison or pre-arrangement. We were having such a good time being together and catching up on each other's news that we lost track of the time. We suddenly realised that

> we had missed visiting time. We looked at each other and said: "Same time and place tomorrow then!"'[110]

However, even when it was in its heyday, not everybody was attracted to Blooms. Some people did not like the food; others chose to eat elsewhere, such as at Strongwaters, or preferred home cooking. Stanley Irons recalls: 'Funnily enough, my dad hated Blooms. He was brought up on Barnetts in "The Lane". He would only go there [to Blooms] when forced.'[111] During the 1980s, people living in the Pembury Road area of Dalston could enjoy Bloom's meals without having to make a trip to the restaurant. One of Bloom's employees took orders and customers collected the food from his flat. He was called a 'vouched man'.[112]

Customers of the Golders Green Restaurant During the 1970s and 1980s

Trade at the Golders Green restaurant varied according to the day and the time of day. On Sunday lunchtimes, the main customers were family groups and, according to a *Jewish Chronicle* writer, a 'vocal pantomime-style ("Oh, yes you did" and "Oh, no I didn't") sibling rivalry could be heard above the shouted requests for salt beef, *latkes* and new greens.'[113] Families also ate there on Sunday evenings. Even those Jews who had shunned their religion took their families to Blooms. Will Self recalls: 'When I was a child, my mother whose Semitic anti-Semitism (the most virulent kind) took the form of her frequently admonishing her children that "No one knows I am Jewish", would sometimes crack – usually on a Sunday evening – and take us to Blooms in Golders Green.'[114]

On mid-week evenings, the main diners were 'kosher courting couples gazing moonie-eyed *a deux* [mutually infatuated]', but also 'track-suited long-time marrieds slipping out for a break from the kitchen' – the same people who had been the core customers when the restaurant first opened, just older.[115] Although the delicatessen counter was busier at lunchtimes, there was a steady trade of pin-striped businessmen 'queuing after work for sustenance to be consumed in front of the TV'.[116]

The main trade on weekday lunchtimes was people working in the vicinity or visiting the area. Philip Baigel, who was a regular customer, recalls:

> I used to be a dentist in Willesden Green in the 1980s. A few days a week the desire for a high cholesterol "fress-up" in Blooms was just too much to resist during my one-hour lunch break. The whole expedition was a well-oiled (or should I say a well-*schmaltzed*) operation to enable me to finish a patient by 12.30pm, drive to Golders Green, find a parking spot, walk to the restaurant, get a seat, place an order, eat and savour the foody fare, pay the bill, walk back to the car, drive to the surgery and be seated to greet the 1.30pm patient with a stuffed grin and a more dental version of "open wide". Every minute was critical and crucial, and any delay in traffic, or difficulty in parking could scupper the whole foolhardy endeavour.[117]

Bloom's Wholesale Trade in the 1970s and 1980s

During the 1970s, there was a major shift in the market for Bloom's manufactured products. Whereas in the past customers had obtained their goods from butchers and delicatessens, the supermarkets, the number of which was now growing exponentially, became the main source of Bloom's goods. Mac Fisheries was the first supermarket to contract with Blooms, but the other rapidly expanding chains – Tesco, Waitrose and Sainsbury's – were quick to follow suit. While this was the death knell for the traditional Jewish butchers and delicatessens, the supermarkets continued to ensure the wide availability of kosher products, including Bloom's goods.[118] A buyer for the Sainsbury's chain was quoted as saying: 'We are keen to make kosher foods available as far as possible, where there is a known Jewish community.'[119] Norman Bookbinder, who played a prominent role in securing the supermarket contracts for Blooms,[120] comments:

Once we had expanded into Tesco, it was a fairly simple roll out. As soon as Tesco had a kosher range, everybody wanted a kosher range and they quickly understood the snowball effect of a kosher shopper going into one of their stores to buy a pack of Viennas, sliced meats and turkey products and then going on to spend over a hundred pounds on other goods.[121]

During the 1970s, the demand for frozen goods continued to grow, which Blooms was able to exploit since many of its meat products, such as the salami and the sausages, lent themselves to freezing. Blooms negotiated a large contract with Bejam, a frozen goods firm based in Milton Keynes.[122] Even more interestingly, Blooms was also beginning to build up custom for its meat products amongst non-Jews, selling to non-Jewish delicatessens, especially in London.

108. Advertisement appearing in the *Marylebone Mercury*, 6 May 1977.

The Customers of the Aldgate Restaurant in the 1990s

By the late 1980s, the transformation of the East End described in Chapter Six was having a major impact on the core custom of the Aldgate restaurant. Whereas in the past its peak dining times had been evenings and Sundays, the restaurant was now at its busiest at lunchtimes, when it was mainly filled with workers – stockbrokers and financial traders – from the nearby City of London and those working in central London within easy travelling distance of Aldgate, who were mostly non-Jewish. One commentator said that Blooms was now the diner of choice for 'sleek city types entertaining Jewish clients and colleagues from the Big Apple, or from Moscow and St Petersburg'.[123] Apparently, the non-Jewish City workers were attracted by its white tablecloths and celebrity status.[124]

What is ironic about this, is that when mass immigration commenced in the 1880s, one of the barriers between Jews and non-Jews was their very different diets. In addition to accusations about Jews reducing housing and employment opportunities open to non-Jews, there were unfavourable comments about their food, which looked and smelled 'different'. Kosher butchers were described as 'alien butchers', and Jewish food shops and cafés were frequently criticised for their low levels of hygiene, as previously mentioned. Jewish food gradually became an integral part of the local culture, with non-Jews sampling Jewish food sold on street corners and from takeaway businesses. However, by the late 1980s, the situation had moved on again. Geoffrey Alderman comments: 'It became a status symbol amongst gentiles to dine at Blooms. "Have you eaten in Blooms?", they would ask each other.'[125]

The non-Jewish diners included people from the different ethnic groups, living either in the East End or further afield. The legendary head waiter, Lou Dein, (mentioned in Chapter Eight) once told a visiting reporter that a number of Indian people were regularly dining at the Aldgate restaurant in the years leading up to its closure,[126] and Harris Bokhari recalls that when he was young, he and his Punjabi-born father, Naz (the first Muslim secondary school headteacher in the UK), ate regularly at Blooms in Aldgate and later in Golders Green.[127]

At the beginning of the 1990s, the Aldgate takeaway trade was still buoyant on weekday lunchtimes, again mainly due to custom from City workers. Daniel Appleby recalls:

> At the beginning of the 1990s, I was working as an in-house lawyer for an oil company in central London. My colleagues were an agreeable but very English bunch, and I would try to dream up places for lunch that might be something of a surprise for them. On a couple of occasions, I took them to Blooms in Whitechapel. I liked going to the East End and I knew it well from accompanying my father there as a child. My father, who ran a jewellery shop in Earls Court, would go "down The Lane" every Sunday to visit Black Lion Yard to collect or deliver customers' repairs. However, by the 1990s, the world I had known had virtually disappeared and Bloom's restaurant was one of its final vestiges and it seemed diminished by that time. I do not recollect it being packed with customers and my gentile colleagues were surprised that such "dull" food could be so lionised. It takes time and some sympathy fully to appreciate a salt beef sandwich on rye bread, heavily flavoured with mustard and accompanied by a new green cucumber and a *latke*.[128]

In the evenings, the restaurant was increasingly devoid of diners. According to a *Jewish Chronicle* writer, the main evening diners were 'designer-clad Chigwellians, Woodfordians or Loughtonians, stopping off for a plate of salt beef as they wended their way home from a tiring spell of slapping down the Gold Card in South Molton Street or Beauchamp Place'.[129] At lunchtimes, the Jewish diners were mainly 'nostalgia chasers', those who were participating in the plethora of guided walks and heritage tours of the East End organised by people such as the historian Bill Fishman.[130] As a result of the declining trade, from the mid-1980s the restaurant began reducing both its weekday and Sunday opening hours.[131]

However, there were still reports of high-profile people dining at Blooms, some of whom were rather unexpected. In 1994, the *Jewish Chronicle* reported that Afif Safieh, the head of the PLO delegation in London for peace talks, had been spotted lunching in Blooms with Jewish journalists. 'Reliable reporting sources' said:

> Having started with *gefilte* fish, smothered in *chrein,* he went on to demolish a plateful of salt beef and *latkes*, and washed it all down with a cup of black coffee. Mr Safieh – an aficionado of French cooking – declared himself particularly impressed with Bloom's famous new green cucumbers. However, deciding that discretion was the better part of valour, he declined to take on the ultimate challenge of *lokshen* pudding.[132]

Although by the 1990s Jewish diners were few in number, in 1993 a few years before the restaurant closed, a group of well-known figures staged a party at Blooms to celebrate the eighty-third birthday of the artist and cartoonist Harry Blacker. It started around breakfast time and lasted all day. The former East Enders present at the celebration included Bill Fishman, Rabbi Lionel Blue, the novelist Barnet Litvinoff, and the first lady of the Yiddish theatre, Anna Tzelniker. The art critic Brian Sewell was the guest of honour. They spent the day reminiscing and telling jokes about the 'Old East End'. Cameras captured the affair, and the footage was used to produce a documentary film named *East Endings*, narrated by Alan Dein.[133]

When the Aldgate restaurant closed in February 1996, the *Jewish Chronicle* journalist Jan Shure commented that at one recent midweek lunchtime, just half the tables had been occupied and the diners were almost exclusively non-Jews. She commented that Morris Bloom's original customers 'had moved on both geographically and aspirationally', and Blooms was no longer valued by Jewish diners for either its location or its style and ambience.[134] The restaurant had remained in American guidebooks, and one US tourist arrived too late to enjoy it. In May 1999, the *Los Angeles Times* published an article by the travel writer Dan Falk, who reported that he had been recommended by one of his guidebooks to visit Blooms only to find that it was now a Burger King.[135] Jeremy Dein, the son of the head waiter, Lou Dein, reflects on the changes:

> When my brother and I were small, our mother sometimes took us to the East End to collect our father from Blooms on a

> Sunday and to pick up a salt beef sandwich as a special treat. The restaurant would be buzzing and packed with people. It was just chaos! When I went back at the same time on a Sunday as a young man, it was very quiet; indeed, it simply wasn't the same place.[136]

Bloom's Manufacturing Arm

The demand for Bloom's manufactured goods was a very different story. During the 1990s, the availability of Bloom's meat products in supermarkets continued to grow. Despite the decline in religious observance amongst Jews and the reduced consumption of fresh kosher meat, the demand for processed and packaged goods was still growing, partly because of the expansion of the newer chains of supermarkets such as Asda. This growth came not just from Jews, but also from outside the Jewish community. In 1998, Norman Bookbinder explained that many British Muslims were now finding kosher meat products acceptable as an alternative to halal food.[137] However, the finances of the wholesale side of Blooms were inextricably linked with those of the Aldgate restaurant and the wholesale business eventually had to be sold despite the huge demand for the Bloom's canned and packaged goods.

Customers at the Golders Green Restaurant Before it Closed

In Golders Green, trade remained steady because of the general boom in demand for kosher food in that part of London, but the restaurant continued to seek out new customers. As previously mentioned, in 1991 the restaurant extended its opening hours with the aim of attracting young people. The move was successful and on winter Saturday nights and very late on summer Saturday nights, the young 'pavement posers', who were described as 'London's Dolce & Gabbana-clad, 16-plus-crowd' arrived.[138] According to a press report, the extended opening hours resulted in around 500 young people meeting and eating at Blooms each weekend: 'They came marching in from about midnight.'[139] Rob Marco, who was one of these young people, recalls how he and his friends welcomed the opportunity to enjoy a late-night soup and sandwich before going home.[140] The takeaway meals, which could be ordered into the early hours of the morning, also proved to be popular with younger people.[141]

However, the success of this initiative did not last into the twenty-first century. The restaurant's main trade, like its staff, became noticeably older and people started to joke that to dine at Blooms you had to show your bus pass.[142] The restaurant no longer had a multigenerational clientele, except on Mothers' Day and Fathers' Day, Bloom's busiest days in the year. On those days, grown-up children brought their parents to the restaurant, knowing how attached they were to Bloom's food.[143] In 2007, when the restaurant was refurbished, an attempt was made to attract young, modern orthodox Jews to eat there alongside the older, middle-of-the-road Jews, but the move was unsuccessful.[144]

After the Aldgate restaurant closed, a few celebrities transferred their custom to Golders Green. One regular customer in the early years of the twenty-first century was Vanessa Feltz:

> Blooms was always an energetic experience, dodging the waiters carrying soup, catching a boiled *gefilte* fish in your hand with carrots flying everywhere. It made you feel like you were getting some exercise, a bit like 'It's a Knock Out', when in reality you were probably consuming more cholesterol than a sensible person should eat in a year. The food was an affront to man and beast really, but it was always my fall-back restaurant.[145]

The food critic Giles Coren also dined in Blooms occasionally:

> I would always take some gentile girlfriend to Blooms as part of breaking it to her that I was Jewish. And I would explain to her, "Here's a *latke*, yes, it's supposed to taste like that; this is how you pronounce *kreplach, kneidlach, tsimmis.*" I once took a blonde,

> Swedish-looking girl, who did really well, ordered everything perfectly and I was very proud of her. But then she turned round and said, "And can I have a glass of milk please?" I was so mortified but looking back, I do think it was terribly sweet.[146]

The dwindling number of diners included several non-Jews who enjoyed the *heimische* food and the ambience of Blooms. On one occasion, a television crew was present when a rabbi and an imam sat down to eat together in the restaurant and the scene was caught on camera.[147] However, the presence of these celebrity and non-Jewish diners was not enough to prevent the restaurant from continuing to lose custom and eventually closing in 2010.

The next chapter examines in more detail changes in Jewish diet, food and eating illustrated by the Bloom's story.

Notes

1. Quoted in Panikos Panayi, 'The Anglicisation of East European Jewish Food in Britain', in the *Journal Immigrants and Minorities*, 30.2-3, pp.300–301.
2. Gerry Black, *Jewish London, An Illustrated History* (Derby: Breedon Books, 2007), p.141.
3. See Chapter Ten for further discussion of the food served at Blooms in its early days.
4. Emanuel Litvinoff, *Journey Through a Small Planet* (London: Penguin Modern Classics, 2008).
5. See Yohanan Petrovsky-Shtern, *The Golden Age of the Shtetl: A New History of Life in East Europe* (Princeton NJ: Princeton University Press, 2015), p.129.
6. Rabbi Scott Aaron, 'Meat and Jews: A Mixed Grill Relationship', *Times of Israel*, 19.9.2012.
7. Hasia R. Diner, *Hungering for America: Italian, Irish and Jewish Foodways in the Age of Migration* (London: Harvard University Press, 2001), Kindle location 2064.
8. Interview with Connie Stanton, 7.10.2022.
9. *JC*, 30.8.1940.
10. *JC*, 12.4.1935 and 1.5.1935.
11. Todd Edelman, *The Jews of Britain 1656—2000* (Berkeley CA: University of California Press, 2002), p.170.
12. See various advertisements in the *Jewish Chronicle*.

13. *JC*, 10.11.1939.
14. A. B. Levy, *East End Story* (London: Vallentine Mitchell and Co. Ltd., 1951), p.99.
15. Christopher Driver (ed.), *The Good Food Guide 1975* (London: The Consumers' Association and Hodder and Stoughton, 1975), p.348.
16. Ruth Janis Williams, post on Facebook page The Jewish East End of London, 29.10.2016.
17. Quoted in *JC*, 18.6.2010.
18. Brian Scott Lee, post on Facebook page I Grew up in Golders Green Station in the 1960s and 1970s, 19.8. 2022.
19. Charles Haslett, post on Facebook page East End of London and East London – History and Memories, 26.6.2020.
20. Jo Harrison, post on Facebook page East London Days Gone By, 31.8.2018.
21. Pat Cook, post on Facebook page East End of London and East London – History and Memories, 7.7.2017.
22. Interview with Helen Blairman, 1.9.2022.
23. Interview with Philip Luxembourg, 10.10.2022.
24. Interview with Stewart and Ruth Spivok, 6.9.2022.
25. Alan Avraham Brummer, post on Facebook page Jewish Britain, 15.5.2016.
26. Message from Martine Kaufman, 5.9.2022.
27. Kelly Sherwood, post on Facebook page Bethnal Green and East London, 20.1.2021.
28. Saleem Raja, post on Facebook page East End of London and East London – History and Memories, 8.9.2020.
29. Barry Silkman, post on Facebook page Memories of Petticoat Lane and Surrounding Areas, 1.11.2016.
30. Tom Jaine (ed.), *The Good Food Guide 1990* (London: The Consumers' Association and Hodder and Stoughton, 1990), p.42.
31. Ian Gold, post on Facebook page The Jewish East End of London, 29.10.2016.
32. David Ziants, post on Facebook page Memories of Hessel, Langdale Mans, Cannon Street Rd and Cable St, 2.12.2019.
33. *Diss Express*, 5.3.1954.
34. Jacquie Braham Lynam, post on Facebook page Memories of Hessel, Langdale Mans, Cannon Street Rd and Cable St, 8.5.2020.
35. Interview with Alan Dein, 2.1.2023.
36. Conversation with Beverley-Jane Stewart, 14.4.2023.
37. Interview with Marilyn Lovell, 28.3.2023.
38. Jack White, post on Facebook page The Jewish East End of London, 29.11.2016.
39. Adele Winton, post on *ibid.*, 29.11.2016. The review of Blooms was written in 1967 and was contained in a publication named *Quest*, Volume 2.
40. Barbara Jacobs, post on the Facebook page The Jewish East End of London., 29.11.2016.

41. Message from Philip Baigel, 24.3.2022.
42. See Pam Fox, *Jews by the Seaside, The Jewish Hotels and Guest Houses of Bournemouth* (London: Vallentine Mitchell, 2022) p.335.
43. For example, interview with Marsha Bloom, daughter of Connie Shack, 13.12.2022.
44. 'Dooally Danny's Visit to Bloomin' Britain', *The Stage*, 27.12.2003.
45. David Feldman. 'Bloom, Solomon Sidney', in *Oxford Dictionary of National Biography*, Oxford University Press, March 2009.
46. Simon Schama, 'The King's Pugilist, Daniel Mendoza, 1764–1836', in Franklin Foer and Marc Tracey (eds), *Jewish Jocks: An Unorthodox Hall of Fame* (NY: Twelve, 2012), p.12. I would like to thank Professor Tony Kushner at Southampton University for drawing my attention to this anecdote.
47. *JC*, 16.7.1965.
48. *JC*, 13.7.1962.
49. Message form Philip Baigel, 24.3.2023.
50. Interview with Martin Malin, 22.9.2022.
51. Neville Filar, post on Facebook page The Jewish East End of London, 13.11.2020.
52. Kevin Greenland, post on Facebook page East London Days Gone By, 30.6.2020.
53. Interview with Anthony Gerstler, 6.9.2022.
54. See https://web.archive.org/web/20061018044059/http://www.eastlondonhistory.com/blooms.htm.
55. See Pam Fox, *The Jewish Community of Golders Green* (Stroud: The History Press, 2016).
56. Interview with Alan Dein, 3.1.2023.
57. Quoted in the *JC*, 17.6.2010.
58. Interview with Martin Malin, 22.9.2022.
59. Anonymous interviewee, 31.8.2022.
60. See Fox, *The Jewish Community of Golders Green.*
61. Interview with Norman Bookbinder, 5.12.2022.
62. Ted Merwin, *Pastrami on Rye: An Overstuffed History of the Jewish Deli* (New York and London: New York University Press, 2018), p.118.
63. Anonymous interviewee, 22.8.2022.
64. See Fox, *Jews by the Seaside.*
65. Information from 1960s Bloom's advertising brochure, courtesy of Jonathan Fishburn.
66. Interview with Professor Geoffrey Alderman, 31.10.2022.
67. *JC*, 10.7.1964.
68. Conversation with Alan Jacobs, 20.4.2023.
69. *Ibid.*
70. Fiona Griffin, post on Facebook page The Jewish East End of London, 30.1.2018.
71. *JC*, 8.7.1994.

72. *JC*, 16.7.1965.
73. John Gowers (son of Dick Gowers mentioned in Chapter Seven) on Facebook page Memories of Petticoat Lane and Surrounding Areas, 8.5.2020. See Chapter Seven for further information.
74. *JC*, 16.7.1965.
75. Barry Mingay, post on Facebook page East End of London and East London - History and Memories, 8.12.2017.
76. Conversation with Benita Singer and her son Stuart Singer, 21.4.2023. Marc Bolan, who was born in Hackney, had a Jewish father.
77. See https://web.archive.org/web/20061018044059/http://www.eastlondonhistory.com/blooms.htm.
78. *JC*, 5.8.1994.
79. *JC*, 6.11.1992
80. See mention in Chapter Eight.
81. See https://web.archive.org/web/20061018044059/http://www.eastlondonhistory.com/blooms.htm.
82. Sylvia Moe, post on Facebook page The Jewish East End of London, 13.11.2020.
83. Barry Din, post on Facebook page Memories of Hessel, Langdale Mans, Cannon Street Rd and Cable St, 27.12.2017.
84. Vivienne Thompson, post on Facebook page Memories of Hessel, Langdale Mans, Cannon Street Rd and Cable St, 25.8.2015.
85. Jack Chandler, post on Facebook page The Jewish East End of London, 25.5.2020.
86. Interviews with Alan Dein, 3.1.2023 and Lawrence Reuben, 7.9.2022.
87. Anonymous interviewee, 31.8.2022.
88. Christopher Driver (ed.), *The Good Food Guide 1980* (London: The Consumers' Association and Hodder and Stoughton, 1980), p.38.
89. Conversation with Rochelle Berlyn, 22.8.2022. See Chapter Seven for more information on Rochelle Berlyn.
90. *JC*, 24.8.2001.
91. Interview with Stewart and Ruth Spivok, 6.9.2022.
92. Interview with Georgina Phillips, 29.5.2023.
93. Message from Sheila Finesilver, 16.9.2022.
94. Nicole Schlagman, post on Facebook page The Jewish East End of London, 13.11.2020.
95. Jackie Joannides, on *ibid.*,13.11.2020.
96. Message from Philip Baigel, 24.3.2023.
97. Robert Elms, *London Made Us: A Memoir of a Shape Shifting City* (Edinburgh: Canongate Books, 2019).
98. Elizabeth Whycer, post on Facebook page Jewish East End of London, 30.1.2018.
99. Message from Philip Baigel, 24.3.2023.

100. *JC*, 10.7.1964.
101. Angela Harrell, post on Facebook page The Jewish East End of London, 19.11.2019.
102. Sandy Slotnick, post on Facebook page Memories of Hessel, Langdale Mans, Cannon Street Rd and Cable St, 7.8.2022.
103. Paulette Lerman, post on Facebook page The Jewish East End of London, 19.11.2019.
104. Interview with Pauline Halpern, 31.8.2022.
105. Hazel Capal, post on Facebook page The Jewish East End of London, 13.11.2020.
106. Conversation with David Hallgarten, 17.4.2023.
107. Interview with Georgina Phillips, 29.5.2023.
108. Peter Beresford, post on Facebook page East London Days Gone By, 16.12.2019.
109. Susan Berman, post on Facebook page Memories of Petticoat Lane and the Surrounding Areas, 17.9.2021.
110. Conversation with Howard Cohen, 20.5.2023.
111. Stanley Irons, response to article on Blooms in *The Times*, 13.4.2020.
112. David Boldinger, post on Facebook page Jewish Britain, 21.8.2022.
113. *JC*, 19.1.1996.
114. Will Self, *Feeding Frenzy* (London: Penguin, 2022).
115. *JC*, 19.1.1996.
116. *Ibid.*
117. Message from Philip Baigel, 24.3.2023.
118. Interview with Norman Bookbinder, 30.12.2022.
119. *JC*, 19.1.1996.
120. See Chapter Five.
121. Interview with Norman Bookbinder, 30.12.2022.
122. Bejam was later absorbed into the firm Iceland.
123. *JC*, 19.1.1996.
124. Alan Dein quoted in Rachel Lichtenstein, *On Brick Lane*, (London: Penguin Books, 2007), p.105.
125. Interview with Geoffrey Alderman, 31.10.2022.
126. *JC*, 2 .9.1988.
127. *Jewish News*, 30.12.2022.
128. Email from Daniel Appleby, 4.9.2022.
129. *JC*, 19.1.1996.
130. See mentions in Author's preface.
131. See *JC*, 18 7.1986.
132. *JC*, 12.8.1994.
133. The film was made by Crossfire Films Ltd and is available from Film London.
134. *JC*, 23.2.1996.

135. Dan Falk, 'A Walk on the East Side', *Los Angeles Times*, 30.5.1999.
136. Interview with Jeremy Dein, 7.9.2022.
137. Julian Kossoff, 'Sausage dispute just isn't kosher, say London Jews', *The Independent*, 12.9.1998.
138. *JC*, 19.1.1996.
139. *JC*, 31.5.1991.
140. Rob Marco, post on Facebook page Jewish Britain, 15.5.2016.
141. *JC*, 15.9.1991.
142. *JC*, 5.10.2007.
143. Anonymous interviewee, 20.12.2022.
144. *JC*, 27.4.2007.
145. Quoted in *JC*, 19.6.2010.
146. *Ibid.*
147. Anonymous interviewee, 20.12.2022.

Chapter Ten

Bloom's Food

The Centrality of Food in Jewish Culture

In Jewish culture food is revered and sacred; it gives meaning to Jewish life. The intimate connection between food and holiness, between good food and a good life, is enshrined in biblical sources through to modern religious writings. For Jews, food is not just about consuming enough calories to survive but is a tangible manifestation of divine will.[1] In Isaiah 55,1-3, it is commanded that human beings should not only eat, but that they should 'be satisfied'. The Jerusalem Talmud, Tractate *Kiddushim* 4:12; 66b, contains a warning that those who fail to partake of good foods they have seen, will be punished. In Jewish teachings, a particular emphasis is placed on good food being consumed on *Shabbat*, during festivals and on holy days. Appreciating food at special times is seen as being the closest that Jews can come to achieving paradise on earth, as reflected in the *erev Shabbat* (eve of the Sabbath) table song '*Mah Yedidut*'.[2]

However, Jewish teachings do not only dictate the importance of food, but they also proscribe the food that can, and more critically, cannot be consumed by Jews, how it must be prepared for consumption and how and when it should be eaten. These are the laws of *kashrut*, which are mainly set out in the book of Leviticus, but they have been interpreted, elaborated upon and debated by Jewish sages in the Talmud and many subsequent codes.

The basic tenets of *kashrut* are that observant Jews must not store, prepare, cook or consume together, meat and dairy foods, allowing a gap between the consumption of these different foods;[3] must not eat meat other than that obtained from cud-chewing animals with fully cloven hooves and which have been slaughtered to specific standards (*shechita*) by a professional butcher (*shochet*); and must only eat fish that have both fins and gills. The laws of *kashrut* also dictate the types of food to be eaten (or not eaten) during festivals and holy days, notably during *Pesach*.

Observing the laws of *kashrut* has always served to make Jews conscious of their identity, but in Eastern Europe *kashrut* also acquired a cultural significance as a means for distinguishing Jews from their non-Jewish neighbours. The cultural distinctions were particularly apparent in respect of the cooking fats used by Jews – mainly those derived from chicken and geese – the smell of which is said to have permeated every Jewish home.[4]

The Wandering Jew and the Impact on Jewish Food

Due to Jewish history, there is no such thing as typical Jewish food.[5] As Jews have moved around the globe, often escaping from persecution and social and economic discrimination, they have taken with them the foods and flavours they had absorbed while living in the countries they left behind. They then acquired a liking for different cuisines as they assimilated into their new homelands, adapting hitherto unfamiliar dishes to comply with the laws of *kashrut*. The renowned food writer Claudia Roden has commented: 'Every cuisine tells a story. Jewish food tells the story of an uprooted, migrating people and their vanished worlds.'[6]

In addition, although some foods are generally regarded as being ubiquitous to Jews, such as *cholent* (a stew of meat and vegetable prepared and cooked slowly in advance of *Shabbat*) and *charoset* (a sweet paste made of fruit and nuts eaten at *Pesach*), both appear in different forms in every land that Jews have lived. Even within the Pale of Settlement there were wide variations. Whereas Polish Jews ate sweet *gefilte* fish, Lithuanian and Ukrainian Jews ate *gefilte* fish as a savoury dish. The sweet *gefilte* fish eaten in Poland was accompanied by *farfl* (small squares of dough), which were not generally consumed by Jews anywhere else in the Russian Empire. Similarly, Polish Jews traditionally ate *lokshen* as a pudding rather than as a savoury dish, which is how it was consumed by Lithuanian and Ukrainian Jews. While Polish Jews had a penchant for pickles as a means for making a stodgy and monotonous diet (see below) more palatable, their Lithuanian neighbours had no predilection for pickles, but used 'sours', beetroot, cabbage and sorrel, in the same way.[7] These culinary variations, which reflected the tastes of the wider communities in the areas where Jews lived, were particularly pronounced in relation to food consumed during Jewish festivals. There were also variations in terminology, with Jews sometimes using the same words to refer to different dishes. According to the American food historian Hasia Diner:

> Those who lived in the more northerly and easterly regions ate a soup called "*rosl*" made of beets, while those living towards the south-west made "*rosl*" without beets. They knew *rosl* as meat soup, more akin to pot roast than to the beet soup of their "fellow" Eastern European Jews.[8]

These regional differences led Claudia Roden to pose the question of whether it is possible to define what constitutes 'Jewish food'. She concluded that the food consumed by Jews in different places only became Jewish when it travelled with Jews to new homelands and that because a food culture is complex, it does not mean that it does not exist.[9] She has also commented: 'There is much more to Jewish food than cooking and eating. Behind every recipe is a story of local traditions in far-off towns and villages.'

As a result of Jewish wanderings, Jewish diet in Eastern Europe did not remain static. Jews travelled far and wide, oblivious of national boundaries, for work (seeking ways to make a living or as peddlers), religious purposes (to study or to teach) and for markets and fairs. They stayed in homes, inns or, if they were very poor, communal lodging homes. As a result of eating with Jews in other parts of the Pale of Settlement, the travellers picked up both ingredients and information about different dishes and ways of cooking them, which they took home to add to the repertoire of what they ate.[10] This was especially the case for wealthier Jews who could afford to sample new dishes and tastes.

Marriage arrangements between Jews from different regions of Eastern Europe often led to a fusion of diets, as did the general movement of Jews from smaller communities to large towns and cities that took place over the course of the nineteenth century. Hasia Diner has commented that the urbanisation of the Jewish population of the Pale of Settlement meant that cities such as Warsaw, Lodz, Kyiv, Minsk, Bialystok and many others became culinary melting pots, 'blending different styles and ingredients from near and distant places.'[11]

Food in Eastern Europe Prior to Emigration

During the nineteenth century, the Russian authorities introduced hundreds of repressive edicts aimed at forcing Jews to relinquish their identity and assimilate into the wider population. Particularly punitive was the antisemitic legislation of 1882, known as the 'May Laws', governing the economic and social lives of Jews in the Pale of Settlement. As a result of these laws, Jewish communities generally became increasingly impoverished. Class differences between Jews and disparities in their wealth also became more apparent. Inequalities were particularly obvious in respect of food. While the rich ate well, in both quality and quantity, throughout the year, most Jews usually ate the most basic foods on weekdays and consumed only slightly better meals on *Shabbat* and during festivals, holy days and life-cycle events. The divisive impact of these differences between Jews is evidenced by a Yiddish alphabet song which was widely taught in *chederim* (Jewish elementary schools) across Poland and Lithuania:

Aleph: The rich man eats fruit preserves [*ayngemachts*];
Beys: the poor man gnaws bones [*beyndelekh*].
Giml: The rich man eats geese [*gendzelekh*];
Daled: the poor man has poverty [*dales*].
Heh: Small chickens [*hindelekh*] eats the rich man;
Vov: the poor man has pain [*veytikn*].
Zayin: The rich man eats buttered rolls [*zemelekh*];

Khes: the poor man has sicknesses [*kholasn*].
Tes: The rich man eats roasted pigeons [*taybelekh*];
Yod: sorrows [*yesurim*] suffers the poor man.
Kof: The rich man wears rubbers [*kaloshn*];
Lamed: the poor man wears straw sandals [*laptyes*].
Mem: The rich man drinks whisky [*mashke*];
Nun: the poor man is sober [*nikhter*].
Samekh: The rich man wears satin clothing [*sametene*];
Ayin: the poor man is in tatters [*opgerisn*].
Pey: The rich man eats fried chicken stomachs [*pupkes*];
Tsadik: sorrows [*tsores*] has the poor man.
Kof: The rich man eats veal chops [*kotletn*];
Reysh: radishes [*retekh*] eats the poor man.
Shin: The rich man smokes Shereshevski's [superior] cigars;
Tov: the poor man puffs at inferior [*tutin*] tobacco.[12]

Although Jewish teachings mandated Jews to eat well at sacred times, this was impossible for many people, and they were therefore reliant on communal charity to comply with the teachings. Jewish law dictated that it was a non-negotiable *mitzvah* (good deed) for those who could afford it (a thin layer of wealthy merchants and the top religious leaders) to ensure that their impoverished co-religionists ate good food when they were required to do so. While this ensured that the poor did not starve, being assured of a decent meal at least once a week, this charity served to make hungry Jews more aware of their social status and their lack of means. This robbed them of the pleasure of eating the food they were supposed to enjoy and diminished the meaning of what were meant to be special days. Hasia Diner comments: 'Food obtained through charity came with an emotional price tag and created conflict between the desire for self-respect and the hunger for food.'[13] It was this problematic relationship with food that impelled many poor Jews to leave the Pale of Settlement.

As crushing poverty rather than religion became the main determinant of what they consumed for most Eastern European Jews, the range of dishes they ate became ever narrower. The main components were black bread, potato (which had relatively recently taken over from grains as a dietary staple due to its high calorific content),[14] cabbage, herrings, *kasha* (cooked buckwheat) and *krupnik* (vegetable soup).[15] In many parts of the Pale of Settlement, Jews were forbidden from growing vegetables, which meant that they generally ate few vegetables. There was very little variation between the food eaten at the different meals during the day. Meat was a rarity, even though meat had become a commanded element of Jewish diet after the great flood, albeit with the caveat of the animal's blood not being ingested. Claudia Roden declares: 'Jews have always had a passion for meat, and it has always been their most highly prized food.'[16]

Although the Talmud dictates that there is no joy without meat and wine, most Jews could not afford to buy it. The dearth of meat in the Eastern European Jewish diet was exacerbated when the Russian government imposed a tax on kosher meat known as the *korobka* (meaning box and referring to the chest in which the payments were deposited), the proceeds of which went into the state treasury, on top of the existing taxes levied by Jewish communal authorities to support *schechita*.[17] The government tax hit the poor harder than the rich and its impact was not evenly spread across the Pale of Settlement. The tax was repealed in Russian Poland in 1863, which resulted in more Polish Jews, even poorer ones, eating meat more often.[18]

It is also important to note that, on the rare occasions when most Jews living in the Pale of Settlement were able to eat meat (usually as an act of charity), what they consumed was not the pickled and cured meats and sausages that were common in Jewish diets in other parts of Europe (most notably in France, Germany and Romania), but the most inexpensive cuts of meat, especially offal – feet, spleen, lungs, brains, liver and intestines.

Bloom's Food in the Firm's Early Years

When Morris acquired his first premises at 58 Brick Lane, the main foods that he served in the small café and as takeaway snacks were the meat products that he was manufacturing in the yard at the rear of the premises – salt beef and Vienna sausages made with veal –

alongside other simple Eastern European fare – herrings, soups and stews served with bread – and snacks that did not need much preparation, including the salt beef sandwiches that became Bloom's signature offering.[19]

The Bloom's menu therefore struck a balance between the familiar and the new, allowing Bloom's customers to retain a connectedness with the lands from which they had fled, but at the same time affording them a sense of optimism since, even if they were on the lowest rung of the economic ladder, food was now both more abundant and affordable than it had been in Eastern Europe. After all, this is why Jews had left the Pale of Settlement. The food served at Blooms, and other establishments like it in the Jewish East End, would have been anathema to the already acculturated Jewish establishment (the 'English Jews' as they were called to distinguish them from the recent immigrants). Judging by Jewish cookbooks of the day, the assimilated Jews dined almost entirely on English dishes suitably adapted to comply with *kashrut*.[20]

While the ability to eat meat more often would have been seen as an improvement, initially not everybody would have been attracted to eating Morris Bloom's salt beef or his Viennas since, as already mentioned, such meat products were beyond the ken of most Eastern European Jews. However, the speed of Morris's success suggests that his customers were quick to overcome any misgivings they might have harboured about eating salt beef and sausages. Speaking about the American experience, Hasia Diner has commented: 'Although East European Jews had not eaten these foods [sausages and cured meats] before migration … they learned to think of them as traditional.'[21]

This means that, from the outset, Blooms was facilitating what food writers call a 'foodway', the way in which immigrant communities adapt what they eat to suit the countries in which they live as they become assimilated into a new culture. According to a later commentary, when he set up in business, Morris Bloom was convinced that his own style of kosher food would 'delight the public's palate'. His judgement and timing proved to have been sound.[22] It is unlikely that his meat products would have been so rapidly successful during the war years when anti-German feelings ran high and Jews were reticent about displaying any Germanic connections.[23] Salt beef was a common dish in Central Europe and, as their name suggests, Vienna sausages have their origins in Austria. However, by the early 1920s, these concerns were less potent.

Since Morris Bloom and his wife Rebecca both came to London from Eastern Europe, it is worth pausing to consider why, when Blooms first opened, it mainly sold products that neither of them is likely to have consumed on a regular basis prior to their emigration. Although salt beef is brisket that is made kosher by the salting process, Jews in Eastern Europe could rarely afford to eat beef (except perhaps at *Chanukah*, the Jewish festival of lights[24]), even if it were a cheaper cut like brisket, which comes from the tough meat and fat that covers a cow's breastbone.

The answer is possibly two-fold: that the skills in curing and salting and sausage making, which Morris Bloom is said to have acquired in Lithuania prior to his emigration,[25] were supplemented on his journey across Europe,[26] and that on his arrival in the East End, he possibly worked for Barratts in Middlesex Street, one of the few meat establishments then producing kosher salt beef and 'German' sausages.[27] It is also interesting to ponder on the extent to which Bloom's early food repertoire represented a fusion of the different culinary traditions known by Morris Bloom from Lithuania and Rebecca from Poland. It is possible that there was a significant amount of fusion since this would have helped to attract a wider range of customers.

The Pre-War Years

The culinary assimilation, which had started to take place in the 1920s, was even more apparent during the 1930s when the range of goods manufactured by Blooms expanded to include 'special garlic' and plain *worsht*, breakfast sausage, both veal and beef, Viennas, pickled tongues, pickled beef, smoked beef, liver sausage, 'postrema' (pastrami), salami and pressed beef. The goods were not only more cosmopolitan (pastrami originated from Romania; salami, originated from Southern Europe; and *worst* originated from German[28]), but also included more expensive cuts of meat.

This expansion and diversification reflect the fact that the immigrant Jewish community was generally becoming more affluent and discerning in what it ate. This was particularly the case for second-generation Jews, whose aspirations had been raised by their education in British state schools. Upwardly mobile Jews who had moved away from their first area of settlement in the East End and were becoming part of mainstream society, had expanded their diet, but they were still inclined to return to their roots to eat familiar food. Even those first-generation immigrants remaining in the East End would have had higher culinary expectations. Having sampled good food, they wanted more.

By the end of the decade, luxury goods had been added to the Bloom's product list. Packaged goods to be consumed in a variety of locations, not just the East End, and in a variety of social settings (the 'picnic snacks') were also now available. Jews were no longer huddling together in a *shtetl* atmosphere. The following quote demonstrates how, by the 1930s, the consumption of Bloom's food was regarded as a symbol of social mobility:

> Blooms had their place on the corner of Old Montague Street. And on Monday they'd have the offcuts of *vorsht* from the weekend, all different kinds of *vorsht*, you see, like salami … You'd either fry this *vorsht* or some would have it cold. That was delicious. Oh God, you thought you were so wealthy if you had some of that. And sometimes you would get the little sausages like Viennas. You thought you were the tops when you bought some of those.[29]

However, despite the firm's move upmarket, at the centre of Bloom's menu, and for which it was rapidly becoming a household name, were large portions of salt beef, usually eaten with bread, *chrayn* (a red sauce made of grated horseradish and beetroot juice) and pickles.[30] As a result, Bloom's salt beef sandwiches were fast becoming an important vehicle for facilitating the assimilation of Eastern European Jews into British life, representing a kind of 'halfway house'.

Food During the Second World War

There was a hiatus in the development of Bloom's food offer during the Second World War due to several factors, including the lack of staff to prepare and serve the food, the fluctuations in custom as the result of evacuation, bombing and service in the armed forces, and the squeezing of the restaurant into the factory premises after 2 Brick Lane was demolished in 1941. Blooms would also have been adversely affected by the disruptions in food supplies that led to rationing and the legal restrictions placed on the consumption of food. Beef, the mainstay of Bloom's menu, was in very short supply. The situation was compounded by the reduced availability of people with the skills to porge meat.[31] It is therefore likely that most meals served by Blooms during the war would have included poultry of some description.

While there is no evidence to support the suggestion, it is possible that Blooms, like some other Jewish (and non-Jewish) food establishments, resorted to using 'black market' sources to bolster the range and amount of food they were able to offer their customers. There might have been some trading of ration coupons, such as those for bacon, to allow Blooms to obtain the ingredients used heavily in Jewish cooking. Stan Alfert, who was taken to Blooms during the war, recalled that coats were placed on empty seats to enable Blooms to claim additional meat rations.[32] However it was procured, Blooms appears to have had sufficient food to be able to offer a hot meal at any time of the day in its restaurant. During the war years, the Jewish licensing and supervising bodies took a more lenient approach to the requirements of *kashrut*, which would have helped Blooms to cope with food shortages.

BLOOM'S RESTAURANT
2, BRICK LANE, E.1
'Phone: BIShopsgate 6311
Under the supervision of the Beth Din

Well known for their unsurpassed cooking and service have pleasure in announcing that they are still able to provide

Luncheons
Dinners
Suppers

A hot meal at anytime

DELICATESSEN COUNTER. OUTDOOR AND INDOOR CATERING FOR ALL FUNCTIONS.

M. BLOOM
Wholesale Sausage Manufacturers
Send your orders direct to
111, WENTWORTH STREET, E.1
'Phone: BIShopsgate 3937
AND BE ASSURED OF SATISFACTION

109. Advertisement in the *Jewish Chronicle*, 2 August 1940.

The Post-War Years

The years of austerity and continuing rationing immediately after the war, curtailed the developing eating habits of the Jewish community emanating from Eastern Europe. However, by the time that the new Bloom's restaurant opened in Whitechapel High Street in 1952, things were very different. The extent to which Bloom's food both reflected and acted as an agent of assimilation had become even more apparent. However, the emphasis was different. Prior to the Second World War, the focus had been on helping recent immigrants to make the transition between their old and their new lives, with the rapid assimilation of the post-war years, the role of Bloom's food was to assist former immigrants (and, more particularly, their offspring) feel comfortable in British society without abandoning their roots entirely. This can be seen in the ever-longer menus of food available in the new restaurant. As previously mentioned, back in Eastern Europe, the Jewish diet had been very limited for most Jews, but now they could exercise choice.

Remarkably, when people are asked about their memories of Blooms in this post-war period, few speak in detail about what they ate, perhaps because recollection of the individual dishes and tastes have not remained as strong as other aspects of the Bloom's experience (to be discussed further in Chapter Eleven). However, what does come over loud and clear is the impact that consuming Bloom's food had on them. One former diner recalls:

> When the food arrived and I took my first bite, a wave of Jewishness washed over me like a tide. The food gave me a sense of identity I have found in few other places. I was eating my family's history.[33]

This memory is important because it not only demonstrates how Jewish identity was passed from one generation to the next through the medium of food, but it also suggests that, for some people, the act of eating was more important than food itself, what has been termed 'kitchen Judaism'.[34]

An analysis of Bloom's menus for the late 1960s and early 1970s[35] provides some very useful insights. What is immediately obvious is that Bloom's repertoire remained heavily dominated by food that was emblematic of Eastern European (as opposed to Central European) Ashkenazi food (see Glossary of Hebrew and Yiddish Terms) culture: *latkes, lokshen, gefilte* fish, *kneidlach, kreplach, blintzes, schmaltz* herrings, *farfel, borscht* and *tzimmis* (see Glossary of Eastern European Jewish Foods at Appendix One). The dishes were described in Yiddish and prepared in a traditional Eastern European way, such as the *gedempte* veal and *gedempte* potatoes (types of pot roast), *pechta* (calves' foot jelly) and *heimische* barley soup. These Eastern European menu items make it clear that although Jews could now afford to eat what had been once been special-occasion foods more regularly, they had not lost sight of the everyday foods that were still helping them to preserve their Eastern European Jewish identity. What had once been regarded as 'normal foods' had taken on cultural significance just as *kashrut* did in Eastern Europe.

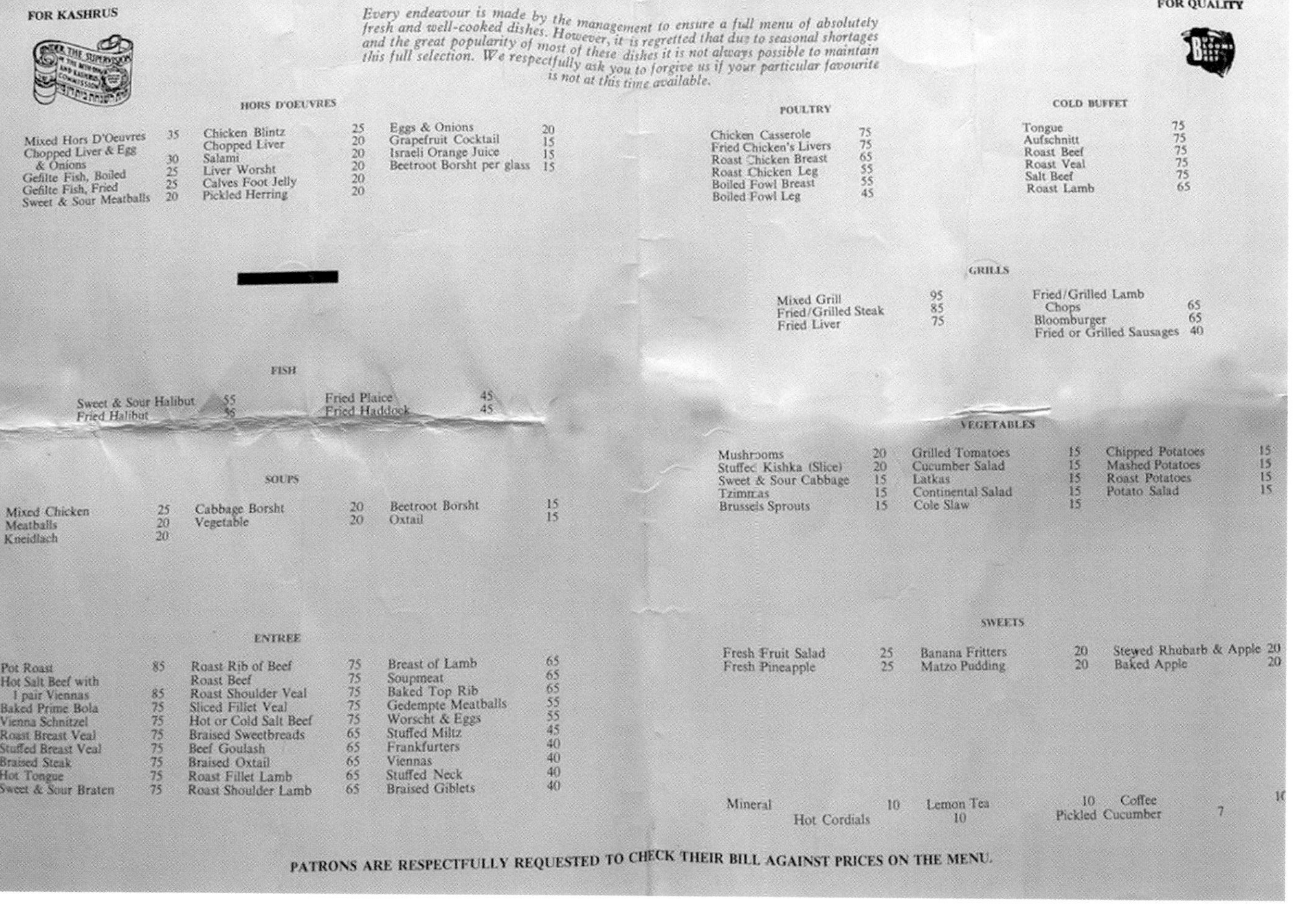

FOR KASHRUS

FOR QUALITY

Every endeavour is made by the management to ensure a full menu of absolutely fresh and well-cooked dishes. However, it is regretted that due to seasonal shortages and the great popularity of most of these dishes it is not always possible to maintain this full selection. We respectfully ask you to forgive us if your particular favourite is not at this time available.

HORS D'OEUVRES

Mixed Hors D'Oeuvres	35	Chicken Blintz	25	Eggs & Onions	20
Chopped Liver & Egg & Onions	30	Chopped Liver	20	Grapefruit Cocktail	15
Gefilte Fish, Boiled	25	Salami	20	Israeli Orange Juice	15
Gefilte Fish, Fried	25	Liver Worsht	20	Beetroot Borsht per glass	15
Sweet & Sour Meatballs	20	Calves Foot Jelly	20		
		Pickled Herring	20		

POULTRY

Chicken Casserole	75
Fried Chicken's Livers	75
Roast Chicken Breast	65
Roast Chicken Leg	55
Boiled Fowl Breast	55
Boiled Fowl Leg	45

COLD BUFFET

Tongue	75
Aufschnitt	75
Roast Beef	75
Roast Veal	75
Salt Beef	75
Roast Lamb	65

GRILLS

Mixed Grill	95	Fried/Grilled Lamb Chops	65
Fried/Grilled Steak	85	Bloomburger	65
Fried Liver	75	Fried or Grilled Sausages	40

FISH

Sweet & Sour Halibut	55	Fried Plaice	45
Fried Halibut	56	Fried Haddock	45

SOUPS

Mixed Chicken	25	Cabbage Borsht	20	Beetroot Borsht	15
Meatballs	20	Vegetable	20	Oxtail	15
Kneidlach	20				

VEGETABLES

Mushrooms	20	Grilled Tomatoes	15	Chipped Potatoes	15
Stuffed Kishka (Slice)	20	Cucumber Salad	15	Mashed Potatoes	15
Sweet & Sour Cabbage	15	Latkas	15	Roast Potatoes	15
Tzimmas	15	Continental Salad	15	Potato Salad	15
Brussels Sprouts	15	Cole Slaw	15		

ENTREE

Pot Roast	85	Roast Rib of Beef	75	Breast of Lamb	65
Hot Salt Beef with 1 pair Viennas	85	Roast Beef	75	Soupmeat	65
Baked Prime Bola	75	Roast Shoulder Veal	75	Baked Top Rib	65
Vienna Schnitzel	75	Sliced Fillet Veal	75	Gedempte Meatballs	55
Roast Breast Veal	75	Hot or Cold Salt Beef	75	Worscht & Eggs	55
Stuffed Breast Veal	75	Braised Sweetbreads	65	Stuffed Miltz	45
Braised Steak	75	Beef Goulash	65	Frankfurters	40
Hot Tongue	75	Braised Oxtail	65	Viennas	40
Sweet & Sour Braten	75	Roast Fillet Lamb	65	Stuffed Neck	40
		Roast Shoulder Lamb	65	Braised Giblets	40

SWEETS

Fresh Fruit Salad	25	Banana Fritters	20	Stewed Rhubarb & Apple	20
Fresh Pineapple	25	Matzo Pudding	20	Baked Apple	20

Mineral	10	Lemon Tea	10	Coffee	1
Hot Cordials	10			Pickled Cucumber	7

PATRONS ARE RESPECTFULLY REQUESTED TO CHECK THEIR BILL AGAINST PRICES ON THE MENU.

110. 1960s Bloom's menu. Courtesy of Michelle Spencer.

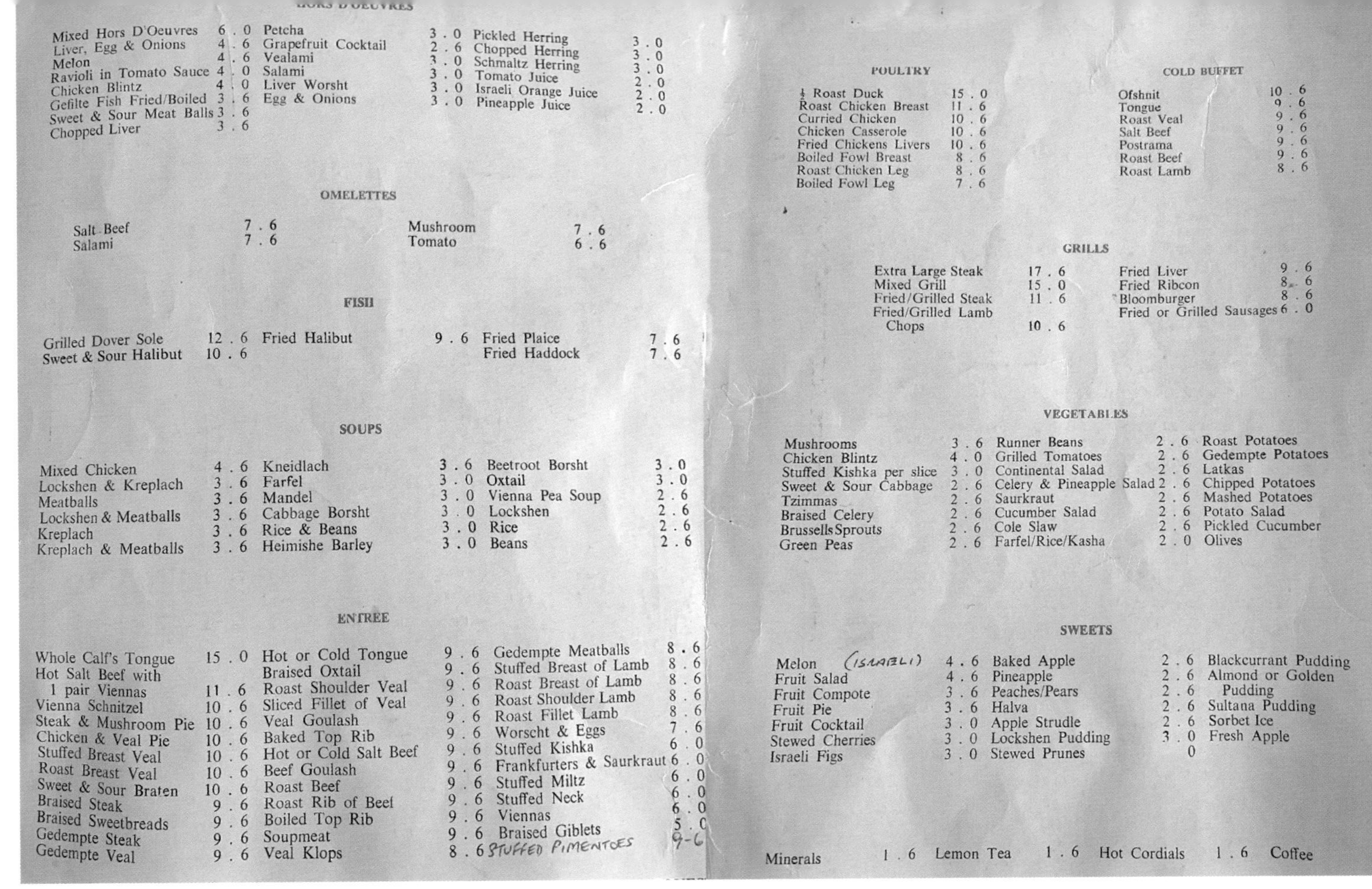

HORS D'OEUVRES

Mixed Hors D'Oeuvres	6 . 0	Petcha	3 . 0	Pickled Herring	3 . 0
Liver, Egg & Onions	4 . 6	Grapefruit Cocktail	2 . 6	Chopped Herring	3 . 0
Melon	4 . 6	Vealami	3 . 0	Schmaltz Herring	3 . 0
Ravioli in Tomato Sauce	4 . 0	Salami	3 . 0	Tomato Juice	2 . 0
Chicken Blintz	4 . 0	Liver Worsht	3 . 0	Israeli Orange Juice	2 . 0
Gefilte Fish Fried/Boiled	3 . 6	Egg & Onions	3 . 0	Pineapple Juice	2 . 0
Sweet & Sour Meat Balls	3 . 6				
Chopped Liver	3 . 6				

OMELETTES

Salt Beef	7 . 6	Mushroom	7 . 6
Salami	7 . 6	Tomato	6 . 6

FISH

Grilled Dover Sole	12 . 6	Fried Halibut	9 . 6	Fried Plaice	7 . 6
Sweet & Sour Halibut	10 . 6			Fried Haddock	7 . 6

SOUPS

Mixed Chicken	4 . 6	Kneidlach	3 . 6	Beetroot Borsht	3 . 0
Lockshen & Kreplach	3 . 6	Farfel	3 . 0	Oxtail	3 . 0
Meatballs	3 . 6	Mandel	3 . 0	Vienna Pea Soup	2 . 6
Lockshen & Meatballs	3 . 6	Cabbage Borsht	3 . 0	Lockshen	2 . 6
Kreplach	3 . 6	Rice & Beans	3 . 0	Rice	2 . 6
Kreplach & Meatballs	3 . 6	Heimishe Barley	3 . 0	Beans	2 . 6

ENTREE

Whole Calf's Tongue	15 . 0	Hot or Cold Tongue	9 . 6	Gedempte Meatballs	8 . 6
Hot Salt Beef with		Braised Oxtail	9 . 6	Stuffed Breast of Lamb	8 . 6
1 pair Viennas	11 . 6	Roast Shoulder Veal	9 . 6	Roast Breast of Lamb	8 . 6
Vienna Schnitzel	10 . 6	Sliced Fillet of Veal	9 . 6	Roast Shoulder Lamb	8 . 6
Steak & Mushroom Pie	10 . 6	Veal Goulash	9 . 6	Roast Fillet Lamb	8 . 6
Chicken & Veal Pie	10 . 6	Baked Top Rib	9 . 6	Worscht & Eggs	7 . 6
Stuffed Breast Veal	10 . 6	Hot or Cold Salt Beef	9 . 6	Stuffed Kishka	6 . 0
Roast Breast Veal	10 . 6	Beef Goulash	9 . 6	Frankfurters & Saurkraut	6 . 0
Sweet & Sour Braten	10 . 6	Roast Beef	9 . 6	Stuffed Miltz	6 . 0
Braised Steak	9 . 6	Roast Rib of Beef	9 . 6	Stuffed Neck	6 . 0
Braised Sweetbreads	9 . 6	Boiled Top Rib	9 . 6	Viennas	6 . 0
Gedempte Steak	9 . 6	Soupmeat	9 . 6	Braised Giblets	5 . 0
Gedempte Veal	9 . 6	Veal Klops	8 . 6	STUFFED PIMENTOES	9-6

POULTRY

½ Roast Duck	15 . 0
Roast Chicken Breast	11 . 6
Curried Chicken	10 . 6
Chicken Casserole	10 . 6
Fried Chickens Livers	10 . 6
Boiled Fowl Breast	8 . 6
Roast Chicken Leg	8 . 6
Boiled Fowl Leg	7 . 6

COLD BUFFET

Ofshnit	10 . 6
Tongue	9 . 6
Roast Veal	9 . 6
Salt Beef	9 . 6
Postrama	9 . 6
Roast Beef	9 . 6
Roast Lamb	8 . 6

GRILLS

Extra Large Steak	17 . 6	Fried Liver	9 . 6
Mixed Grill	15 . 0	Fried Ribcon	8 . 6
Fried/Grilled Steak	11 . 6	Bloomburger	8 . 6
Fried/Grilled Lamb Chops	10 . 6	Fried or Grilled Sausages	6 . 0

VEGETABLES

Mushrooms	3 . 6	Runner Beans	2 . 6	Roast Potatoes	2
Chicken Blintz	4 . 0	Grilled Tomatoes	2 . 6	Gedempte Potatoes	2
Stuffed Kishka per slice	3 . 0	Continental Salad	2 . 6	Latkas	2
Sweet & Sour Cabbage	2 . 6	Celery & Pineapple Salad	2 . 6	Chipped Potatoes	2
Tzimmas	2 . 6	Saurkraut	2 . 6	Mashed Potatoes	2
Braised Celery	2 . 6	Cucumber Salad	2 . 6	Potato Salad	2
Brussells Sprouts	2 . 6	Cole Slaw	2 . 6	Pickled Cucumber	1
Green Peas	2 . 6	Farfel/Rice/Kasha	2 . 0	Olives	1

SWEETS

Melon (ISRAELI)	4 . 6	Baked Apple	2 . 6	Blackcurrant Pudding	2
Fruit Salad	4 . 6	Pineapple	2 . 6	Almond or Golden Pudding	2
Fruit Compote	3 . 6	Peaches/Pears	2 . 6		
Fruit Pie	3 . 6	Halva	2 . 6	Sultana Pudding	2
Fruit Cocktail	3 . 0	Apple Strudle	2 . 6	Sorbet Ice	2
Stewed Cherries	3 . 0	Lockshen Pudding	3 . 0	Fresh Apple	
Israeli Figs	3 . 0	Stewed Prunes	0		

Minerals 1 . 6 Lemon Tea 1 . 6 Hot Cordials 1 . 6 Coffee

111. 1970s Bloom's menu. Courtesy of Michelle Spencer.

FOR KASHRUS

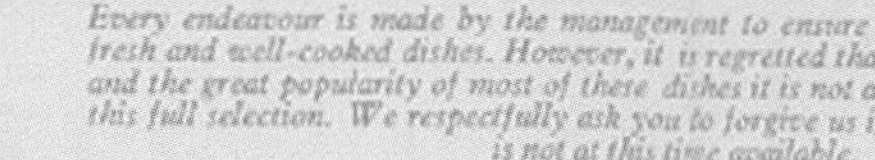

FOR QUALITY

Every endeavour is made by the management to ensure a full menu of absolutely fresh and well-cooked dishes. However, it is regretted that due to seasonal shortages and the great popularity of most of these dishes it is not always possible to maintain this full selection. We respectfully ask you to forgive us if your particular favourite is not at this time available.

HORS D'OEUVRES

Mixed Hors D'Oeuvres	35p	Petcha	20p	Grapefruit Cocktail	15p
Liver, Egg & Onions	30p	Vealami	20p	Beetroot Borsht per glass	15p
Melon	25p	Salami	20p	Tomato Juice	15p
Gefilte Fish Fried/Boiled	25p	Liver Worsht	20p	Israeli Orange Juice	15p
Ravioli in Tomato Sauce	25p	Egg & Onions	20p	Israeli Grapefruit Juice	15p
Chicken Blintz	25p	Pickled Herring	20p	Pineapple Juice	15p
Sweet & Sour Meat Balls	20p	Chopped Herring	20p		
Chopped Liver	20p	Schmaltz Herring	20p		

OMELETTES

Salt Beef	50p	Mushroom	45p
Worsht & Eggs	50p	Tomato	45p

FISH

Dover Sole	75p	Fried Halibut	55p	Fried Haddock	45p
		Fried Plaice	45p		

SOUPS

Mixed Chicken	25p	Kreplach	20p	Rice & Beans	20p
Lockshen & Kreplach	20p	Kneidlach	20p	Heimishe Barley	20p
Kreplach & Meatballs	20p	Beetroot Borsht		Oxtail	20p
Lockshen & Meatballs	20p	with Potato	20p	Vienna Pea Soup	20p
Meatballs	20p	Cabbage Borsht	20p	Lockshen	20p
		Farfel/Kasha	20p		

ENTREE

Hot Salt Beef with one		Roast Beef	75p	Stuffed Breast Lamb	65p
pair of Viennas	85p	Hot Salt Beef	75p	Roast Breast Lamb	65p
Steak & Mushroom Pie	75p	Sweet & Sour Braten	75p	Roast Shoulder Lamb	65p
Vienna Schnitzel	75p	Baked Prime Bola	75p	Roast Fillet Lamb	65p
Stuffed Breast Veal	75p	Braised Steak	75p	Baked Klops	55p
Roast Breast Veal	75p	Gedempte Steak	75p	Gedempte Meatballs	55p
Gedempte Veal	75p	Baked Top Rib	65p	Stuffed Miltz	45p
Roast Shoulder Veal	75p	Beef Goulash	65p	Stuffed Neck	40p
Sliced Fillet Veal	75p	Braised Oxtail	65p	Frankfurters &	
Veal Goulash	75p	Braised Sweetbreads	65p	Sauerkraut	40p
Roast Rib of Beef	75p	Soupmeat	65p	Viennas	40p
Hot Tongue	75p				

POULTRY

Fried Chickens Livers	75p
Curried Chicken	75p
Chicken Casserole	75p
Roast Chicken Breast	65p
Roast Chicken Leg	55p
Boiled Fowl Breast	55p
Boiled Fowl Leg	45p

COLD BUFFET

Aufschnit	75p
Roast Veal	75p
Tongue	75p
Salt Beef	75p
Roast Beef	75p
Roast Lamb	65p

GRILLS

Mixed Grill	95p	Fried/Grilled Lamb	
Fried/Grilled Steak	85p	Chops	65p
Fried Liver	75p	Bloomburger	65p
		Fried or Grilled Sausages	40p

VEGETABLES

Mushrooms	20p	Grilled Tomatoes	15p	Potato Salad	15p
Stuffed Kishka per slice	20p	Continental Salad	15p	Latkas	15p
Sweet & Sour Cabbage	15p	Celery & Pineapple Salad	15p	Farfel/Kasha/Rice	15p
Tzimmas	15p	Sauerkraut	15p	Roast Potatoes	15p
Braised Celery	15p	Cucumber Salad	15p	Gedempte Potatoes	15p
Brussels Sprouts	15p	Cole Slaw	15p	Chipped Potatoes	15p
Green Peas	15p	Mixed Vegetables	15p	Mashed Potatoes	15p
Runner Beans	15p	Broccoli	15p		

SWEETS

Fresh Pineapple	25p	Israeli Figs	18p	Halva	18p
Melon	25p	Lockshen Pudding	18p	Blackcurrant Pudding	18p
Fruit Salad	25p	Stewed Prunes	18p	Almond or Golden	
Fruit Compote	25p	Peaches/Pears/		Pudding	18p
Stewed Cherries	20p	Pineapples	18p	Sultana Pudding	18p
Fruit Pie	20p	Apple Strudle	18p	Sorbet Ice	
				Lemon or Orange	18p

		Lemon Tea	10p	Hot Cordials	10p
Minerals	10p	Coffee	10p	Pickled Cucumber	7p

PATRONS ARE RESPECTFULLY REQUESTED TO CHECK THEIR BILL AGAINST PRICES ON THE MENU.

112. Bloom's *Pesach* Menu, early 1970s. Courtesy of Michelle Spencer.

Additionally, there are examples of the fusion of various Eastern European ways of serving food: the sweet and sour meatballs and sweet and sour cabbage, and the appearance on the menu of *lokshen* as both a savoury and sweet dish and a dessert, blending the preference of Polish Jews for sweet dishes and with the preference for savoury food of Lithuanian and Ukrainian Jews mentioned earlier in this chapter. This fusion can probably be attributed to Jews from different parts of the Pale of Settlement living near one another in the East End and sharing their different food traditions, and marriage between Jews from different parts of Eastern Europe.

The range of food available at Blooms in the post-war years also included dishes that recent Jewish immigrants might not have even known about, yet alone tasted. Examples of the new foodstuffs included some typically British dishes, such as stuffed breast of lamb and shoulder of lamb, vegetables like broccoli (which had become prevalent in Britain in the eighteenth century), runner beans (brought to England from South America) and Brussel sprouts (which, despite their name, originated in Afghanistan, Iran and Pakistan, and came to England via Belgium in the late nineteenth century). These items reflect the anglicisation of Jewish diet that was taking place, food transfer in action, which might have been accelerated by the evacuation of Jews from the East End during the war when many people (especially young people) were living with or alongside non-Jews who fed them unfamiliar foods. Jews who served in the armed forces alongside non-Jews were also introduced to unfamiliar foods.[36]

However, British dishes were supplemented by both non-Jewish dishes from various parts of Europe: ravioli in tomato sauce from Italy, halva from Greece, beef goulash from the Austro-Hungarian world, braised celery from Turkey and the Balkans, sauerkraut from German speaking countries, coleslaw from the Netherlands and strudel from Austria and German. The inclusion of an increasing number of dishes that were German in origin might have been due to the influence of the continental Jews who arrived in the country before, during and after the Second World War. This international aspect of the menus indicates that Jews were not only entering mainstream society in Britain, they were now also people of the wider world rather than of the *shtetl* (small Jewish village or town in Eastern Europe).

Other interesting aspects of Bloom's menus during the post-war years are the use of foreign terminology, such as 'Entrées' and 'Mixed Hors d'Oeuvres', the inclusion of continental salads and the availability of a wider variety of meat dishes, especially the steak and mixed grill items. These are further signs of social and cultural integration and internationalisation,[37] as well as indicating increasing affluence. In Panikos Panayi's seminal paper on changes in Jewish food over the course of the twentieth century, 'The Anglicisation of East European Jewish Food in Britain',[38] he shows that these various changes were equally apparent in the evolving content of Jewish cookbooks, which were important in shaping the tastes of assimilating Jews.

Further features of the menus that must be briefly mentioned are: the specification of certain drinks as being Israeli, the result of the upsurge in Anglo-Jewry's loyalty towards Israel following the Six-Day War (and perhaps also of the Bloom family's love and support for Israel), and the inclusion of fried *gefilte* fish and fried haddock on the menus, 'Jewish' food items that are found only in Britain, the result of the influence (through intermarriage and other means) of Jews of Portuguese origin on immigrants from Eastern Europe.[39] Also notable is the prominence of side dishes. Many former Bloom's diners speak with passion about eating 'new green' pickled cucumbers, described as 'a more Mediterranean form of the *heimische* cucumbers'.[40] Mediterranean influences on the food eaten by Jews mirrored what was happening amongst the British population as a whole, largely as result of the books written by Elizabeth David.[41]

What is not so obvious from the menus is the most germane aspect of eating at Blooms reflecting the assimilation process: the quantity of food that was being consumed by Bloom's customers. Bloom's diners would typically order three cholesterol-laden and highly calorific courses. This phenomenon was also a prominent aspect of the Jewish hotels of Bournemouth in the post-war years, where dining has been described as 'a mind-blowing, waistline expanding experience, almost a practically non-stop eatathon'.[42] One GP practice located near the largest Jewish hotels in the town received numerous calls during the summer months to treat guests with digestive problems caused by overeating.

A variety of reasons have been posited for the copious eating by Jews in the immediate post-war years, including that it was a source of solace from the pain of the Holocaust. Geoffrey Alderman states: 'They were celebrating their endurance and vitality after the horrors of the 1940s – eating, perhaps, to assuage the guilt of their own survival and attempting to enter into a dialogue with their Maker through the medium of food.'[43] Another explanation is that the emphasis on eating was a reaction to the limited availability of food, and sometimes even hunger, experienced during the war. However, as time progressed, it became more obvious that enthusiastic eating was also a way of demonstrating the success of those able to afford to eat to their hearts content, and as a symbol of how far people were now removed from the poverty of *shtetl* life. Jews were now entering an expanding range of middle-class occupations, small shops were being replaced by significant businesses and small-scale landlords were becoming property dealers. Given the importance of food in Jewish life, what better way to celebrate material success than with lavish amounts of food? By the 1960s, Bloom's portions ranged from 'generous' to 'gargantuan' and were noted for being 'more gourmand than gourmet.' In 1964, the *Jewish Chronicle* writer Tracy Miller reported:

> I once dined with a Mancunian visiting London. He insisted on going to Blooms, so Blooms it was. My friend worked his way steadily through the menu: *lokshen* soup, a plate of salt beef with sweet and sour cucumbers, chips, *lokshen* pudding, and coffee. Hardly able to move at the end of his meal, he suddenly remembered that he had missed out on a course, and calling the waiter over, ordered a portion of chopped liver, concluding a very palatable meal with an *hors d'oeuvre*![44]

Valerie Isaacs remembers: 'I once ordered stuffed breast of veal with braised celery. The veal was enough for a family of four and on a separate plate was a whole head of celery. We didn't share in those days. It was delicious!'[45] The size of the Bloom's salt beef sandwiches became legendary. Reminiscing, the comedian David Schneider once commented: 'I don't know if they counted as sandwiches because the meat to bread ratio was so large. That was the joy of them.'[46] However, not everyone could afford to eat lavishly. Some less affluent families still living in the East End went to Blooms once a week, not to buy the large salt beef sandwiches that could not be split, but to purchase slices of pressed beef to take home to make a meal for several people, eking out the meat by serving the slices with chips.[47]

In the period between 1945 and 1970, membership of the United Synagogue continued to grow. As Jews left the first areas of settlement to live in the suburbs, they did not recreate the *chevrot* (small places of worship) that had sustained them as newly arrived immigrants. Instead, they set up new synagogues, which often become affiliated to the mainstream United Synagogue, since this was seen as a symbol of respectability and upward mobility. Although there were differences in levels of synagogue attendance and Jewish observance, and signs of secularisation became gradually became more apparent, well into the 1960s, Bloom's *kashrut* status was still important as an expression of Jewish identity, even for less and non-observant Jews. However, that was about to change because of far-reaching changes taking place in Anglo-Jewry.

The Late Twentieth Century

By the 1970s, the immigrant community was fully acculturated, and had made the transition from being 'would be British' to a successful cultural grouping. Whereas in previous decades the practice of Judaism was largely a private affair and one confined to safe Jewish spaces, the public display of Judaism, such as wearing *kippot* (skull caps) had become more commonplace. However, the size of the Jewish community fell dramatically from 400,000 in the post-war years to 283,000 in 1996 due to trends such as declining birth rates, intermarriage and Jews moving to Israel.[48]

Even more salient from Bloom's point of view was that the reduced Jewish community was changing religiously. Although the community overall moved to the right and became more observant, reversing the trend of previous decades, the community was also polarising and becoming less cohesive. There was a growth both in the progressive movements (Liberal and Reform Judaism) and what is now called the *charedim*, the various denominations of ultra-orthodox Jews (see Glossary of Hebrew and Yiddish Terms). The fully acculturated immigrant community was no longer in need of the 'comfort blanket' of eating traditional Jewish food in a kosher restaurant to provide a sense of identity and, whereas in the past Blooms had appealed to a broad cross section of Jews, this was no longer the case. While for some Jews, Bloom's *kashrut* status was not a major concern, for others it was not sufficient, even though, by the 1990s, the requirements of the Beth Din and the Kashrus Commission (now Kosher London Beth Din, KLBD) had become far more stringent. Despite this, Blooms chose to retain its kosher licence, probably to avoid offending the dwindling number of its Jewish customers to whom it did matter.

While Bloom's food was starting to lose its appeal for Jews, Jewish food was entering the mainstream. As discussed in the previous chapter, a greater number of non-Jews were now dining at Bloom's restaurant as an 'ethnic experience', especially in the Aldgate restaurant, and were purchasing the Bloom's packaged and canned goods that had flooded the supermarket shelves nationwide. However, the number of non-Jews eating *heimische* food remained small and, as one writer has commented, compared to America, the type of food Blooms provided 'never really turned heads outside the Jewish community'.[49] In addition, only a limited number of traditional Jewish foods made their way into the wider community. For example, it seems that while salt beef sandwiches were popular, there was no real appetite for dishes like *lokshen* and *gefilte* fish.

The fact that Jews no longer wanted the same thing in terms of dining is reflected in the growth of both 'glatt' kosher eateries, those that were licensed by ultra-orthodox Kedassia, and 'kosher-style' restaurants and cafés that were not licensed by the communal authorities. It is interesting that several of the non-kosher eateries that opened in the suburbs of north-west London and elsewhere were run by people who had previously worked for Blooms, as mentioned in Chapter Seven. Emulating Bloom's menu and food presentation, they became successful. One such kosher-style eaterie was Michael Bloom's Knosherie in Hatton Garden.[50] The food critic Jay Rayner commented trenchantly: 'It was too much hassle to have [a licence] and anyway his [Michael Bloom's] new City-Worker clientele didn't care whether a rabbi had muttered over their lunch or not.'[51]

Non-Jews had also moved on. When the restaurant opened at Bevis Marks Synagogue in 2003, it was welcomed enthusiastically by both high-powered Jewish businessmen, who had sorely missed having a restaurant on their doorstep where they could take clients wishing to eat a kosher meal, and non-Jews seeking to impress valued Jewish clients by taking them somewhere with a 'modern take' on Jewish food. The Bevis Marks restaurant also attracted tourists and Jews looking for an 'innovative venue' for a celebration.[52] A *Jewish Chronicle* food critic pronounced that the restaurant had 'assumed the mantle once occupied by Blooms – though with a completely different cuisine – of being the City's kosher eating place'.[53]

In addition to the changes taking place within the Jewish community, there were major shifts in British society that impacted on the appeal of Bloom's food. In the post-war years, wave after wave of different ethnic groups arrived in the country, which led to Britain becoming a multiracial society. Each of the new immigrant groups brought with them their own cuisine. Now part of mainstream society, Jews, like the wider population, wanted to sample the new foods that were on offer, a kind of culinary tourism. In response, commencing in the early 1980s, a plethora of eateries opened serving kosher versions of food from across the world – Chinese, Italian, Indian, Japanese and French. This phenomenon was particularly noticeable in Golders Green and the other suburbs of north-west London with burgeoning Jewish communities. The move towards a more cosmopolitan diet was accelerated by the advent of cheap flights and package holidays, of which Jews were quick to take advantage, exposing them to a wide range of cuisines and tastes.

As a result, Blooms, which had once been virtually 'the only show in town', was relegated to being just one dining option amongst a constellation of kosher cuisines. Eating Bloom's food was now a matter of choice rather than necessity, and the decision to do so was made less often because of the availability of many other options. Dining at Bloom's became something that people did on occasion rather than on a regular basis. When Michael Bloom appeared on the BBC's 'Restaurant Show' in 1994, he maintained that Bloom's customers did not want to eat food in fancy surroundings that 'did not leave them feeling like a balloon after *fressing* [eating a heavy meal]'.[54] Two years later, even though the food had become noticeably lighter and the portions smaller, the Aldgate restaurant closed.

The upsurge in loyalty towards Israel that followed the Six-Day War in 1967 led to many Jews taking their main holidays in Israel rather than in resorts such as Bournemouth,[55] and to make regular visits to Israel to visit friends and relatives living there. As a result, British Jews, who had previously existed on traditional Ashkenazi food, were exposed to the Middle Eastern Sephardi (see Glossary of Hebrew and Yiddish Terms) diet that predominated in Israel. This was another important factor in broadening Jews' taste in food. In Israel, they discovered that kosher food did not begin and end with chicken soup and *lokshen* pudding.

Over the same period, larger numbers of Israelis were coming to London to work or to study, mainly settling in north-west London. They found the Ashkenazi-style food that predominated devoid of taste, and this led to an explosion of Israeli-owned restaurants and takeaways, especially in Golders Green, which as a result was dubbed 'Little Tel Aviv'. The new eateries included Dizengoff, Taboon, SOYO (serving Israeli breakfasts), Zaki's and Pita. The most popular of the new eateries was Solly's, run by Solly Sade, who had at one time worked in the Bloom's restaurant in Aldgate.[56] Solly's endured for many years, became a 'foodie favourite' and was frequented by many celebrities, including some former Bloom's diners.[57] The new Sephardi dishes very quickly appealed to Jews of different backgrounds, but particularly to the younger generation who did not have the same emotional attachment to traditional Ashkenazi food still being served by Blooms, which they saw as a throwback to an earlier age. The boom in Sephardi eateries was matched by a growth in Israeli-owned grocery stores selling Sephardi produce, which became a rival to Bloom's manufactured goods.

The Twentieth-First Century

By the turn of the twenty-first century, the tide had well and truly turned against what was pejoratively characterised as 'immigrant food', 'peasant food', or the 'food of poverty and oppression'. The food critic Matthew Norman derided Ashkenazi food in general and Bloom's food in particular for its 'Teutonic lumps of meat' and for being tasteless. He commented: 'If a chilli was ever found in Blooms, a fire alarm would go off and everyone would have to be disinfected.'[58] Jay Rayner saw Ashkenazi food as a 'thin, etiolated affair compared to the extraordinary cookery of the Sephardi Jews'.[59] He described the food available at the booming Sephardi eateries as follows:

> … light and sunny. It's about grilled meats and couscous, marinated vegetables and hummus, stuffed peppers and roast aubergines and, like the Sephardi Jews themselves, comes from all points of the compass: Iran and Iraq, Morocco and Spain, Turkey and Syria and Egypt. It is, in short, much more in tune with Britain's increasingly eclectic tastes than Ashkenazi comfort food could ever be.[60]

He concluded by saying: 'And so, while Blooms in Whitechapel closes, a new restaurant like Kinneret in Edgware opens, offering a wide range of Sephardi dishes.'[61] Even people for whom Bloom's food retained a 'Proustian quality'[62] were seduced by the new array of Sephardi eating options, both kosher and non-kosher, and they quickly traded fatty *heimische* food for dishes cooked with oil and new vegetables imported from Israel, such as aubergines, peppers and avocados. The boom in Sephardi food intensified and broadened as

Israel saw an influx of Jews from the Middle East and North Africa, leading to a 'Levantathising'[63] of Israeli food and also the arrival in Britain of Sephardi Jews originating from Tunisia, Algeria and Morocco and a range of Middle Eastern Sephardi backgrounds (referred to collectively as *Mizrahi* (Eastern) Jews (see Glossary of Hebrew and Yiddish Terms)). Mainly coalescing in Jewish strongholds like Golders Green and Hendon,[64] the new wave of arrivals left their imprint on the eateries and shops in those areas. There had been an influx of *Mizrahi* to Britain in the years following the establishment of the independent state of Israel, but their numbers were comparatively small, they were more dispersed and the time was not ripe for them to influence Anglo-Jewish food as Ashkenazi Eastern European cuisine was still in its ascendency. The culinary climate at the beginning of the new century was very different and open a wide range of influences.

The widespread availability of Sephardi food, combined with an increasing awareness that the type of food served and sold by Blooms was unhealthy, resulted in many Jews seeking food that was 'less dense'. Jay Rayner described traditional Ashkenazi foods as being 'to light, healthy eating what Slobodan Milosevic is to the Nobel Peace Prize', and as 'light and feathery as, ooh, whipped lead'.[65] Anne Karpf was one of the few writers to defend Bloom's-type food, which she saw as an 'antidote to anxiety, a promise of plenitude' and warned other writers: 'Hands off our heritage.' However even she admitted that traditional Ashkenazi food 'celebrates the longevity of the tribe, even while actuarially it shortens the lives of its individual members'.[66]

A few years earlier, the *Jewish Chronicle* cookery editor Evelyn Rose, who championed healthy eating amongst Jews, mainly by incorporating Sephardi dishes into their diet, revealed:

> Whenever I talk to groups, I find enormous interest in healthy eating and a healthier lifestyle. Forty or thirty years ago, more food meant more love. Today, everyone realises that

> what's important is what is in the food that they're serving. They are more concerned about low fat, low sugar, additives and cholesterol.[67]

Evelyn Rose launched a range of soups that were marketed by the major Jewish food firm Rakusens as 'healthier' than traditional Jewish soups. Her legacy was taken forward by her daughter Judi, who with her GP-nutritionist cousin Dr Jackie Rose, launched *To Life! Healthy Jewish Food*, a cookbook containing healthy kosher recipes, drawing on Jewish cooking from around the world, fragmenting the two main categories of Ashkenazi and Sephardi food into many different local cuisines, and fusing different cooking styles.[68]

Appeals made by Evelyn Rose and other leading cookery writers to make Ashkenazi dishes more appealing to the modern Jewish palate by-passed Blooms for many years. In 2002, it was reported that a meal at Blooms usually commenced with 'the squadron of soups' – *lokshen*, *kneidlach* or *kreplach* soup, barley soup and beetroot *borscht* – as well as the *schmaltz* herring, the chopped liver and the *gefilte* fish. To follow, diners often selected from '*gedempte* meat balls, and roast chicken, liver and onions, *tzimmes*, *latkes* and pickled cucumbers', which was 'waiting to be rounded off with a plate of satisfying *lokshen* pudding or apple strudel …' The famed Bloom's salt beef sandwich, that 'sultan of sandwiches', had apparently become even larger, now being packed with slices of smoked turkey and salami as well as salt beef, which were interspersed with coleslaw, almost a parody of itself.[69]

When the Golders Green restaurant reopened after its refurbishment in 2007, the new menu was more cosmopolitan, featuring chicken curries, grilled Dover sole, grilled tuna, duck salad and spaghetti Bolognaise, but the loyal customers were largely eating the 'old favourites'. According to some food reviewers, Blooms, still flying the flag for *heimische* food, was 'stuck in a time warp', 'marooned in the past'[70] or was a 'timeless rock against a sea of trends'.[71]

113. Advertisement in the *Jewish Chronicle*, 16 March 2007.

Until 1980, neither of the Bloom's restaurants held a licence to sell alcohol. For most customers this did not present a problem since alcohol was generally of less interest to Jews, giving rise to the often repeated saying 'Gentiles drink and Jews eat.' A dinner at Blooms was usually rounded off with lemon tea or coffee, or blackcurrant juice (or later Coca-Cola) for children and young people. Initially, diners in the Aldgate restaurant wishing to partake of alcohol ordered their drinks from a waiter, who went to the pub next door to Blooms, the White Hart, to fetch them. Apparently, the waiters were sometimes seen either spilling the drinks or sipping them on the way back to the restaurant.[72] Later, Bloom's started purchasing kosher Israeli wines to serve in the restaurants. Reviews in *The Good Food Guide* suggest that these wines were 'nearly drinkable' and that customers were best advised to drink lemon tea instead.[73] The non-Jews who dined more than once at the restaurant knew to bring their own alcohol with them, even if it meant that they had to pay a cover charge.

By the time that ownership of Blooms in Golders Green passed to Jonathan Tapper in 1999, it had started to offer a wide range of good quality Israeli wines, including what was described as a 'very acceptable Israeli Carmel red'.[74] By 2007, the restaurant had a separate wine list, which featured more expensive wines and champagne. Bloom's customers were apparently now more discerning about what they drank than they had been half a century earlier when the writer Chaim Bermant commented that very few of the guests staying in Bournemouth at the luxurious Green Park Hotel were wine connoisseurs, even though the hotel had 'the best wine list in a kosher establishment anywhere'.[75]

The Final Years

In the last years of its operation, Bloom's restaurant did introduce lighter dishes as a nod to health-conscious Jews. However, this was regarded as being too little, too late. Potential customers seeking something healthy were now eating elsewhere and the decreasing numbers of customers dining at Blooms were largely older people still wedded to the traditional food it served. Philip Baigel recalls:

> I remember that at some point shortly before the closure of the restaurant, some bright spark had the idea of bringing the menu more up to date, and to include some "healthy options". Mysterious words, never before seen or heard within those hallowed walls, suddenly appeared on the menu. Terms like "side salad" and "greens" were now up there on a par with *schmaltz* and chopped chicken livers. I remember asking the waiter innocently "What happened to the *kishke*?" He replied, "Oh that stuff isn't considered healthy anymore, sir – and we have decided to take it off the menu." It was the same with the roast stuffed breast of lamb and all the other high cholesterol delicacies, which although they could be the harbingers of your next heart attack, were the only reason why anyone chose to come to Blooms in the first place. Ironically, the time at which Blooms rushed to embrace healthy eating was exactly the point when the slow death of the restaurant began.[76]

One former employee tells the story of daughters and sons of long-standing customers who would bring their parents into the Golders Green restaurant to eat but would not eat a meal themselves.[77] Because of its past reputation, people were tempted to try a meal at Blooms once or twice but found it 'out of date'. Whereas, the Bloom's menu had once been the epitome of the Jewish cultural experience, its time had come and gone, and it had failed to modernise for the twenty-first century at a time when it could have made a difference.

Notes

1. Gillian Feeley-Harnick, *The Lord's Table: The Meaning of Food in Early Judaism and Christianity* (Washington, D.C.: Smithsonian Institution Press, 1981), p.72.
2. See https://www.zemirotdatabase.org/view_song.php?id=9.
3. Observant Jews use different crockery, cutlery and cooking implements for meat and non-meat ('milky') foods.
4. Claudia Roden, *The Book of Jewish Food, An Odyssey from Samarkand and Vilna to the Present Day* (London: Penguin Books, 1999), p.56.
5. It is helpful to distinguish between the words diet and cuisine. Diet is a plan for eating, it is not a culture. Cuisine is the assembly, preparation and serving of different food items to produce dishes that do not exist in nature. These two concepts were defined by the Italian historian, Massimo Montanari. See Massimo Montanari, *Food Is Culture* (New York, Chichester, West Sussex: Columbia University Press, 2006), p.52.
6. See Roden, *The Book of Jewish Food,* p.3.
7. John Cooper, *Eat and be Satisfied: A Social History of Jewish Food* (Northvale, NJ: Jason Aronsen Inc,1993), p.149 and p.165.
8. Hasia R. Diner, *Hungering for America: Italian, Irish and Jewish Foodways in the Age of Migration* (London: Harvard University Press, 2001), Kindle location 1908.
9. See Roden, *The Book of Jewish Food*, pp.8–9.
10. *Ibid.*, p.10.
11. See. Diner, *Hungering for America,* Kindle location 1924.
12. See https://www.jhom.com/bookshelf/topics/letters/kheder.html.
13. See Diner, *Hungering for America,* Kindle location 2200.
14. See Cooper, *Eat and be Satisfied,* p.147.
15. See Diner, *Hungering for America*), Kindle location 2082.
16. See Roden, *The Book of Jewish Food*, p.116.

17. *Ibid.*, p.116.
18. See Cooper, *Eat and Be Satisfied*, p.147.
19. Some Jewish food writers trace meat sandwiches back to a rabbi, Hillel the Elder, who invented the first sandwich to commemorate the enslavement of Jews by the Pharaohs of Egypt in what he called *korech* (to encircle or envelope). What has become known as 'the Hillel sandwich' was devised as a way of fulfilling a Torah injunction that Israelites should eat *matzah* and bitter herbs. The Hillel sandwich also traditionally included meat, representing the Temple sacrifice. It is eaten during the *Pesach seder*. See Glossary of Eastern European Jewish Foods at Appendix One.
20. See Roden, *The Book of Jewish Food*, p.157.
21. See Diner, *Hungering for America*, Kindle location 2573.
22. 1960s Bloom's marketing brochure, courtesy of Jonathan Fishburn.
23. During the First World War, many German bakeries and butchers were ransacked.
24. In Eastern Europe, large numbers of cattle would be slaughtered in the winter as they became a liability during the harsh, cold months. This meant that there were plenty of cheap brisket cuts available, and so it became a *Chanukah* tradition to opt for brisket.
25. See various obituaries for Sidney Bloom on his death in 2003.
26. See Chapter Two.
27. See Chapter Three.
28. See https://www.seriouseats.com/guide-to-jewish-deli-food.
29. 'Miss Z' interviewed by Jerry White for *Rothschild Buildings, Life in an East End Tenement Block 1987–1920* (London: Pimlico, 2003), p.154.
30. Interview with Connie Stanton, 7.10.2022
31. See Glossary of Hebrew and Yiddish Terms.
32. Conversation with David Alfert (may his memory be for a blessing), Stan's son, 20.5.2023 (this is how he remembered the story his father told him).
33. Anonymous interviewee, 22.8.2022.
34. The term was used by the late Rabbi Lionel Blue to describe his talks and writings about East End history, the hallmark of which were his reminiscences about *heimische* food.
35. Images of Bloom's menus available online on various Facebook pages and at the Jewish Museum of London. Menus kept by Bloom family descendants, Martin Malin and Michelle Spencer, have also been used for this analysis.
36. See Jonathan Romain, 'They Looked for Horns', *Manna*, 26, article 12. He said: 'The dietary laws suffered greatly. Few non-Jews were familiar with the regulations concerning *kashrut*. Even if they were knowledgeable, kosher food was rarely available. Countless Jewish children had their first taste of bacon and, whilst it was eaten nervously to begin with, it soon lost its awesome connotations.'

37. Rabbi Scott Aaron, 'Meat and Jews: A Mixed Grill Relationship', *Times of Israel*, 19.9.2012.
38. Panikos Panayi, 'The Anglicisation of East European Jewish Food in Britain', in the journal *Immigrants and Minorities*, 30.2-3, pp.292–317.
39. See Roden, *The Book of Jewish Food*, p.96.
40. Conversation with Hannah Jacobs, 5.5.2023.
41. See https://en.wikipedia.org/wiki/Elizabeth_David.
42. Geoffrey Alderman, quoted in Pam Fox, *Jews by the Seaside, The Jewish Hotels and Guest Houses of Bournemouth* (London: Vallentine Mitchell, 2022) p.152.
43. Geoffrey Alderman, 'Abundant Southern Comforts', *JC*, 29.9.2014.
44. *JC*, 10.7.1964.
45. Valerie Isaacs, post on Facebook page The Jewish East End of London, 29.10.2016.
46. Quoted in *JC*, 18.6.2010.
47. Anonymous interviewee, 22.4.2023.
48. Marlena Schmool and Frances Cohen, *A Profile of British Jewry, Patterns and Trends at the Turn of the Century* (London: Board of Deputies, 1998), p.5.
49. *JC*, 1.1.2013.
50. See Chapter Six.
51. Jay Rayner, writing in *The Guardian*, 3.7.2000.
52. *JC*, 30.7.2010.
53. *JC*, 29.9.2006.
54. Quoted in *JC*, 8.7.1994.
55. See Fox, *Jews by the Seaside*, pp.130–131.
56. *JC*, 27.2.2000.
57. For further information on the Israeli eateries in Golders Green see Pam Fox, *The Jewish Community of Golders Green, A Social History* (Stroud: The History Press, 2016), pp.136–137.
58. Quoted in *JC*, 18.6.2010.
59. See Rayner, writing in *The Guardian*, 3.7.2000.
60. *Ibid.*
61. *Ibid.* His comment is somewhat ironic since the premises occupied by Kinneret were briefly taken over in 2007 for a new branch of Bloom's restaurant (see Chapter Five). While it was open, Kinneret apparently regularly attracted customers from as far afield as Luton and St Albans. *JC*, 12.11.1999.
62. David Schneider quoted in *JC*, 18.6.2010.
63. See Rayner, writing in *The Guardian*, 3.7.2000.
64. See Fox, *The Jewish Community of Golders Green*, p.77.
65. See Rayner, writing in *The Guardian*, 3.7.2000.
66. *JC*, 12.3.2004.
67. *JC*, 23.2.1996.

68. Judi Rose and Dr Jackie Rose, *To Life! Healthy Jewish Food* (Bishops Castle, Shropshire: YouCaxton, 2020).
69. *JC*, 7.6.2002.
70. See *JC*, 5.10.2007 and *JC*, 18.6.2010.
71. *JC*, 30.7.2004.
72. Stewart Levinson, post on Facebook page Memories of Hessel, Langdale Mans, Cannon Street Rd and Cable St, 29.11.2017.
73. Drew Smith (ed.), *The Good Food Guide 1983* (London: The Consumers' Association and Hodder and Stoughton, 1983), p.55.
74. *JC*, 12.11.1999.
75. Quoted in Fox, *Jews by the Seaside*, p.159.
76. Message from Philip Baigel, 8.12.2022.
77. Anonymous interviewee, 20.12.2022.

PART FOUR
Conclusions

Chapter Eleven

Bloom's Historical Significance and its Legacy

This book has explored the ninety-year history of Blooms as it evolved from a modest neighbourhood café and takeaway store, supplied by a small-scale butchery, became an internationally famous restaurant, operating in tandem with a national manufacturer and wholesaler, through to its ultimate demise. It is story that needed to be told and one that has proved to be well worth the telling because of the remarkable contribution that Blooms made to Anglo-Jewish life. While not ignoring the fact that Blooms was not the only successful restaurant, delicatessen and meat manufacturer in the East End, there are many aspects of Blooms that make it quite unique, and which become more apparent as the story unfolds.

Telling the Bloom's story is like holding up a mirror to Anglo-Jewry. At any point in the firm's history, it reflected what was happening in the Jewish community. However, its significance is much more than being a microcosm of Anglo-Jewish life. Blooms was an iconic institution that became legendary because it lasted so long. Like several other Jewish institutions that had a glorious past, notably the Jewish hotels and guest houses of Bournemouth, Blooms is surrounded by a significant amount of nostalgia and sentiment. More than a decade after the Bloom's restaurant in Golders Green closed, there are still regular cries along the lines of 'Bring back Blooms!'. The large amount of attention that Blooms continues to receive on social media is staggering.

Bloom's Changing Contribution to Anglo-Jewry

This understandable nostalgia and laudable desire to keep the memory of Blooms alive does not detract from, and even highlights, the key part it played in supporting and facilitating the assimilation of an immigrant community into mainstream life in Britain. The way in which it achieved this varied at the different stages of its existence.

In the firm's early years, Blooms (like similar establishments in the area) played a vital role in helping recent immigrants to make the adjustment from life in Eastern Europe to starting afresh in a new country where the dominant culture was alien to them. At Blooms, they could come together in an environment reminiscent of the 'Old Country' to share food (such an important component of Jewish life) with people who spoke the same language and understood the trauma of leaving a homeland being a refugee in a strange land. This communal experience made them feel connected to the life they had left behind while acting as a bridge to their new lives.

Blooms also provided a safe space where Jews, who in Eastern Europe had not been used to eating outside their homes, were able to enjoy in public the foods that they associated with their heritage (the concept of *oyesessen* referred to in Chapter Nine). At this early stage, little attention would have been given to how the mainstream population, or even the established Jewish community, viewed the ambience of the place; the emphasis was on the immigrants' cultural roots. Therefore, even when it was still a very modest undertaking, Blooms was already more than a place to buy or eat food.

As the immigrant generation became more settled and felt ready to move on from the *shtetl* life that they had initially aimed to recreate in London, they began to develop higher aspirations. Since they had been through the resettlement experience themselves, Morris and Rebecca Bloom were attuned to a change of outlook, and their enterprise expanded to meet rising expectations by producing a greater range of food, including foods that would have been regarded as luxuries in Eastern Europe.

Blooms also recognised and met the aspirations of the offspring of the immigrant population, who were coming of age in the late 1920s and early 1930s. Having been brought up and educated in Britain, their outlook, both culturally and religiously, was different from that of their parents; they occupied an uncertain space between two very different worlds. Although they were less cautious than the previous generation, many of these younger people were not yet ready (or able) to leave their segregated Jewish life. They wanted food and a convivial meeting place, a kind of 'secular synagogue', which kindled their optimism that a better life lay within their grasp. With its larger premises and 'restaurant' designation, Blooms was able to satisfy their needs.

The desire for moving on amongst both first and second-generation immigrants became more obvious as the 1930s progressed. As discussed in Chapter Ten, the concepts of place and displacement are central to determining what Jews eat and by the pre-war years, the dynamic between place and displacement are evident in Bloom's food offerings with a continuing nostalgia for the food of the Old Country beginning to combine with an embryonic Jewish identity in a new land.

The third group of Jews for whom Blooms facilitated assimilation during the 1930s was the upwardly mobile Jews who had left the East End, but who still had strong emotional ties to the area. Just as Blooms had initially functioned as a conduit between Eastern Europe and London, by providing a venue where they could meet and eat, Blooms was now serving to span the gap between the East End and the suburbs where an increasing number of Jews were living. With its delivery vans and increased production of kosher goods in its new 'electric factory', Blooms also helped to support Jewish life in the places to which Jews had dispersed. Whereas in the early days Bloom's role had been a simple one, it was now meeting a variety of needs and was fast becoming much more than a neighbourhood enterprise.

During the war, Blooms valiantly endeavoured to provide food throughout the day for those resilient Jews remaining in the East End despite the enemy bombs raining down on the area, and those making their way there from other places. Blooms was a beacon in the bomb-ravaged streets, offering both comforting food and emotional sustenance to war-weary Jews who were disproportionately affected by enemy action. For many Bloom's customers, the restaurant was probably seen as providing a safe 'Jewish space' at a time when British society in general was not welcoming of Jews. This role continued, even when the whole of the Bloom's enterprise had to be squeezed into the Wentworth Street premises.

When the war ended, there was a short hiatus while Blooms prepared for the next stage in its development, which was to be a huge leap forward. The relocation of the restaurant from the teeming backstreets of the Jewish quarter to 90 Whitechapel High Street was highly symbolic – not only was Blooms going upmarket, it was also making its way into the wider world. Even its location adjacent to Aldgate East underground station can be read as a sign of its links to a world beyond the East End. The much larger establishment, with its plate-glass window and lit shop sign, matched the rising aspirations of the rapidly assimilating immigrant community. The general upward mobility of the community was also signified by the extended menu, the white-clothed tables, the team of waiters wearing jackets and bow ties and the countermen wearing longer jackets and ties. For Blooms customers, these features conveyed that they were now able to enjoy a dining experience that was comparable to that of the majority population of the country. When in 1960 the claim that the restaurant was 'The Most Famous Kosher Restaurant in Great Britain' was added to the external signage, it was not just a reflection of the ambition of the Bloom family, but also of its customers' growing desire to be part of British society.

114. External signage of Bloom's. Courtesy of Ruth Plaut, *c.* 1985.

When the new restaurant opened in 1952, it was possibly a small step ahead of the progress being made by the community, but the Bloom family, perhaps because of their regular stays in an ostentatious hotel in Bournemouth,[1] recognised the emerging trends, and its customers were quick to catch up. By the mid-1950s, the main narrative amongst the descendants of immigrants was: 'We arrived as penniless migrants, but we put down roots and began to prosper. We survived the war and the Holocaust, and we are now becoming British citizens, living alongside non-Jews. We want to make our mark on society and share in its rewards for hard work and have some fun.'

Blooms in Aldgate restaurant was a perfect match for this mood. However, Blooms not only reflected the demographic, social, economic and psychological shifts in Anglo-Jewry, it also helped to support and accelerate the changes by providing a secure space where, just for a short while longer, immigrants and their offspring could stay in touch with their origins at a time when their lives were swiftly changing. At this time, the Jewish world was very fluid and sometimes confusing, but Blooms was a constant. It was like a magnet to an immigrant community's past lives and helped to bridge the social gap between Jews' old and new lives.

In the decade following the Second World War, Blooms also became a hub for 'nostalgia trips' for Jews who were aware that the East End that they knew had virtually disappeared. The décor of the restaurant was consciously designed to feed this nostalgia. Blooms became what the historian Pierre Nora refers to as a 'site of memory', a place where people, either as individuals or as part of a group, interact with a place, believing that it provides them with access to the past.[2] The firm's East End credentials were similarly promoted in Bloom's marketing materials.

115. Line drawing depicting and East End street market. Extract from 1960s Bloom's marketing brochure. Courtesy of Jonathan Fishburn.

It is important to remember that Blooms in Aldgate was not just a restaurant, it also had a very busy takeaway counter, filled with food that conveyed a sense of abundance through its plate-glass window, and which provided a link with the wider world of the streets of the East End, increasingly derelict as they were becoming. The takeaway therefore heightened Bloom's connections to the area and its history, which after all is why its diners were there. Even the experience of buying takeaway food helped to create a sense of Jewish history. In its location opposite Gardiner's corner, Blooms was symbolic of the confidence and pride of Jewish culture in an area that had been, and continued to be, on the frontline between fascism and anti-fascism.[3]

As Britain entered an era of abundance in the mid-1950s, Bloom's manufacturing arm was also supporting assimilation by extending its reach further and further beyond the East End by establishing the new distribution networks, described in Chapter Five, which enabled it to feed Jews not only in their suburban homes, but also in leisure and recreational locations. In addition, the factory was producing an increasing number of luxury lines as well as packaged goods that satisfied the aspirations of the generally more prosperous and middle-class community. Evocatively, Fiona Hulbert recalls:

> When I was growing up in the late 1950s and early 1960s, at weekends the whole family – myself, my two brothers and our parents – would bundle into my father's Bedford van that he used during the week at his garment factory in the East End. It had bench seats in the back, which meant that we were often joined by various friends and relatives. We drove to places like West Wittering on the south coast, taking with us a picnic, the centre piece of which was Bloom's canned goods – usually Viennas and meat balls – which we heated on a small primus stove and ate with bread, sitting amongst the sand dunes on a tartan rug.[4]

By the mid-1960s, Bloom's restaurant was reaching its heyday. A *Jewish Chronicle* writer declared that 'a legend has been born'.[5] Its role was also changing once more. Jews from many walks of life and countries of origin, with ranging levels of observance and at different stages in the assimilation process gathered at Blooms and engaged with each other in forging a unitary Anglo-Jewish identity. This identity brought together Jews who had previously defined themselves in terms of the many different countries from which they had originated, as well as the remnants of the established, pre-1880 community. Blooms was a place where gossip was exchanged, deals were struck and diners ruminated on life. Being Jewish, Bloom's customers bonded with intensity when they were eating together. With Bloom's emerging celebrity status, it was somewhere they wanted to be.

When it opened in 1965, the Golders Green restaurant was very popular, but it did not serve the same functions as the Aldgate restaurant. Its clientele was much narrower and more predominantly middle class than at the older East End establishment, and in its suburban environment it lacked the connection with immigrant history. The atmosphere of the Aldgate restaurant proved hard to replicate when diners were looking out onto streets lined with high-class clothes, shoes and accessory shops: 'It never had the same emotional significance or meaning as the Aldgate restaurant.'[6]

In the post-war period there was a discernible shift in the relationship between Blooms and its female customers. In Chapter Nine mention was made of traditional Jewish attitudes (based on Jewish teachings) towards the role of women in respect of the preparation and serving of food, which meant that initially they were largely excluded from buying food from Blooms. The small café is likely to have been filled with men having loud conversations, talking with their mouths full and making friends and forging contacts over red meat with its masculine overtones. This situation might have changed slightly in the decade leading up to the Second World War, but women customers would still have been viewed principally in their roles as wives and mothers rather than customers.

By the 1960s, more British women were entering the workforce and gaining other freedoms. As a result of their rapid assimilation, which had exposed Jews to different social norms, women now appear to have been eating at Bloom's restaurant as equals, even though the

Bloom's workforce remained male dominated. The shift in attitudes towards women might have been assisted by Evelyn Bloom and Sylvia Malin and the leading, high-profile roles they played in the business. Although she sometimes referred to herself as a *Yiddishe Momma*, the glamorous image that Evelyn overtly cultivated was very different. Women and their changing lifestyles also seem to have gained more influence in shaping Bloom's manufacturing and wholesale activities, evidenced by the dramatic increase in the production of canned and packed goods, which reduced the domestic burden on women. In addition, the way in which they were portrayed in Bloom's advertising materials was as 'modern' rather than in the pre-war years when they were absent from Bloom's marketing information.

The great stride forward in Bloom's manufacturing and wholesale operations came much later than at the restaurant. It occurred in 1971 when the factory moved from its overcrowded premises in Wentworth Street to a much more spacious building in Tunmarsh Lane, Plaistow. This move gave the firm the opportunity to modernise and expand its non-restaurant activities. While it was the restaurant that was in the public eye, a revolution in Bloom's role took place behind the scenes in Tunmarsh Lane as the factory geared itself up to stock the shelves of the burgeoning supermarkets up and down the country with Bloom's produce. The major expansion in the production and distribution of Bloom's goods made it a household name nationally and vastly increased the contribution the firm was already making to sustaining Jewish life, even in smaller communities. By curing meat and pickles and packaging them, Blooms enabled Jewish culture to survive and thrive in a British setting.[7]

However, while business was booming at the factory, the Aldgate restaurant was on the brink of less positive change. Ironically, it was to become evident that one of the reasons for the changing fortunes of the restaurant was the increased availability of packaged food, which Jews could consume at any time to fit in with their new lifestyles, often while they were doing other things, such as watching television or being at a football match; it was 'convenience food'.

At the beginning of the 1970s, Jews were still eating large meals at the restaurant or queueing at the delicatessen counter to buy copious amounts of takeaway food. They could afford to eat out lavishly and doing so was a symbol of their prosperity. Blooms was imbued with the aura of abundance and celebrity, and eating there was 'the thing to do'. However, by the end of the decade, far-reaching changes within Anglo-Jewry (particularly the polarisation of the community) and in wider society were impacting on Jewish eating habits, as discussed in detail in Chapter Ten. A fourth generation of descendants of the immigrants was coming of age, who felt no need to connect with their roots through the medium of eating *heimische* food in the East End; this had no resonance for them. They wanted to define their Jewishness in their own way, rather than those of their grandparents and great-grandparents. Even their parents wanted to spread their wings and try the world foods that were coming on stream.

By the 1990s, the Aldgate restaurant was largely the preserve of non-Jews, tourists and die-hard Bloom's diners from the suburbs of north and north-east London. As the East End historian Bill Fishman was wont to say, Blooms was 'the last of the Mohicans', almost an act of defiance.[8] When it closed in 1996, it had long since ceased to function as a major gathering place for the Jewish community. Since the different arms of the Bloom's business were interdependent, the closure of the restaurant impacted on the manufacturing activities, even though they still had a major role to play in Jewish life.

Norman Bookbinder comments: 'By the 1990s, the restaurant had expertise and experience galore, but it was entirely the wrong place.'[9] However, the East End was changing rapidly. Had the restaurant been able to remain open for another decade, it would have been well-placed to take advantage of the 'Big Bang' in the City and to serve the vibrant multicultural community that now epitomises the East End, which includes a significant number of younger Jews who have once again settled in the area. Rinkoff's bakery in Jubilee Street and Vallance Road and Beigel Bake in Brick Lane have blossomed because of the East End's changing character.[10]

The transfer of Bloom's manufacturing and wholesale activities to the large enterprise of Gilbert's Kosher Foods had implications for Bloom's former customers. On one hand, it led to goods being produced on a larger scale, resulting in lower prices in the supermarkets. On the other hand, it meant that decisions on the choice and content of products were in the hands of a large corporation and that customers had less influence than they had previously. The growth of pre-packed and ready-prepared food helped to erode further traditional views on the role of women in relation to food to the point where communal bodies were concerned about the reduction of women's skills in food preparation and their knowledge of recipes handed down through generations. However, for many women (less so perhaps for *charedi* women), this was a small price to pay for their liberation from stereotypical roles, especially since the reduction in food knowledge related to a type of food that was increasingly unpopular with a new generation of Jewish women.

The Golders Green restaurant was the only part of the Bloom's business to survive following the closure of the Aldgate restaurant. It struggled on for another fourteen years, but without a clear niche or role in relation the Jewish community. When it too closed in 2010, Blooms had been flying the flag for kosher restaurants for the best part of a century, and many people were saddened by the news of the closure of the iconic restaurant. One former customer commented: 'Blooms was an institution and I was sad when it closed, rude waiters and all, but the food wasn't that great any longer.'[11] However, the reality was that, by then, very few people wanted to eat traditional Eastern European food (or to do so on a regular basis) because they had more cosmopolitan tastes and the demand was now for a full range of restaurants providing kosher versions of world cuisine, much as customers in the non-kosher market expected.

The many types of food being savoured by Jews calls into question the often-quoted statement made by the French philosopher Jean-Anthelme Brillat-Savarin in 1825: 'Tell me what you eat: I will tell you what you are.'[12] Jews were trying many different cuisines, but it had no impact on their, by now, firmly established Anglo-Jewish identity; they did not become what they ate. Brillat-Savarin could not have foreseen the impact of the globalisation of the food industry. In addition to the world foods that they were eating, there was also an increased demand by Jews for 'healthy' food. It is ironic that while the first generation of immigrants were preoccupied with having enough to eat, born out of scarcity and famine in Eastern Europe, several generations on, their descendants were worried about consuming too many calories.

It is worth analysing two further aspects of the historical significance of Blooms, the first of which is the way it acted as a welcoming gathering space and became an anchor for community life. Especially in its heyday, the Aldgate restaurant was a prime example of a 'third place', a term coined by the American sociologist Ray Oldenburg in his 1989 book, *The Great Good Place*,[13] to describe casual and informal settings that occupied an intermediate realm between home ('first' place) and work ('second' place).

Oldenburg identified eight key characteristics of a third space, each of which Blooms readily satisfied: neutral ground (Bloom's diners had no obligation to be there, it was their choice to eat at the restaurant and they could come and go as they pleased); a leveller (Blooms placed no importance on socio-economic status and there were certainly no qualifying characteristics for eating there, other than perhaps a willingness to devour large quantities of highly calorific food); conversation (Blooms was abuzz with people engaging with each other, often in tandem with eating); accessibility (the restaurant was reachable by road and rail and the car park was an additional perk. It was also psychologically accessible); regulars (Blooms had a core of customers who set the tone for the place); low profile (despite its neon sign outside, Blooms prided itself on its 'no frills' interior); playful mood (the atmosphere of the restaurant was light-hearted and there was great deal of banter); and a 'home from home' (the Bloom family were keen to *schmooze* with their customers, the diners felt encouraged to regard the restaurant as a place where they belonged). Bloom's role as a third place was fully recognised by contemporary commentators. In 1966, the writer Jo Joseph, asserted in the *Jewish Chronicle*:

> Blooms has become a rendezvous for interesting people on every rung of the social ladder. The food is relished by MPs, GPs and VIPs. It is the eating–meeting–greeting place for old *landsmen* and reviving the past over steaming dishes, where

> bewitching aromas dance the *hora* [popular Jewish dance] around the nostrils, relaxing furrows, keeping time at bay.[14]

The second feature of Blooms that would benefit from further comment is its cultural characteristics. Blooms was not just a neutral space that allowed Jews to transcend long-standing divisions between them based on class and country of origin, it was also an intensely, and some would say, eccentrically Jewish space. Like the Jewish hotels of Bournemouth, it enabled Jews to relax and be themselves. Jews visited Blooms to sample the Jewish culture as well as the food. News spread around the community and it quickly became a 'destination of choice' for Jews. Writing in the *Jewish Chronicle* in 1964 about Jewish seaside hotels, but equally relevant to Blooms, Ben Azai commented:

> Jews, I am aware, are gregarious, and they like to be where they are reasonably certain others will be, and the concentration then tends to be cumulative, more going where more go, while the less-popular resorts become less popular. The word only needs to go around that a place is full of Jews for them to descend upon it from every quarter.[15]

Similarly, David Hallgarten recalls: 'It was such a Mecca for Jews from all over the place, and it was not unusual to see someone you hadn't seen for five or ten years.'[16]

Bloom's restaurant was also a non-threatening space where Jews could test out their recently acquired middle-class manners without exposing themselves to the derision of the longer-established upper and middle classes, although over-pretentiousness was likely to have been deflated by the irreverent Bloom's waiters.

As time progressed, Blooms became an increasingly secular environment, a place where diners could embrace, maintain and develop their Jewish identity, rather than practise their religion:

> You were definitely going to a restaurant and not to synagogue; you were experiencing Jewish culture, but you were not experiencing religion, not sitting through three hours of a

> *Shabbos* service. It might incidentally reinforce a religious outlook, but people did not go to Blooms to pray; they were going to be with Jewish people and, at that time, there were very few places that they could do that.[17]

In his 1984 paper, 'Des Espaces Autres', the French philosopher Michel Foucault wrote about 'other spaces', what he referred to as 'heterotopia', which function as a counter-site to everyday life.[18] He put forward four categories of heterotopias, including spaces that allow for the affirmation of differences and have more layers of meaning than immediately meet the eye. Bloom's restaurant in its heyday was a prime example of such spaces. This is evident in the way in which former diners talk about the Jewishness of the place and how Jewishness was toned up rather than toned down at Blooms. Beverley-Jane Stewart comments:

> We Jews are not shy and retiring. We are always listening to other people's conversations and arguing. This kind of boisterousness for which Blooms was known would only have happened in a Jewish restaurant. We were always looking around to see who we knew. People went to Blooms to see and be seen.[19]

What is perhaps most interesting about this analysis of the part played by Blooms in Anglo-Jewish history, is what it says about the assimilation of Eastern European Jews. Until relatively recently, historians tended to portray the 'alien Jews', as they were often referred, as pliable subjects, whose religious outlook and way of life was capable of being shaped by philanthropy and education by the already assimilated Jews. However, the Bloom's story shows that, from the outset, the immigrants and their descendants were determined to be in control of their own destiny. They generally assimilated at their own pace and on their own terms, finding their own social space. On occasion, it almost appears that there was an air of defiance against British traditions and customs, with the immigrants creating their own institutions and support systems (of which Blooms might be regarded as one), and remaining connected to their roots and their traditions until they felt sufficiently secure as British citizens (largely not until the third and fourth generations) to substitute a new identity with which they felt comfortable. As David Feldman has stated, the immigrant Jews were 'active participants' in their anglicisation.[20]

The path taken by Eastern European immigrants and their descendants in Britain diverged from both the experience of preceding Jewish settlers in Britain and the American immigrant experience. While earlier, much smaller waves of Jewish immigrants to Britain had found it necessary to obliterate their culture almost completely to gain acceptance, the Eastern European immigrants were determined not to be moulded into 'good Anglo-Jewish citizens' by forsaking their Yiddish identity. Their achievement was no mean feat given the strong pressures for assimilation, both within and outside the Jewish community. By comparison, the pressures for Jews to assimilate in America were not nearly as strong and since Jews there were far more numerous, they were better able to withstand any coercion to conform. Ironically, because of the more conducive climate, the Eastern European immigrants assimilated more quickly in the United States.

The desire of immigrant Jews to control their assimilation, which Blooms helped to facilitate, was also a salient factor in accounting for Bloom's success and its longevity, to which we will now turn.

The Reasons for Bloom's Success and its Decline

Although several chapters of this book have been devoted to examining specific aspects of the Bloom's business – the staff, the waiters, the customers and the food – what becomes abundantly clear is that the key to Bloom's success is that no single element of the business was more important than another in making it work; it was the package as a whole and the interplay and synergy between the component parts of that package that led to it becoming a legend. While some customers were more interested in certain aspects of Blooms, say the food rather than the pantomime provided by the waiters, or meeting long-lost friends and relatives, rather than being focused on what they ate, they nevertheless recognised that there was much more to Blooms than its famous salt beef sandwiches. Today, we might refer to Blooms as a theme park.

However, in addition to the staff, customers and the food, there is a fourth and vital element of the package, which must not be overlooked – the role of the Bloom family. From its inception, Blooms was run as a family enterprise and family members played a leading part in its operation. As a result, the family's views and interests dominated the ethos of Blooms. The family was the firm and the firm was the family, the success of one reinforcing the power and glory of the other. While this process is apparent in many family-owned and run businesses, it is even more pronounced when a family is Jewish, a culture in which family pride and traditions are especially potent. In particular, the family's commitment to *tzedakah*, instilled in the business by Morris Bloom, and handed down from generation to generation, permeated the business.

The family were not only prominent in leading the business, but they were also very visible and 'hands on'. Martin Malin comments:

> I often used to think that my uncle Sidney was a bit like a ringmaster in a circus, managing all the different, larger-than-life and forceful people who worked for Blooms. And he did this at the same time as making sure that the kitchen ran smoothly, always watching to see that the customers were happy and enjoying themselves. Somehow, he made it all work.[21]

A significant proportion of the firm's employees was made up of close family friends, many being people with whom Sidney and Sylvia had grown up, which reinforced the family atmosphere of Blooms. Even if what might have been seen as 'nepotism' by outsiders might have reduced the profitability of the business, it did give Blooms a branding that enhanced its reputation and which was readily understood by its Jewish clientele.

The 'family feel' of the business was retained even after Blooms became a famous institution and made a major contribution to generating both staff and customer loyalty. The prominence of family members and their positive impact on the business is very similar to other Jewish enterprises, most notably the celebrated Jewish hotels in Bournemouth when they were in their heyday. With their drive and commitment and their social and managerial skills, Rebecca and Evelyn Bloom and Sylvia Malin were very similar to the powerful women proprietors of the hotels, the so-called 'Grande dames of Bournemouth', who were 'queen bees in an era when few women had top jobs'.[22]

In addition to the family atmosphere of Blooms, several people interviewed for this book saw the way in which family members supported, encouraged, guided and acted as role models for staff as being important in the ascent of the business. However, the feature of the Bloom family, which appears to have been the most influential in securing the international reputation of its restaurants and its manufacturing and wholesale activities, was the cohesiveness of the Bloom family unit. The business moved seamlessly from Morris and Rebecca to Sidney, Evelyn Bloom and Sylvia Malin who worked as a team, contributing complementary skills. The team was at its most cohesive when the firm was at its most successful. Strong family bonds led to a robust business and helps to explain the longevity of Blooms.

What the Bloom family did supremely well for an extended period was to manage a business package so that it became more than the sum of its parts. However, as it emerged, organising a successful business package and managing it well were not the only factors in determining continued success. It was also about timing – spotting opportunities to launch or modernise different elements of the business – reading market trends, harnessing technological developments, monitoring people's eating habits and their tastes in food and recognising consumer concerns. However, as his own son admitted, Sidney Bloom was a cautious man.[23] While some East End businesses (notably the Rinkoff bakery[24]) were able to achieve long-term sustainability by maintaining a balance between continuity and change, the Bloom family appear to have erred on the side of adhering to traditional values and approaches instilled in the business by Morris and Rebecca. Elissa Bayer comments: 'I have always worked in the City, so I went more to the Aldgate branch than to Golders Green. The big thing about Blooms was that it never changed. They always did things their way, and the way that they had always been done.'[25]

It can also be argued that Blooms traded for too long on the success of a business model that had relied on its East End credentials. In 1966, a contemporary writer remarked that, at Blooms, 'nosh was wrapped up in nostalgia'.[26] Not only did the image of the Jewish East End that Blooms sought to portray fail to reflect the reality of a rapidly disappearing entity and the deteriorating environment of the area, but it also failed to recognise the impact of the changing outlook of successive generations of the offspring of immigrant Jews. Over time, the nostalgia that was an integral theme of Bloom's *raison d'être* became increasingly irrelevant. For each new generation, there was a diminishing interest in maintaining connections with the East End and the nostalgia that Blooms had encouraged.

The success of Blooms relied heavily on the cohesiveness of the family unit, but there are indications that, over time, the family became less cohesive. The reasons for reduced family cohesiveness include: the loss of a vital family member – the death of Evelyn Bloom in 1990 at a relatively young age (certainly the business declined very rapidly after her death); the weight of pressures created by changes in the meat industry and the '*kashrut* wars' (in 1986, Michael Bloom revealed that the company was on the point of being 'brought to its knees' due to 'inflated prices and limited meat'[27]) and the publicity the rows attracted; reducing trade in the Aldgate restaurant and mounting signs of decline, such as failing machinery at the factory; and increasingly unfavourable reviews of the restaurants.

By the 1980s, there were some difficult decisions to be taken on issues, such as investment in technology and the adaptation of traditional Bloom's recipes, as mentioned in Chapter Six. There were also the issues of location and the business forms that work in different locations. Alan Dein comments:

> When Bloom's restaurant opened in Whitechapel High Street in 1952, it was in a superb location. You came out of the underground station and stumbled into Blooms. It was probably the savviest things that the Bloom family did when they moved there. But 40 years on, it was in entirely the wrong location for Jewish customers, although its life was extended by the restaurant being within walking distance of the City of London. When the Golders Green restaurant opened in 1965, it was also in a good location, that's where the Jewish community were, and there were very few other kosher eating options. However, the formula that worked so well in the East End wasn't a good fit for the new environment. By the time it closed, the Golders Green restaurant was still in the right place, but everything else had changed and Blooms had failed to see this.[28]

In 2012, a lengthy article by Marcus Dysch appeared in the *Jewish Chronicle* analysing the reasons for the end of Blooms, which he thought were numerous: the super abundance of kosher restaurants; the difficult economic climate (Blooms was not the only kosher eaterie to close at around the same time); the decline in the number of people keeping kosher; the hard work and long hours involved in running a restaurant; and rising meat prices.[29]

Although all the factors cited by Marcus Dysch clearly contributed to the final demise of Blooms, what the article failed to mention was that, in addition to Bloom's decision to adhere to its long-standing business model, to a large extent, Blooms was a victim of its own success. By playing a role in helping to produce an assimilated, self-confident and thriving Jewish community, bolstered by growing prosperity and the rise of a multicultural society in which diverse groups were now being encouraged to celebrate their origins, Blooms was no longer necessary. The formula that had worked so well for three decades in supporting assimilation had outlived its contribution, especially in the setting of Golders Green in the twenty-first century. Some of the events that precipitated the closure of the two restaurants, rendered the demise of Blooms sadder and more painful than it might otherwise have been, but without major changes to the way in which it operated, the end of Blooms was probably inevitable.

Blooms: A Very British Phenomenon

Blooms was not only intensely Jewish; it was also very British. The way in which it developed and the form it took were very much a reflection of the nature of British society and British culture. This was highly apparent to the Canadian journalist and travel writer David Sax when he visited London in the early years of the twenty-first century to explore what he described as the 'Deli Diaspora'. He commented:

> While working class roots are a source of pride in the United States, the rigors of the monarchy-based upper class in Britain place a great emphasis on one's lineage. While the Hollywood studio executive can rhapsodize about being raised in a Brooklyn tenement, the same cannot be said about a peer in the House of Lords who grew up in Brick Lane. This affected how London's Jewish delis evolved.[30]

The impact of its British environment on the character of Blooms can be evidenced by comparing and contrasting the firm with the traditional New York Jewish delicatessen ('deli'),[31] the history of which was coincidentally being prominently exhibited in Los Angeles as this book was being written.[32] There is more to be said about the differences and similarities between the New York delis and the many other Jewish delis that operated in the East End and elsewhere in London, but the focus of this discussion in this book is Blooms.

The beginnings of the New York delis and of Blooms are remarkably similar. They both originated in the latter part of the nineteenth century, starting life with the selling of salt beef (called corned beef in America), sausages and pickles, mainly by German-Jewish butchers, to other Jews. In both countries, this practice was emulated by Jews from Eastern Europe when they started to arrive in large numbers at the end of the century, making sure that everything was kosher and adding their own, more familiar dishes. In America, one of these traditional dishes was pastrami, a form of smoked and seasoned salt beef imported by Romanian Jews, of which a notably larger proportion settled in New York than in London. As in London, the experience of eating beef and other meats on a regular basis only became possible for the Eastern European immigrants to New York after their arrival in a new country.

The new generation of butchers was mainly involved in the small-scale manufacture of meat products, which they sold from a simple storefront. As with Blooms and similar East End eateries of this era, the New York delis were the first places where Eastern European Jewish food became visible to the wider world and subsequently came to represent 'Jewish food'. The American scholar, Seth Wolitz, comments that the deli was 'the epitome of Jewish culinary experience in New York. It was the first (and most beloved) venue for Jewish food outside the home and a favourite neighbourhood institution.'[33]

In both London and New York, these immigrant businesses did not evolve to become more than storefronts until the 1920s, which is when the divergences between Blooms (and other businesses like it) and the New York delis begin to become apparent. In London, the kosher cafés and restaurants that opened in the interwar years were mainly, but not exclusively, located in the streets of the East End,[34] serving the teeming Jewish quarter. In New York, the new wave of delis, including the renowned Reuben's deli, mainly opened in the city's theatre district, where they became synonymous with the showbiz culture of Broadway.[35] It was only subsequently that they began springing up in Jewish strongholds in the city, such as the Lower East Side, the Bronx and Brooklyn, where they could be found on the corner of almost every block. The New York delis became such an iconic institution that their presence marked a Jewish neighbourhood more clearly than a synagogue.[36] Due to differences in the size of their respective Jewish populations, the delis in New York were always much more numerous than in London. It is estimated that by the early 1930s, there were 1,550 delis operating in the five boroughs of New York.[37]

In New York, many of the so-called 'Mom and Pop' businesses, like Blooms was in its early years, quickly went on to become larger delicatessens with extensive sit-down areas. Many also featured in-house bakeries and 'appetising sections' as well as a deli counter. Their names and specialities were often displayed in ostentatious neon lights. By comparison, the Bloom's café (later referred to a restaurant) remained small and relatively unassuming until after the Second World War, probably because of its location in the East End of London and its relative lack of competition.

The New York delis reached their zenith in the interwar years, several decades before Blooms experienced its heyday. Unlike Blooms, which soldiered on during the war and flourished after it ended, a significant proportion of the New York delis closed in the war years due to food shortages and lack of patrons. Many more closed during the 1950s as Jews left New York to live in the suburbs, taking their delis with them. Those delis that remained in New York struggled to make a profit due to lack of custom, the rising cost of meat, especially kosher meat, difficulties in securing staff and the increasingly dangerous environment of many parts of New York. The New York delis were therefore reaching their nadir at the time that Bloom's restaurant was at the height of its celebrity status and its factory was entering its boom time. The traditional New York delis that survived increasingly became the preserve of non-Jewish tourists and occasional nostalgia hunters, but this was decades before the same happened to Blooms.[38]

It is not just the timeline that is different. Almost from the outset, the delis that opened in Manhattan were patronised by Jews and non-Jews, particularly those operating near Broadway, where Jewish stars of the stage socialised with non-Jewish actors escaping from the antisemitism that was rife in America at the time. The delis that opened in other parts of New York were popular with Jews, who as they became more secular, used them as meeting places to talk politics, hold community meals, and meet their spouses.[39] Non-Jews were quickly attracted to these convivial and inexpensive eateries and they became immersed in their Jewishness, which rubbed off on them.[40] The non-Jewish deli customers of the interwar years were particularly numerous on Sundays (like Blooms, this was the delis' busiest day) when the takeaway counters became 'nothing short of a lifesaver' for those entertaining unexpected guests, or those who had returned from holiday to an empty larder.[41]

Unlike Britain, America has always been a country made up mainly of immigrants, creating a cultural melting pot that has led to a much greater fusion of different cultures and foodstuffs than Britain. By comparison to the New York delis, Bloom's customers remained almost exclusively Jewish, and the restaurant did not become an effective bridge between Jews and non-Jews until the 1970s. Added to the rigours of the British class system previously mentioned, in the post-war years successive governments placed an emphasis on unifying different ethnic and religious groups into a single 'British' identity. As a result, for much longer than in New York, British Jews needed a safe space where they could be overtly Jewish to withstand the forces making for total assimilation.

The early patronage of the New York delis by non-Jews had a major impact on the food that they served. By the middle of the twentieth century, the menus of many delis had become Americanised and were continuing to absorb more and more dishes from other cuisines. In Ted Merwin's outstanding history of the New York delis, he comments that many were now serving more turkey than corned beef and pastrami, especially in the lead-up to Thanksgiving Day.[42] The American food writer Harry Golden once quipped: 'The moment they [the Eastern European Jewish immigrants] settled themselves in the ghetto they did not walk, they ran for the nearest Chinese restaurant to feast on chow mein. Chow mein was a sort of "instant Americanism".'[43] By comparison, the broadening of Bloom's menus, and the fusion of cuisines they incorporated, happened much more gradually and was greeted with far less enthusiasm by Bloom's customers, who generally became more cosmopolitan in their eating habits much later than in New York.

The presence of non-Jews in the New York delis not only exposed Jews to other cuisines, it also introduced them to different eating habits, especially the emphasis on healthy eating, which came to the fore in America earlier than in Britain. The outcome of this was that New York Jews were generally quicker to abandon what were regarded as unhealthy *heimische* foods than Jews in Britain. In New York, the process started in the interwar years when there was a proliferation of both kosher and non-kosher eateries selling healthy and gourmet food.

In addition, the delis' broad-based patronage meant that many were quick to discard their kosher credentials. The kosher meat market in New York was riddled with fraud and there was a great deal of confusion relating to kosher certification due to the city's plethora of licensing bodies. As a result, some delis gave up using kosher meat, saying that they wanted 'no part in the complicated, expensive and often hypocritical world of kosher certification'.[44] Others went a step further, remaining open on *Shabbat* and Jewish holidays and mixing meat and milk dishes,[45] both of which were a violation of the Jewish law. Their proprietors argued that different understandings of kosher could coexist. This trend reflects the fact that, in general, the American Jewish community has always been more religiously progressive than the Anglo-Jewish community.[46]

The appearance of the 'kosher-style' deli was also the outcome of changes within the Jewish community in America. Between 1914 and 1924, there was a 30 per cent decline in the number of Jews keeping kosher, the time of the most rapid growth of New York delis.[47] For some Jews, eating in a deli became a form of religion; they called themselves 'gastronomic Jews'. Ted Merwin suggests that this reflected the desire by many Jews to create a new balance between their Jewish and American identities and to downplay Judaism in favour of a more secular way of being Jewish.[48]

By the 1940s, this kosher-style deli had become the most prevalent form of deli in New York.[49] By contrast, a large proportion of Bloom's customers continued to regard eating in a licensed kosher restaurant and buying packaged kosher food as part of their Jewish identity for much longer, perhaps as a bastion of defence against total assimilation. Whilst New York delis were ambivalent about publicising their *kashrut* status, Blooms ostentatiously displayed its kosher credentials in its signage: 'M. Bloom (Kosher) & Son Ltd', and 'The Most Famous Kosher Restaurant in Britain'. The clear message was that kosher food and the people who ate it were worthy of being part of British society, and loyalty to religious tradition was something to be admired.

A reflection on the comparative history of Blooms and the New York delis makes it apparent that while there was a linear progression in the evolution of Blooms and its contribution to Anglo-Jewish life, in New York the picture was much more complex. Due to the delis' location in many different parts of the city, the New York delis sought to meet the varying needs of their clientele. In the interwar years, the basic and inexpensive delis situated in the Lower East Side, Brownsville and East Bronx, what Ruth Glazer calls '*shlacht*' (literally struggle) stores, were clearly designed to cater for the newer immigrants and to assist them in retaining their connections to Eastern European. They were like the delicatessens in the East End of London, such as Mossy Marks's in Middlesex Street, Barry Rogg's in Canon Street Road (both of which endured until the late twentieth century), and also to Blooms in its very early days. Those delis located in more upscale neighbourhoods like the Upper West Side met the aspirations of the successful manufacturers for eateries with what they saw as having more urbanity and style.[50] These delis were more akin to Bloom's restaurant in the post-war years.

While there are many differences between the New York delis and Blooms, there are some notable similarities. Some of these are so profound that they suggest that the Bloom family might have been on a fact-finding visit to New York or had relatives and friends there who could relay information about the operation of the delis. Like Blooms, the early delis provided a 'grass roots' environment. Ted Merwin comments that the delis' customers 'required no education, no upper-class breeding, no intricate knowledge of manners and mores'.[51] Their general atmosphere also sounds remarkably similar to that in Blooms: 'The very environment of a delicatessen somehow ensures that everyone inside will eat Jewish (lots and fast), get treated Jewish (with tough, sarcastic love) and talk Jewish (loudly).'[52] The historian Barry Kessler sums up the ambience of delis in the title of his article, 'Bedlam with Corned Beef on the Side',[53] which could equally have been applied to Blooms. Like the Bloom's restaurants, the internal décor of delis included images of their owners, neighbourhood scenes and their famous customers, designed to spur nostalgia.[54]

Perhaps because of their roots in the theatre district of Manhattan, the New York delis were famed because of their entertaining employees. The early Jewish waiters in the delis have been described in almost identical terms to Bloom's waiters:

> Jewish delicatessen waiters were frequently bossy and obnoxious to the customers; they told them where to sit and what to order and how to behave … The short-tempered, sarcastic waiter was always ready with a cynical remark that cut the customer down to size like an expert tailor taking a swipe at a garment.[55]

Similarly, David Sax speaks about 'the love-hate relationship' between the Jewish delicatessen waiter and his clients: 'It was a battle of sullen service vs constant *kvetching*, of walking misery vs predetermined disappointment.'[56] Ted Merwin explains the relationship between waiters and deli diners as follows:

> Who else could talk to you obnoxiously other than a close friend or family member? … The waiter was a kind of surrogate uncle or grandfather for the duration of the meal; he paradoxically made you feel at home by treating you with undisguised contempt.[57]

Like the Bloom's waiters who transferred from the Aldgate to the Golders Green restaurant, some of the deli waiters worked for the same family owners for many decades. Another similarity was that, as in Blooms, the Jewish deli waiters were replaced by waiters from far-flung places, who learned the '*shtick* and banter' from those who preceded them, which, according to David Sax was 'passed down almost like Talmudic knowledge'.[58] However, there is one notable difference, from the earliest days, the New York delis employed women waiters, who were apparently equally feisty.[59] This difference might have been yet another outcome of the earlier exposure of New York Jews to the thinking of other population groups.

The 'countermen' who carved the meat and made the sandwiches were also key characters in deli life, as they were in Blooms. Their 'deft ability with steaming meat and sharp blades [was] a source of wonder'.[60]

Despite these similarities, there is no denying that Blooms was very much the product of its British environment, and even more so of its East End setting. It has become increasingly fashionable amongst young Jewish people today to look to America for a source of their Jewish identity. In an age of globalisation this is understandable, but the Bloom's story demonstrates how much, until relatively recently, British Jewish institutions were predominantly shaped by influences much closer to home.

Bloom's Legacy

Bloom's legacy is enormous. While many young people will never have heard of Blooms, most of those people who remember Blooms, especially those who dined at its restaurants or ate its food elsewhere, speak of Blooms with warmth and pride. It was a big Jewish success story that has left a long afterglow, and which looks set to remain an essential part of Anglo-Jewish folklore for as long as there are a significant number of people who remember Blooms when it was famous.

Bloom's most profound legacies are the part it played in supporting the assimilation of the descendants of the Jews who arrived in Britain *en masse* in the period from 1880 until the start of the First World War, and its undeniable contribution to fostering and shaping the Anglo-Jewish identity discussed earlier in this chapter. By providing a congenial meeting place and serving food that allowed diners to feel connected to their origins, Blooms reinforced their Jewish identity, be that predominantly cultural or religious. Although there is no obvious way of substantiating this suggestion, it is not implausible to suggest that, without Blooms, some Jews might have left Judaism. One commentator has suggested that the generation of Jews that came of age in the decades following the end of the Second World War 'twin tracked': they 'dressed British and thought Yiddish', striking a delicate balance between British norms, whilst simultaneously retaining their Jewishness.[61] Blooms was a powerful agent in catalysing this new identity, which was quite distinctive from other Jewish identities that emerged in the post-war years in America and in mainland Europe.

One of the ways in which Blooms helped to retain and shape Jewish identity was by performing an educative function, aiding young diners to understand the culinary traditions of previous generations at a time when an increasing number of them had a diet at home that bore little resemblance to what their grandparents ate. A former diner recalls:

> By the time that I started going to Blooms, none of my grandparents were keeping kosher and my parents never did. At home, we had quite an anglicised diet, so it was at Blooms that I learned about traditional kosher food. Neither of my grandmothers would have stuffed a neck to save their lives and that was one of the standard dishes at Blooms and, even though I never ate it myself, I did watch other people eat it. If I hadn't gone to Blooms, I wouldn't have known what *tzimmes, farfl* and *lokshen* pudding tasted like, and I wouldn't have picked up this knowledge anywhere else.[62]

Bloom's function of providing an informal cultural education is reinforced by the comments of another former diner living in a place lacking an institution like Blooms. Leslie Green recalls:

> My family used to travel from Glasgow to Cornwall and on route we would go to Blooms in Whitechapel. I was about ten years old and was fascinated with the whole *gesheft* [the entire set up]. We didn't have anything like it in Scotland, so it was a real education for me![63]

Blooms was also a place where young people heard about Jewish life in the East End, and sometimes also Jewish life in Eastern Europe, because of being party to conversations in which their parents and grandparents, aunts and uncles reminisced. While eating with family members, children were not just learning about Jewish food, but also the social conditions that produced it. Eating traditional food on its own was not sufficient to convey meaningful cultural messages.

In addition, Blooms had an educative function for the non-Jews who dined at the Aldgate restaurant and ate alongside Jews. As a result, some (but not all), developed a liking either for Jewish food generally or for certain dishes, which led them to buying Bloom's products when they started appearing on supermarket shelves (see further discussion below). Geoffrey Alderman comments:

> Blooms was not only a major provider of manufactured foods and meat products, it also established kosher restaurants as worthy of a visit by people from the non-kosher world (both Jews and non-Jews) and, as a result, raised the status of kosher restaurants and put Jewish food on the map. No other kosher restaurant in the land had the same impact. That's a very important legacy.[64]

There is also anecdotal evidence that eating at Blooms not only introduced non-Jews to Jewish food but also to Jewish culture, which might have assisted in improving inter-faith understanding and relations.

> When my son worked in the City during the 1990s, he offered to provide some of his clients with an 'ethnic' experience by taking them to Blooms. The first thing they did was to order wine. They were somewhat taken aback when chunky lemonade glasses were unceremoniously plonked down on the table. My son told them: "Don't ask for wine glasses, this is what you are going to get here." They consulted the menu and decided to order fried fish. They were surprised when the fish arrived and it was cold, which is how it was served in Blooms. They queried this with the waiter, who shrugged his shoulders and said: "You want hot fish, then you should have come yesterday." It turned out to be an "experience", but not quite in the way that they expected. They learned a lot about "Jewish style"![65]

It must be recognised that *heimische* Jewish food has not become mainstream to the same extent as it has in America and has never succeeded in competing in the non-Jewish restaurant and takeaway market to the same extent as Indian and Chinese food. However, via another legacy of Blooms, the appeal of traditional Jewish food originating in Eastern Europe lives on. As mentioned in Chapter Seven, several of the staff who worked for Blooms went on to open their own kosher-style restaurants and salt beef bars, which proved to be very popular with Jews and non-Jews alike. The most remarkable example of this legacy is Bambos Georgiou, who left Blooms to open the Brass Rail salt beef bar at Selfridges, which is still thriving, before opening the two B&K eateries in Edgware and Hatch End. The more recent Tongue and Brisket cafés in central London run my Bambos's descendants, show how food made popular by Blooms, especially its salt beef sandwiches, is still being mainstreamed.

Not all former Bloom's employees went on to open their own businesses, but in this discussion of Bloom's legacy it is worth noting that, as mentioned in Chapter Seven, over the years, Blooms provided 'on-the-job' training for many employees in skills that they might not otherwise have acquired, notably the many staff who started work as kitchen porters and went on to become qualified chefs. The head chef at the former kosher-style Madison's delicatessen in Stanmore learned his trade at Blooms.[66]

While the legacy of Bloom's restaurants is perhaps more apparent, the continuing impact of the firm's manufacturing and wholesale activities is also significant. As a result of Bloom's foresight, and particularly the skills of Norman Bookbinder in contracting with the supermarket chains to stock Bloom's products, kosher food went nationwide and played an important role in sustaining Jewish life, even the smallest of communities. This legacy is evident in the vast amounts of Bloom's products that are still sold by Gilbert's Kosher Foods. The goods bearing the Bloom's brand are purchased not only by Jews, but also to a significant number of non-Jews, including many Muslims, when halal products are not available. They are sold in supermarkets (and more recently online) throughout Britain and across mainland Europe. With sales of Bloom's manufactured and packaged goods at an all-time high, Norman Bookbinder, the managing director of Gilberts, comments: 'We go on producing Bloom's goods with great care and to a high standard because that's what people want and what they expect.'[67] The nostalgia attached to the products was evident when Gilberts introduced a 'healthier' version of Bloom's Viennas, and former Bloom's customers lobbied Gilberts, asking for the traditional recipe to be reinstated.[68] See Plates Section, Plate 13.

The Future of *Heimische* Food

When immigrants started arriving in Britain at the end of the nineteenth century, 'Jewish food' was seen as what was eaten by the established and fully assimilated Jewish community, which was mainly English food that had been adapted for a kosher diet. Anything more 'exotic' was mainly limited to Jewish festivals and holy days. The Sephardi diet that had once predominated had been virtually obliterated by assimilation.

Over the course of the twentieth century, but especially in the years following the end of the Second World War, Eastern European Ashkenazi food became the dominant form of Jewish food, with lingering memories of lands left behind combining with the desire to memorialise Jewish culture after the horrors of the Holocaust.[69] Not in small part, this shift was due to the influence of Blooms, but also as a result of *heimische* food being featured in post-war cookery books, novels, autobiographies, memoirs and plays, such as Arnold Wesker's 'Chicken Soup With Barley'. However, by the latter decades of the twentieth century, food writers, particularly Claudia Roden, were planting the notion that there were many other types of Jewish foods, including Sephardi dishes, and they succeeded in constructing a global identity for Jewish food culture. As a result, *heimische* food became 'unfashionable' and lost ground to a host of other Jewish cuisines from around the world.

When Blooms closed its doors in 2010, many people believed that this signalled the death knell of the traditional Eastern European Jewish food that Blooms had helped to put on the map and kept in the public eye for many decades. However, this has proved not to have been the case, and over the last ten years there have been indications that there is a renaissance of interest in *heimische* food, especially in London. Whereas food writers were once highly disparaging of Eastern European Jewish food, particularly writers such as Jay Rayner, it is no longer *de rigeur* to condemn this type of food. Back in 2013, one journalist discerned 'something strange was happening' in the world of Jewish food:

> The trend-setters were looking for something new. They had got tired of Thai, grown weary of Moroccan and had about as much fusion as they could stomach. How about something old-fashioned, comfortable and Eastern European? Old-style Jewish food.[70]

An ever-increasing number of eateries, which are mainly non-kosher (the revamped *glatt* kosher Reubens in Baker Street is an exception), are featuring traditional Jewish food on their menus, sometimes alongside several other cuisines. Atypically, the menu at the Tongue and Brisket cafés is a limited one, its owners having taken the business decision to concentrate on what they do well. In some eateries, the *heimische* food items being served are sometimes healthier versions of traditional dishes (for example, at Mishkins in Catherine Street, WC2), or traditional dishes with a twist (for example, by the Bell and Brisket in various locations, its food vans being reminiscent of the food barrows that once trundled around the East End). However, some eateries are featuring unashamedly fatty, salty Ashkenazi food, such as the Jewish Deli that operates in Broadway Market in Hackney on Saturdays. Some of the new restaurants and takeaways have been short-lived due to the challenging economics of running a successful food business, but as one restaurant or takeaway serving *heimische* food closes, another opens, suggesting that the taste for such food does exist.

What is interesting about these various businesses selling *heimische* food is that, except for the B&K salt beef bars in Edgware and Hatch End, they are in areas where there are few Jews and attract a broad range of customers, including young people. The Beigel Bake in Brick Lane, which has been operating since the 1970s and has reinvented itself several times in response to changing tastes and eating habits, is open 24 hours a day. It is at its busiest in the early hours of the morning, serving salt beef bagels to hungry young clubbers mingling with taxi drivers and early risers. This trend suggests that some traditional Jewish dishes are becoming more mainstream, but it is unlikely that most of those consuming the food, even Jews, are aware of (or interested in) its religious origins, its cultural significance, or the part it played in facilitating assimilation.

It is notable that the main impetus for the revival of traditional Jewish food has come from outside rather than within the Jewish community. In New York, where '*heimische* food is venerated', Jews are seeking to be innovative and ambitious with their culinary inheritance, making traditional dishes 'vibrant and exciting', such as in Zabars and Barney Greengrass's eaterie, both in the Upper West Side of the city.[71] Although they are willing to eat the food, British Jews seem less inclined than non-Jews to redeem the dishes of their forebears. This has been attributed to differences between American and British Jewish culture:

> In America, New York in particular, they [Jews] are proud, unabashed and central operators in a culture they helped form. In Britain, we are quieter and more peripheral. In America there is a bigger clientele, more money and bolder displays of heritage.[72]

These differences between Britain and New York have led Josh Glancy, special correspondent to *The Sunday Times*, to call upon British Jews to be more adventurous: 'I'd like to see some of Britain's – and Anglo-Jewry's – gastronomic fervour focused in the direction of *heimische* food. Spicy short-rib cholents, sweet potato kugels, red snapper *gefilte* fish, pan fried chicken liver on brioche.'[73]

Traditional food may be coming round again, but the settings in which it is served are from a more modern era. The experience of eating it is also very different. It is now devoid of the meaning that it once had, and it is no longer a reference point for a rapidly assimilating Jewish community. One of the hallmarks of Jewish identity is the way in which it constantly reinvents itself. In the third decade of the twenty-first century, a significant proportion of Jews do not define themselves purely in terms of their Jewishness, with their self-image being defined to a greater or lesser extent by factors such as gender, occupation and where they live. Amongst those Jews who do still view being Jewish as the core of their identity, many no longer view Jewishness as stemming solely from the origins of their ancestors or what they ate.

Whatever the new and revamped eateries do or do not provide, they are clearly not anything like Blooms in that they do not function as a 'third place' as discussed earlier in this chapter. Not only is there no longer a need for Jews to come together to bond by sharing of food, there are now many other ways, perhaps more suited to the needs of a more fully assimilated community, in which Jews can savour and reaffirm their Jewish culture: participating in events such as Jewish Book Week and Jewish Film Festival, or the wide programme of activities organised by the JW3, the Jewish Cultural Centre in Hampstead. Increasingly important are what may be described as 'virtual third places', such as the online communities and social media groups aimed at Jews, which have been so pivotal in the research carried out for this book.

Without question, this book has shown how much Blooms contributed to Anglo-Jewish history, how much its success deserves to be celebrated and cherished as a Jewish historical signpost and as a crucial repository of a gradually evolving Anglo-Jewish identity, even by those who never experienced it themselves. However, the cries for 'Bring back Blooms' are misplaced. It is not possible nor necessary to turn back time. The journalist Josh Glancy quoted above has encouraged British Jews to: 'Imagine a new Blooms, featuring your grandma's food reinvented in ways you hadn't even imagined. It's time to rethink our culinary heritage. If we will it, then it is no dream.'[74]

However, if Blooms were to be reinvented in the way that Josh Glancy suggests, then it would not be the Blooms that became an icon, the Blooms that played such a significant role in Anglo-Jewish history, or the Blooms that has left such a strong legacy.

Notes

1. See Pam Fox, *Jews by the Seaside, The Jewish Hotels and Guest Houses of Bournemouth* (London: Vallentine Mitchell, 2022).
2. Discussed in Barbara E. Mann, 'Space and Place', in Laurence Roth and Nadia Valman (eds), Routledge Handbook to Contemporary Jewish Cultures (London: Routledge, 2014), p.192. See also https://en.wikipedia.org/wiki/Lieu_de_m%C3%A9moire.
3. Conversation with Alan Dein, 12.6.2023.
4. Conversation with Fiona Hulbert, 17.4.2023.
5. *JC*, 15.7.1966.
6. Interview with Alan Dein, 22.8.2022.
7. This was also the case in America in relation to the Jewish delis. Ted Merwin, *Pastrami on Rye: An Overstuffed History of the Jewish Deli* (New York and London: New York University Press, 2018), p.2.
8. Quoted in interview with Alan Dein, 3.1.2023.
9. Interview with Norman Bookbinder, 9.12.2022.
10. See Pam Fox, *History in the Baking: The Rinkoff Story* (London: The Rinkoff Bakery, 2019).
11. 'Jake', responding to an article on Blooms in *The Times*, 'Waiters were the stars at celebrity kosher joint Blooms', 13.4.2020.
12. Jean Anthelme Brillat-Savarin, *The Physiology of Taste*, originally 1925 (London: Penguin, 1994), p.13.
13. Ray Oldenburg, *The Great Good Place* (New York: Paragon House, 1989).
14. *JC*, 15.7.1966. Jo Joseph was a TV and radio script writer and broadcaster, as well as being responsible for writing Bloom's marketing materials. See Chapter Nine.
15. *JC*, 7.8.1964.
16. Interview with David Hallgarten, 17.4.2023.
17. Interview with Alan Dein, 3.1.2023.
18. See https://foucault.info/documents/heterotopia/foucault.heteroTopia.en/.
19. Conversation with Beverley-Jane Stewart, 14.4.2023.
20. David Feldman, *Englishmen and Jews: Social Relations and Political Culture, 1840-1914* (New Haven: Yale University Press,1994), p.382.
21. Interview with Martin Malin, 9.4.2023.
22. See Fox, *Jews by the Seaside*, pp.85–86.

23. See mention in Chapter Six.
24. See Fox, *History in the Baking.*
25. Email from Elissa Bayer, 5.5.2023.
26. Jo Joseph writing in *JC,* 15.7.1966.
27. *JC*, 5.9.1986.
28. Interview with Alan Dein, 3.1.2023.
29. *JC*, 23.2.2012.
30. David Sax, *Save the Deli, In Search of the Best Pastrami and Rye and the Heart of the Jewish Delicatessen* (Toronto: McClelland and Stewart Ltd, 2010), p.232. The author mentioned a visit to Blooms. His impressions were not positive.
31. Delicatessens came to America from the German-speaking countries in Europe. Delicatessen means delicacies in German, and Webster's dictionary defines the word as 'prepared cooked meats, smoked fish, cheeses, salads, relishes, etc., or 'a shop where such foods are sold'.
32. See https://www.nyhistory.org/exhibitions/ill-have-what-shes-having-the-jewish-deli.
33. Seth Wolitz, 'The Renaissance in Jewish Cuisine', Policy Forum 18 (Jerusalem: Institute of World Jewish Congress, 1999).
34. There were several Jewish cafés and restaurants in the West End of London, mainly in the Soho area (where there was an established but smaller Jewish community than in the East End), such as Isow's, Goodys and B.B. Blooms mentioned in Chapter Four.
35. An indication of their 'showbiz' connections is that several deli owners named their sandwiches after Broadway stars.
36. Annie Polland and Daniel Soyer, *Emerging Metropolis New York: New York Jews in the Age of Immigration* (New York: Basic Book, 1997), p.133.
37. See https://untappedcities.com/2022/01/19/history-of-jewish-deli-nyc/.
38. Ironically, many of the tourists eating at Blooms were American.
39. See https://untappedcities.com/2022/01/19/history-of-jewish-deli-nyc/.
40. See Merwin, *Pastrami on Rye*, p.11. This was like the way in which the Jewish humour that grew up in the Catskill resorts permeated American culture.
41. *Ibid.*, p.76.
42. *Ibid.*, p.11.
43. Quoted in *JC*, 15.7.1966.
44. See Sax, *Save the Deli*, p.30.
45. Ruth Glazer, 'The Jewish Delicatessen: The Evolution of the Institution', *Commentary* Vol I, (March 1946), pp.58-63. https://www.commentary.org/articles/ruth-glazer/from-the-american-scene-the-jewish-delicatessen/.
46. Selma Berrol's comparative study of the Lower East Side in New York and the East End in London suggests that the Eastern European Jews who migrated to New York were generally less religious than those who settled in London, which may account for these differences relating to attitudes to *kashrut*. Selma Berrol, *East Side/East End: Eastern European Jews in London and New York, 1870–1920* (Westport, Conn: Praeger, 1994), pp.10–11.
47. See Merwin, *Pastrami on Rye,* p.79.

48. *Ibid.*, p.52.
49. See Glazer, 'The Jewish Delicatessen.
50. See Merwin, *Pastrami on Rye*, p.78.
51. *Ibid.*, p.xiv.
52. See Sax, *Save the Deli*, p.45.
53. Barry Kessler, 'Bedlam with Corned Beef on the Side', *Generations*, Fall 1993, pp.2–7.
54. Claudia Roden, *The Book of Jewish Food, An Odyssey from Samarkand and Vilna to the Present Day* (London: Penguin Books, 1999), p.119.
55. See Merwin, *Pastrami on Rye*, p.68.
56. See Sax, *Save the Deli*, p.43.
57. See Merwin, *Pastrami on Rye*, p.69.
58. *Ibid.*, p.158.
59. See Sax, *Save the Deli*, p.42.
60. See Merwin, *Pastrami on Rye*, p.69.
61. Commentator in the film, 'The Green Park', directed by Jack Fishburn and Justin Hardy.
62. Anonymous interviewee, 22.8.2022.
63. Leslie Green, post on Facebook page Jewish Britain, 16.4.2016.
64. Interview with Professor Geoffrey Alderman, 31.10.2022. Alan Dein points out that although Blooms certainly raised the profile of kosher food to a new level amongst non-Jews in the post-war years, as early as the 1935, the jazz singer Max Bacon recorded a track that proudly extolled the virtues of bagels available in the 'cosmopolitan' area of Whitechapel and Aldgate to an audience beyond the Jewish community. Conversation with Alan Dein, 12.6.2023. See https://www.youtube.com/watch?v=BVIBztBxBLI.
65. Anonymous interviewee, 22.4.2023. The fish would have been fried fresh for its first serving and then refrigerated and served as a cold dish subsequently.
66. *JC*, 25.4.2003. His name is unknown.
67. Interview with Norman Bookbinder, 9.12.2022.
68. *JC*, 8.1.2015.
69. This was the case even though Florence Greenberg's ground-breaking Jewish cookery book, first published in 1947, did not contain any Eastern European dishes. They were deliberately excluded on the grounds that they were 'unhealthy'. See Florence Greenberg, *Florence Greenberg's Cookery Book*, First edition, p.5. It was not until 1961 that she recognised *heimische* food. See *JC*, 21.7.1961.
70. *JC*, 1.2.2013.
71. Josh Glancy in *JC*, 17.9.2021.
72. *Ibid.*
73. *Ibid.*
74. *Ibid.*

Appendices

Appendix One

Glossary of Eastern European Jewish Food

Name	Description
Borscht  Courtesy of Wikipedia	A sour soup often associated made with red beetroots as one of the main ingredients, which give the dish its distinctive red colour. The same name, however, is also used for a wide selection of sour-tasting soups without beetroots, such as sorrel-based green borscht, rye-based white *borscht*, and cabbage borscht. Brisket is also sometimes added to *borscht*. There are hot and cold versions.
Blintz  Courtesy of Wikipedia	A thin, crepe-like pancake usually rolled up around fruit. Traditionally served on the festival of *Shavuot*.
Calves' foot jelly, see *Petcha*	
Cholent  Courtesy of Wikipedia	A slow-cooked stew, traditionally served for *Shabbat* lunch.

Name	**Description**
Chopped liver  Courtesy of Shutterstock	Traditionally from the chopped liver of geese, but later using chicken and beef livers mixed with egg. Often served as an appetiser for Jewish holidays.
Chrain  Courtesy of Wikipedia	A spicy horseradish sauce used for topping *gefilte* fish (see below).
Farfel  Courtesy of Wikipedia	Small pellets or flake-shaped pasta. It is made from egg noodle dough and is often toasted before being cooked. Typically, it is added to soups or served as a side dish. During *Pesach*, when dietary laws pertaining to grains are observed, it is replaced with *matzah* (see below) broken into small pieces.

Name	Description
Gedempte  Courtesy of Wikipedia	Yiddish for pot roast that involves braising together inexpensive cuts of meat like brisket, beef chuck or shoulder roast that are cooked for hours to soften. Other ingredients used in the sauce often include sauteed onion, carrot, and celery, minced garlic, paprika, thyme, basil and stock or wine.
Gefilte fish  By Mushki Brichta – Wikipedia Commons	Ground fish mixed with *matzah* (see below) meal and other ingredients and rolled into balls or cylinders, which are then poached or boiled. Traditionally served on at *Pesach* and on *Shabbat*.
Holishkes  By Loyna - Wikimedia.org	A cabbage roll dish prepared from blanched cabbage leaves wrapped in a parcel-like manner around minced meat and then simmered in tomato sauce. Sometimes rice is added to the meat filling. While the dish is eaten all year round, it is customarily served on the Jewish festivals of *Sukkot* to symbolize a bountiful harvest, and on *Simchat Torah* because two stuffed cabbage rolls placed side by side resemble Torah scrolls.

Name	Description
Kasha  Creative Commons	Buckwheat or groats, prepared in a pilaf and often served with *farfalle*.
Kishke  Courtesy of Wikipedia	A sausage-like dish, traditionally packed inside beef intestine.
Kneidlach  Courtesy of Wikipedia	Yiddish for *matzah* ball, a dumpling made of *matzah* meal, eggs and oil, usually served in chicken soup.

Name	Description
Knish  Creative Commons	A savoury pie frequently stuffed with potato filling. Often includes meat and other vegetables. It may be baked or deep fried.
Kreplach  Creative Commons	A triangle-shaped dumpling, usually filled with either chicken or ground meat (liver and onions for example) and served in chicken soup. Often referred to as Jewish Wonton or ravioli.
Kugel  Courtesy of Wikipedia	A sweet or savoury baked casserole usually made with some type of starch (often noodles or potatoes), eggs and a fat. A sweet or savoury baked casserole usually made with some type of starch (often noodles or potatoes), eggs and a fat.

Name	Description
Latkes  Creative Commons	Fried potato pancakes, traditionally served on *Chanukkah*.
Lokshen  Courtesy of Wikipedia	The term for a range of egg noodles commonly used in a variety of Jewish dishes including chicken soup, *kugel*, *kasha*, and as a side dish to brisket, sweet and sour meat balls, and many other dishes. It is also served as a pasta dish with either melted butter or a basic tomato sauce. In addition, it is sometimes served as a sweet dish.
Matzah  Courtesy of Wikipedia	Unleavened bread traditionally eaten on *Pesach*.

Name	Description
Matzah Meal  Creative Commons	Finely ground *matzah* bread which resembles coarse flour. It is used during *Pesach* when yeast products and leavened breads are forbidden.
Petcha  Courtesy of Wikipedia	Also known as 'calves' foot jelly' is a kind of aspic prepared from calves' feet.
***Schmaltz* herring**  Courtesy of Wikipedia	Herring cooked with fat rendered chicken (or other poultry).

Name	**Description**
Stuffed miltz  My Jewish Learning	A cow's spleen usually stuffed with *matzah* meal (see above), onions and spices.
Tzimmes  Kosher.com	A dish usually made of a mixture of carrots and honey, cooked over low heat and typically sweetened with honey or sugar. Often served at *Rosh Hashanah* when it is traditional to have sweet and honey-infused dishes in honour of the New Year. Tzimmes sometimes includes a medley of root vegetables such as potatoes, sweet potatoes, parsnip, carrots), which are slowly simmered with prunes or other dried fruit or with beef or brisket added to the vegetables.

Plates Section

Plate 1. Painting of Young Communists meeting at 'Bloom's Corner' in the 1930s by John Allin. Reproduced courtesy of Sharon Allin, John Allin's daughter.

Plate 2. Bloom's pickle dish. Courtesy of Mark Nagle.

Plate 3. Bloom's postcard, advertised as one of London's top tourist destinations. Courtesy of Alan Dein.

Plate 4. 'I'm a Bloom's Beefeater' badge for young customers. Courtesy of Alan Dein.

Plate 5. John Allin's painting of Wentworth Street, showing Blooms on the right and its near neighbours to the left. Reproduced courtesy of Sharon Allin, John Allin's daughter.

Plate 6. Diagram showing kosher and non-kosher parts of a cow. Kosher Catering London blog.

Plate 7. Jigsaw of Bloom's Golders Green, based on a picture painted by Philip Baigel. Courtesy of Philip Baigel.

Philip Baigels' painting contains a number of jokes including: Polite waiter needed badly. No double/triple parking. Everything with chips and health warning. Dog looking at Hot Dog poster. Healthy special: Kishke in schmaltz. Clean glass sign. Fresh food from 1920. Best Kosher - runner up - 1985 Shidduch Row. Reserved sign for Family Chazer. Winner latke eating price 1985. Sign in Carmellis - In case you were still hungry.

Plate 8. New décor of Golders Green restaurant in 2007 showing the replacement murals. Courtesy of the *Jewish Chronicle*, 27 April 2007.

Plate 9. Bloom's restaurant in Edgware. Courtesy of Wikipedia.

Plate 10. Advertisement in the *Jewish Chronicle*, 9 November 2007.

Plate 11. Tongue and Brisket, Wardour Street, London. Courtesy of the Georgiou family.

Plate 12. Famous people who ate at Blooms. *The Times*, 13 April 2020.

129. Bloom's Viennas produced and sold by Gilbert's Kosher Foods.

List of Images

List of Illustrations

Index of People

Page numbers for illustrations marked i., page numbers for photographs and other images marked p. and endnotes marked n.